D1591089

Richard Wollheim on the Art of Painting

Art as Representation and Expression

Richard Wollheim is one of the dominant figures in the philosophy of art, whose work has shown not only how paintings create their effects but why they remain important to us. His influential writings have focused on two core, interrelated questions: How do paintings depict? How do they express feelings?

In this collection of new essays, a group of distinguished thinkers in the fields of art history and philosophical aesthetics offers a critical assessment of Wollheim's theory of art. Among the themes under discussion are Wollheim's explanation of pictorial representation in terms of seeing-in, his views of artistic expression as a type of complex projection, and his notion of the internal spectator. In the final essay, Wollheim himself responds to the contributors.

Given the high level of international recognition that Wollheim's work has enjoyed for many years, this book will be eagerly sought out by all serious students of the theory of art, whether in departments of philosophy or art history.

Rob van Gerwen is Lecturer in Philosophy at the University of Utrecht.

Richard Wollheim on the Art of Painting

of Painting

Art as Representation and Expression

Edited by

ROB VAN GERWEN

Utrecht University

PUBLISHED BY THE PRESS SYNDICATE OF THE UNIVERSITY OF CAMBRIDGE
The Pitt Building, Trumpington Street, Cambridge, United Kingdom

CAMBRIDGE UNIVERSITY PRESS
The Edinburgh Building, Cambridge CB2 2RU, UK
40 West 20th Street, New York, NY 10011-4211, USA
10 Stamford Road, Oakleigh, VIC 3166, Australia
Ruiz de Alarcón 13, 28014 Madrid, Spain
Dock House, The Waterfront, Cape Town 8001, South Africa

http://www.cambridge.org

© Cambridge University Press 2001

First published 2001

Printed in the United States of America

Typeface Times Roman 10/12 pt.   *System* DeskTopPro$_{/UX}$ [BV]

A catalog record for this book is available from the British Library.

Library of Congress Cataloging in Publication Data
Wollheim, Richard, 1923–
Richard Wollheim on the art of painting : art as representation and expression / edited
by Rob van Gerwen.
p. cm.
Includes bibliographical references and index.
ISBN 0-521-80174-5
1. Painting – Philosophy.   2. Aesthetics.   I. Gerwen, Rob van, 1957–   II. Title.
N66.W63 2001
750'.1–dc21
00-052952

ISBN 0 521 80174 5 hardback

Contents

List of Contributors

Svetlana Alpers is in the Department of History, University of California at Berkeley, Berkeley, CA, U.S.A.

Michael Baxandall is in London, Great Britain

Malcolm Budd is in the Department of Philosophy, University College London, Great Britain. E-mail: m.budd@ucl.ac.uk

Paul Crowther is in the Centre for Professional Ethics, University of Central Lancashire, Great Britain. E-mail: p.crowther1@uclan.ac.uk

Caroline van Eck is in the Department of Art History, Free University, Amsterdam, Netherlands. E-mail: eck_van_ca@let.vu.nl

Susan L. Feagin is in the Department of Philosophy, University of Missouri, Kansas City, MO, U.S.A. E-mail: feagin@philosophy.umkc.edu

Rob van Gerwen is in the Department of Philosophy, Utrecht University, Netherlands. E-mail: Rob.vanGerwen@phil.uu.nl.
WWW: http://www.phil.uu.nl/~rob/

Andrew Harrison is in the Department of Philosophy, University of Bristol, Great Britain. E-mail: Andrew.Harrison@Bristol.ac.uk

Robert Hopkins is in the Department of Philosophy, University of Birmingham, Great Britain. E-mail: HOPKINRD@m4-arts.bham.ac.uk

Jerrold Levinson is in the Department of Philosophy, University of Maryland, U.S.A. E-mail: JL32@UMAIL.UMD.EDU

Graham McFee is in the Chelsea School, University of Brighton, Great Britain. E-mail: G.J.McFee@bton.ac.uk

Michael Podro is in the Department of Art History and Theory, University of Essex, Great Britain. E-mail: MPodro@TALK21.com

Monique Roelofs is at Brown University, in the Pembroke Center for Teaching and Research on Women, Providence, RI, U.S.A.
E-mail: Monique_Roelofs@Brown.edu

Anthony Savile is in the Department of Philosophy, King's College, London, Great Britain. E-mail: Anthony.Savile@kcl.ac.uk

Renée van de Vall is in the Department of Cultural Sciences, Maastricht University, Maastricht, Netherlands.
E-mail: R.vandeVall@LK.UNIMAAS.NL

Carolyn Wilde is in the Department of Philosophy, University of Bristol, Bristol, Great Britain. E-mail: Carolyn.Wilde@bris.ac.uk

Richard Wollheim is in the Department of Philosophy, University of California at Berkeley, Berkeley, CA, U.S.A. E-mail: wollheim@uclink.berkeley.edu

Relevant Works by Richard Wollheim and Their Abbreviations as Used in This Volume

AM	1973. *On Art and the Mind*. London: Allen Lane.
AO1	1968. *Art and Its Objects: An Introduction to Aesthetics*. New York: Harper & Row.
AO2	1980. *Art and Its Objects, second edition*. Cambridge, U.K.: Cambridge University Press.
CR	1980. Criticism as Retrieval. AO2, 185–204.
CPE	1993. Correspondence, Projective Properties, and Expression in the Arts. MD, 144–58. [Originally: 1991. Kemal, S., ed. *The Language of Art History* 51–66. New York: Cambridge University Press.]
MD	1993. *The Mind and Its Depths*. Cambridge, MA: Harvard University Press.
PA	1988. *Painting as an Art*. Princeton, NJ: Princeton University Press.
PS	1993. Pictorial Style: Two Views. MD, 159–70. [Originally: 1979. Lang, B., ed. *The Concept of Style*, 129–45. Philadelphia: University of Pennsylvania Press.]
SC	1993. The Sheep and the Ceremony. MD, 1–21. [Originally: 1979. *The Leslie Stephen Lecture, University of Cambridge*. Cambridge, UK: Cambridge University Press.]
TL	1984. *The Thread of Life*. Cambridge, UK: Cambridge University Press.
W-IPU	1986. Imagination and Pictorial Understanding. *Proceedings of the Aristotelian Society, Supplement*, 60: 45–60.

Where an article has been reprinted in a collection of Wollheim's essays, the page references in the text refer to that collection.

Preface

This book presents the offspring of a three-day conference on Richard Wollheim's aesthetics, which was held (in Wollheim's presence) in May 1997 in Utrecht, the Netherlands, augmented with a symposium from the *Journal of Aesthetics and Art Criticism* and Wollheim's reply to the essays. The theme of the book – as of the conference – is the troubled conceptual relations in the art of painting between expression and representation. The conference, which took place in the best of spirits, benefited from a lively and ongoing discussion on one singularly coherent and stimulating body of thought, that is, Wollheim's. Almost every chapter originating from the conference has been rewritten where appropriate in response to the discussions at the conference and to other chapters in this volume. This argumentative coherence is further served by Wollheim responses to the chapters. Thus, this volume presents a coherent body of work addressing issues raised by Wollheim but that are of importance far beyond his theory.

I would like to thank the authors for their supportive and stimulating cooperation, and particularly Graham McFee for his assistance in the editorial process. I would also like to express a word of thanks to the institutions that made it all happen: the Department of Philosophy of Utrecht University, the Leiden-Utrecht Zeno institute for research in philosophy, the Royal Dutch Academy of the Sciences (KNAW), the Foundation for Philosophy and Theology (SFT) of the Netherlands Organization for Scientific Research (NWO), and the Research Institute for History and Culture (OGC) of the department of Humanities, Utrecht University. Thanks also to Laura Lawrie, Matthew Lord, and Terence Moore of Cambridge University Press for their assistance in producing this book. Last, and emphatically, my thanks are due to Richard Wollheim for his supportive and energetic attitude and his never-diminishing strength of argument.

Rob van Gerwen
Utrecht, October 13, 1999

Richard Wollheim on the Art of Painting

Art as Representation and Expression

Introduction

ROB VAN GERWEN

In the discipline of philosophical aesthetics and that of art history, Richard Wollheim is renowned and appreciated for the intelligence and coherence of his philosophy of art, and for having based his thoughts on a sensitive appraisal of actual works of art. The present volume is meant to (critically) honour him for his achievements. It contains contributions from leaders in both fields. Before summarizing their arguments, I shall present some of Wollheim's main theses concerning the theme of this book.

If we were to assume a landscape painting, expressive of a melancholy weariness, that shows us three trees and a red-roofed farm, then what intuitively acceptable characterization could we produce of the complex conceptual relations between what this painting depicts and what it expresses? We can see the three trees and the red-roofed farm by merely looking at the painting, but in contrast, for us to recognize the scene's weary atmosphere of melancholy, our "mere looking" seems in need of an imaginative supplement of some sort. Should we say that the melancholy is integral to our experience, such that we might best characterize it as *evoked* in us, or is it, rather, a property of the painting? If the former, then we would still have to specify which properties of the painting supposedly cause us to have the feeling; if the latter, however, then an explanation is needed of how a non-sentient thing such as this painting can have a mental state among its properties. Alternatively, if it were no property of the painting, but one of the landscape it depicts, then we would need an account of how the expression of a landscape (assuming we can conceive of such a thing) is to be depicted, and why we should still need the extra imaginative effort to recognize it in or through the painting. Assuming then that we are interested in expression as something based in the work, two questions arise: Is the melancholy a property of the painting in the same way the redness of the farm's roof is, and, second, is it a property of a painting *like* it normally is a property of a person?

In addressing these questions we must first cast doubt on the idea that images are recognized by mere looking. If we assume – as we normally and rightly do – that the redness of a daub of paint is a property of the canvas, this does not tell us whether or not the redness of the roof is also a property of the canvas – even though it is depicted by way of the daub. The trees and the farm are not in that same space and time where the daub and its beholder are. There is, therefore, no need for any properties of the painting to be straightforwardly *transparent* to properties of the represented. So we do not recognize what a painting depicts by merely looking at it. Instead, we see the paint as something it isn't (as part of a roof), or better: We see the roof in the painted surface. Indeed, Wollheim does not think that our recognizing a picture is a case of switching between looking at a canvas and looking right through it at what it represents. The objection to the latter view is that it treats perceiving a painting as though it were like perceiving a farm (which it obviously isn't), or as if we see the painting *as* a farm (which we obviously don't). By contrast, we may wonder whether the perceptual capacities whereby we recognize a tree in real life suffice for recognizing one in a painting. Wollheim thinks not. Instead, representational seeing, or, in Wollheim's term, "seeing-in," is a fundamental capacity of perception distinct from plain seeing. Seeing-in should be so distinct from seeing partly because looking at, for instance, a real tree – that is, a tree that one can touch and smell, and circle around – is so vastly different from looking at a painted one. The notion of seeing-in also incorporates Wollheim's conviction that while we see a tree in a painting, we see both the tree and the painting at the same time. Both elements partake in a single act.

After having introduced the seeing-as account of representational seeing in Sections 11 through 14 of his *Art and its Objects*, in a later edition of that book Wollheim added an essay arguing against it. The seeing-as account stems from Wittgenstein's remarks on the ambiguous duck-rabbit picture. It takes the subject of a painting as an aspect of it, and suggests that we see the painting *either* as a surface *or* as its subject. We presumably switch between the two – surface and subject – without being capable of seeing them both in the same act. At least one argument is more in favour of the seeing-as account than of its rival. Aspect perception allows the dawning of an aspect a major role: One can be staring in disbelief at some painting, trying to make sense of what others attribute to it, when finally it dawns upon one. It is not clear how the seeing-in account can accommodate this, as although it allows for dual attention to surface and subject matter, it seems to have little patience with slow recognition. However, Wollheim did spell out quite a few drawbacks to the seeing-as account, and, overall, his notion of seeing-in indeed appears to fit the bill much better than seeing-as does.

For one thing, seeing-as cannot explain how we can see something *happen* in a picture: We cannot see a still thing *as* an event, but only as one or more particulars. Seeing-in does admit of events: We can see in a picture *how* one person is in pursuit of another. Aspect perception theory would conceive of this in something like this manner: We see part of the picture *as* one character and another part of the picture *as* the other character, but what part of the picture between these two parts are we to view *as* their being in pursuit? Second, in terms of the classical example of seeing-as, that is, the duck-rabbit picture, the fact that someone sees the picture as a rabbit is revealed by the language he uses to describe the picture: He will use words that are appropriate for describing rabbits, rather than ducks. This suggests that we can actually point at the aspects which these words describe: seeing-as is *localizable*. But localizability is no demand on seeing-in. Therefore, because we are not always capable of localizing everything that we see in a picture, seeing-in is the more adequate concept for understanding our perception of pictures. Third, with seeing-in, the possibility of seeing both the surface and the subject at the same time is not precluded; indeed, it is stressed: Seeing-in expresses the twofoldness of our attention. We don't see a picture *as* the thing it portrays, but we see the portrayed *in* the picture. This twofold nature of representational seeing also explains the difference between seeing Holbein's picture of Henry VIII and seeing Henry VIII in person: One who sees the picture of the king is aware of it as a picture. In itself, this does not yet prove that the seeing-in view should be adopted, because other accounts might be equally well equipped to deal with the distinction. However, Wollheim also provides two stronger arguments.

The first he derives from the psychology of perception: Movements of the beholder do not normally lead to perspectival derangements of what is seen in a picture, whereas in plain, stereoscopic perception they do. The fact that we realize this while looking at a painting implies that we are aware that the painting first of all is a surface. Seeing-in – implying the dual attention to surface and subject – explains this. Second, seeing-in meets our idea that great works of art lead us to appreciate the way in which the artist has handled his material; that is, to appreciate *how* something is depicted, instead of merely *what* is depicted. An account which does not explicate this fact of art appreciation does not do justice to art (AO2 215). Twofoldness is merely *appropriate* to viewing any representation, but it is *required* where – in contrast to what we see in a stained wall – the intentionality of the artist's manipulations give it a rationale (AO2 219). Thus, Wollheim's account links the way we perceive paintings to how they are produced.

The first chapter of Wollheim's *Painting as an Art* contains a keen account of how a painter produces his pictures. It specifies some of the types of considerations that guide him while realizing his intentions, and the mechanisms which can be distinguished in the creative process. The upshot of this account is that a painting realizes the artist's intentions, and these, as realized, sustain a notion of correctness for our attributions. The way the artist steers the beholder's perception therefore not only makes the beholder see something in the picture, but it also forms his ticket to enter the worldview of the artist. Again, the fulfilled intentions found our vision of the artist's style. Our interest in individual style fades at the realization of being confronted with something painted by a child or chimpanzee, or with the drawings of schizophrenics – paintings which lack a notion of correctness connected to the intentions of their creators, because they – the creators – necessarily lack a formed style. Our interest in individual style is a necessary condition for our aesthetic interest in paintings.

In "Pictorial Style: Two Views," Wollheim, following Wölfflin, distinguishes two types of style: general and individual. Under the former, Wollheim places the styles of schools, periods, eras: conventions, rather, which can be taught and learned. Individual style, on the contrary, an artist must find through his own creativity: It must be achieved. An artist does not *acquire* his individual style, but *forms* it. From this, individual style derives its psychological reality, the fact that it is internalized in the artist's personality. *Individual style* is, therefore, to be distinguished from possibly contingent elements of *signature*, which merely betray the hand of the artist, such as the types of paint he utilizes or the way he, accidentally, depicts the nails on a hand's fingers or, indeed, his signature. That individual style has psychological reality means that it is something that no artist starts out with, and that can be lost. Thus, some of an artist's works may be pre-stylistic, while others are post-stylistic, whereas perhaps only a few are in his style. According to Wollheim, individual style cannot be grasped by merely attending to properties of paintings: One has also to refer to the artist's psychology. General styles, on the contrary, can be thus assessed, because they answer first of all to art historical problems of classification. They are describable in terms of regularities between paintings, and conventions, and presuppose a *taxonomic* view of style. To identify and describe individual styles, however, a *generative* conception of style is needed, one which meets the psychological nature of art and accounts for the process of its creative emergence. On this view, art historians should reckon with non-linear relations between paintings, as it is psychological considerations that make a trait stylistic, not lawfulness or mere regularity (PS 182ff.).

Some connection with artistic expression imposes itself on us here, with an expression, that is, which is achieved through the manipulation of external material. In "Correspondence, Projective Properties, and Expression in the Arts," Wollheim argues that our reasons for taking a landscape to correspond to a specific state of mind involves a *projection* on our behalf. Expressive properties are projective properties, and, as with secondary qualities – such as colours – our experiences are caused by and about them. Yet, projective properties differ from secondary qualities in being affective rather than merely perceptual, and related to objects that may be absent to the senses. Also, when seeing a frightening thing, we are not merely aware of the thing itself but also of past experiences of fear, with which we built our sense of the thing's fearfulness. Projective properties thus bring to mind the causal history of an emotional awareness. This general psychological phenomenon seems, however, to endanger the idea of a correspondence of our appreciation of an art work's expressive properties with the intentions of the artist, because projection in extreme cases need not have anything to do with the properties of the object under consideration. Obviously, such extreme projections as these should be excluded from any adequate account of expression, but how?

Wollheim tackles this problem by elaborating on the psychology of projection. At first, he says, people project their own feelings, in order to control them, onto another person. Such projections may be arbitrary – for instance, when people project their anger onto other persons by claiming that they are out to hurt them. More adolescent projections, however, presuppose an affinity between the object and the feeling. By introducing this notion of affinity into the account of artistic expression, Wollheim thinks we can retain the idea of correspondence. We should only project on account of a property which however weakly inheres the work.

The objection may be raised now that this conception of artistic expression is not descriptive but evaluative in nature. The postulated affinity between object and feeling resides somewhere in between two extremes: Some work may hardly show an affinity at all, while with other works it may be far too evident. In neither case do we think that the work is expressive. Instead, the requested affinity must hold some middle ground between the two extremes; and whether or not it does so becomes a matter of critical evaluation. Expression – much like individual style, I submit – may, in the end, be an evaluative notion, rather than, or as well as, a descriptive one. This tension in the theory is intentional. Wollheim refuses to view our descriptive account of art as independent from art's very value, and he tries just as hard not to reduce the former to the latter. In all, Wollheim explains the relations between pictorial and expressive aspects of paintings by referring to the psychologies of art creation and art appreciation. But these psychologies he keeps firmly fixed on to the work itself. Nowhere does he depart from the properties of the work; he merely sees these as inducing psychological questions next to art historical ones.

One other, connected, contribution of Wollheim's will be assessed in this volume: that of the internal spectator – present in certain pictures, but not in others – which Wollheim sees as assisting us in viewing what the picture depicts. The internal spectator is a spectator with his own psychological repertoire who is somehow included in certain pictures without being depicted. In such pictures, it is as though the depicted scene is viewed by someone who resides within it. The external spectator centrally imagines seeing the scene from the point of view of the internal spectator – as if able to move within the represented space. In Chapter 3 of *The Thread of Life*, Wollheim reserves the term 'imagination' for a specific mental act of fantasizing what it would be like to be in some situation, either centrally – that is, imagining oneself as the subject who perceives the event – or acentrally. The external spectator is not asked to somehow finish the painting, since he does not form part of it. Nor is this effect a matter of illusion. Illusion paintings present parts of their subject as though they were in the external spectator's space, an effect which is supposed to thrive on our belief that such a strange spatial inclusion could be the case. Internal spectators are a marginal phenomenon, but they are interesting for what they teach us about the transition between the space of the beholder and that of the represented scene. Wollheim gives us examples of works by Caspar David Friedrich and Edouard Manet, where the beholder's *imagination* is allowed to play a role it is denied in seeing-in and projective perception. Representation and expression are perceived, instead of imagined, but seeing the depicted world through the eyes of an internal spectator involves the beholder in an act of imagining. The discussion of this rare enough phenomenon of the internal spectator once more illustrates Wollheim's perceptive understanding of the many effects of paintings.

To sum up, the following are among the most important concepts that Richard Wollheim has contributed to our aesthetic understanding of the evaluative and descriptive appreciation of the art of painting. *Seeing-in* is a *twofold, perceptual* attention both to the surface which (hopefully) is painted in an *individual style*, and to a subject that can be seen in it. Recognizing a work's expression involves a *projection* of mental properties with a personal history on our behalf depending on an *affinity* between that personal history and the very same *individual style* the subject is painted with. In general, what we need, according to Wollheim, is an art-critical approach of art, a "Criticism as Retrieval" which answers to the many notions of correctness I have just alluded to. With Wollheim, this is no mere academicism. Whoever studies Wollheim's texts will soon find out that critical conclusions reached too hastily can seriously damage one's insights. One who takes this theory to heart finds himself or herself forced to look afresh at paintings, and this time more critically and with a better eye for art's psychological origins. It is therefore no coincidence that among the authors in the present volume we find philosophers as well as art historians.

For all the contributions in the present book, it will be helpful to sketch the main arguments, without (of course) offering any judgement on their soundness. Wollheim's views of pictorial representation form the core subject of six chapters, and we begin with Wollheim's own recently elaborated defense of them. In Chapter 1, Wollheim discusses three demands on theories of pictorial representation. He argues, first, that if a picture depicts, then a suitable experience can establish what is depicted in it. Second, a suitable spectator will have such suitable experiences. Third, the spectator must have the suitable capacities or be able to acquire them, and these capacities concern the visual experience of the depicted. With these demands in hand, Wollheim addresses (and dispatches) the subtle theories of depiction of Christopher Peacocke and Malcolm Budd, who understand depiction and our recognition of pictures in terms of the experienced resemblance between the structures or, respectively, shapes, of visual fields of a picture and its real-life subject. Wollheim's main argument against this view is that there need not be a separate experience of the two visual fields resembling one another, just as there needn't be an experience of the real-life subject, for a picture to be recognized as picturing what it depicts. Thus, the demands this theory of experienced resemblance puts on our perception of pictures do not meet Wollheim's first, minimal requirement that there be a suitable experience.

The next chapter is by Jerrold Levinson, one of the two contributors who had ready access to Wollheim's present text (the other being Susan Feagin). Levinson finds himself in much agreement with Wollheim's present views, but poses several questions concerning Wollheim's account of seeing-in. He doubts whether the experience of seeing-in has a uniform nature in all the relevant cases. For instance, Levinson argues, imagination is implied in a different way in the experience of seeing columns in a painting, in contrast to seeing "[. . .] them as having been thrown down some hundreds of years ago by barbarians" (Wollheim, this volume, 24). Andrew Harrison, in Chapter 3, urges that the twofoldness of representational perception does not fit well with the strict division Wollheim proposes between pictorial and descriptive representation, because as is the case with linguistic understanding, we start our understanding of pictures from principles (a "pictorial syntax") which guide the production of a picture from the basic elements an artist starts out with. These basic elements are in themselves non-pictorial combinations of colours and forms, what Harrison calls the "pictorial mesh." If this is correct, as Harrison thinks, the strict division should be abandoned, not the twofoldness. In Chapter 4, Monique Roelofs disputes Wollheim's idea that seeing-in should be treated as a primitive type of perception. She thinks seeing-in can and should be further analysed. Roelofs proposes to view seeing-in as a process of advancing and testing hypotheses concerning what we see before us. Among other things, she sees an answer in this to the question of the role of background knowledge in our appreciation of works of art. Chapter 5 is dedicated to the question of art's beginning and continuation. Anthony Savile argues here that the development of art over time can best be understood as motivated by the idea of wanting to pass on taste and artistic values. This theory, Savile thinks, is compatible with Wollheim's ideas on individual style and its psychological reality. But what about Wollheim's thesis that art works

8   ROB VAN GERWEN

need not be motivated by the wish to communicate? For Savile, Wollheim
cannot make sense of the idea of communication, because he takes the artist
as producing his work for unknown, hypothetical spectators. Against this
position, Savile urges that any artist's aimed for spectator isn't as unspecified
as Wollheim has it.

Because Wollheim thinks of seeing-in as a perceptual capacity, he doesn't
see a role in it for imagination. (Only when there is an internal spectator in
some painting is the imagination activated to assist in the perceptual process).
But one can see that the following is neutral as to this issue: seeing-in ". . .
allows us to have perceptual experiences of things that are not present to the
senses" (AO2 217). Obviously, only those things that are represented in the
picture present themselves to our perception, and of these it remains to be
seen whether or not they present themselves to the imagination or – more
strictly – to the senses. Therefore, in the present volume, four authors –
Levinson, Crowther, Podro, and van Gerwen – disagree that Wollheim's
characterization of seeing-in rules out imagination. Apart from Levinson,
these authors do not necessarily take imagination restrictedly as fantasy. In
the sixth chapter on representation, Paul Crowther investigates the role of
imagination in our twofold attending to pictures. He views the imagination as
a basic function in cognition in the transcendental sense which Kant ascribed
to it: not as the actual thinking up of fantasies, but as the often unconscious
mental power that is presupposed for experience, which puts before the mind
image-like representants of things that are absent to the senses. In Wollheim's
view, this may be incorporated in visual perception, but Crowther thinks it is
rewarding to shuffle the distinctions in the way he does this, because this
very transcendental type of imagination, he thinks, is what is being objectified
in paintings.

Wollheim's characterization of perception is challenged from other angles,
too. Thus, Malcolm Budd (Chapter 7) sees a problem with Wollheim's account of *expression* as a kind of perception that corresponds to a feeling one
doesn't have. We see something in the picture, then become aware of an
affinity with some emotion, only then to reperceive the subject which is then
coloured by the emotion. Or do we first see the affinity, only to find that there
is no way to see the subject without the emotion with which it has an affinity?
What determines what? And, Budd asks, how does Wollheim account for the
correspondence between the thing perceived and the feeling not being had?
Concerning expression's relation with representation, Michael Podro (Chapter
8) distinguishes three aspects in pictures that cannot be conceived of as
independent: the power of depicting a subject, the singularly specific and
complex coherence of a painting, and our experience of seeing the way the
painting is painted as loaded with expressiveness. Expressiveness derives
from the way something is rendered. Starting, like Wollheim, from a psycho-

analytic theory, Podro treats these three aspects in relation to how a child places a transitional object between himself and his mother. The child projects onto such a transitional object both his mother's and his own emotions, so as to repair the separation he is experiencing. Podro perceives certain analogies with expression, which introduce new subtleties into Wollheim's account.

In Chapter 9, Carolyn Wilde argues, via the case of forgery, that style forms the very basis of artistic value. She quotes Wollheim saying that "application of the concept of style to a work of art is a precondition of its aesthetic interest," and argues that individual style is the product of the artist's attention to a subject, which as such steers the beholder's attention to the right spots. A forger will use a style as a kind of matrix for his painting, whereas the painter applying his own style will use it as a way of perceiving the world in order to supplant that way of perceiving onto the picture plane. The authenticity of a picture and its expression is a function of the picture's individual style. Therefore, individual style is as important to understanding expression as it is to our understanding of depiction. Rob van Gerwen's (Chapter 10) approach to representational perception starts from the acknowledgement that a picture addresses only the perceptual modality of vision (while recognizing that vision is embodied). Seeing a horse in a picture implies an anticipation on the capability of recognizing such an animal's depicted visual characteristics if ever one were to be within the depicted reality. (The anticipation removes all talk of experienced resemblance from the analysis of depiction.) Thus, the perception of representation is characterized generally as an anticipation of some unimodal recognition. This general notion enables van Gerwen to understand the analogy of artistic expression to depiction, taking the difference between the two as that between the beholder's respective modalities of mind that are addressed. Pictorial representation is of the visual, whereas expression represents the experiential, and the latter's relevant perceptual modality is imagination. Therefore, according to van Gerwen, both depiction and expression function, similarly, as types of representation albeit with distinct types of subject matter. In Chapter 11, Graham McFee questions the combination of the projective nature of expressive properties with the realist undertone of Wollheim's approach. If expressive properties depend on the contribution of the beholder, how can they objectively be there in the work? Wollheim thinks that the perception of expression does not merely depend on the presence of an extra stock of knowledge, but rather on the ability to mobilize that extra cognitive stock in one's experience, to have it play a role in one's perception of the work. But if perceiving artistic expression becomes such an esoteric ability, then how can people still be educated aesthetically? Can people be taught to appreciate art? McFee offers a solution to Wollheim's difficulty by seeing what follows from the (obvious) "yes" answer.

In Part Three, the contributions which address the internal spectator are collected. Art historian Svetlana Alpers (Chapter 12) takes a close look at that other significant spectator, the artist, by analysing Rembrandt's painting *Bathsheba* – in particular, the artist's position towards his own canvas. She disagrees with Wollheim that the crucial position for the artist with regard to his own work is an upright stance frontally opposed to it, which would as such be a stance available to every spectator. She shows that the spectator of *Bathsheba* cannot quite take up the same position Rembrandt held towards his painting. Two other contributors – van Eck and van de Vall – propose to expand Wollheim's analysis of the internal spectator in the direction of the external spectator. Caroline van Eck (Chapter 15) argues that Wollheim is too dismissive with regard to illusion, and that the use of linear perspective can be understood as a rhetorical device that fulfils the very conditions that, according to Wollheim, point to the presence of an internal spectator. Consequentially, van Eck thinks that the phenomenon of the internal spectator is more widespread than Wollheim thinks it is. Renée van de Vall (Chapter 13) investigates the distinction between the external and the internal spectator by developing the notion of staging. Installations stage their spectators, luring them into the work so as to dissolve the very separation between work and spectator and (so to speak) make the external spectator an internal one. She then applies her insights to a painting by Barnett Newman, showing how it lures one inside while itself entering the beholder's space. Like van Eck and van de Vall, Susan Feagin (Chapter 14) addresses the way a painting addresses its beholder. However, unlike them, she does not loosen up Wollheim's sharp conviction of *trompe l'oeil*, but, instead, defends it. She explains the difference between presentation and representation by analysing the four characteristic differences between *trompe l'oeil* and representation, and argues that although the former is not an instance of the latter, it does lead us to applaud the technical powers of an artist if only he uses them to empower his representation. Robert Hopkins (Chapter 16) questions whether Wollheim really needs an internal spectator with his own psychological repertoire on top of the already very rich phenomena of seeing-in and projection. This criticism becomes all the more pressing in the light of the problem of whether or not external spectators are capable of retrieving the internal spectator's psychology. In Chapter 17, Michael Baxandall considers it the task of the art critic to show the external spectator where to aim his projections. He – the critic – must in this process maintain a certain openness. He must point out the visual connections, but not the psychological ones, which he must leave for the beholder to fill in. The last word on each of these topics is left, as expected, for Richard Wollheim. In Chapter 18, he has defences on offer, as well as further questions. The debate is not over yet, far from it.

Part One
Representation

Chapter 1
On Pictorial Representation

RICHARD WOLLHEIM

1. Philosophical theories of representation abound

This tells us something, in fact it tells us two things, two philosophical things, about representation. The first thing is that, when we set out to ascertain the extension of the concept representation, armed with the re-sources we should expect to be adequate – that is, such intuitions as we have, plus the careful consideration of examples – we encounter many hard cases. Are maps representations? Are traffic signs representations? The second thing is that these hard cases are totally resistant to stipulation. No one (I find) will take it on trust from me that, say, *trompe l'oeil* paintings are not representa-tions, but that most abstract paintings are. The centrality of representation within the pictorial arts means that any answer that is not supported by a theory, moreover a theory that meshes at once with a general account of perception and with broad cultural practices, will not do.

Hence the abundance of theories of representation.

2. However many such theories fall short of a certain minimal require-ment, which has as its aim to safeguard our strongest intuition about represen-tation, this time about, not its extension, but its nature. And that is that pictorial representation is a perceptual, more narrowly a visual, phenomenon. Imperil the visual status of representation, and the visual status of the picto-rial arts is in jeopardy. And for the duration of this lecture, I shall take what is nowadays called the "opticality" of pictorial art as given.

But how is the minimal requirement upon a theory of pictorial representa-tion to be framed? I start with the following: (1) if a picture represents something, then there will be a visual experience of that picture that deter-mines that it does so. This experience I call the "appropriate experience" of the picture; and (2), if a suitable spectator looks at the picture, he will, other things being equal, have the appropriate experience.

Some explanations.

A suitable spectator is a spectator who is suitably sensitive, suitably in-formed, and, if necessary, suitably prompted. The sensibility and information must include a recognitional skill for what is represented, and "other things being equal" means that, in addition to viewing conditions being good enough, the spectator must recruit all these qualifications to the task to hand. As to "suitably prompted," that is intended to forestall a possible oversight and to neutralize an all too common prejudice. What may be overlooked is that sometimes, even if a spectator has the relevant recognitional skills, he may not be suitably informed unless he is told, thing by thing, what the picture before him represents. Without this information, he will not have the appropriate experience. And the prejudice is to assume that if, without this information, the spectator is unable to experience the picture appropriately, then, with this information, he will still not be able to. The information may affect what he says, but how could it affect what he sees?

Elsewhere I have argued that to dispel this prejudice we should recall those childhood days when we were given a line-drawing and asked to say what was in the foliage, and we said nothing, because, turn it this way, turn it that way, we saw nothing, and then we were prompted, we were shown the key, and we said "Boy," "Camel," "Fish," "Rabbit," "Deer," and what had changed was not just what we said. What had also changed was what we saw. Hence prompting, and the need for reference to it in even so skeletal a version of the minimal requirement.

What makes this version skeletal is that though it insists that, for each representational picture, there is an appropriate experience, it says nothing about what this experience is like. Later we shall have to make good this deficiency. Meanwhile are there any theories that fail the minimal requirement even in this version?

3. Suspicion falls first on the theory, or rather family of theories, that I have called semiotic, which have in common that they ground representation in a system of rules or conventions that link the pictorial surface, or parts of it, with things in the world.

If, in our day, the most vociferous of these theories are those which model the rules of representation upon the rules of language, they are also the most vulnerable since, true to the analogy that inspires them, they hold that representational meaning depends upon pictorial structure. But, in the relevant, or combinatory, sense, pictures lack structure. There is no non-trivial way of segmenting pictures without remainder into parts than can be categorized functionally, or according to the contribution they make to the meaning of the whole.

Accordingly what is specifically wrong with linguistically oriented semiotic theories of representation can come to obscure what is essentially wrong with semiotic theory. To bring this out I propose (1) to concentrate on the most plausible version of the semiotic theory, which is one that not merely drops the commitment to pictorial structure but insists that the rules of representation cannot be applied, either by artist or spectator, without recognitional skills for the things represented, and (2) to consider whether such a theory meets the minimal requirement by seeing what it makes of the process by which representational meaning is assigned to pictures by a spectator. Of course, on the face of it, there is no smooth transition from what representational meaning is to how representational meaning is assigned, or *vice versa*. No theory of representation should neglect the fact that one of the best ways of finding out what a picture represents is by looking at the label. However, for any theory of representation, there is a way of assigning meaning to pictures that tracks how that theory says that pictures come by their meaning, and my current strategy is to see whether the way associated with the most plausible kind of semiotic theory allows sufficient room for perception. Does it allow room for an appropriate experience?

The answer will turn out to be, No. No, in that, though the most plausible semiotic theory lets perception in at two distinct points in the process of assigning representational meaning to pictures, at a third, and what is the crucial, point it excludes perception.

Any semiotic theory, linguistically oriented or plausible, lets perception in at point one: The spectator must be visually aware of the surface to which he then applies the rules of representation. Any plausible, as opposed to linguistically oriented, semiotic theory, lets perception in at point two: for the spectator must have the relevant recognitional skills if he is to apply the rules of representation. However semiotic theory of all kinds is debarred from finding any further need for perception. And that is because, from this point onwards, all the spectator has to do is to apply the rules to the surface, and the rules will take him, without any help from perception, to the thought of what is represented, which is his destination.

A way of putting the point is to say that, on any semiotic theory, the grasp of representational meaning is fundamentally an interpretative, not a perceptual, activity. In consequence no appropriate experience is postulated, and it is thus that the semiotic theory fails the minimal requirement.

4. If it shows how wide of the mark semiotic theory is that it fails the minimal requirement even in this skeletal version, this also suggests that, if further theories of representation are to be tested, the minimal requirement needs to be amplified. It will have to say, for every representation, what the appropriate experience is like.

At this point help comes from another strong intuition that we have, again about the nature of representation. It is this: If before an otherwise suitable spectator, looking at a representation, can have the appropriate experience, he must have the relevant recognitional skills, the corollary is that, if he lacks these skills, he can, through looking at the representation and being suitably prompted, acquire them. Other things being equal, he will simultaneously have the appropriate experience and acquire the recognitional skill. It is thus that children acquire a very large number of their recognitional skills from looking at illustrated books. My daughter, on seeing her first elephant, aged two, exclaimed, "Babar."

This being so, if we want to know what the appropriate experience is like, we have only to ask, "Through what kind of experience do we gain a recognitional skill?" The answer to that question is surely this: We gain a recognitional skill through an experience in which we are visually aware of the thing, or the kind of thing, that we are thereby able to recognize. Arguably there could be degenerate cases in which we learn to recognize one thing on the basis of being shown something very like it and then getting ourselves to see the lookalike as the thing in question. But this method could as readily leave us with a merely inferential, as with a truly recognitional, skill. If all this is so, then we can fold this conclusion into our minimal requirement as clause three so that the whole thing now runs as follows: (1), If a picture represents something, there will be an experience of it, called the appropriate experience that determines that it does so; (2), if a suitable spectator looks at the picture, he will, other things being equal, have this experience; and (3), this experience will be, or include, a visual awareness of the thing represented. I call this the amplified, as opposed to the skeletal, version of the minimal requirement.

Thus rearmed, I turn to the next theory on which suspicion falls, though it is also that on which common wisdom settles: that is, the Resemblance theory. It too is a family of theories, members of which may be divided up two ways.

The first way of dividing up such theories is between those which do not, versus those which do, insist that the resemblance, which holds, of course between something pictorial and something extra-pictorial, is experienced. However what these latter theories insist upon is not that there is a resemblance between two such things, and that this resemblance is experienced. All that they ask for is that the two things are experienced as resembling, which is compatible with a very wide range of actual resemblance or actual dissimilarity. Clearly it is only the latter kind of Resemblance theory that will satisfy the minimal requirement, indeed that will satisfy it even in its skeletal version. For it is only it that finds room for an appropriate experience.

Second, Resemblance theories may be divided up according to the terms between which the resemblance relation holds. (And, since, from now onwards, I shall confine myself to theories of experienced resemblance, and since experienced resemblance, unlike resemblance itself, is non-symmetrical, I shall be able to talk about the right-hand, or resembled, term and the left-hand, or resembling, term.) Now disagreements about the resembled term are, in effect, disagreements about the scope of representation, and I shall return to that topic later. As to disagreements about the resembling term, the crucial issue is whether it is, at any rate in the first instance, something on the pictorial surface or some part of the spectator's experience on looking at the pictorial surface.

Finally, and still on the issue of the resembling term, let us be on our guard against those versions of the Resemblance theory which rely upon generalizing remarks of a sort that we indisputably make in front of representational pictures, and which are of the form "That looks like a Saint Bernard," "That looks like Henry VIII."

For note that, when we make such remarks, the demonstrative picks out, not some part of the pictorial surface, not some part of the spectator's experience, but the represented thing: the very breed of dog, the very royal person, that the picture represents. In other words, in each such remark, the resembling term is an artifact of, or has been brought into existence by, representation. In consequence, any generalization of such remarks will not be a theory that explains representation by reference to resemblance. It will be a theory within, not of, representation, which it presupposes.

It was received opinion that the Resemblance theory was dead, and then in the last few years two singularly subtle versions of it have appeared, raising second thoughts: one advanced categorically by Christopher Peacocke,[1] but renouncing the label, the other, coming from Malcolm Budd[2] accepting the label, indeed expressly looking to see the best that can be done under it, and hence advanced only hypothetically.

Both theories are theories of experienced resemblance, and both introduce the visual field of a spectator so as to obtain the left-hand or resembling term. However the two theories conceive of the visual field somewhat differently. Peacocke conceives of it as having both representational and sensational properties – but it is the sensational properties that provide the resembling term in the case of pictorial representation. For Budd the visual field has only representational properties, and it is therefore these which provide the resembling term. Indeed for Budd my visual field is nothing but how the world, as I look out on it, is represented by vision, *with one proviso*: that we have abstracted away all properties involving distance, or outwardness. (Whether such an abstraction is possible, or whether the most that we can do in this direction is to conceive of the different things we see as represented to us as all equidistant from us, is an important matter, but not to be pursued here.) It follows from there being these differing conceptions of the visual field that, for Budd, when something in the visual field is experienced as resembling something else, something non-pictorial, so too is the corresponding part of the pictorial surface. But not so for Peacocke, who introduces another relation holding between the picture and what it represents, and this relation goes through, and is defined partly in terms of, experienced resemblance.

And just a word on what both theories take to be the resembled term. It is another visual field, a possible visual field: more precisely, it is that visual field which the spectator of the representation would have were he, instead if looking at it, the representation, to look at what it represents. But, for any represented thing, there is a myriad of ways in which it can be seen, and to each of these ways there corresponds a different possible visual field. Accordingly the second visual field, or the resembled term, fixes, not only what is represented, but how it is represented: that is to say, what properties it is represented as having. Take two of Monet's *Grainstacks* that represent the same two stacks. Evidently they represent them differently, or as having different properties, but how are we to account for these differences? On the present theory we are to do so by first taking the visual fields to which looking at these two pictures gives rise, and then asking of each, "Which of the myriad visual fields to which looking at two grainstacks in nature gives rise would a suitable spectator experience it, the present visual field, as resembling?" So one of these pictures, that on the left, represents a large grainstack, and it represents this as in full sunlight, and it does so for this reason: that the visual field generated by looking at it pairs itself off with the visual field that would arise when looking at a large grainstack and seeing it in full sunlight.

The further details of both theories are more complex than I have need to take account of, but let me, at this stage, express a preference between the two theories. Peacocke's theory specifies that the experienced resemblance between the two visual fields is specifically in respect of structure. In doing so, it gratuitously comes down on one side rather than the other of Heinrich Wolfflin's famous distinction between the linear and the painterly modes of representation, between the art of stressed, and the art of unstressed, edges.[3] Peacocke's theory aligns itself with the linear mode. Budd professes to avoid this partiality by substituting experienced resemblance in structure for experienced resemblance in shape. If – and I repeat "if" – there is a real difference that correlates with this distinction, then Budd surely improves on Peacocke in substantive adequacy.

So now to the question whether the Resemblance theory thus refined can meet the minimal requirement. So long as the minimal requirement remains skeletal, the answer is Yes. The Resemblance theory clearly insists on an appropriate experience. What each picture represents is determined by some experienced resemblance. But amplify the minimal requirement along the lines suggested, and the answer is, just as surely, No. And that is because the experienced resemblance, which is between two visual fields, does not include a visual awareness of the second field, let alone of what the second field is of, or what the picture represents.[4] True: In order to experience the resemblance, we must have dispositionally a recognitional skill for what the second field is of, or what the picture represents. But it is no more required by the Resemblance theory than it is by the Semiotic theory that this skill is manifested in an actual or non-dispositional awareness of the represented thing. And that, if I am right in characterizing the appropriate experience, is what is called for.

At the beginning of *Philosophical Investigations,* II, xi, pages which cast alternating beams of light and darkness on the topic of this lecture, Wittgenstein distinguishes between two situations in which I can experience or observe a resemblance.[5] The first is this: Two faces confront me, and I observe a resemblance between them. The second is this: One face confronts me, and I observe its resemblance to another face, which is absent. Now, it is only if representations gave rise to experienced resemblance of the first sort that a Resemblance theory could be constructed that satisfied the minimal requirement for a theory of representation. But it is only the second sort of experienced resemblance that it is plausible to think of in connexion with representation. For, in looking at a representation, we see the representation: but not the represented.

At this point it might be objected that the amplification I have laid upon the minimal requirement, or that there must be a visual awareness of what is represented, is excessive, and that I have done this by reading too much into the conditions in which a recognitional skill is acquired.

I shall not follow this line of reasoning. Instead I shall turn to the theory of representation that I have long advocated, for this theory appears to meet the amplified requirement, and the question that I shall address is whether it does so at a cost in cogency or (some would add) intelligibility.

5. Central to this theory is a special perceptual skill, called "seeing-in," which we, and perhaps the members of some other species, possess.[6] Seeing-in is prior, both logically and historically, to representation. Logically, in that we can see things in surfaces that neither are nor are taken by us to be representations; say, a torso in a cloud, or a boy carrying a mysterious box in a stained, urban wall. And historically, in that doubtless our remote ancestors did such things before they thought of decorating the caves they lived in with images of the animals they hunted. However, once representation appears on the scene, it is seeing-in that furnishes, for each representation, its appropriate experience. For that is the experience of seeing in the pictorial surface that which the picture is of.

What is distinctive of seeing-in, and thus of my theory of representation, is the phenomenology of the experiences in which it manifests itself. Looking at a suitably marked surface, we are visually aware at once of the marked surface and of something in front of or behind something else. I call this feature of the phenomenology "twofoldness." Originally concerned to define my position in opposition to Gombrich's account,[7] which postulates two

alternating perceptions, Now canvas, Now nature, conceived of on the misleading analogy of, Now duck, Now rabbit, I identified twofoldness with two
simultaneous perceptions: one of the pictorial surface, the other of what it
represents.

More recently I have reconceived twofoldness, and now I understand it in
terms of a single experience with two aspects, which I call configurational,
and recognitional. Of these two aspects I have claimed that they are phenomenologically incommensurate with the experiences or perceptions – that is, of
the surface, or of nature – from which they derive, and what I had in mind
was something of this order: Sometimes we experience a pain in the knee.
This is a complex experience, but it is not to be understood by seeing how
one part of it compares with having a pain but nowhere in particular, and
how the other part compares with being aware of one's knee and where it is.
What I never wanted to deny was that each aspect of seeing-in might be,
through its phenomenology, functionally equivalent to the experience from
which it derives. The fact that we can acquire recognitional skills through
looking at representations, a point on whose theoretical significance I have
always insisted, conclusively proves this to be so.

Criticism – that is, sympathetic criticism – of my theory of representation
has largely taken the form of asking for more: specifically, more about the
phenomenology of seeing-in.[8]

On this request, some methodological remarks.

First, we must not respond to such a request as though there were a
canonical mode of describing phenomenology so that we could, taking some
experience, and proceeding region by region, finish up with a tolerably
comprehensive account of what it is overall like.

Second, we must not expect from ourselves, or allow anyone else to do so,
a description from which someone who had never had the experience could
learn what it would be like to do so. In fact, the demand for such a description
is implicitly a denial that the experience exists.

Third, we must never lose sight of the philosophical point of phenomenological description. It is not to teach us the range of human experience. It is
for us to see how some particular experience can, in virtue of what it is like,
do what it does. It pursues phenomenology only to the point where function
follows from it. In the case of seeing-in, we need to know how it can provide
an appropriate experience for each and every representation, or how (the
same thing) the scope of seeing-in can coincide with that of representation.

I shall pursue this last line of inquiry, but first I want to consider a proposal,
which many might find plausible. This is that, granted that seeing-in grounds
representation, experienced resemblance grounds seeing-in. In other words,
whenever we see something in a surface, this is in part because of a resemblance that we experience between it and the something else.

There are, I believe, three considerations that militate against such a view.

6. The first consideration is this: The surface of any picture can contain elements that, though individually visible, make no contribution to what the picture represents. In Budd's phrase they lack "pictorial significance." Consider, for instance, the punchmarks in a Gothic painting, or the dabs of complementary colour, red, say, in a field of green, that Monet used to enhance vivacity.

Now, if seeing-in rested on experienced resemblance, we would need an antecedent way of filtering out such elements, otherwise we shall think of a picture as representing those things which we can experience these elements as resembling. We shall think that Orcarna represents the Madonna's halo as embroidered, or that Monet has scattered tiny scarlet blossoms through the reeds.

If however we retain seeing-in as prior, then we shall be encouraged to look at the picture, to see in it whatever we are inclined to, and it is only if we have reason to suspect what we have seen that we shall start to check the surface for elements that might have led us astray. However, since elements that are indubitably insignificant need not lead us astray, there is, so long as the priority of seeing-in is maintained, no necessity for an antecedent principle of exclusion. And this, as I see it, is fortunate, since none seems available.

The second consideration is this: If experienced resemblance is basic, then what we must be expected to do is to attend to each pictorially significant element that we can identify and be visually aware of it at least to this degree: that we experience it as resembling something or other. Perhaps additionally we need to experience it as having that property in respect of which the resemblance strikes us. And this is because, since, on this view, the only way in which anything can be represented in the picture is through some part of the picture being experienced as resembling it, neglect one pictorially significant element, and, we shall lose some part of what the picture represents.

At this point the question arises whether a theory of experienced resemblance, like a linguistically oriented semiotic theory, requires that pictures be capable of systematic segmentation. If the answer is, No, which seems, on general grounds, more plausible, and pictorial elements can in principle swell so as to engulf both small groups of marks *and* the circumambient surface between them, a danger lurks. Consider, by way of example, "the small black circle" of which Roger Fry made so much in his formalist onslaught upon Breughel's great *Procession to Calvary*[9] – how are we to say for certain that we experience such elements as resembling something in the world that the picture represents, rather than as resembling a representation of those things? In other words, can we prevent the theory of experienced resemblance from declining into what I have called a theory within, as opposed to a theory of, representation.

By contrast, when seeing-in is given priority, all that is required is that we are visually aware of the surface, and how detailed this awareness must be is an open matter. And this is because there is no perceptible feature of the surface corresponding to every feature of what is represented. The representational content of a painting by Gainsborough or Turner is not constrained by what I have called "localization."

The third consideration against the priority of experienced resemblance is this: That this view requires us not only to be aware of what properties the pictorially significant elements have, but to infer from these properties how the corresponding object is represented, or what properties it is represented as having. But such inferences can be wild. Parmigianino's Madonna, the woman herself, is not represented as having a long neck, nor did Ingres, who despised anatomy, show his odalisques – again the women themselves – with, as contemporary critics maintained, one vertebra too many.

A final observation: Those who find a place for experienced resemblance in an account of representation think it in their favour that such an account readily yields a criterion of naturalism in representation. If it does, I, on the contrary, see that as a mark against their account. For, once we start to survey the very different kinds of representation that we think of as naturalistic, it seems crude to believe that there is a single, let alone a simple, criterion, least of all one in which experienced resemblance plays a primary role, of naturalism, ahistorically conceived.

7. I return to the question how the scope of seeing-in and the scope of representation can be identical, and I start by asking, What is the scope of representation?

The answer falls into two parts. The first part is ontological, and it gives us the various kinds of thing that can be represented, or what I call the varieties of representation. The second part consists in an overarching constraint, and this is imposed by the limits of visibility. As Alberti put it, "The painter is concerned solely with representing what can be seen."

The varieties of representation are given by a cross-classification. Along one axis, we have representations of objects *versus* representations of events. Women (objects) can be represented, and so can battles (events). Along the other axis we have representations of particular objects or events *versus* representations of objects or events merely of a particular kind. So we can have a representation of Madame Moitessier (particular object), or a representation of a young woman behind a bar, perhaps a young woman of some specificity – but no particular young woman (object merely of a particular kind). Alternatively we can have a representation of the Battle of San Romano (particular event), or a representation of a cavalry skirmish – one fought at dusk, on level terrain, between sides evenly matched, muskets reinforcing sabres – but no particular skirmish (event merely of a particular kind). Representations that are of things merely of some particular kind, whether objects or events, are, I believe, best identified through their intrinsic failure to sustain answers to the question, Which object?, Which event?, or, Which woman?, Which battle?

Nelson Goodman has pointed to another variety of representation: that is, a representation of all things of a certain kind.[10] These are to be found in dictionaries or manuals, but seldom in pictorial art.

However, in considering the scope of representation, I believe that the better starting-point is with the second part of the account: the *constraint* upon representation, or visibility. It gives us more immediate insight into how the scope of representation and the scope of seeing-in coincide. And that is because of what this constraint asks for. Representation does not have to limit itself to what can be seen face-to-face: What it has to limit itself to is what can be seen in a marked surface.

But what is the difference? For is there anything that can be seen in a surface that cannot be seen face-to-face?

The answer is, Yes, and we already know at least part of the reason. For we can see in pictures things merely of a particular kind, and these we cannot see face-to-face. We cannot see face-to-face women and battles of which we may not ask, Which woman? Which battle?

But some might insist that, though we can see in pictures kinds of thing that we cannot see face-to-face, we cannot see them as having *properties* that we cannot see, or cannot see things as having, face-to-face. It was in elaboration of this doctrine that Lessing famously denied that pictures can represent events unfolding in time; that is, that they can represent events as unfolding in time.

It is arguable that where Lessing was really at fault was in the limits he attributed to what can be seen face-to-face rather than in those he consequentially imposed upon what can be represented. Without opening up this issue, let me simply point out that pictures can represent things as having properties that lie extremely close to the limits of face-to-face visibility, and leave it open on which side they actually lie. So pictures can represent a man as singing and a woman as listening to him: They can represent kings as seeing things that are not given to the human eye: They can represent a man as renouncing all earthly goods but one, and why: And they can represent a woman as hearing news the greatness, the terribleness, of which she struggles to take in.

8. If we now ask, How this is so?, we are asking for a general account of what it is for something to be visible in a surface.

Consider the following experiment: I look at a picture that includes a classical landscape with ruins. And now imagine the following dialogue: "Can you see the columns?" "Yes." "Can you see the columns as coming from a temple?" "Yes." "Can you see the columns that come from the temple as having been thrown down?" "Yes." "Can you see them as having been thrown down some hundreds of years ago?" "Yes." "Can you see them as having been thrown down some hundreds of years ago by barbarians?" "Yes." "Can you see them as having been thrown down some hundreds of years ago by barbarians wearing the skins of wild asses?" (Pause.) "No."

At each exchange, what "Yes" means is that the prompt has made a difference to what has been seen in the scene, just as the "No" signifies that, for at least *this spectator here and now,* the limits of visibility in this surface have been reached. Now, let us assume that this spectator is the suitable spectator for this picture. In that case we can understand the "No" as a refusal on his part to be forced beyond the appropriate experience, hence a refusal to force upon the picture something that it doesn't represent.

What this thought-experiment primarily shows is the central phenomeno-logical feature of seeing-in, which is its permeability to thought, whether the thought is caused by the marked surface or is prompted by another. And it is this feature that in turn accounts for the wide scope of seeing-in, wider, as we have seen than that of seeing face-to-face. It is the permeability of seeing-in to thought that accounts for the wide range of things that can be repre-sented and for the wide range of properties they can be represented as having.

However two observations are called for.

The first is this: Just because it is true that, on looking at a picture, we can recruit a thought to our perception so that what we see in the picture changes, it does not follow from this that we have any way of indicating where the change occurs, or what it amounts to – apart, of course, from repeating the thought that has brought about the change. Second, in insisting that thought, conceptual thought, can bring about changes in what we see in a surface, I am not taking sides on the issue whether the experience of seeing-in has a conceptual or non-conceptual content. Tasting soup has a non-conceptual content, but, if we are prompted conceptually about what is in the soup, the soup can taste different.

9. Another psychological phenomenon that is highly permeable by thought is imagination, and it is tempting to think that imagination, specifi-cally in its more perceptual mode, or visualizing, grounds seeing-in.

A simple version of this proposal is that, when I see a face in a picture, I am led, by the marks on the surface, to imagine seeing a face. However imagining seeing a face, which is now assigned the role of the appropriate experience, floats free of the representation. Though it determines what the picture represents, it and the seeing of the pictorial surface are only externally related.

A more complex, and a far superior, version of this proposal, which has been championed by Kendall Walton,[11] is this: I see the pictorial surface, I imagine seeing a face, and of my seeing the surface I imagine it to be an experience of seeing a face. Furthermore the veridical experience of the surface and the imaginary experience of the face, both perceptual, form, in Walton's phrase, "a single experience": twofoldness again.

My difficulty with this second proposal is how to understand the core project, or imagining one perceptual experience to be another. For, if we succeed, in what way does the original experience retain its content? For what is left of seeing the surface when I successfully imagine it to be some other experience? However, if I do continue to see the surface, or this experience retains its content, how have I succeeded in imagining it, the experience, to be an experience of seeing a face? And note two things. First, that imagining one experience to be another is something more experiential than simply imagining that one experience is the other. And, second, note that this problem arises exclusively where (1) what we imagine to be something different from what it is is something perceptual *and* (2) what we imagine it to be is also something perceptual. There is clearly no fundamental difficulty in my moving my hands and arms in a jerky and irregular fashion and imagining of it that I am conducting some great orchestra, nor, for that matter, in my looking hard at an old enemy and imagining of it that I am burning him up with my gaze.

10. I too find a place for imagination in my account of representational meaning, but it is a place that is ancillary to seeing-in, and is relevant only to certain paintings.[12] These are paintings in which the suitable spectator is offered a distinctive form of access through the presence in the represented space – though not in that part of it which is represented – of a figure, whom I call the Spectator in the Picture. The Spectator in the Picture has, amongst other things, a psychological repertoire: a repertoire of beliefs, desires, attitudes, responses. What then happens is that the suitable spectator, the suitable *external* spectator we might say, starts to identify with the internal spectator: that is, to imagine him centrally, or from the inside, interacting with the represented scene as the repertoire assigned to him allows or constrains him to. The net result will be that the external spectator will find himself in a residual state analogous to that of the internal spectator, and this state will in turn influence what he sees in the picture when he reverts from imagination to perception.

Take as examples of representations that contain a spectator in the picture some of Manet's single-figure compositions: say, *The Woman with a Parrot* or *The Street-Singer*. When I look at either of these paintings, I see in its surface a woman momentarily but intensely preoccupied. She is distracted by a secret. Then I recognize from a variety of cues the existence of a second figure, male perhaps or perhaps indeterminate as to sex, who stands in the represented space somewhere just this side of the picture plane. I then start centrally imagining this figure trying, trying hard, trying in vain, to make contact with the represented figure. The tedium, the frustration, the despair that I come to imagine, to imagine from the inside, the spectator in the picture's experiencing will trickle back into me and reinforce how I see the woman. I recapitulate this account of the Spectator in the Picture, taken from *Painting as an Art* – though omitting all discussion of what evidence we might have, in the case of any given picture, for there being such an intervention – in order to emphasize the difference in role, and the division of labour, as I see it, between perception and imagination in our interaction with representational paintings. But, note, none of this is intelligible unless we acknowledge the existence of a form of imagination that contemporary philosophy has, implicitly at any rate, rejected. And that is centrally imagining someone other than oneself. Currently imagination from the inside is treated as though it must be de *se*. If I imagine anyone from the inside it can only be myself; and, if I *seem to* imagine another, what I really imagine is either myself in another's shoes, which falls short of the project I am assuming, or myself being another, which is incoherent. Much recent discussion of the role of imagination, or (as it is currently called) simulation, in grounding our knowledge of other minds is vitiated by this failure to recognize the scope of imagination.

11. Let me, even at this late date, point to a surprising omission in this lecture: surprising, since the phenomenon not only figures large in many accounts of representation, but it is the keystone of my own account. There has been no mention of artist's intention: "intention" being the word that has come to mean those psychological factors in the artist that cause him to work as he does.

The most schematic way of fitting the artist's intention into the account that I have given is this: With any representational picture there is likely to be more than one thing that can be seen in it: there is more than one experience of seeing-in that it can cause. However the experience of seeing-in that determines what it represents, or the appropriate experience, is the experience that tallies with the artist's intention. With omission of the artist's intention from the argument, I have had to put the point more obliquely in terms of the suitable spectator, who is identified as the spectator with suitable sensitivity and suitable information and suitably prompted. But it is the same point, for consider what "suitable" here means. It means the sensitivity, the information, the prompting, that are required if the spectator is to see the picture as the artist desires him to.

However there has also been an advantage in putting the matter as I have had to: that is, in terms of what the suitable spectator sees rather than of the artist's intentions. For it has made it clear why, for some representations, there will be no appropriate experience. Such an experience will elude even the suitable spectator, and that is because the artist failed to make a work that can be experienced in a way that tallies with the artist's intentions. In such cases the work, we must conclude, represents nothing – though, of course, to put it like this obscures the fact that failure, failure to realize intention, is always a matter of degree. Balzac's Frenhofer apart, can it ever be total?

Representational meaning, indeed pictorial meaning in general, is, on my view, dependent, not on intention as such, but on fulfilled intention. And intention is fulfilled when the picture can cause, in a suitable spectator, an experience that tallies with the intention. And note that the spectator's knowledge of the artist's intention, however acquired, can legitimately mould what he sees in the picture. However what this, or indeed any other, knowledge cannot legitimately do is to substitute itself for perception. If all the suitable spectator can do is to pick up on the artist's intention, and interpret the work accordingly, and there is no register of this in his experience of the picture, the conditions of representation have not been satisfied.

Representation *is* perceptual.

NOTES

This lecture was originally delivered as the Gareth Evans Memorial Lecture at the University of Oxford, on 26 November 1996. It is reprinted here from the *Journal of Aesthetics and Art Criticism* 56: 217–26, by the kind permission of the editor.

1. Peacocke, Depiction.
2. Budd, How Pictures Look.
3. Wölfflin, *The Principles of Art History*.
4. Peacocke expressly makes this point when he contends that, in the case of the representation of, for example, a castle, his theory demands that the concept castle enters the content of the appropriate experience in a more embedded fashion than it would if that experience were an experience as of something falling under that concept. He also says that, if the appropriate experience were an experience as of a castle, that would favour an illusionistic account of representation (Depiction, 403). My thesis of twofoldness is intended to block that line of reasoning.
5. Wittgenstein, *Philosophical Investigations*.
6. See Seeing-As, Seeing-In, and Pictorial Representation (AO2 205–26), and PA, Lecture II.
7. Gombrich, *Art and Illusion*.
8. For example, Budd, On Looking at a Picture, and Walton, Seeing-In and Seeing Fictionally.
9. Fry, *Transformations: Critical and Speculative Essays on Art*, 15–16. For a discussion of this passage, and of formalist criticism, see Wollheim *On Formalism and its Kinds*.
10. Goodman, *Languages of Art*, Chapter I.
11. Walton *Mimesis as Make-Believe: On the Foundations of the Representational Arts*.
12. PA, Lecture III.

Chapter 2
Wollheim on Pictorial Representation

JERROLD LEVINSON

I. Richard Wollheim offers us in the first chapter an elegant precis of the view of pictorial representation he has developed over the past thirty years.[1] In addition, he comments on competing views of the matter, and responds to criticisms or calls for elaboration that his own view has elicited. Somewhat regrettably from the point of view of one charged with producing a critical discussion, the extent of my accord with Wollheim on this topic is rather large, as I now indicate.

First, I agree with Wollheim that the concept of pictorial representation, or depiction, cannot be explicated without appeal to a characteristic sort of *experience*, the sort of experience Wollheim has denominated "seeing-in." Sustaining an appropriate seeing-in experience, that is, a seeing-in experience that conforms with the artistic intention governing a given picture, is what is criterial of such representation, and not anything else.

Second, I agree with Wollheim, as against Budd, that seeing-in is generally prior to, and not to be analyzed in terms of, the perceiving of resemblances as such, whether between objects or experiences.

The fundamental rationale for so insisting is this. Though perception of resemblance, or more narrowly, structural isomorphism, between object aspects or visual fields, may be a concomitant, trigger, or consequence of seeing-in, it is not equivalent to seeing-in. Seeing-in can occur without such perceptions, and vice versa, and so there can be no identifying them. The experiences of perceiving resemblances and seeing-things-in-other-things are different, and irreducibly so; the former is inherently relational and comparative, the latter not.[2] We may observe, in addition, that were seeing-in to be identified with perception of structural isomorphism, then since the latter is clearly a degree notion one would expect the former to be as well. But seeing-in is not evidently a notion of degree, nor is that of depiction, which seeing-in underwrites; seeing-in and depiction are closer, if anything, to being on-off or all-or-nothing affairs.

What is likely true in this matter is that a nonzero degree of structural isomorphism between a representation and its subject is required for seeing-in to take place, that is, that some such isomorphism may be a causal precondition of seeing the subject in the representation; the mechanisms whereby seeing-in – a kind of seeing, after all – is enabled to occur seem to require as much. But even if that is so, the perception of such isomorphism, as opposed to its mere existence, remains strictly unnecessary to the occurrence of the distinct experience of seeing-in.

Third, I agree with Wollheim, as against Walton, that seeing-in is generally prior to, and not to be analyzed in terms of, imagined seeing.

A reason for that insistence, beyond those hinted at by Wollheim, is as follows. If seeing-in is equated with imagined seeing of a certain kind, that is, if every case of the former is made out to be a case of the latter, then we lose a resource for explaining some of the special character, whether of immediacy, intimacy, absorbingness, or emotional impact, of some pictures as opposed to others (or alternatively, of some occasions of experiencing pictures as opposed to others), by appeal to the idea that although all pictures in being perceived as such induce seeing-in, only some pictures induce (or only some occasions of experiencing involve), actually imagining seeing the object that a picture represents. Imagining seeing X in viewing Y implies, as a default, imagining you are face-to-face with X; but it seems doubtful one is standardly doing that merely in virtue of seeing X in Y, that is, recognizing the look of X in the design of Y.[3]

II. The basic shape of Wollheim's position on pictorial representation is thus one I find congenial. But I have come to have various qualms about its specific articulation, qualms that prompt me to a friendly interrogation of some of its constitutive elements. As a result I will be led to venture certain claims that Wollheim would, I am sure, be reluctant to embrace. Still, the picture of picturing that I uphold remains, in broad outline, a recognizably Wollheimian one.

The elements of Wollheim's position that I will examine are these: the treatment of *trompe l'oeil*; the status of twofoldness in seeing-in; the recognitional aspect of seeing-in; the scope or range of seeing-in; and the appeal to the artist's fulfilled intention as a standard of representation. At more length, the questions I want to pursue are as follows. (1) Is *trompe l'oeil* precluded from being understood as representational because designed to forestall an apprehending experience characterized by twofoldness?; (2) Is the experience of seeing-in in fact necessarily characterized by twofoldness, that is, simultaneous awareness of medium and of subject, such that seeing-in has always a configurational as well as a recognitional aspect?; (3) What can be said about the recognitional awareness that is arguably at the core of seeing-in, especially if configurational awareness, or awareness of medium, is not always present as well?; (4) Is seeing-in really the same phenomenon or mental state across all the sorts of things it is said can be seen in pictures?; and (5) Is the artist's fulfilled intention to depict such and such an apt criterion of what it is correct to see in a picture, and so of what it depicts?

III. That *trompe l'oeil* pictures pose a problem for the seeing-in theory of depiction is, I think, undeniable. If being a depiction requires inviting and sustaining seeing-in, and if seeing-in is an experience that necessarily involves twofoldness, and if twofoldness necessarily implicates awareness of and attention to pictorial surface, at some level, then it seems that *trompe l'oeil* pictures cannot be depictions. Though Wollheim is content to accept this consequence of his seeing-in account, it strikes me, as it has others, as counterintuitive.[4]

Now, there is in fact a way to understand *trompe l'oeil* pictures as supporting appreciative experiences with something like twofold character, and thus as thereby having clear claim to depictive status, before adressing the question of whether simple seeing-in is necessarily characterized by strict twofoldness. It is this. When we see *trompe l'oeil* pictures as pictures, that is, when we are aware that they are pictorial contrivances, when we are past the point of being taken in by them, when we recognize them as *trompe l'oeil* while allowing them to continue to "fool the eye," then something on the order of twofoldness, or simultaneous awareness of subject and medium, is present, even though the medium is, in a way, transparent. In such cases there is a kind of awareness, perhaps even visual awareness, of the surface, in the sense that visual attention is carried to it, despite the fact that with a perfect *trompe l'oeil* the surface remains invisible. Once you grasp that something is a *trompe l'oeil* you can attend to its surface, and in its visual aspect, even though you cannot by hypothesis see the surface as such. What you can do with a *trompe l'oeil* painting, as with any painting, is mentally focus on the surface before you at the same time as you register its pictorial content, notwithstanding the fact that in such cases the surface does not end up arresting your vision.

But let us put aside that resolution of the difficulty, appealing as it does to an exceedingly liberal construal of twofoldness, and consider again the problem generated for the theory of picturing by *trompe l'oeil*. It seems there are two options open to us. We can either allow that seeing the pictorial content of a *trompe l'oeil* painting without realizing it is such, and so *a fortiori* without any awareness of the painting's surface, is still an instance of seeing-in, and thus that such seeing does not always involve twofoldness (first option), or else deny that seeing the pictorial content of a *trompe l'oeil* painting without realizing it is such is an instance of seeing-in, thus retaining twofoldness as a necessary feature of such seeing (second option).

One might argue in favor of the second option that naively registering the pictorial content of a *trompe l'oeil* does not involve seeing the picture *as* a picture, and for that reason should not be accounted a case of seeing things in the picture. In addition, since attention to form concurrently with content, or to content-as-embodied-in-form, is often taken to be the heart of what it is to carry *aesthetic* attention to an object,[5] one might further argue, against the first option, that by its lights seeing-in would not necessarily exhibit aesthetic character.

However, as is probably apparent, such an argument would be weak, since the considerations on which it turns seem more convincingly deployed in the opposite direction. Plausibly *not* all seeing-in or registering of pictorial content is aesthetic in character, or even informed by the awareness of pictures as pictures; for instance, that directed to or had in connection with postcards, passport photos, magazine illustrations, comic strips, television shows, or movies.[6] Thus, any view that builds aesthetic character, or even awareness of pictures as pictures, directly into seeing-in would seem to have something amiss. It seems perfectly reasonable to hold that one can be seeing things in pictures, in virtue of looking at pictures, even when one is *not* seeing them as pictures, and a fortiori, *without* appreciating them aesthetically.[7]

I propose, then, that we embrace the first option, whereby simple *seeing-in*, and what we might call *pictorial seeing* proper, are distinguished, with only the latter definitionally implying twofoldness. Pictorial seeing, or seeing pictures as pictures, is indeed a *sine qua non* of aesthetic appreciation of pictures, but the fact is that there can be seeing-in in connection with pictures that is not even pictorial seeing, that does not involve any awareness of pictorial properties or the medium in which they are embedded.

If you see a woman in a picture in virtue of visually processing a pattern of marks, then of course in some sense you are thereby perceiving the medium in which those marks inhere or consist. But it is far from clear that when you see the woman in the picture you must in some measure be attending to, taking notice of, or consciously focusing on the picture's surface or patterning as such. Yet that does appear to be part of the import of twofoldness as Wollheim construes it: "Looking at a suitably marked surface, we are visually aware at once of the marked surface and of something in front of or behind something else. I call this feature of the phenomenology 'twofoldness'."[8] That twofoldness as Wollheim understands it means that the experience of seeing-in involves, in its configurational as well as its recognitional aspect, *some* level of conscious apprehension and not, say, merely unconscious registering – is confirmed by this more extensive passage from *Painting as an Art*: "The twofoldness of seeing-in does not, of course, preclude the one aspect of the complex experience being emphasized at the expense of the other. In seeing a boy in a stained wall I may very well concentrate on the stains, and how they are formed, and the materials and colours they consist of . . . and I might in consequence lose all but *a shadowy awareness* of the boy. Alternatively, I might concentrate on the boy, and on the long ears he seems to be sprouting . . . and thus have only *the vaguest sense* of how the wall is marked" [my emphases].[9]

A crucial issue, then, would seem to be what, exactly, *being visually aware of* a picture surface amounts to. Not, surely, *receiving information from* the surface, or *being sensitive to changes* in features of the surface; such construals are too weak for the purpose, since too easily satisfied by mental states, for example, subdoxastic ones, that lie below the level of consciousness. Not, surely, *thinking or reflecting that* one is seeing the surface as one sees it; such a construal would be too strong, collapsing visual awareness per se and selfconscious visual awareness. Perhaps, then, something like this: *attending to the surface as one views it and is affected by it.* But if anything like that construal is adopted, it is indeed doubtful that the seeing-in involved in grasping pictorial content always entails or includes visual awareness of the surface as well. At any rate, Wollheim has not indicated an intermediate notion of awareness that might be apt to the needs of the case but that does not import any degree of attention whatsoever.

IV. The task remains, though, of saying what simple seeing-in consists in, given it does not inevitably involve visual awareness of medium, that is, attention in some degree to medium, and yet is not just seeing in the ordinary sense.[10] As has rightly been observed,[11] clarifying what Wollheim calls the "recognitional aspect" of seeing-in – and what we may now take to be the very core of seeing-in – seems incumbent on a supporter of the seeing-in approach to pictorial representation.

Here, then, is a stab at what such recognition amounts to. In looking comprehendingly at a picture of a woman, say Kees van Dongen's engaging and mildly fauve canvas, *La chemise noire*, one does not necessarily perceive an isomorphism between experience of the picture and experience of a woman (Budd), nor does one invariably imagine seeing a woman (Walton), nor, in all probability, does it seem to you that a woman is actually before you (Gombrich). Rather, I suggest, it seems to you *as if* you are seeing a woman (alternatively, you have an *impression* of seeing a woman), in virtue of attending visually to portions of the canvas.[12] The core of seeing-in, in other words, is a kind of *as-if* seeing that is both occasioned by visually registering a differentiated surface and inextricably bound up with such registering.[13]

Of course, more needs to be said about the tight relation required here between the registering of visual information and the perception of pictorial content.[14] The relation has to be such as to rule out nonstandard causal routes by which a picture's visual array might lead one to have an impression of seeing a woman, for example, one where such an array triggered, at a subperceptual level, a chemical change that in turn issued in a localized hallucination of a woman just like the woman seeable in the picture. The impression of seeing, or as-if seeing, at the core of seeing-in is one intimately bound up with the registering of the visual data afforded by the picture, whereby the latter in a sense constitutes or realizes the former.[15]

V. None of this is to deny that much of the interest and appeal of seeing-in lies in the possibility of twofoldness in one's experience of a picture, that is, simultaneous awareness of both picturing pattern and pictured object, where one's seeing-in thus becomes seeing pictorially, properly speaking. Yet equally important, I would suggest, is the option, in which one might at turns indulge, of switching back and forth between awarenesses or focussings of attention of those two kinds, seeing sometimes only pure pattern, sometimes only pure object. In fact it would seem reasonable to include, within the ambit of pictorial seeing, that is, seeing of the kind normative for pictures understood and appreciated as pictures, both seeing where there is *simultaneous* awareness of design and content (or twofoldness), and seeing in which there was *alternation* back and forth between phases of simultaneous awareness of design and content and phases of exclusive or near-exclusive focus on one or the other. It seems that our knowing engagement with pictures does in general display an alternation between phases of simultaneity, often sustained without deliberateness, and ones of switching, often occasioned by deliberate reflection on what one's experience is like. Pictorial seeing might thus conveniently be stretched to cover such activity in all its phases.

It is hard to overestimate the keen interest that viewers of painting naturally take in bringing simultaneously into relation, or alternating systematically between, the recognitional and the configurational, or the pictured and the picturing, in different styles of depiction. This is one of the obvious, but nevertheless deep, sources of fascination with the differences among Neo-Classical, Impressionist, Post-Impressionist, Expressionist, Cubist, Surrealist, and Abstract-Expressionist treatments of what is in some sense the same subject. We are endlessly amazed with the variety of ways there are to pictorially "construct" familiar objects, so that patterns or designs that would seem to have little in common, compared as such, are revealed to have an affinity in supporting equally a visual impression of, say, a cow. That a cow can be "made," visually speaking, out of dots, dashes, lines, angles, masses, smears, or mere chiaroscuro, is something we delight in bringing home to ourselves through this activity of regularly correlating design and content in our apprehension of a painting. Each time, after absorption in the represented world, that we attend primarily to the configurations afforded by a painting, we derive anew the pleasure of seeing of what the objects of that world have been made.

But there is yet more than that. Different styles of representational painting arguably give us access to unique kinds of beings, allowing us to see things not encountered in the real world at all, rather than merely allowing us to see familiar things in a new way. What I have in mind are "beings" such as these: Ingres-women, Picasso-women, and De Kooning-women; Kirchner-men, Beckmann-men, and Grosz-men; and finally, Miró-dogs, Klee-dogs, and Dubuffet-dogs. Paintings of the respective artists familiarize us with extraordinary creatures of that sort, ones that can enter importantly into one's imaginative and interpretive repertoire; such paintings do more than simply show us how those artists, or their implied personae, may be said to have viewed ordinary women, men, and dogs.[16] Of course, after making the acquaintance of Ingres-women, Kirchner-men, or Miró-dogs, one may then be in a position to spot their instantiations, or near-instantiations, in the world around one, *hors de peinture*. That is to say, we achieve acquaintance with kinds of beings whose exemplars are not all of them, or not necessarily, fictional.

VI. I have concentrated so far mostly on seeing-in as it applies to objects. But as Wollheim urges, seeing-in may be held to range over actions and events as well, and even over individuals-merely-of-a-certain-kind as opposed to particular individuals. Concern arises, however, as to whether the range of seeing-in is usefully taken to be as wide as Wollheim proposes. The concern might alternatively be expressed as one of whether the seeing-in involved in all such cases is sufficiently of a piece as to merit the single label. Let us look to what Wollheim says about the outer limits of seeing-in as he descries them, as illustrated in the example of the classical landscape with ruins.[17]

Wollheim suggests that a suitably prepared and prompted viewer plausibly can see, in such a painting, all the following: columns, columns-as-having-come-from-a-temple, columns-as-having-been-thrown-down, columns-as-having-been-thrown-down-hundreds-of-years-ago, and columns-as-having-been-thrown-down-hundreds-of-years-ago-by-barbarians. But such a viewer cannot, Wollheim submits, see in the painting columns-as-having-been-thrown-down-hundreds-of-years-ago-by-barbarians-wearing-the-skins-of-wild-asses.

But why not? Why are all those other *qua*-objects seeable in the picture – which I take to be roughly interconvertible with the seeability therein of corresponding states of affairs – but not the last? What principle of cut-off for the *qua*-objects or states of affairs that can be seen in a picture does Wollheim have in mind? What he offers is an operational test: propose for seeing-in a candidate state of affairs and note whether it makes a difference in the suitable spectator's experience. Yet, in the absence of a clear idea of the bounds of seeing-in, it is hard to know how one would interpret the results of such a test. It is not entirely obvious what would rule out seeing the columns as having been thrown down by barbarians wearing the skins of wild asses. After all, we no more see the vandals and their destructive acts than we see the equine pelts they may very well have sported.

Of course, we can speculate on what it is that makes a non-manifest state of affairs or condition a reasonable candidate for seeing-in as Wollheim conceives that. Possibly a condition being such that perceptual inference to it is highly compelling, or a condition possessing visual traces of a relatively unequivocal sort, at least for a properly backgrounded viewer, makes such a condition something that can be seen in a picture. But I am not concerned to further worry these or any similar suggestions. The real problem, I think, is that seeing non-manifest states of affairs in pictures, seeing occurrent actions in pictures, and seeing objects in pictures may be importantly different phenomena, whose differences, say as regards spatial localization or permeability by thought, may be more obscured than illuminated by considering them together as members of a species. "Seeing-in" may not be univocal across its putative instances, especially if, as suggested earlier, twofoldness is not even an invariant feature of the experience of seeing one thing in another.

It is not clear that the same sort of activity or perception is involved when going from seeing-in of objects to seeing-in of events to seeing-in of conditions, or from seeing-in of physical events or conditions to seeing-in of psychological events or conditions. For example, localization, the property of such-and-such's being seeable more-or-less right where the relevant pictorial design is, may be characteristic of the seeing in paintings of physical objects, but somewhat less so of the seeing of events, and very much less so of the seeing of psychological entities, whether objects or events. And the permeability of seeing-in to thought, reflection, or conceptualization seems progressively more pronounced, in general, as one moves from the seeing of objects to the seeing of events to the seeing of only indirectly evidenced states of affairs in a painting. And finally one might add, for good measure, that a role for imagination in the robust sense appears considerably more plausible in regard to seeing-in of this latter sort than to seeing-in of the former two sorts. These divergences make suspect, at the least, the assumption that seeing-in in all the cases claimed by Wollheim is of a uniform nature.

VII. Lastly, there is to my mind a problem about Wollheim's appeal to fulfilled representational intentions as a standard for what a picture represents. Here is a formulation, though from an earlier paper: "Very roughly, P represents X if X can be correctly seen in P, where the standard of correctness is set for P by the fulfilled intentions of the artist of P."[18] A difficulty lurks here that Wollheim and other actual intentionalists about meaning have some tendency to gloss over. It is this. What it is for the pictorial intentions of the artist of P to be *fulfilled* cannot be specified apart from what suitable viewers are *enabled* to see in P. Such intentions are fulfilled if viewers are in fact enabled – and enabled without undue thematic prompting or inordinate mental contortion – to see in P what the artist intended be seen there. The artist's *fulfilled* intention cannot be thought of as an independent condition to which viewers' responses can be held accountable, but can only be understood in terms of the responses of appropriately primed and backgrounded viewers being the ones they were intended to be. Another way of making my point would be to say that the standard of correctness for depiction is not, as Wollheim sometimes puts it, the *fulfilled* intentions of the artist, but merely the intentions *simpliciter* of the artist for a certain sort of seeing-in, given they are capable of being complied with by the picture's intended viewers. The artist's representational intentions only *are* fulfilled if suitable viewers are enabled, on reasonable prompting, to see-in the painting in accord with the artist's representational intentions. Thus it arguably makes little sense to say they comply with the artist's *fulfilled* intentions in this regard, since such do not, as it were, preexist such compliance.[19]

VIII. Richard Wollheim's theory of pictorial representation is the fruit of long reflection, deep insight, and an intense love of painting. In the course of this essay I have criticized that theory in a number of respects, notably, its treatment of *trompe l'oeil*, its conception of seeing-in, and its appeal to the artist's fulfilled intention as a standard. Note, however, how much remains of what Wollheim has urged in what I am willing to affirm on this vexed topic: Pictorial representation involves the intentional marking of a flat surface so as to elicit a distinctive sort of visual experience in appropriate spectators, an experience we may continue to call seeing-in as long as we understand that this sometimes amounts only to what may be more transparently labeled seeing-from, where such experience is indeed elicited from those spectators in virtue of their attending to the surface as marked.[20]

NOTES

This paper is reprinted here from the *Journal of Aesthetics and Art Criticism* 56: 227–33, by the kind permission of the editor.

1. Notable bulletins in that development include Seeing-as, Seeing-in, and Pictorial Representation, in AO2; W-IPU; Art, Interpretation and Perception, in MD; and above all, PA.
2. To elaborate: perception of resemblance between visual field 1 and visual field 2 explicitly involves relating and comparing those items, while seeing object X in painting Y does not involve a parallel relating and comparing of those items. The second term in such an experience, that is, Y, does not enter into the *content* of the experience involved – though naturally it is involved in generating the experience and in fixing what experience it is. The content of the experience, consisting as it does in "seeing X," in a manner of speaking, is basically just X. (I say "basically," since it might be held that the content in question is slightly other than X per se, for instance, *image of X*. But the point would remain that such content was nonrelational, or at least, not involving a relation to Y.)
3. On my conception of it, *imagining* is necessarily *active or contributory* (though not necessarily something one is aware of initiating, and not necessarily some-

thing under the complete control of one's will). By contrast, *seeming to one as if* – what I propose captures, as well as anything can, the experience at the heart of pictorial seeing – is *passive or receptive*, not something one brings about and actively sustains but something that, in the last analysis, simply occurs. Seeing X in Y is something that happens to one, even where deliberate mental actions of various kinds, for instance, framings, thinkings, or suggestings, serve as triggers to such happening.

4. See, for example, Lopes, *Understanding Pictures*, Chapter 2.
5. See Eldridge, Form and Content: An Aesthetic Theory of Art; Budd, *Values of Art. Pictures, Poetry and Music;* and Levinson, *The Pleasures of Aesthetics*, Chaps. 1 and 2.
6. I am not, of course, denying that we may often be cognizant of such pictures as pictures, or carry aesthetic attention to them, only that we must or even usually do so.
7. I have been influenced by Lopes's critique of seeing-in theory on these points in *Understanding Pictures*.
8. On Pictorial Representation, 19.
9. PA, p. 47. We might, appropriating words of Willy Loman in *Death of A Salesman*, underline that "notice must be taken" in order for something to count as awareness.
10. To say it does not involve visual *awareness* of the medium is not, of course, to say that it does not involve visual *processing* of the information embodied in the medium.
11. See Walton, Seeing-In and Seeing Fictionally.
12. Note that "seeming to one as if P," or "having the impression that P," are not locutions that entail "believing that P" or even "thinking it probable that P." For example, "It seems to me as if I am falling unsupported," said in a rapidly descending elevator.
13. There is a real question whether the experience I have continued to refer to as simple seeing-in should in fact be so called. Two reasons give pause. The first is that the association of seeing-in – which is, after all, a term of art introduced by Wollheim – and twofoldness is so entrenched that an experience of seeing-in *sans* twofoldness sounds almost oxymoronic. The second is that conceiving such experiences as the "seeing-in" label encourages one to do, as a matter of seeing things *in* surfaces, does undeniably occasion strain where *trompe l'oeil* pictures are concerned, since in such cases the surfaces are, by hypothesis, neither seen nor seeable. One might thus concede that the visual experience of pictures I have been calling *simple seeing-in*, and that is present even when twofoldness is not, might in certain cases with more justice be called *seeing-from*.
14. It is a virtue of Walton's account of depiction, of course, that it secures the desired intimacy in the most direct fashion, by making the act of perceiving the picture that which the viewer imagines to be an act of actually seeing the subject of the picture. But it seems to me that what necessarily happens in such a case of seeing-in is at most that one *takes* one's apprehending of a surface's forms and colours to be a seeing of a woman, in a sense that does not imply that one believes or suspects that one is seeing a woman, but not that one *imagines* of such apprehending, more actively, that it is a seeing of a woman.
15. One might worry, finally, that if simple seeing-in is construed so as not to necessarily involve awareness of a picture's surface, then simple seeing-in and simple seeing will collapse. But this worry is unfounded. In the case of simple

seeing-in you seem to see X, that is, you have an as-if-seeing experience of X, in virtue of visually registering certain configurations of a surface, rather than in virtue of being in the visual presence of X. In the case of simply seeing X, it is true as well that you seem to see X, that is, have an as-if-seeing experience of X, but then there are differences. With simply seeing X there is, first, the *belief*, or tendency to believe, that X is before you, and second, it is X, and not merely a surface configured to afford an impression of X, that indeed *is* before you. This is all admittedly rough and ready, not intended as careful analysis. The point is just that the experiences of simple seeing-in and simple seeing can surely be discriminated, though once twofoldness is abandoned as a *sine qua non* of seeing-in such discrimination may not be a wholly internal matter, but may instead rest on matters such as what is precipitating the experience and what sort of mechanisms are involved in its doing so.

16. A story from the golden era of *The New Yorker* seems relevant here. James Thurber, one of the early great cartoonists of the magazine, was once the subject of discussion at the weekly art meeting being presided over by the then editor, Harold Ross. The point at issue was the seal perched on the headboard of a bed in one of Thurber's most famous cartoons, in which the wife is vocally skeptical of her husband's claims to have heard a seal bark. Someone at the meeting, noting the somewhat loosely drawn character of the seal, asked "Do seals look like that?," To which Ross's reply was "Thurber's seals look like that." (From an interview with *New Yorker* Cartoon Editor Robert Mankoff, *The Washington Post*, December 7, 1997.)

17. On Pictorial Representation, p. 23–4.

18. W-IPU, 46.

19. To be fair to Wollheim, the formulation of the intentional condition on representation in the present paper almost entirely escapes the problem, highlighted here, to which earlier formulations were subject: "Representational meaning, indeed pictorial meaning in general, is, on my view, dependent, not on intention as such, but on fulfilled intention. And intention is fulfilled when the picture can cause, in a suitable spectator, an experience that tallies with the intention" (On Pictorial Representation, 27). Still, it seemed worth drawing attention to, if only to forestall backsliding.

20. Thanks to Gregory Currie and especially Alessandro Giovannelli for helpful comments on a draft of this essay.

Chapter 3
The Limits of Twofoldness: A Defence of the Concept of Pictorial Thought

ANDREW HARRISON

Introduction

What Richard Wollheim has taught us, which has put us all in his debt, is that pictures are a proper subject for the traditional enquiries of analytical philosophy. However, I believe that he has not pushed this topic as far forward as it can go. Some quite deeply embedded assumptions of analytic philosophy need to be challenged rather more forcibly than Wollheim has been inclined to. Wollheim's extensive and deeply illuminating discussions of pictorial art contain as indications of crucial themes a number of not very technical terms of his own coining. The two that are most salient are, I suggest, "seeing in," his name for that sort of projective visual imagination from which he derives the psychology of pictorial recognition and "twofoldness." "Twofoldness" is his name for how we need to incorporate within our proper responses to pictures in art a simultaneous awareness both of what the picture depicts and of the qualities of the marked surface which renders such depiction possible. It is the implications of this latter concept that I want to explore here, since I believe they go far further than Wollheim himself wishes to acknowledge. It is a traditional, often tacit, assumption of analytic philosophy that the sole domain of the cognitive is linguistic communication, more particularly that the communication of thought can only be conceived of in terms of what can be expressed in how declarative sentences may succeed or fail to establish the truth conditions of what they say. But then it seems to follow that so long as we take pictures seriously in their own right – that is as not having a content that can be reduced to a linguistic equivalence – any cognitive account of the pictorial must be radically out of place. My view, however, is that if "cognition" means "thought," taking pictures seriously "in their own right" must invite us to consider the claims of genuinely *pictorial thought* that is not reducible to the linguistic but which is for all that a form of thinking articulated by the picture-maker and recoverable, via the picture, by an appropriately sensitive beholder.

The excitement I have derived from reading Richard Wollheim's writing about pictures encourages me in this belief, but I suspect that he himself would resist it. For throughout his writing he has, I am sure rightly, resisted all attempts to assimilate the understanding of the pictorial to the model of linguistic understanding, but he has argued as if this should further commit us to a systematic rejection of forms of cognition which are as much located within the practices of picture-making as linguistic thought may be located within our practices of language production. In his account of pictorial understanding his preferred starting point is to be found in what he calls "seeing in," that is to say in the psychology of our projective visual imagination. I certainly do not wish to deny that this exists in much the way he describes it, but my claim in what follows is that the very general phenomenon of projective seeing of this sort cannot on its own provide a full enough account of the pictorial to be adequate to an understanding of pictorial art. I do believe, however, that what he has called "twofoldness" can do this. The most important reason why it can is that it is the necessity of setting limits to the application of this idea that it makes it illuminating. My further contention is that if we take what he tells us about "twofoldness" seriously what it implies is then at odds both with the idea that the psychology of a beholder's visual imagination can provide a grounding account of pictorial understanding in art and also with *how* he contrasts pictures with language. Faced with that choice we should choose "twofoldness."

2. The Denial of Differential Attention

Like most important philosophical ideas, "twofoldness" is both deceptively simple and profound in its implications. How deep these implications are is, I think, still inadequately explored, but it is best to begin by running over the old ground of a crucial disagreement of Wollheim with Gombrich. "Twofoldness" is the term introduced by Wollheim to encapsulate his denial that pictures, especially painting and drawing, demand from us "differential attention."

In a crucial opening passage in *Art and Illusion*, Gombrich lays great emphasis on the difficulty we can have in capturing the precise point at which attention to a picture's marked surface switches over into attention to what the picture depicts.[1] It is central to Gombrich's account of our response to pictures that attention to pictorial surfaces and to what they depict are mutually exclusive. It is significant that he presents the issue here as if it were a matter of precise introspective awareness, where we may nonetheless fail to catch hold of the exact point at which we can switch between two alternative states of mind or modes of attention. Gombrich illustrates this with Wittgenstein's famous example of how we may switch between attention to a marked surface as *a picture of* a duck or as *a picture of* a rabbit. Here, the elusive "moment of change" is a change between *exclusive* alternative experiences of an interpretations of an ambiguous picture. However, as many readers of Gombrich, most particularly Wollheim, have noted, this is a misplaced analogy. Switching between two exclusive "picture interpretations," or "recognitions" is quite a different matter from switching between some "picture interpretation" and another and no pictorial interpretation at all. It is the latter which surely has to constitute simply attending to the marked surface in its own right. However, such a corrective, while right enough, might well be used to strengthen Gombrich's point, which was that once we do attend to a marked surface *as a picture* this excludes attending to it as "merely" a marked surface. Introspective report can be quite variable in these cases, but in the case of the simpler example of the Necker Cube (the familiar outline drawing of a transparent box) most people do seem to find that the switch between seeing it as a drawing of an "inside out" cube to an "outside in" cube happens quite spontaneously and unpredictably while it can be a difficult task of concentration to attend to the pattern of lines in such a way that it is *merely* seen as just that. In this case it can indeed seem as if *any* response on the part of the beholder to the marked surface *as a picture* does somehow drive out the non-pictorial response. However, insofar as we have evidence here it seems that much depends on the sorts of pictures we take as examples. If we take not the very simple linear diagrams that are typified by psychologists' drawings but far more graphically "expressive" drawing the experience can be quite different. Different drawing and painting styles themselves seem to attract twofold, as opposed to differential, attention and may do so in a variety of different ways. They do so most strongly when we have to do with pictures that demand from us a serious aesthetic response.

Wollheim's concept of "twofoldness,"[2] then, opposes Gombrich's account with the claim that in all serious responses to pictures that have been handmade we have no option but to engage in *dual* attention, both to the qualities of the marked surface and to what that surface depicts as aspects of the *same response*. If this were not so we would have no access to an understanding of the primary aspect of a painter's or a draftsman's style.[3] For those styles of drawing and painting that have to engage our aesthetic understanding require that we have to attend to the essential role of a work's *facture* – that is to say the visual evidence of *how* the depicting surface has been made – within our understanding of its depictive function. On this view, what on Gombrich's account is elusive to introspection is simply not there to be captured within any serious aesthetic response. Attention, or aspect, switching of the sort Gombrich insists on cannot be in question so long as we are concerned with a proper response to the expressive content of that sort drawing and painting that make use of the physical resources of its medium as integral with the resources of depiction. We owe much to Wollheim for insisting on this deceptively simple fact as being of fundamental importance for our understanding of pictorial art.

However, despite their disagreements both Wollheim and Gombrich share the same assumption that the general issue *is* something that has to do with a kind of experience within us. More particularly, and far more importantly, the force of this assumption is then that our theoretical access to the kind of thing that pictures depict must be *via* a route *from* the quality a picture-beholder's experience – the beholder's inner landscape – *towards* an understanding of depiction – the outer, public, landscape of the picture. I think this assumption should have been questioned as well. For it is this assumption that underlies, in my view, much of Richard Wollheim's strategy that steps from the phenomenology of "simple" perception *via* that of a specific form of projective seeing ("seeing-in") towards a theory of pictorial understanding. This leaves Wollheim's concept of "twofoldness" inadequately explained with regard to how the role of such dual attention is to be located within further explanation. The issue is how we should order our explanatory categories.

3. The Wider Implications of "Twofoldness"

The topic of "twofoldness" is central to wider issues than we sometimes suppose. To reject differential attention, either as Wollheim does or in any other way, is far from rejecting a minor mistake in analysis. It is, rather, to turn away from a major influence on our attitude to the visual arts. It is well to dwell briefly on just how powerful this influence can be. Consider how well the doctrine of differential attention runs with the Albertian assumption that a paradigm for pictures is an imaginary window.[4] (It would, of course, be unfair to blame this widespread conception on Alberti alone: it provides a paradigm case of a 'non-deceptive illusion').[5] We are to imagine a *real* framed surface through which we may imagine ourselves seeing a world we merely imagine. Each use of "imagine" here plays a vital, and subtly different, role in the account. The role played in this imaginative exercise by the use of a picture's (normally rectangular, thus window-like) frame is of deep importance. It is significant how far it still has a huge grip on us despite all the vicissitudes of subsequent uses and theories of depicting methods. This ought to be more surprising than it normally is. Frames are, of course, highly convenient devices for transporting and exhibiting finished pictures, and thus of announcing to the beholder that the work is in full dress and on artistic display. But there is far more to the matter than that. Other exhibiting devices may readily be found and rectangular frames are manifestly not essential to the construction of compositional pictorial space. The frame can evoke, rather, a quite particular kind of imaginative fiction whose ghost continues to haunt us as if it were part of the very idea of full dress display. In the description of this fiction both occurrences of "imagine" – that we are to *imagine* a window through which we see an *imagined* world – are essential. One fiction, as it were, *encloses* the other rather as the narrative of one play or story may enclose another. In the Albertian account pictures are irreducibly a form of visual narrative in their own right. We are invited to suppose a sense of a deep connection between pictures and narratives, of how pictures come to seem to take over what we might think to be the supreme task of language, that of complex story-telling: here the story is an implicit narrative of our real and imagined visual experience.

But, in fact, *by themselves* pictures do *not* tell stories; there is nothing in the pictorial record itself that can correspond to those words of consequence, of likelihood or possibility that articulates the telling of a tale. Suppose a picture, as it might illustrate a children's storybook of three cats on a wall and a dog looking at them from the ground. Will they run off? Are they friendly to the dog? Will this perhaps be the very last time they will so happily sit on the wall? Nothing in the picture itself can answer such questions. Such questions and their possible answers belong to the story that the picture illustrates. As I have argued elsewhere, we would do well to adopt the term "illustration" for the widest category of how we bring narrative – an essentially linguistic mode – to the imaginative contextualizing of pictures. We often think of illustration as minor pictorial art, confined to picture books, but really the relation of pictures to overt or tacit story telling is just the same whether we think of children's books or of the highest religious or history painting. Historical or religious beliefs or intentions belong as much outside the purely pictorial as any story belongs outside its illustrations. Quite properly, a great deal of the work of art historians consists therefore not in discussing the pictures themselves but in filling out for us their narrative, that is essentially linguistic, contexts. This restriction is a "logical" one, to do with the mode of communication we adopt, not a matter of our imaginative psychology. In simple cases, we may so readily tell an appropriate story to ourselves when shown a picture that it may seem an inevitable consequence of our grasping what it is that is depicted, but it is we who bring the narrative to the picture from a non-pictorial context of understanding. This applies just as much to the "visual narrative" of the imagined window as to any story we match to a pictorial illustration.

What makes the image of pictures as visual narratives powerful is that it links the idea of pictorial narrative with a specific sort of visual phenomenology, redolent with metaphorical possibilities that take us directly back not merely to the topic of differential experience, even, in many belief systems, of visions of different kinds of reality. Compare George Herbert's "*A man who looks on glass may on it stay his eye/Or if he pleases through it pass and then a Heav'n espy.*" This metaphor for how religious experience may reach through, and beyond the mundane refers to the Pauline metaphor of seeing though "a glass darkly" as opposed to "face to face," but its point has also to do with a certain sort of choice: In the case of windows (or mirrors, since the metaphor may be read either way) he may do as he please but cannot do both at once – and here we do have a case of willed phenomenology, of controlled attention to the content of visual experience. If pictures were imagined windows through which we see an imaginary world then attention to pictorial surfaces *would* have to be an *alternative* option to attention to what they depict.

The obvious objection to this is that pictures are not like that. The problem, however, is *how* they are not like that. We must take sides between two deeply contrasting accounts of pictures – between "experience-replication" and something far more reflective – more "cognitive," however irreducibly pictorial. The tension between these two conceptions of the pictorial runs through just about all traditional accounts of these matters. It is with us still. It is the concept of "twofoldness" that can force the issue.

For if "twofoldness" is a fact about the *experience* of picture-seeing we might either say that there are *two experiences* that somehow *must go together*, or that there is *one experience* with *two aspects*.[6] The most natural way of putting this might then be to refer to one aspect as attending to a marked surface "in a certain way" the other to what it depicts "in a certain way." The problem is then this. These awkward qualifying clauses seem ineliminable – since in effect the two "ways" have to be able to converge on one another if pictorial understanding is to succeed. They only become explicable when we notice that the apparent option (which "twofoldness" should make no option at all) is between *the marked surface* as it can be seen to articulate a *manner of depiction* of a real or imaginary landscape, person, apple, and to the real or imaginary *subject* (person, landscape, or apple) *as depicted in that way*. But then this cannot be a matter of different, and introspectable, objects. Rather, "convergence" will have to be, not between two "experience contents" but between two *judgements*, that is to say between two intellectual perspectives on the same *intentional object* – namely, *the object of depiction* as it applies to that picture, rightly construed.

Terminology can be troublesome here, whether we are loosely talking about the "phenomenology" of picture-beholding or its "psychology." There is a perfectly good sense in which we may simply wish to refer to "what it is like" for someone to experience a picture or a marked surface in a certain way. This may certainly be a matter for introspection and in a quite proper, if loose, sense this may be termed a phenomenological matter. So in this vein we might ask how different types of experience may, *via* pictures, come to terms with one another, even how the power of the work may somehow bring these different mental experiences together. There is nothing very wrong with this as a first move. But we inevitably approach further analysis with quite inadequate tools so long as we are content to remain with the idea of an introspectable experience. The different concept of an intentional object, whether in the high tradition of phenomenological analysis in the spirit of Brentano or Husserl or in the quite different traditions of discourse of, for instance, Quine, goes far beyond any question of what a particular experience is "like." For intentional objects are the formal objects of certain types of *judgements*. What any adequate account of "twofoldness" demands is to exhibit an articulated structure of judgement that begins, as it were, at the ground floor. What matters is how pictures are construed, and how they are made to be construed. Where they are misconstrued the appropriate "convergence" will not occur.

Generally, in any context where an account of communication is possible it has to be possible to have two intellectual perspectives on the same intentional object, as for instance when "*what S means*" (where S is a sentence) may, be both "*what the speaker meant*" and "*what the hearer understood.*" The positing of two such perspectives is simply one way of claiming that communication occurs. (This is, of course, not to claim in ideal level of success.) Of course any relevant analogy here will be, inevitably, far from exact, but "twofoldness," if taken seriously, inevitably carries with it some analogy with other forms of communication, even if a form of communication that is essentially in pictorial terms. In saying this I am conscious of what may be my first head-on collision with Wollheim in my understanding of "twofoldness."

This consequence is a source of unease. Wollheim has gone as far as to deny that pictures *do* communicate at all, even though at other times his own metaphor of pictures as a "conduit" between the state of mind of the artist to that of the properly informed beholder seems to suggest quite the reverse. For surely "conduits" must communicate. The unease is the suspicion that if we are tempted to think of pictures as a form of communication we will then be trapped into asking *what it is* that is communicated as if the only possible answer must be what can be given a *linguistic* equivalent – as if can be only be one medium of communication – the verbal.[7]

But this simply begs the question of the pictorial.[8] In effect Wollheim seeks to resolve the issue by retaining a concept of the pictorial as a "causal" "conduit" between the mind of the artist and the mind of the beholder, treated in such a way that it resists virtually *any* comparison with the linguistic which is regarded, by contrast, as encoded and "conventional." But the embarrassment is surely misplaced. If pictorial communication *is* a proper category it cannot be *reduced* to that belonging to any other medium of thought, however it may interact or compare with it. This manifestly need not exclude specific common features. This being so, we may say that the analogous dual perspective on the same intentional object in the case of pictures would be: on how the *artist*, achieves, or realizes a representation and on how the *beholder* realizes how the depiction was achieved. As Wollheim has rightly insisted, it matters that these two *roles* must for the painter, be occupied by the same person. This is a constitutive condition of the painter's activity. But then it is by adopting both roles together that the picture-maker communicates, makes clear to him/herself, how it is that he/she conceives of the subject matter within the *process* of picture-making. Something exactly comparable is equally a condition of any communicative activity: we as much *realize*, make clear to ourselves, how we think in the process of articulating our thoughts in language (or in any *other* medium) as we make them potentially clear to others.[9] The idea of picture-making is thus a concept of communication from the start.

It is no accident that the word "realize" like other words in the same area, carries its own double aspect of intention and intentionality – a double aspect common to *all* forms of communication, in whatever medium. Realizing the nature of our own thought is all of a piece with what constitutes enabling others to realize what they are. This is why drawing for the artist – perhaps especially that involved in the preliminary making of a picture – is inevitably a process of thought and knowledge, an activity of realization. But this is then *just not* the kind of issue that could in principle be explored by the mere introspection of the experience of seeing pictures – since it is precisely this dual role that notoriously does *not* apply to introspection. What we are faced with is the highly structured texture of *pictorial-understanding*.

In the present context, perhaps this concept of understanding *should* be controversial. I shall argue for the stronger claim that it is best grounded not (or not merely) in the psychology of *perception* but in the "cognitive" nature of drawing. And that drawing is a "cognitive" matter is, of course, controversial. (I shall return in conclusion to why I think it is indeed *drawing* that should be the key idea here). "Twofoldness" (in my view, not, I think, in Wollheim's) should be shown to embody that fact. For the facts of "twofoldness" saturate the facts of pictorial art. This is most simply demonstrated by the fact that there can be two boundaries beyond which twofoldness falls away, but for radically different reasons, one where the demands of pictorial art weaken, the other where the demands of the pictorial weaken. These limits identify the shape, scope and power of the idea.

4. The Limits of Twofoldness

The first of these limits is so familiar that it can easily be overlooked. This is where our *interest* in a picture is not at all to do with its pictorial status, not at all to do with its expressive style, but simply with its *depictive function* alone. Consider a descriptive scientific drawing, a sketch of an intended artefact, a mug shot, a photograph in an estate agent's window, a collection of family snapshots: none of these invite, nor should invite, twofold attention. More to the point, if it occurs we reject it as irrelevant. It is as if for all that the demands of twofoldness are there in the background, for these purposes we need to resist them. A persistent error in understanding pictorial communication is to see these cases as somehow the primitive, elementary ones since they seem on the face of it simpler. They are, in my view, derived from the others by a need to disregard what is inherent in all pictures. In none of these cases are we concerned with the *object-as-depicted*, only with *the object that is depicted*. All philosophical scepticism aside, it matters greatly that we do use pictures, perhaps most often, in this purely descriptive way. Because lawyers, engineers, scientists, and doting parents may all with justice insist that they are not bothered by the "artistic" qualities of their pictures, it can be tempting to suppose that here we are faced with a boundary between art and something else, something duller, more utilitarian. But this is to neglect the fact that such pictorial roles have their own place within the history of art itself, if in a rather subtler way that is parasitic on the simpler cases. There twofoldness resists *itself* as if *tact concerning style* becomes itself *a form of style*. To seek (pictorially or in other ways) to describe something is to seek something difficult and specific. Sometimes the difficulties on the way may seem too trivial to take seriously. For instance it would be a trivial folly to reject a police artist's pencil drawing on the grounds that the mugger was not after all grey all over. However, such trivia rank high among the many commonplaces that can in their turn be transfigured by art.

The second limit of twofoldness can seem equally dull. This is the fact that any drawing or painting (certainly any hand-made picture) depicts *only when the surface presents an adequate complexity of organization*. The limit here, unlike the first set of cases, does not derive from our interests – from the use to which we put the picture – but from what the marked surface is *itself* capable of. It is far more like a logical than a pragmatic limit. Divide a picture into small areas and we first get details (hands, faces, eyes, instead of whole figures). Below that there must come a point where what results is a quite "abstract" if richly factured surface, which *on its own* has no pictorial force (even though it may have a rich aesthetic or artistic power). My term for this limit is the pictorial "*mesh*," and any given picture, or *area* of a painting or drawing will have its *own* pictorial mesh.[10]

Below the mesh twofoldness falls away, but the "mesh size" itself plays a significant role in how twofoldness functions for our understanding of pictures. Much of the clues to the expressive qualities of a painting derive from how the *relative scales* of significant marks of facture – such as the size of a brush stroke or the continuous movement of a drawn line – relate to the pictures' "depictive mesh." In a restrained style the mesh may be much larger than such marks of facture, in exaggeratedly painterly styles far smaller, in other cases they may approximate. What does affect our introspectable *experience* of picture seeing is how we can thereby begin to "orchestrate," or to "integrate," our perspectives of understanding. It is the latter which is basic, which as it were, "generates" the phenomenology of our response, not the other way about.[11]

It is now very difficult to put forward the idea of pictorial communication without the most naturally available vocabulary carrying overtones of further theory. At this point it is as well to keep the theoretical claims as modest as possible. Minimally then, it is how we make (and are able to make) *pictures* that should be the prime explanatory category for the role the pictorial plays in our lives, and thus of our pictorial *thought* – and I do suppose that there is such a form of thought in its own right. However, it is pictorial methods that themselves provide both the grounding explanation of pictorial recognition and the constraints it imposes. The major constraints are of two kinds: the first, not stressed nearly enough, has to do with the kind of drawing (or painting) instruments we may use: ways of marking lines or spreading pigment in colour or in monochrome themselves limit and determine what visual aspects of things we can depict. In this quite ordinary sense, it is the choice of medium that can be crucial. However, always related to this, is a different, second, type of constraint which I am quite happy to call "pictorial syntax," which (put most loosely) is how our patterns of understanding of the visual world derive from our practices of picture-making, whether we make them for ourselves or others, not from our general experience of visual recognition and perception.

Could Richard Wollheim's concept of a certain sort of "projective seeing," what he calls "*seeing-in*" in principle perform the role allotted to it, which seems to be to provide a grounding for understanding the pictorial? It is not that "seeing-in" is not real enough. One way of putting the matter would be that the issue between us is that while he might well order things as I do here in the case of language, (thus for the aesthetics of literature which must require a essential concept of understanding) for him the order *could not* run that way in the case of pictures. The apparently obvious reason is that pictures simply do not require *that sort of* understanding which language requires. But what does the idea of "that sort of understanding" commit us to? Nobody, as far as I can see, really wants to claim that pictures require to be understood as sentences are understood, but unless we suppose by *fiat* that language can be the only possible location for any concept of understanding something which is communicated, we are here, at best, at the start of, not the terminus of, an enquiry. We cannot foreclose the important questions. So *how* is it that pictures are not like language? What makes the question difficult is that the answer *seems* so obvious: we only have to look to see it. This is, I contend, an illusion.

5. Wollheim's Contrast Between Pictures and Language

I certainly agree with Wollheim that pictures do *not* work like language does. Wollheim's mistake is to make the contrast in the wrong place. Really, neither "contrast" nor "comparison" should be the name of the game: The problem is getting the right differences to run properly with the proper similarities. Wollheim's argument is most emphatically presented in "Pictures and Language." There, he asks us to consider the word "bison," a picture of a bison, and an actual bison.[12] Why a bison? The shock of recognition in the discovery of Western European rock art was stupendous. There on the rock before us, requiring no code of interpretation, no conventions, thus (and importantly) no verbally codified beliefs lost over time, was a bison picture (presumably) as recognizable to us as it was to its maker in 12,000 BC.

Far from all rock art is quite like that, but for all that *there* on the rock were pictures of bison to the life. We just have to look and see. (The shock was, it seemed, *our* recognition of *them* – of our ancient ancestors *via* the bison painting.) Pictures, then, whatever their deficiencies, *can* have a power to communicate that *radically* outstrips language. The ancient bison reinforced a modern European hope, (not much noticed by contemporary analytic philosophers) that pictures might provide an escape from that curse of Babel that divides us by our different languages.

Here we seem to have a paradigm of the power of easy-to-recognize pictures. No learnt pattern of understanding is required of us beyond a simple psychology of recognition. Recognizing actual bisons and recognizing bison pictures go together in ways that could not possibly link recognizing the word 'bison' to either of these. Certainly, we disregard this at our peril. But what should we actually conclude from it?

Since Nelson Goodman's *Languages of Art* the paradigm problem has too often been seen as the mistake of attempting to *ground* pictorial success in visual resemblance.[13] Visual resemblance is, Goodman points out, neither a sufficient condition for pictorial representation nor a necessary one. Furthermore, resemblance being a symmetrical relation while that of one thing representing another is not, to explain the latter by the former could not in principle succeed. But, perhaps more to the point, the idea of resemblance is simply not precise enough to capture the issue. No great harm is done if we report our responses to the pictures here by insisting or denying that they do resemble bison, but not much good is done either.

Wollheim puts the matter differently and certainly better: the point is not about resemblance between pictures and things they depict but about a

Upper Paleolithic (c. 24–20,000 B.C.)
Each of these pictures are dramatically easy recognisable, yet are at the
same time highly sophisticated drawings that celebrate the differing pictorial
functions of line against the different functions of texture and volumetric
colour.

Grotto de la Vache

Niaux

contrast of pictures with words in a language. He contrasts pictures with language in three ways. Each claim he makes seems on the face of it to be more obvious than its denial. For all that I am doubtful about each, or about the interpretation we should give to each.

The first is that, whereas language must have a syntax, which for the purposes of this argument we can take to be "rules" that enable us to construct sentences from words, phrases and clauses, pictures do not have a syntax. "There can be," he says, "no serious expectation that what makes a cave painting a picture of a bison . . . is a rule or convention." (Here he assumes, I take it, that such "rules" or "conventions" have to be consciously and overtly learnt and taught, and are "arbitrary." I see no reason why we should take this for granted.) Wollheim's second claim is that, whereas pictures are not, words are arbitrary signs: It surely is indeed obvious that the word "bison" is arbitrarily connected to a real bison in ways in which this is manifestly not so for the bison picture.

His third claim is that, whereas pictures do, words do not, have what he calls the power of "*transfer*." "Transfer" is Wollheim's term for the following. To be able to recognize a bison picture is to be able to recognize a dog-, or cat-picture and, we might add, also a chimera-picture (in the same style) whereas to have learnt the word "bison" is not to have learnt the word "dog" or "cat" (in the same language).

My second limit to "twofoldness" questions how we should interpret each of these principles. In reverse order, consider, first, "transfer." What Wollheim calls "transfer" of pictorial recognition from what we first recognize to what we can then recognize is certainly important, but we should ask how it contrasts with or compares to a comparable, and equally familiar, fact about language. We need to be sure that with respect to pictures and language we really are comparing and contrasting at appropriate points. For perhaps the most dramatic fact concerning the acquisition of linguistic competence is the "generation" of linguistic understanding, how linguistic competence my readily "transfer" from what we first learn to what we may then recognize. A child who can understand the key phrase in the sentence "Daddy went shopping," can thereby grasp the sense of "Kitty went shopping," even though being perfectly aware that shopping is not the sort of thing that little cats do or could do. Big theories of generative grammar apart, the possibility of linguistic fiction and fantasy is built into language right at the start. But we should note that this fact does not relate to words, such as "dog" or "cat" but to sentences or *clauses*, to linguistic fragments rich enough to have a grammatical structure. Notoriously, and I shall here assume uncontentiously, if simplistically, the "generative" power of such grammatical understanding lies at the heart of the linguistic. Equally, we could say that pictorial "transfer" means that the possibility of picture-fictions (dragons as well as horses,

Cerebus as well as dogs) is built in at the start. It can seem as if, as standard empiricist theories of imagination have always stressed, the primary role for imagination were to operate a kind of construction kit from fragments of recalled experience. In the case of "Daddy shopping" and "kitty shopping" the "instructions" for the kit seem to be located within our grasp of linguistic grammar. Is it outrageous to suppose that something comparable might hold for pictures? Let me stress again that should we wish to compare linguistic "generation" to pictorial "transfer" the appropriate point of comparison will not be of pictures to *words* (such as the arbitrary shape of sound "bison" or "dog") but with grammatically structured *clauses*, phrases, or sentences. Then, conversely, what in the pictorial would pair with unstructured sub-units comparable to words had better be areas of a marked surface *below the mesh* of pictorial significance. The parallel might then be to think of words as below the mesh of grammatical significance. If (most) words are arbitrary in themselves and are then connected with their referents by the enclosing system of language, so equally marks below the mesh are arbitrary unless similarly organized within a pictorial system.

The general principle here is then this: In any system of communication what can be communicated is first of all a matter of the level of complexity. (This is quite compatible with the idea that how we should construe relevant complexity may vary dramatically from one mode of communication to another. For example, a sign for a note in music is insufficiently complex to convey a tune (the difference between notes and tunes may have no convincing parallel in either pictorial or linguistic contexts). Despite all the variations between modes of communication, such as linguistic, musical, or pictorial, the topic of relevant complexity may be perfectly general. Thus (very roughly), in language, a phrase is a natural unit for the communication of states of affairs, a sentence for assertions about them, narratives for longer consequential units, and so on. A theory of pictorial communication should similarly start with the concept of a picture's minimal depictive unit. More complex pictorial levels are likely to be very different from complexity in language.

As far as the doctrine of the "arbitrary sign," a doctrine that at least since Saussure has been supposed to represent the demarcation point between language and other successful or unsuccessful candidates for being systems of communication, we may say this. Below the pictorial mesh marked surfaces are in their own way quite as arbitrary with respect to what the whole picture (or its details) signify as words may (normally) be to their referents.[14] A brush stroke or a single pencil mark "below the mesh" has no more "natural" resemblance (that is to say apart from its place in a picture as a whole) than the word "bison" to a bison. As it were, below the mesh, depictive twofoldness falls away, even though we may still have the expressive abstraction of facture, of paint handling, touch, or linear "gesture."

A partial parallel of pictures with language, which leaves unquestioned other more decisive differences, might then be this: at the level of complexity of phrases, clauses, sentence structure, and so on, it is at least by no means *obvious* that division into subject and predicate forms, noun phrases, or adjectival or verb phrases is at all arbitrary from the point of view of speakers who regard the world as naturally divided into things and their properties or agents and their actions. (If it is objected that many questions are begged by this use of the term "naturally divided into," this merely re-enforces the point, for this is where philosophical questions about language begin). We may ask precisely comparable questions concerning the status of the various devices of drawing *vis-à-vis* our perceptual recognition of the looks of things. These are the characteristic puzzles of the non-arbitrary sign. Certainly how in pictures the move from the arbitrary unit to the non-arbitrary sign (what articulates pictorial significance) is very different from how the parallel is achieved in language. It does not follow, however, that there is no such move; in fact, it is an essential aspect of pictorial significance. For it is in negotiating such a transition that our twofold response to what pictures present to us in visual art becomes most manifest. I would go further: For it is in such a transition, essential to our response to pictorial *art,* that we bring together into a unity of judgement our aesthetic reactions to a work and our understanding of how it achieves its depictive power.

Certainly Wollheim's rejection of the very idea of syntax as applied to the pictorial seems to fit closely with common opinion, but this is, I suggest, very largely because the idea of syntactical "rules" carries with it the further idea of conventions or codes for understanding that have to be learnt and which can be taught. There is no need to assume this. Pictures are *not* like language, not because the pictorial lacks a syntax, but because pictorial syntax is radically *different* from linguistic syntax, even if our grasp of the latter is largely tacit, and certainly requires no formal learning. There is in the pictorial no parallel with subject-predicate structure, no hierarchy of negation patterns, of brackets, of subordinate clauses that would enable a picture to depict the content of a conditional sentence, no capacity of the sort language has to formulate its own principles within itself. Hence, we can have no concept of the "meta-pictorial," nor of a purely pictorial narrative: the principles of pictorial thought and communication do not admit of pictorial expression, nor can pictures, by themselves tell stories. Pictorial syntax, as I have urged elsewhere, is a minimal syntax. But it is not for this reason absent. Essentially the devices of the pictorial in drawing and painting are the devices of making relations in what we see manifest in another relational mode.

Pictures, while not being a species of map, are a species of *that genus* to which maps, models, and diagrams also belong,[15] namely projective systems whose depictive capacity derives not from mere resemblance (however recognized) but from their being structural analogues. Just as it is sufficient to misconstrue a relational sign (of the form "aRb") as a three-object signifier (to mistake the sign for a relation for a sign for a relatum) so, similarly a precisely comparable mistake can be to construe, say, the outline in a drawing (a pattern of relation-signs) for a picture of an object with a black line around it, or even a drawing of a piece of bent wire. The bisons represented by European ancient rock art are not beasts with black lines round them, nor do we see the "naturalistic" rock paintings that make such outlines manifest as depicting such animals. This is not mere visual recognition but pictorial construing. We often tend to suppose that this is somehow limited to serious visual art. In fact, it is all about us, as manifest in the amateur or barbarous scrawls we can find in any graffiti as in the subtlest studies by great artists. Great art is intelligibly better than commonplace scrawls, not in principle different; if this were not so it would not be marvellous but unintelligible. But then what is happening here, straightforward as it may seem, could not in principle be located in the introspectable phenomenology of visual experience alone, but within a much richer context that must incorporate the *understanding* of depictive methods and processes of significance.

6. The Key Concept of Drawing

Understanding drawing and painting is to grasp how the devices and ambiguities of the variety of "syntactical" roles and functions of elements within the marked surface may best be brought to light in the complexities of drawing. A simple example might be that the same marked line may do duty both for the direction of a plane a shadow or a crease. Think of the line that may be drawn to indicate the shape of a forehead or the orbit of an eye: such a line can mark a shadow of a forelock or of the fold of a lower eye lid (a discriminable visual "object") or at the same time the change in direction of a plane making up the solid of the skull (a relation). It may equally have a fluid or hesitant graphic role in itself, as detachable from the figurative as is a flourish in a signature. It is, however, one and the *same* line, playing *separate* roles within different contexts in the totality of the picture. We need to negotiate such ambiguities.[16]

Understanding drawing may reside in details as fine as this: at least as challenging to analysis as is grasping the complexities of a poem, or the nuances of a conversation. (In each case, of course, with a good eye or ear we may "get" it all at once – without much reflective awareness of what we have grasped.) To understand the role of drawing in our grasp of the pictorial is to come to see how for a picture-maker (whether in great art or in the everyday vernacular of amateur scrawls and sketches) these "logical" distinctions and varieties are articulated within the *processes* of drawing. There is a prejudice, not merely a popular prejudice, that has it that drawing stands to painting either as a limited, normally linear and monochromatic, form of picture-making or as a variety of systems of preliminary work that artistic decorum hides in the finished product, so that either way drawing is painting's humble ancillary, only comparatively rarely within the traditions of European Art achieving the status that permits of public presentation. I propose that it is the concept of *drawing* that should be the primary explanatory category of the pictorial.

For example, Michael Baxandall (239 of this volume) illuminatingly explores the role of specifically optical content within the Chardin's *Return from the Market*, while Svetlana Alpers (173–5 of this volume) locates the central clue to a proper grasp of Rembrandt's painting of Hendrickje as *Bathsheba* in the ambiguities of its drawing. The account I am attempting here would, I hope, if carried through, demonstrate how these apparently different strands in a picture's content are themselves essentially inter-articulated through what are, for me, the essentially cognitive strategies of drawing itself. Compare also in this volume (115) Michael Podro's warning not to isolate the recruitment of specific aspects of a line or surface. All this has to do with "drawing" in the sense I intend.

We need not be too anxious to contrast painting with drawing here: there is no real boundary. Often it may seem that painterly richness or "finish" may render the underlying nature of pictorial communication resistant to immediate analysis of how a picture "above the mesh" *must* force twofold attention onto us. To think of drawing as the primary concept for understanding the role of *facture* in our understanding of pictures is to think of the *realization* of visual, more generally, spatial, thought, and experience in the complex processes of marking depictive surfaces. Such acts of the realization of thought and experience constitute the possibility of pictorial communication. It is indeed significant that in making drawings (or sketches) we often, perhaps always, "fix," or articulate, for *ourselves* how we visually explore the world about us before we may be prepared to present that articulation to *others*, but that then indicates just how seriously we should take drawing within a theory of the pictorial.

Traditional contrasts between "painterly" and other pictorial virtues can mislead us here. Even good pictorial criticism sometimes gives the impression of being over-influenced by the negative idea of a child's colouring book, as if the tasks of making a drawing and then converting it into a finished picture could be similarly separated. Sometimes expressively deficient paintings may be criticized as being "merely" coloured-in drawings lacking an essential painterly quality. But there is really no need to restrict our conceptions of drawing to what William Blake called "dear mother outline," important as that may be.[17] "Mere" coloured-in outline (of which Blake was less guilty than his famous slogan might suggest) diminishes the picture by tending to reduce the role of drawing away from the application of pigment. We need to remind ourselves that precisely what we do value as "painterly" is a form of paint handling that by, for instance, using the sensuous dexterity of brush-work, *draws* in colour and texture in precisely that way in which limited monochromatic handling with pen or pencil does. Both uses of the media of picture-making articulate visual and spatial thought directly in the processes of picture making. The best concept we have for this process of the embodiment of thought is thus, I suggest, drawing.

My disagreement with Richard Wollheim's theoretical emphasis is thus something like this. What the phenomena of pictorial mesh show is that there is an unresolved theoretical tension in what Wollheim has to tell us. The power inherent in the concept of "twofoldness" is to enforce a non-contingent connection between our grasp of depictive recognition and of this expressive power of *facture* – that is to say, the evidence of the process of picture-making as a process of the articulation of visual and spatial thought. "Twofoldness" marks the fact that we cannot conceptually grasp one independently of the other. However, it then follows that to take "twofoldness" seriously is to mark the fact that we cannot hope to reach towards a full understanding of the pictorial *via* a simple extension of the psychology of non-pictorial perception and recognition. In the bulk of Richard Wollheim's writing, this tension tends to be disguised in two ways, by, in effect, privileging the experience of the beholder of a picture over that of a picture-maker, and by treating pictures as a (causal) "conduit," whereby the psychological state of the maker is transmitted to the mind of the beholder. The motive for the first move is natural enough: since picture-makers (artists) are beholders of what they make and few beholders are makers (as artists), it can seem that being a beholder is all that we and the artists could have in common. This forgets that in far more humble ways we are equally all picture-makers. It also disguises the fact that without a grasp of what it is to make a picture how the channel of communication could work remains quite mysterious.

I suspect this tension cannot be resolved. But it is the concept of "twofoldness" that, because of its limits, forces us to focus on a central feature of our aesthetic judgement of pictorial art that can in turn provide the key to our more general understanding of the pictorial. Certainly what Wollheim calls "seeing-in" – that sort of imaginatively projective seeing that, as Leonardo recognized, links the play of visual imagination on a randomly marked surface with the impulse to picture-making – is a constant within our visually imaginative lives. But it is the very *ubiquity* of such imaginative play that deprives it of the required explanatory power. What we need to grasp is how these acts of imagination can *sometimes* (for the development is far from inevitable) become embodied in the articulation of visual and spatial experience. The simple answer is that *we make it so*, by the variety of ways in which we make pictures. Paradoxical as it may seem, it is the ways of picture-making (of drawing) that explain our ways of pictorial communication and the recognition of shared visual experience and not the other way about.[18]

NOTES

1. Gombrich, *Art and Illusion*, 6.
2. Richard Wollheim, Reflections on *Art and Illusion*, On Drawing an Object, and PA (see especially his fn. 6 to Ch. 2, 360).
3. For relevant concepts of style for this argument see PS, Goodman, The Status of Style, and Harrison, Style.
4. Alberti, *On Painting*.
5. Elementary fairness to Gombrich's account requires that "illusion" in *Art and Illusion* is primarily non-deceptive – an illusion of fiction we are not, or not normally, taken in by. I certainly do not mean to imply that Gombrich would endorse the Albertian conception itself.
6. See Wollheim *PA*, 360, fn. 6, where he discusses these various options.
7. Compare Alfred Hitchcock's quip that "messages are for Western Union": as if an appropriate concept of communication in film should be where content can be both reduced from one medium to another, and further "reduced" to gists and piths. The joke should rebound on Hitchcock, not on those who try to understand film (or any other medium) in its own terms.
8. See Baxandall, *Patterns of Intention*, and The Language of Art Criticism. See also the paper in the same volume by Catherine Lord and José A. Benardete, Baxandall and Goodman. What matters in these discussions is that they focus very properly on the limits of what we may in principle say about the pictorial.
9. See Roy Harris's stimulating and illuminating emphasis on this fact in *Signs, Language and Communication*. Graham McFee (this volume, Ch. 11, n. 30) says "Art is not centrally an instrument of thought." He endorses Wollheim's claim that ". . . internal employment . . . is a distinctive characteristic of language, to which there is no analogue in art." Insofar as I understand both these assertions, I would reject them.
10. This might seem to put me at odds with at least one interpretation of Nelson Goodman's claim (see Goodman, *Languages of Art*) that pictures are *replete* systems, namely that which would have it that they signify pictorially "all the way down" where this is taken to mean that the smallest (isolated) detail can be pictorially significant. I do not, however, believe that this could be a fair reading of what he means.
11. Talk of "expressiveness" can make for difficulties in this context. The prejudice dies hard that expression or expressiveness in art is tied to the specific idea of expressing emotion. (Rather as if the expressive qualities of painterly handling or the restraint of silverpoint were some version of smiling or frowning.) One response could be to point out that to say of any sign or formula (however broadly we conceive of this) what it is a sign of is to say what is "expressed" by the sign. Thus, we can as readily talk of a mathematical expression as a facial expression. But that would be inadequate. In the context of art expressive features do not target the picture's referent, but something about the mind of the picture's maker. This may be, but does not have to be, the emotions of the maker. Style is thus in this sense irreducibly a concept of expression. Rob van Gerwen's search for a

theory of "expression's connectedness with representation" (135 of this volume) is thus clearly right. Compare Michael Podro (118 *ff.* this volume) where he refers to Wollheim's account of expressive properties in nature. However we elaborate an account of this, it seems that we could not then avoid making the beholder's imaginative projection of feeling onto a feelingless object. If we regard all concepts of expression in this way we will be in trouble. See also Malcolm Budd. I would very much endorse his warning against "a monolithic concept of expression" (this volume 108).

12. Wollheim MD 185–90.
13. Goodman, *Languages of Art.*
14. Exceptions in English would be onomatopoeia, very common indeed for words for sounds (e.g., "whisper," "murmur," "mumble," "hiss," and so on). Spoken, and heard languages attract such natural analogues. We should well expect a parallel set of examples for visual forms of communication, such as sign languages, and, of course, pictures below the pictorial mesh. None of these departures, however undermine the general point here.
15. Many arguments deployed in this area tell against the quite different claim that maps and pictures belong to the same species within a wider genus, perhaps, of graphic signs. I do not maintain this.
16. The "ambiguities" here are like the ambiguities deployed in Empson's account of metaphor yield "conjunctive" rather than "alternative" significance. This need not imply that such multiple roles for depictive marks are in any straightforward sense metaphors. See William Empson, *The Structure of Complex Words,* and *Seven Types of Ambiguity.* There are wider implications here for Wollheim's own account of "metaphoricity" in painting (see PA), which there is not space to pursue here.
17. Keynes, ed., *The Writings of William Blake.*
18. Versions and aspects of the argument in this paper have appeared before in my Representation and Conceptual Change, *Making and Thinking,* Conduits or Conventions? (a review of PA), A Minimal Syntax for the Pictorial, and *Philosophy and the Arts, Seeing and Believing.*

Chapter 4
A Hypothesis About Seeing-In

MONIQUE ROELOFS

On Richard Wollheim's theory, Vermeer's *View of Delft* is a depiction of Delft because it invites a special kind of visual experience, one of "seeing" Delft "in" the picture.[1] A strength of Wollheim's theory, I believe, is its emphasis on the phenomenal aspect of the experience that is criterial of depiction. It is as a phenomenal state that seeing-in fulfills its aesthetic and artistic functions. What is missing from Wollheim's phenomenological view, however, is an experientially and explanatorily adequate characterization of seeing-in. While the make-believe theory proposed by Kendall Walton and the sophisticated similarity theories presented by Malcolm Budd and Christopher Peacocke take steps to remedy this, these accounts, I will argue, encounter three problems. Name these the 'coherence,' the 'location,' and the 'attitude' problems. It is possible to lay the groundwork for an answer to these problems by supplementing Wollheim's phenomenological notion of seeing-in with an explanation in terms of perceptually driven hypotheses, or, in other words, conceptualizations, that enter into phenomenally conscious awareness. Through a combination of the phenomenological view and the conceptualizations hypothesis, we may hope to account for the most striking relations between seeing-in and other forms of mentation. We can locate seeing-in on the spectrum of connective and disconnective experiences constituting the sphere of aesthetic experience generally. What is more, we can articulate a view that coheres with empirical findings on the relation between perception and cognition, as well as the tendency to enlist prototypical features and resemblances in conceptualization tasks. A consideration of Wollheim's phenomenological notion of seeing-in, and Walton's proposed elucidation of it, will clarify how the aesthetic functioning of seeing-in requires at its basis a fine-grained cognitive process.

1. The Phenomenological and the Make-Believe Theories of Seeing-In. Wollheim takes seeing-in to be a single experience possessing two "aspects," an awareness of the pictorial surface and a simultaneous recognition of an entity standing out in front of or receding behind other elements of that surface. He labels these two aspects the "configurational" and the "recognitional" aspects of seeing-in. Here we have reached the point where, in Wollheim's view, further analysis of the experience loses explanatory import.[2]

Walton carries the account beyond the point where Wollheim ends, attempting to fit seeing-in into the moulds of his general theory of representation (MMB, SF). Walton proposes that seeing-in be analyzed in terms of a specific kind of imaginative act. According to Walton, seeing sunflowers in van Gogh's *Sunflowers* is undergoing a single experience wherein we imagine of our viewing of the painting that it is a viewing of sunflowers.

Though Walton's theory is rich in explanatory power, imagination does not recommend itself as a constituent of seeing-in on phenomenal grounds. Experientially, seeing-in is not like an ordinary exercise of the imagination. Ordinary imaginings about one's visual acts are relatively voluntarily and free-floating. But van Gogh's *Sunflowers* directly impel appropriately experienced spectators to become aware of sunflowers. The flowers come to light more automatically and immediately than they would if seeing-in were the kind of imaginative act Walton takes it to be.

Some philosophers have observed a tension between the perceptual nature of seeing-in and an explanation in terms of imaginings.[3] The main problem that I see with the make-believe account, one that seems hard to remedy by specifying the notion of imagination, is that the approach leaves the relation between the imagined seeing and the real perception of the design too loose. As Flint Schier has argued, initiates in a death ritual may imagine of their looking at inscribed stones that it is looking at their grandfathers.[4] That is not the same as 'seeing' persons 'in' stones, however. The content of one's imagined looking in such a case does not have a sufficiently strong basis in the experience of the real looking. A phenomenal integration is lacking. Our awareness of the sunflowers depicted in van Gogh's canvases and the awareness of the design are closely connected. The connection between the two experiential elements is stronger than the relation between the real viewing of the stones and the imagined person sightings.[5]

Call the problem of accounting for the coherence of seeing-in the coherence problem. Walton is well aware of the problem. He qualifies the make-believe proposal by arguing that the imaginative and the visual component of seeing-in are "inseparably bound together, integrated into a single complex phenomenological whole" (MMB, 295). There is, in Walton's words a "mutual interpenetration of seeing and imagining," whereby the imagining is a part of one's visual experience of the canvas" (MMB, 301).[6] In order to ensure that this interconnectedness obtains, Walton requires that the relevant imaginings and perceptions form a single experience. Via this move, Walton may be able to forestall potential counterexamples such as that of Schier's stones.

However, I doubt that the right kind of coherence between the visual and imaginative elements of seeing-in can be produced merely in virtue of this qualification. Weakly and irrelevantly related imaginative and perceptual states can cohere into single experiences. Take a white painting, covered irregularly with black spots. Now, have a dalmatian run by. Surely this allows you, as the dog fades in the distance, to spontaneously hold on a bit to its image by way of the painting: You find yourself imagining of your looking at the canvas that it is seeing a dalmatian. And, given the vivacity of the memory image just imprinted in your awareness, the imaginative perception can certainly form a single, integrated experience. But I do not see that this experience thus becomes a case of seeing a dalmatian in a canvas, even if it might lead to such seeing-in at a later stage. The requirement of a single experience fails to restrict seeing-in to the kind of perception invited by things like Vermeer's *View of Delft* and cloud figurations.[7]

I doubt that it is possible to forge a link between real and imagined looking that can produce the phenomenal entwinement of the recognitional and the configurational aspects of seeing-in. This is especially clear when the depicted content is very rich, as it often is in the movies, and in complex paintings such as *The Disembarcation of Marie de Médici at Marseille* by Rubens. *The Disembarcation* presents a wealth of visual sensation and awareness, a wealth also of cognitive material, much of which we see in the work: pompous, suspicious, hypocritical attitudes, servile, mocking states of mind.[8] But this rich seeing-in experience cannot acquire its content in virtue of imaginings fastening on the perceptual experience of the canvas. Imaginings of a common sort cannot inject so much content so solidly into ordinary visual experience. And that makes it unlikely that imaginings (in a sense that pertains to any other imaginative activity) are constitutive of seeing-in.[9] The coherence problem invites us to look elsewhere for the explanation of seeing-in.

Perhaps Walton does not regard imaginary seeing as a part of the mechanics of seeing-in at the point where I have taken them to operate. The idea may be that once other necessary processes have occurred, imaginative perception arises on the way to a full seeing-in experience, aiding in the fabrication of the complex, cogent phenomenology of pictorial understanding. Imaginary seeing does seem to play this role. But this means that to reach a full understanding of seeing-in we have to retrace some steps in the explanation.[10]

Some of the worries that arise for Walton's theory may be accommodated by specifying the requisite notion of imagining. But in order to do many of the things that imaginings do in Walton's theory, they have to be relatively free, voluntary, and unconstrained, while their supposed role in the creation of seeing-in would require them to be bound and automatic. It will thus be hard to subsume seeing-in together with other aesthetically relevant imaginative states (for example, those that give rise to various participatory acts) under a unitary notion of what it is to imagine.

The sophisticated similarity theories crafted by Malcolm Budd, Christopher Peacocke, and Robert Hopkins avoid the coherence problem in the form in which it confronts the make-believe view. However, the internal coherence of the seeing-in experience also poses difficulties for these theories, as we will see later.

2. *Seeing-In and Other Psychological Attitudes.* I wish now to examine the characteristics of seeing-in in the light of features of other kinds of states (belief, perception, experiences of secondary qualities, imaginings). This will suggest that seeing-in recruits the services of an attitude distinct from these states, and lay a basis for a response to the coherence problem.

Seeing-in shares characteristics with belief. First, like many belief-states, it is declarative and affirmative. To express this point simply, though a bit paradoxically: Viewing *Sunflowers*, in a sense to be explored later, we ascribe yellow-sunflowerhood, that is, the property of being yellow sunflowers to van Gogh's canvas. The declarative import of seeing-in represents a crucial point of correspondence with ordinary states of belief, even if its precise nature is still unclear.

Second, like many belief-states, the seeing-in experience is informed by higher-level reasoning, and in turn, gives rise to more of it.[11] Legion are the cases described by Erwin Panofsky, E. H. Gombrich, and Richard Wollheim in which background knowledge assists in the discovery of what we see in paintings.[12] Informed by contextual awareness, seeing-in experiences form the basis for our interpretative exploration of the meaning of *The Disembarcation*, inviting inferences that lead to further attributions of properties to the represented scene. Consider the conclusions we draw about what we see: from the postures, gestures and expressions in *The Disembarcation* to disrespectful receptions, and on to prefigurings of a doomed marriage, political strategies, and war preparations. The seeing-in experience elicits an abundance of realistic thinking, providing a basis for further explorative thought, that then helps to fine-tune the experience.

The affirmative content of seeing-in and its embeddedness in reasoning both suggest that seeing-in corresponds to belief, in that we mobilize conceptual contents and apply them to paintings. Further evidence for this resides in a third parallel with belief, namely the potentially rich phenomenology of seeing-in, which is often as complex as, or even more complex than the phenomenology of the most intricately structured thoughts that we think to ourselves.

If we can take the three parallels between seeing-in and states of belief seriously, then seeing-in would seem to engage our conceptual scheme much in the way higher-level beliefs do.

But as the critique of illusion theories has demonstrated, seeing-in does not quite fit the category of belief. On reflection, we withold assent from the idea that there are lakes and forests in Jacob van Ruisdael's nature scenes and neither is there a real temptation to approach them for swims or walks. While beliefs paradigmatically evince themselves in their impact on behaviour and cognitive inferences, these manifestations are etiolated in depiction.[13] Placing more weight on the dissimilarities than the similarities between seeing-in and belief-states, recent thinkers distinguish seeing-in from central kinds of belief-states.

Recent work on perception, as it turns out, warrants a revitalization of the belief-based approach to seeing-in. Modularity theory makes it plausible that we have so-called informationally encapsulated beliefs, beliefs that proceed in isolation from vast repertoires of stored information.[14] The similarities between seeing-in and forms of belief may thus find an explanation on the view that seeing-in is underwritten by such insulated beliefs. Accordingly, seeing sunflowers in van Gogh's *Sunflowers* would involve believing that there are sunflowers on the canvas, where this belief is protected from beliefs that testify to the fictional or conventional character of the depiction.

However, since seeing-in is extensively informed by higher-level beliefs, there is no chance that it is the office of a misled perceptual mechanism channeling its products into conscious experience, outside the reach of higher-level cognition. How could we achieve impressions such as those of the turbulent energy of Rubens' sketches through a prior bracketing of our awareness of the behaviours of objects and human figures?[15] The trouble with a strong kind of encapsulation hypothesis is that it exposes seeing-in to a great cognitive reservoir while granting it protection from a very specific body of beliefs. I see little ground for assuming that we are in the grip of such peculiar cognitive divisions. The case for a belief hypothesis seems to be weak.

But there is more to learn from the comparison with belief states. Seeing-in shares important features with perceptual beliefs. The perception of sun-flowers in Van Gogh's canvases typically proceeds as immediately, automati-cally, and mandatorily as the perception of real sunflowers. In these respects, seeing-in is closer to everyday perceptual identification of objects such as flowers and pianos than to central, higher-level thinking or imagining. This suggests that seeing-in, at base, consists in perceptually driven identifications, rather than the slow, voluntary deliberations of higher-level reason. For all its cognitive plasticity, the seeing-in experience derives its substance in large measures from relatively low-level perceptual stimuli.[16]

Another point of correspondence between seeing-in and certain perceptual states is that seeing-in, like perceptual experiences such as yellow-impressions and other experiences of secondary properties, and unlike deliberate entertaining, thinking or spontaneous imagining, involves a projection of conscious mental content onto picture planes. In other words, seeing-in manifests a non-veridical localization of conscious content external to oneself. We experience the sunflowers that we see in van Gogh's paintings as anchored in the picture plane, somehow attributing properties to the canvas that are not really there, at places where other properties are located.[17] Seeing-in shares this non-veridical attribution of experiential features with experiences of secondary properties. For while the world arguably comes in colour and reflectance properties, it does not come in colour phenomena, even if it seems to, in experience. This experiential projection, our sense that in some way there is sunflowerhood of a sort "out there," on the canvas, with the green and the yellow, is not adequately captured if, à la Budd, Peacocke, or Hopkins, we explain seeing-in in terms of experienced similarities of shape or structure. Why would we locate sunflowerhood "out there" if the content of our experience is "similar-to-the-shape/structure-a-sunflower-would-have-if-seen-from-a-certain-angle?" Call this problem the location problem. How do similarity theories introduce notions of sunflowers into the seeing-in experience, rather than more parsimoniously, notions of sunflower-shapes? What motivates us to make transitions from attributions of sunflower shapes to attributions of "sunflowerhood?" More on this later.[18]

Seeing-in then, appears to share features with perceptual beliefs (projection, immediacy, automaticity) and with higher-level cognitive and imaginative states (sensitivity to a wide range of central cognitions; a rich phenomenology; embeddedness in reasoning).[19] How can we reconcile these characteristics of seeing-in? We must locate the experience in the right range of a spectrum from perceptions to imaginings and beliefs. Sophisticated similarity theories push it too close to the perceptual extreme, while illusion theories place it too near the extreme of higher-level mentation. The phenomenological and the make-believe theories reproduce this distribution by dividing the experience into two elements. The task is to allot the attitude that underwrites seeing-in a suitable place within the mental. Call this problem the attitude problem.

3. The Mechanics of Seeing-In. Definitely we are not always aware of the precise kinds of propositional attitudes we are engaging in.[20] Given the difficulty with modelling seeing-in after either perception or higher-level belief and imagining, I suggest that seeing-in solicits the services of an attitude distinct from these states. Let us try to get clearer on what this attitude may consist in.

As I have argued, the complex phenomenology of seeing-in, its affirmative character, and its embeddedness in reasoning indicate that seeing-in shares with deliberate cognition and perceptual identification the deployment of conceptual content. In view of recent work on perception, I propose then the following: As a first approximation, seeing-in is grounded in hypotheses about pictorial surfaces. We form hypotheses in which we apply concepts to features of the work that do not exemplify these concepts.[21] For example, seeing a lake in a Ruisdael painting involves applying the concept "lake" (or a related concept like "water plane") to pictorial shapes. We categorize shapes and colours under concepts of ordinary objects ("lake").[22] These concepts are responsible for what Wollheim calls the recognitional aspect of seeing-in. Call these concepts, accordingly, 'recognitional concepts.' Seeing-in experiences deploy perceptually driven, conscious hypotheses in which we characterize design features in terms of recognitional concepts at varying levels of complexity.[23] We encode a red shape in *The Disembarcation* as a red shape, as similar in shape to a flag, and, at different levels, employing recognitional concepts, as a ceremonial flag, as one of Marie de Médici's regalia, and so on.[24] Pictorial properties (e.g., red shapes) serve in the first instance as evidential grounds for the relevant hypotheses, and in the second instance as referential objects of these hypotheses – the objects to which we apply recognitional concepts.[25] Pictorial properties function in this one respect in the same way as the ordinary perceptual stimuli that lead to the perceptual categorizations underwriting seeing-as experiences.

In ordinary seeing-as, the requisite evidential grounds are sufficiently strong to issue in "recognitional" beliefs. When we see entities in pictures, on the other hand, the evidential grounds remain too weak and conflicting to generate such beliefs. But they are sufficiently persuasive to mobilize and retain in consciousness a wide range of recognitional hypotheses, sustaining an intermediate level of commitment, a level that stops short of the level of commitment attached to beliefs, but rises above that of imaginings and merely entertained ideas. It is these hypotheses, entering into phenomenal consciousness, that underwrite the seeing-in experience.

My proposal is, then, that we perceive pictorial properties through concepts that fail to apply, entertaining in phenomenal consciousness perceptual hypotheses to which we are committed more strongly than to imaginings, but less strongly than to beliefs. In what follows, I will explain how this idea, call it the "hypothesis view," accounts for the features of seeing-in that have come to light in the comparison with other forms of mentation.

We have seen that seeing-in has a remarkable coherence that sets it off from species of imaginative experience and is thus hard to explain on the principles of the make-believe theory. The hypothesis view holds that perceptual hypotheses (non-veridically) attribute recognitional properties to design elements. In the application of recognitional concepts to perceptual material, I see a way to ensure the coherence of the experience. The connection between what

Wollheim calls the configurational and the recognitional aspects of seeing-in is supported by the attribution of conceptual content to the perceptual features of the picture plane.[26] It is then through the notion of concept application that the hypothesis view hopes to answer the coherence problem.

Unlike imaginings, which are higher-level states, seeing-in solidly locates properties in pictorial surfaces since – like basic perceptual categorizations – it is predominantly perceptually driven, even if it is to some measure affected by top-down processing, that is, it may be primed, steered, or interfered with by higher-level states. Here we have a response to the location problem.

Since seeing-in is perceptually driven, its scope is narrower than that of imaginings, which range freely over any kind of content – from the a posteriori, to neuroses, to democracy, and other states that we can imaginatively import to pictures, but less often see in them.

Seeing-in shares with perceptual beliefs its potential immediacy and automaticity because it is to a large extent perceptually driven. While it permits interference by higher-level cognition, it is at base a perceptual process, one that potentially (and frequently) is no less commanding or fast than the basic categorizations informing ordinary seeing-as. Unlike belief and perception, however, seeing-in is shielded from action because our commitment to the relevant hypotheses falls short of the degree of commitment we attach to higher-level beliefs and lower-level perceptions.

At this stage of the analysis, we are in a position to see why experiential similarities are relevant to the generation of seeing-in, even if, *contra* Budd, Peacocke, and Hopkins, they do not suffice to yield an account of what the experience consists in. Let me explain.

At the basis of the rich phenomenal experience and the elaborate inferential connections of seeing-in lies a fine-grained, progressive process of categorization. The pictorial properties in which we see objects must possess enough differentiation to give rise to this detailed categorization. A substantive measure of differentiation arises at the perceptual level, which provides experiences of primary and secondary properties. In cooperation with these experiences, a variety of factors invite the process of hypothesis formation that permits seeing-in. Perhaps the most influential factors are experienced similarities of shape, colour, brightness, or texture between design elements and depicted objects, as these objects could be seen in certain ways. We experience the shapes and colours of *Sunflowers* as similar to the shapes and colours of real sunflowers. This is the insight that motivates traditional and sophisticated similarity theories of depiction.

However, as testified to by caricatures, variously stylized representations, and clever "abstractions," experiential formal similarity may be marginal.[27] A city depiction need not produce a significant experienced similarity to a city when viewed from a certain perspective. Experienced formal similarity also is not sufficient for seeing-in. We can experience the black-spotted white surface of my earlier example as similar in shape, structure, brightness, and colour to a dutch cow, a dalmatian, a snow-covered volcano landscape, the dirty bottom of a swimming pool, an earlier study for itself, a marked white board, and more. But this falls short of seeing cows or other things in the canvas – even if we conceptualize its shapes as similar to the shapes of cows or dalmations, and so on.[28] Here we encounter the coherence problem. The difficulty is to forge a sufficiently tight connection between experienced similarities of form and correlative elements of recognition. The hypothesis view explains why depictions push us beyond the level of experiential similarities to the level of recognitional objects, while also admitting informational transference between these levels.

Constructing seeing-in in terms of experienced similarities or isomorphisms, Budd, Peacocke, and Hopkins accord constitutive significance to factors that at most help to realize seeing-in experiences.[29] Besides experienced similarities or isomorphisms, many other factors help to generate seeing-in experiences. Some of these are iconographic conventions, references set up by individual artists,[30] face-recognition mechanisms, emotions we feel for design elements, and interpretations of a feature's function in the work.[31] These factors are relevant because they help to mobilize recognitional hypotheses, rendering some hypotheses more active, or lowering thresholds for their activation. Different mobilizing factors are responsible for the varying degrees of mandatoriness, rapidity, stability, degree of commitment, and so on, of the seeing-in experience.

In the view that seeing-in involves the formation of perceptually driven, conscious hypotheses, we can then find a basis to account for its most significant relations with other mental states.

Evidence in this context, as I suggested earlier, is the scope of objects over which seeing-in ranges. Notably, the objects that we see in artworks are usually entities that many of us in normal life readily perceive to be present without much deliberation: bodies, violins, concrete actions (writing, pouring). We do not typically have the experience of democracy, neurotic disorders, or the a posteriori. This, together with the rapidity and mandatoriness of seeing-in, suggests that rough and ready perceptual categorizations lie at the heart of the seeing-in experience. Perceptual stimuli have a hard time triggering hypotheses about things like democracy, even though we may imagine or think all we want about these entities.

The idea that seeing-in enlists basic perceptual categorizations allows us to find confirmation for the hypothesis view in another area of cognitive psychology, that of conceptual categorization. I have postulated a process of hypothesis formation that involves the application of concepts to a surface in spite of the awareness that the surface is something else. This kind of conceptualization is not unique to seeing-in. Concept application often ignores significant facts about the object in question. Typically, concepts participate in reasoning only under partial activation of their contents, that is to say, our thinking with a concept does not necessarily involve reasoning with the full notion we have formed of its extension. There is experimental evidence that categorization is based on factors that are not determinative of the identity of the object. For example, common-sensically we tend to see whales as fish because they swim, ignoring higher-level knowledge that we have acquired about their circulatory and reproductive systems. This rough and ready mode of thought is the norm in everyday categorization practices. We categorize objects by way of concepts on the basis of stereotypical features or similarities to exemplars, without assessing whether the considered beliefs we have about the extension apply.[32] Our grasp of depictions can then be seen as an instance of a broader capacity to apply concepts on evidential grounds that fail to satisfy central conditions of category membership.[33] As triggers of categorization processes, the colours and shapes of pictures are in the company of other kinds of "deficient" evidence. At crucial levels of pictorial processing, the evidential force of colours and shapes outbalances the weight of occurrent beliefs to the effect that it's "only pictures" that we're looking at.[34] This leaves us with successive and parallel stages of conceptualization, realizing the rich phenomenology of seeing-in, in spite of the fact that we "know better."

Given the parallels and differences between the workings of these hypotheses and the workings of ordinary beliefs, perceptions, and imaginings, it is enlightening to speak of a psychological attitude that borrows elements from other kinds of mentation, without reducing to them, an attitude, both distinct from and similar to belief, perception, and imagination, one that must be further explored.[35]

Considering that seeing-in is affected by higher-level beliefs, inferences, associations, and imaginings, we must address, before ending, the suspicion that certainties about picture frames, flatness, and their like may dispel the relevant perceptual hypotheses from consciousness. What, precisely, explains the potential stability of the seeing-in experience in the face of abundant cognitive disconfirmation?

To be sure, "better knowledge" about the flatness and frames of pictures informs the process of hypothesis formation. However, it leaves the phenomenology of seeing-in intact because the confirming evidence from shapes and colours is more powerful than the disconfirming evidence from flatness and frames. This is why the relevant hypotheses enter and remain in conscious awareness, as opposed to the many perceptual hypotheses that we unconsciously entertain but reject in the absence of sufficient supporting evidence.

My proposal is then, in short, that seeing-in engages us in the formation of conscious perceptual hypotheses, a process that is driven by perception, and fine-tuned and expanded by a variety of higher-level reasonings and imaginings. In the conjunction of Wollheim's notion of seeing-in as a phenomenal state and an explanation in terms of such hypotheses, we can find a basis for a response to the coherence, the location, and the attitude problems, and an account of the relations between seeing-in and other forms of mentation.[36]

The hypothesis view invites two small shifts in the experiential terrain. First, it construes seeing-in as a special form of seeing-as. The phenomenology of these two states provide confirmation for this. Twofoldness marks some kinds of seeing-as, as well as in seeing-in. Seeing Union Station face-to-face can be equally twofold as seeing it in Hitchcock's *North by Northwest*. It is easy to be immersed in the surface-look of water to the point that under a dark sky, it looks like an oily asphalt plane, or if the sky is white, like plaster, marble, or viscous plastic. And, yet, such surface impressions may not for a moment dispel the awareness that we are actually seeing water. What is more, such rich textural experiences, as can also be had from viewing, say, a crowd of people in a square, an assembly of roofs from a high point in a city, or a patch of ice-covered trees illuminated by the moon, are quite capable of combining with the awareness of what we are seeing, so as to form a single but complex experience. This is precisely what makes these rich seeing-as experiences so surprising and delightful. The configurational aspect of such seeing-as experiences can be as prominent and involved as what we get in a Rubens painting. Seeing-in shares central aspects of its phenomenology with certain kinds of seeing-as.[37]

Second, on the hypothesis view, seeing-in may in principle range over wide arrays of contents. I am open to the possibility that an experienced viewer is able to see "something revolutionary" shimmer in Malevich's *Red Square* if the painting and her understanding of Malevich's artistic program help her to summon enough content and instill it in the experience of the work's colours and shapes.

The distinctive aesthetic achievements of seeing-in lie in its capacity to locate representational contents seamlessly and effectively onto picture planes. Forging a tight connection between representational and configurational elements, one that finds a match only in some forms of expressiveness, perceptually driven, conscious hypotheses lend seeing-in its special standing among the states that structure aesthetic experience.[38]

NOTES

1. Wollheim, AO2 (sections 11–13; Essay V); and PA (Ch. 2, section B).
2. Wollheim, PA (46–7). In his chapter in this collection, Wollheim offers additional clarification of his reasons for terminating the explanation here (19–20).

3. Jerrold Levinson objects to the make-believe account of depiction that imagining is a kind of thinking while seeing-in is a species of perception. For this reason, he considers seeing-in an irreducible perceptual experience (Levinson, Making Believe, 294).

4. Schier, *Deeper into Pictures. An Essay on Pictorial Representation* (13–26) envisions a ritual in which appropriately trained ancestor worshippers who project images of their grandfathers onto runic stones inscribed with the grandfathers' names. According to Schier, this ritual invalidates Wollheim and Walton's analyses of depiction because it satisfies their requirements for seeing-in, but fails to produce the kind of experience that is characteristic of depiction. While Schier's argument presents difficulties for the make-believe theory of seeing-in, I think it leaves the seeing-in theory of depiction untouched. Projected imagery by itself, no matter how appropriate, falls short of seeing-in and neither need it satisfy the requirements for seeing-in. Whether the stones do or do not cause seeing-in, and hence do or do not qualify as depictions, depends on the impact that their precise markings and shapes make on visual experience, under appropriate conditions of observation. This is not something that can be specified through the stipulations involved in a ritual. Accordingly, Schier's example fails to de-couple seeing-in and depiction.

5. A reply along Walton's lines would be that the imagined person sightings fail to satisfy the rules of make-believe governing the practice of depiction, even if they may conform to personal or ritualistic codes (Walton, *Mimesis as Make-Believe: On the Foundations of the Representational Arts* (MMB), 303; see also 296, n. 4). The problem with this is that we are analyzing depiction by way of the phenomenal state of seeing-in. We are not unpacking seeing-in in terms of antecedently given depictive practices. Seeing-in can occur outside the strictures of social or personal games. This is the import of the fact that we can see grandmothers in the clouds. In the last analysis, the rules of the game depend on the nature of seeing-in, and not *vice versa*. There is more friction between Wollheim's phenomenological analysis and Walton's make-believe account than Walton suggests.

6. Another condition for depiction in Walton's theory, and probably for seeing-in, is that this integrated state lead to rich and vivid games of make-believe (MMB 295, n. 3 and 296). But my worry is that such richness and vivacity may ensue in the absence of seeing-in, for example through contextual priming or acculturation. We must find more meaningful connections between the elements of seeing-in, as the following example indicates.

7. Within the frame of Walton's theory, the problem is to find a relevant connection between real and imagined looking. Another way of expressing the problem is to ask how seeing-in relates to what Michael Baxandall labels the "ocular" in this volume.

8. For Wollheim, the scope of seeing-in is given by the limits of what is visible in a painting (23–7) this collection). I am in agreement with this insofar as visibility is a phenomenological criterion. This means that hypocritical servility must be included in the scope of seeing-in, since it is "visible" in Rubens' painting with no less ease, cogency, or stability than sunflowers can be seen in van Gogh's work.

9. Another difficulty for the make-believe account is what I call the "location problem" later in this chapter. The theory fails to explain how the sunflower-content ends up being located with the paint on van Gogh's canvas, rather than,

say, in the eyes, with the act of looking, or nowhere in particular. We do not normally experience imaginative contents as being located outside of us.

10. The coherence of seeing-in helps to differentiate the experience from various broader or narrower aesthetic states that come to envelop it, incorporate it, lead up to it, or follow from it but are marked by weaker internal connections. Under such states I would include Walton's imaginative acts, but also, for instance, elements of friendship and other moments of subject positioning. See Svetlana Alpers' and Renée van de Vall's discussions of spectatorship in this volume.

11. I follow Jerry Fodor in distinguishing between perception and higher-level cognition (Fodor, *The Modularity of Mind* (MM) 86–8). In Fodor's view, perceptual processes are restricted to a narrow range of informational input. Higher-level cognitive processes cut across cognitive domains (ibid., 101–3). Cognitions and imaginings, as I use these terms in this paper, are higher-level processes.

12. See Wollheim, W-IPU and CR.

13. This needs qualification. Some behaviours towards real objects carry over to their depictions, viz, ripping photographs, hiding from pictures, petting stuffed animals. Consider the attitudes and actions of the spectator identified by Van de Vall in this collection. Such responses, however, can find explanation in imaginings, desires, and so on, rather than in the analysis of seeing-in.

14. For the notion of informationally encapsulated belief, see Fodor (MM).

15. Baxandall's account of the perception of nervous inner movement in Chardin's *Return from the Market* throws light on the contributions of both higher and lower level mentation to a seeing-in experience (this collection, 234–5).

16. See Fodor on basic perceptual categorizations, the categorizations that allegedly issue from modular systems (MM, 94–7). See Churchland, Perceptual Plasticity and Theory Neutrality on the notion of plasticity.

17. Some argue that objects have reflectance properties, but lack the reflectance-looks (or visual appearances) which experientially we take them to have. See Boghossian and Velleman, Colour as a Secondary Quality. I should add that strictly speaking, of course, we do not locate properties on picture planes, but property instantiations.

18. I think that the location problem lies at the heart of one of Wollheim's objections to sophisticated resemblance theories (17–19 of this volume). Resemblance theories also fail to characterize the strong connection between the experienced recognitional and configurational content. Furthermore, they do not give us sufficient reason to think of the pictorial shapes in terms of sunflowers and hence fail to account for the way seeing-in is embedded in reasoning. While Peacocke and Budd, on the one hand, do not attribute enough content to the seeing-in experience, they also attribute too much content to it in requiring us to compare representations in visual fields. On a literal reading of the sophisticated similarity theory considered by Budd, seeing-in includes (a) an awareness of isomorphism; (b) an awareness of a visual field representation of the subject as seen from a certain point of view; and (c) an awareness of the visual field representation of the picture. I find it implausible that the basic experience of depictions includes these higher-order cognitive elements.

19. In my view, a substantive part of the experience proceeds fairly automatically, while other parts of it occur more or less deliberately.

20. Introspectively, we often regard states of dissociation, self-deception, and denial as ordinary beliefs, thus ignoring crucial differences in their psychological and epistemic status. Discrepancies between common-sensical typologies of mental

states and scientifically defensible construals of them is one of the motivations for Churchland's eliminative materialism (Churchland, *Matter and Consciousness*).

21. L. Gregory (*Eye and Brain: the Psychology of Seeing, The Intelligent Eye*, Perception, Perception as Hypotheses) and Irvin Rock (*Perception*) endorse a view of perception as hypothesis formation and testing. The broader notion of perception as an inferential process also informs recent information-processing theories of vision to which I am indebted (see, e.g., Marr, *Vision*). Simply put, Marr analyzes perception in terms of progressively developing layers of information, whereby only some of these layers reach conscious visual experience.

    A point of clarification. Seeing-in is distinct from metaphorical description in the sense that the conceptualizations it engages play a different psychological role than ordinary metaphors. Conceptualizations, as opposed to metaphors in the ordinary sense, are involved in an attitude that differs from belief and imagination in ways I hope to clarify in the following pages.

22. In view of the nuances of seeing-in, it is plausible that we can see a lake in a Ruisdael painting without using the concept "lake," but instead something like "outdoor body of water," or "water-filled valley." The substantive perceptual basis and the variable degree of specificity of the requisite conceptualizations comes out, for instance, in the ability to see various kinds of things simultaneously in one and the same configuration. See Harrison's example in this collection of a line that depicts both the direction of a facial plane, and a shadow of a forelock or the fold of an eyelid (59). I am in sympathy with Harrison's call for a convergence between two judgements in seeing-in but would resist his demand that they pertain to the same object of depiction (39–40).

23. A view of seeing-in as a differential, multi-level mental process is essential to its function in pictorial experience, its ways of inviting and resulting from imaginings, cognitions, acts of attention, affective states, and so on. Consider Baxandall's analysis of the perception of nervous inner movement in Chardin's painting through visual and imaginative work of the mind on "fine and coarse channels of information" (239 of this collection).

24. This formulation is schematic. I endorse a picture of progressively arising phenomenal and conceptual differentiation. While part of my argument is that concepts must come into play at fairly early stages of the informational processing (earlier than Wollheim seems to suggest in W-IPU, 49), I leave it open at which precise levels of the experience this happens. In his contribution to this volume, Paul Crowther recognizes in the configurational aspect of seeing-in structures of "unity, diversity, reality, limitation, negation, and, overall, balance between these relations" (94). Such levels of experience seem to me to include conceptual as well as nonconceptual, sensational elements.

25. Michael Podro's remarks on the inextricability of depicted light and light reflected from pictorial surfaces are illuminating in this context (Chapter 8, this collection). My proposal traces such inextricability to our conceptualizing the latter in terms of the former. I suggest the same for Podro's point about the projection of shape and movement onto one another. The multiple, interconnected levels of conscious experience that on my view, realize seeing-in permit the interdependencies Podro identifies between the perception of a line's shape, the sense of represented movement, the awareness of the line's apparent impulse, the implications of form set up in the drawings, and the compositional complexity of the drawing. The conceptualizations underwriting seeing-in, furthermore, sustain imaginings such

as those about shadows turning into ink and make it meaningful to wonder about the extension of fictive elements across boundaries of the frame.

26. A coherence that in some respects is potentially no less strong than what we may find in cases of seeing-as in which we attend closely to an object's look.

27. Dominic Lopes, *Understanding Pictures* offers a persuasive critique of similarity theories. Lopes argues that the recognition of similarities depends to a great measure on a prior recognition of objects. My problem with Lopes' positive account of pictures in terms of aspects is that it sidesteps the phenomenological nature of seeing-in.

28. Note that such intentional and stylistic codes as structure interactions with pictures in specific depictive media do not straightforwardly turn these states into seeing-in experiences.

29. Exploring a sophisticated similarity theory, Budd, How Pictures Look analyzes depiction on the basis of experienced isomorphism between the structure of a picture's surface as experienced and an experienced representation of the picture's subject matter. Peacocke, Depiction considers experienced similarities of shape criterial for depiction. Peacocke's analysis lends too much significance to experienced shape (cf. ibid., 392). The colour/brightness/texture dimensions can be equally important. It is not clear exactly what relevance Budd's theory accords to these factors, since he leaves the notion of experienced isomorphism underspecified.

30. Beuys, for instance, gave special meanings to brown, Malevich to red.

31. Several chapters of this collection highlight factors that contribute to seeing-in. Carolyn Wilde draws attention to the embeddedness of seeing-in within processes of substitution, compensation and reconstitution. Svetlana Alpers emphasizes the importance of an awareness of the studio situation to the specification of Bathsheba's resistance and noncomplicitous pose in Rembrandt's painting. Renée van de Vall identifies contributions of the spectator's attitudes and movements to the phenomenal qualities of Newman's zips. Michael Baxandall, Paul Crowther, and Michael Podro describe functions of imaginative perception. Cf. also Walton's principles of generation (MMB Ch. 4).

32. Eleanor Rosch, Principles of Categorization (35–41) advances data about speed of processing, speed of learning, priming, and the use of qualifying terms such as "almost," "virtually," or "technically" as evidence to the effect that categorization involves thinking with prototypical representations. For further discussion of issues of categorization, resemblance, and stereotypes, see Rosch and Mervis, Family Resemblances: Studies in the Internal Structure of Categories, Smith and Medin, eds., *Categories and Concepts*, 166–72 and Smith and Medin, Concepts and Concept Formation, and Rey, Concepts and Stereotypes.

33. A complication, presented to me by Bob Howell in his ASA conference commentary, is that seeing-in differs from quick, basic, perceptual categorization in that seeing-in, on my view, takes place in spite of the awareness that the object of categorization, the pictorial surface, is something else, while rough and ready perceptual categorization does not normally involve perceiving what we know to be false. (The latter only occurs in the case of perceptual illusions that are not also cognitive illusions.) I explain this difference between seeing-in and seeing-as by arguing that perceptual processes rapidly bypass the relevant kind of higher-level awareness, commending its favored hypotheses before higher-level awareness can produce enough interference to boost its favored hypotheses. Perceptual processes, as I will argue momentarily, effectively limit the inferential

efficaciousness of higher-level perception, even if they do not neutralize it. While I believe that a radical encapsulation hypothesis along the lines of modularity theory conflicts with actual pictorial experience, my own view grants perceptual evidence a measure of informational protection in virtue of its own evidential strength. The complexities of the issues here make it attractive to explore the division of labor between perception, hypothesis formation and belief in seeing-in through a careful study of borderline cases, that is to say, examples that just barely permit seeing-in, and that have us constantly on the verge of losing the experience.

34. I am simplifying here. The evidential powers of colours and planes join forces with the effects of priming and contextualization.

35. The hypothesis view, as it stands, is schematic. We can hope to develop it by exploring how seeing-in utilizes concepts, beliefs, low-level perceptions, imaginings, and phenomenal experiences. A functionalist view of mental states that postulates mental representations may offer suggestions for further substantiation (see Block, What is Functionalism? and Fodor, *The Language of Thought*). Some have extended such approaches to other phenomenal states such as experiences of secondary qualities, for example, Rey, Sensational Sentences. However, my account remains neutral on the adequacy of such views.

36. Elsewhere, I argue that seeing-in shares the location, coherence and attitude problems with experiences of varieties of musical expressiveness and stylistic properties in art (*The Cultural Promise of the Aesthetic*, bookmanuscript). The recurrence of these problems testifies to the proximity and interdependence of artistic expression and representation, which are defended by Rob van Gerwen and Michael Podro in their articles in this volume.

37. In a longer version of this chapter, I argue that we cannot identify the characteristic phenomenology of seeing-in in terms of the criteria that we can find in or extrapolate from Wollheim's account: depth appearance; twofoldness; singularity of experience; independence from conventional symbol interpretation; or non-illusory attribution of features that are not present. The characteristics with which Wollheim hopes to capture the seeing-in experience fail to pinpoint a distinctive phenomenology. The fact that seeing-in shares crucial aspects of its phenomenology with forms of seeing-as is one of several reasons why Wollheim's phenomenological theory stands in need of supplementation in terms of the processes underwriting seeing-in.

38. I thank Jerry Levinson, Bob Howell, Eric Lormand, Kevin Meehan, Georges Rey, and Mark Rollins for discussion and comments. Versions of this paper were delivered at the meetings of The American Society of Aesthetics (Eastern Division, Corning, NY, March 1996) and The Society for Philosophy and Psychology (San Francisco, May 1996).

Chapter 5
Communication and the Art of Painting

ANTHONY SAVILE

The chapters of this volume are devoted to two areas of Richard Wollheim's aesthetics, to his thought about representation and his thought about expression. My own contribution is not concerned with either of them directly but rather with the background against which they find their place in the whole. In particular, I shall be engaged with his contention in *Painting as an Art* that that art is misunderstood if it is conceived of in terms of communication. Why this theme is background to what will be to the fore in most of the other chapters will become apparent.

1. In his Mellon lectures, Wollheim says (PA 90) that while the painter may perhaps construct his art as communication, he need not do so. In consequence, we are advised to think of his partner, the beholder, as a hypothetical figure rather than a categorical one. This thought opposes a widespread *idée reçue* about the nature of the painter's art, and even before one asks just what it comes to, Wollheim's striking proposal is apt to provoke resistance.

One way of severing any intrinsic connection between art and communication is obvious, but that it is obvious tends to escape many to whom the underlying conjunction of the two appeals. This severance arises from the thought that when it comes to the proper understanding of a painting, the appropriate criterion of success is tied only very loosely to the mind of the work's maker. Rather, it is said, either we should look to the mind of a well selected hypothetical painter and to what such a person would most probably have intended by his canvas, alternatively (and less plausibly perhaps), that we have regard to the favoured critical reception his work has enjoyed, and be guided by that. In either case, communication in any strong sense is absent, for the simple reason that each of these routes bypasses the psychological realities of the actual artist's mind, and thus blocks appeal to that which alone renders communication possible – a thought that was once the author's own and which might be passed on to a prospective communicatee.

Against this background, we may see how someone alert to the conflict between the initial *idée reçue* and the mooted criteria of correct understanding could come to give up the doctrine of art as communication, and in doing so suppose himself to be a disciple of Wollheim's. He would say the

principles for proper understanding dominate our adherence to a communi-
cation-based conception of art, and recognizing the incompatibility I have
just alluded to, would elect to reject the latter while retaining the former.
Wollheim, though, will have none of this: For as everyone here knows, he
has no hesitation about appealing to the actual history of the artist's psyche
in setting the standard for proper understanding of his work. Hence, there is
nothing to stop categorical reference to the actual artist's intentions here, and
that might well seem to indicate a communication-oriented understanding of
art straightway. Once this easy route to adoption of the negative position is
rejected, the appeal of some version of a communication based thesis may
look irresistible. As I said, rejection of the *idée reçue* provokes resistance
even before we ask what it comes to. Yet before succumbing to temptation let
us first ask just what Wollheim's thought might be.

2. To start with, we should get out of the way any thought that painting
might not be communicative simply because it often falls upon blind eyes or
upon no eyes at all, and then of course communicates nothing. That truth is
something that anyone wedded to a communicative conception of painting
must accept anyway. It presents no challenge to any party to the debate. What
is at issue is whether a pictorial work of art must as such be constructed with
a view to communication of its content to a beholder, whether or not communication is actually effected. This formulation of the idea must hold whatever further refinement is added when we come to give Wollheim's thesis any
more precise content.

Even if there are hosts of paintings whose genesis is not rightly explained
in terms of intentions to communicate, I don't suppose anyone would want to
deny that there are plenty which are, and many more that could be. Indeed,
Wollheim himself allows that painting can be executed as communication,
insisting only that it does not have to be so executed. If I set my mind to
produce a work of figurative communicative art, I may very well succeed,
even if my success should turn out to be no more than modest in quality.
Wollheim will not dissent: so the way to take his thesis will not be as saying
that art is essentially non-communicative. More restrainedly, it will be that it
is not communicative in essence. Its achievements *need not* be communicatively engineered, even if often enough they are.

Now, it is a merely logical point that on this way of looking at things the
more restrained non-communication thesis could be true even if all the figurative art we have were in fact communicatively conceived. Faced with this
observation, I take it that the proponent of the modestly conceived doctrine
will say that as a matter of fact a great deal of the art that we have and which
is of the highest interest to us is non-communicative in its origin, even though
it is a purely logical possibility that none should actually be so.

Even so, put like this, hasn't the original idea been unnecessarily enfee-
bled? At least, someone who was impressed with the idea of communication
as descriptively adequate to the range of painting that he encounters might
say that his claim is not meant as a metaphysical one at all, only one that fits
the phenomena as they present themselves to us well enough. A more robust
reading of Wollheim's thought would take him not merely to be denying that
claim of descriptive adequacy to our actual stock of pictorial art, but more
strongly as affirming that what we regard as its central cases are not, and
could not rightly be, thought of as executed with communicative intent.
Painting is not essentially non-communicative in that we can make perfectly
good sense of painting that is produced in that mode, but that said, our grasp
of the concept of the art of painting should not allude to communication in
its central cases. In this very specific sense, its non-communicative nature
would be of the art's essence, and that being so we could not envisage a
situation in which all its instances turned out to be cases of an intentional
communicational exercise. Leaving in the air for the moment all consideration
of the motivation that might lead one to adopt the stronger of these two
readings of the non-communicative thesis, I shall simply assume that it is the
stronger and more interesting of them that we have to test.

3. Any decent account of an art, painting, music, or whatever, must make
plain how it is so much as possible for that art to come into being, and then
for it to sustain itself in existence. That is, the account's adequacy to the
phenomena must be not only synchronic but diachronic as well. The initial
question of genesis may be resolved by the introduction of an autonomous
aesthetic interest in the appropriate area that comes to supplant such functional concerns as in our own case we like to suppose originally sustained a
practice of commonly embellished craft. Then, once this step is taken, elaboration of the many ways in which our aesthetic interest can be publicly
satisfied is what may be called on to account for the persistence of this art or
that, in ways that are deeply enough rooted in the social fabric. In contrast
with many features of the natural world that persist until interrupted, the
institution of art needs constantly to renew itself since, setting aside the issue
of expanding of social spread, repetitious production of what the past hands
down to the present satisfies no interest not already satisfied already. Without
constant renewal, art in its institutional aspect is moribund.

For the most part, concern for these diachronic matters has been treated in
empirical fashion by historians of art, focusing, as they have, on the course
of stylistic change that art's development has in fact taken. Broadly speaking,
their explorations have fallen into two broad strands: those who privilege
endogenous forces to account for development (e.g., Vasari, Winckelmann,
Wölfflin, Riegl) and those who have pursued an ambition of systematicity in

ways that at the time looked more likely of success through concentration on exogenous, social and economic, forces (viz., Semper, Viollet-le-Duc, Taine, Antal, and Hauser).

The very idea of systematic art-history has fallen out of favour in our day, in part, I dare say, on account of Wollheim's own work. For him, the historical concentration on development of styles, *generic* styles as he has called them, is beside the point, since generic style is seen as no more than a taxonomic device that enjoys no psychological reality in the artist's mind. However, since it is precisely to the mind of the artist that we must look to forge an adequate notion of the content of art as it changes over time, any success that the systematically oriented historian may seem to have enjoyed will have been misdirected. Once we redirect our interest and concentrate on what matters, on the changes that the painter's art has undergone in its content, and in doing that honour the primacy of the painter's own psychology, we have to acknowledge that systematic history replete with *ex post* predictive powers is not to be had. For that, we should need to suppose that there are laws governing the direction of artistic change, and it is common philosophical currency today that the concepts of common-sense psychology with which the artist's mind is stocked are ill-suited to deliver any such thing.

I shall not question this line of reasoning. However, it would be a mistake – not a mistake that Wollheim makes, I hasten to add – to suppose that on this account the diachronic issues I have raised can be dismissed as out of place. What we learn from Wollheim's reflections is that if explanation of artistic development is to be had it will be piecemeal explanation, and not aspire to predictive power (even when viewed *ex post*). Moving away from the empirical domain of the art historian, who may still hope to provide the piecemeal account of change case by case, we may in pursuing this diminished ambition still quite properly require the philosopher to indicate the structure of a general mechanism through which artistic change can take place and that may be expected to operate via endogenous psychological means rather than exogenous, sociological ones.

A quite general objection to my insisting on the diachronic aspect of the matter could be that the persistence of art over time as a public institution is itself merely a contingent matter. Our art has certainly persisted and developed, and, true, that is the only art we shall ever know about. Nonetheless, our concept of art could extend to possible cases that may be supposed to have enjoyed an autonomous aesthetic interest for only a brief while and then just have petered out. If that is so, no matter what conclusions concerning communication might flow from the general mechanism of change that I envisaged asking the philosopher to delineate, they could not enter into the essence of the art of painting. Consequently, in discussing the topic of communication we have nothing to learn from considerations of the proper methodology of art history. So it may be said.

This is not an idea that should impress us. The art we have does indeed display change, so it is captured only through a concept whose structure at the very least makes room for the possibility of art's development and change, whether in the various instances of it that we like to imagine such change is realized or not. Hence, it is perfectly legitimate for the philosopher to say that given that the possibility of change is written into the heart of the concept, whatever is involved in making room for that possibility may itself properly belong to art's essence. Whether the methodology of art history in fact generates interesting consequences of this sort is a perfectly open matter, not a closed one.

4. Let us start by considering the transition from a practice of craft to the emergence of art as a publicly recognized endeavour. For convenience, to mark the requisite publicity that is involved, I shall talk of the institution of art, though that may not be the best choice of term. To avoid misunderstanding, I stress that in my use of it there is nothing to turn us towards the so-called institutional theory of art, much less to the silly view that for something to be art is for it to enjoy a certain status. So, I ask by what steps is the transition made from institutionalized craft to the institution of art? That some such transition is called for seems self-evident. For the gods there was no pre-history of art maybe, but for us humans it could not have sprung up fully armed as if from the head of Jupiter. A little ontogenetic speculation is in order.

(a) We might imagine the bright apprentice of some guild (shop-sign painters perhaps) finding his work engrossing enough to be worth pursuing not just to fulfil some publican's commission but for his own satisfaction. For him, his painting comes to acquire an autonomous aesthetic interest.

(b) His efforts are found pleasing by other members of the guild and so they are stimulated to emulate him on their own account. Still, we don't have the institution of art for members of the sign-makers' group are each one painting for himself and impervious to the activities of the others.

(c) Various of the group's products are admired for their aesthetic qualities by non-producing outsiders. Maybe they are acquired for the pleasure they bring their owners, are then exhibited to friends and acquaintances to bring them a measure of delight, too, and perhaps also do something to enhance the standing of their possessors.

(d) There arises in the society a generalized demand for such objects, and this demand can be thought of as the engine for the production of further works of the kind. At this fourth point, I think we stand on the threshold of the institutionalization of art if we haven't already over-stepped it. And here it makes sense to ask whether the artist isn't incipiently in the business of communication. Certainly I am envisaging him, or better them – a mark rather of presumptive plurality than uncertain gender – as responding to external demands. However, we haven't yet got to a stage at which we have to say that the painter produces what he does to convey to another, that is, to his indefinitely identified patron, the thought that he struggled to capture for himself on his canvas. This isn't obligatory, because even if the work he produces would not have existed but for the new public demand for it, it is perfectly possible that as far as the artists' psychology goes, they see themselves merely as incited to produce works for their own satisfaction (for the satisfaction of making them, that is) even if they would not have done so but for the novel external stimulus. At this stage of the proceedings we have nothing that amounts to *negotiation* between the two parties that must play their roles in the institutionalization of art, and if communication is to make any noteworthy appearance on stage it will be negotiation that brings it in its train. (Of course I do not mean *financial* negotiation – there is ample room for that in what we have already.)

I have said above that if nothing more happens than this initial institutionalization of art, after a while the practice will be liable to lapse – not maybe that isolated individuals may not continue to find a pleasure in the autonomous activity but as far as the wider public is concerned. Without the incursion into my fable of some development in the content of the art that is produced that carries the broader public with it after the saturation of the original impetus. At this point, we need to introduce the a priori mechanism of which I spoke before.

5. Unsurprisingly, the mechanism I have in mind is the mechanism of negotiation, the negotiation of taste and value that is, not of price. What I mean by this is that overtly or covertly artist and patron have to settle on a variation of what was originally perceived as an autonomous aesthetic good which both parties can recognize as of aesthetic value. For success here, the artist needs to be sensitive to what the patron can (come to) appreciate, and the patron similarly sensitive to what the artist can find himself motivated to produce.

It could, of course, happen, as if by magic, that acting independently of the patron's interest the artist should light upon a development of his early work that took the public's fancy, and this could in logic be a repeated process that kept the institution alive. Only when we remember that artist and patron here are both plural figures and that the concordance between them is public concordance, such a purely logical possibility is not one that we should spend time on. In our world, that is not how things can come about.

For the sake of realism, it is important to stress here that both artist and patrons can be sensitive to each other's tastes and interests and indeed can play a decisive part in moulding them. Neither party should be assumed to have a predefined closed aesthetic horizon.[1] So through their negotiation the artist will be able to assist his public acquire taste, judgement, and discernment, and likewise the patron encourage the artist to find where his capacities lie. (Recall by way of singular example how Michelangelo responded to the stimulus provided by Pope Julius II.) And, I submit, the outcome of this kind of negotiation will be publicly established and constantly developing work that occupies the post-initial stages of the institution and informs the course taken by their successors.

If my fable comes anywhere near the mark it suggests that a sensible non-systematic programme for art history would be to trace the course that such negotiations have taken. On such a basis explanation of developmental change is entirely non-predictable (even *ex post*) but it does follow a comprehensible pattern and to follow its traces would be genuinely enlightening. As far as Richard Wollheim is concerned, such history would not stray from the creditable path of tracing the psychological realities of the minds of artists and their public which must be respected if we are to understand the course that the changing content of art has taken. (I even wonder to myself whether there may not be room here to exploit a notion of generic style which is more than a mere taxonomic convenience, but this is not an issue I can pursue now.)

6. What I now have to ask as a matter of urgency is whether the mechanism of negotiation I find so significant can be thought to work in the absence of any concern on the part of the artist to communicate his thought to the public patron whose taste and judgement he is in the process of forming and whose taste and judgement plays its part in guiding what the artist himself fashions. If there is negotiation proper here, then it seems inevitable that there should be communication in at least one minimal sense of that word. For a thought that the painter has is offered to the beholder-patron for his delectation and judgement. An experience is proposed for him to internalize as a good that the painter himself has laboured to realize in his atelier, and in doing that has himself entertained before passing it on through his brush. Something like this, I imagine, is the kind of thing that Wollheim envisaged as possible, though we know not as necessary.

Even if this thought is correct, there are, however, at least two ways in which its import may be diminished. The first derives from my rather loose use of the terms 'artist' and 'patron' to speak less of individuals than as personae in the social weave. For it will be said that as far as my beholder goes, he is not an individual like Giulio della Rovere, but just someone or other who has the role of keeping the institution of the painter's art alive. And as the Mellon lectures went, once the beholder comes to be seen as a hypothetical rather than a categorical figure, the notion of communication seems no longer to be in play.

How seriously this particular implication was offered is uncertain, but in general it must be right to think that the hypothetical nature of a message's intended recipient does nothing to impugn its communicational power. Prisoner in his German tower, Richard Coeur de Lion could have sung his favourite song to alert any passing vassal in his camp to his plight. The fact that he did not have a particular person, such as Blondel, in mind should not deter one from saying that he was attempting to communicate his plight, to the world at large perhaps.

Waive this reservation. In speaking of the patron, to whom if anyone the painter's communicative work is addressed, I have surmised that it might be proper to think of him as a plurality rather than an individual. Once we do this an analogy invites itself that might make that plural figure categorical rather than hypothetical anyway. When Sergeant Grey, drilling his men on the barracks' square, orders his platoon halt and come to attention, he communicates his desire not just to whoever happens to be in the squad, to White, to Green, and to Black as it happens, though he may not know that, but to the platoon as a whole. The platoon is to halt as a man, so to speak, and the platoon here is a categorical target of Grey's commands. What this might suggest is that in the maintenance of art over time a sufficient number of practising artists need to work in communicative vein to keep the institution alive, and that in doing so they need to direct their efforts at that categorical plurality of patrons sometimes rather coarsely dubbed "the artworld." That at least is a possibility to be entertained.

The second response I envisage is this. When we recall the most interesting formulation of the thesis I have been discussing, namely that it is essential that central cases of a developed art of painting not to be produced with communicative intent, it is entirely possible that it should consist with the proposal I have been canvassing. For my own suggestion says no more than that for art to persist as the institution it is, a sufficiently large core of works must be produced as communication. There is absolutely nothing in that that forbids one also accepting that many of the art's central cases are not communicationally conceived of. If this matter of logic is urged upon me, equally of course Wollheim could allow that, while there must be central cases that are not envisaged as communication, enough must be so to keep the institution afloat.

7. Maybe that complex two-track position is the right one to adopt. But to be persuaded to adopt it we need to be motivated to do so, and earlier on I

simply bypassed the issue of motivation. Yet, the gap has to be filled because if not, the non-communication thesis that recommends itself will be the weaker one that holds merely that a descriptively adequate account of the art of painting need make no allusion to communication. We have seen that once diachronic matters are allowed into the picture, this claim is dubiously true. Then, also, it is in all likelihood less substantial than anything that Wollheim would like to attach his name to.

Here I am more or less obliged to speculate. One thought urging the strong interpretation might be that in making communication central we would invest communicative conventions, rules and norms with far greater importance than they deserve. The artist would be putting the content of his work in the hands of devices which in their day to day employment might elude his control. So his work would risk acquiring a content that did not match the psychological reality that fashioned its vehicle. To avoid this danger, stress must be laid on non-communicational material.

Second, there is the idea that reliance on those norms that communication depends on would be restrict our ability to pay full honour in our philosophy to the artist's potential generosity in what he fashions. We would cut ourselves off from a truthful account of art's value. The very works we care most about are so often those that we say break the bounds of convention, and since these are the very works that underpin the normative aspects of art's achievements, we would through overplaying the role of communication in effect be sacrificing them.

I do not find either of these considerations compelling. The appeal to conventions and norms that bind the communicationally oriented painter do admittedly allow his work to take on a character that did not occur to him and thus put it on occasion beyond his control. A painter might think that according to the conventions he is using, his work represents Henry I, whereas in fact properly deployed they determine that he has painted Henry II instead. Maybe one could think of cases that also did for expression what I here instance in terms of depiction. Even so, this should worry no one: For to recognize that on occasion the artist has not exercised control or his work in no way implies that he did not have control of the conventions he was relying on in creating his work. Deviations from the situation in which he both has control and also exercised it must be exceptions and carry no deep threat to the importance of the psychological reality of the artist in fixing his work's content *even when it is thought of in communicational terms.*

As for the point about value, one must not minimize the generative scope of the rules and norms that form the framework within which communication is conducted. I have been at pains to insist that the collectively envisaged patron be thought of as no less imaginative and inventive than the artist himself. So even if one were to restrict one's attention to cases in which communication is allowed to be afoot, it is far from clear that that will impose debilitating limits on the value that may be found in the work that is so produced. Anyway, if the upshot of the motivational considerations is that we don't adopt the two-tracked essence thesis that is open to us, but simply rephrase Wollheim's original remark that while painting can be a matter of communication it need not be to read while painting cannot always fail to be communication sometimes it must be, there would be plenty of scope for the existence of painting that was not engineered as communication and whose value is quite unconstrained by anything that communication brings with it. Just how much violence such an outcome does to Wollheim's own thought is something that we may have the good fortune to discover.

NOTE

1. This interplay may not always work beneficially. Cf. Zola in *Après une Promenade au Salon (1881)*: "Le pis est qu'il y a, entre les peintres et le public, une démoralisation artistique, dont la responsabilité est difficile à déterminer. Sont-ce les peintres qui habituent le public à la peinture de pacotille et lui gâtent le goût? Ou est-ce le public qui exige des peintres cette production inférieure, cet amas de choses vulgaires?"

Chapter 6

Twofoldness: From Transcendental Imagination to Pictorial Art

PAUL CROWTHER

Introduction

In *Art and its Objects*, Wollheim observes that "the seeing appropriate to representations permits simultaneous attention to what is represented and to the representation, to the object and to the medium. . . ."[1] This provisional characterization of "twofoldness" or "seeing-in" is then hardened by Wollheim. Twofoldness is not only permitted in our perception of pictorial art, it is actually demanded. The most interesting and important justification of this consists in Wollheim's claim that

seeing-in derives from a special perceptual capacity, which presupposes, but is something over and above, straightforward perception. This special capacity is something which some animals may share with us but almost certainly most do not, and it allows us to have perceptual experiences of things not present to the senses: that is to say, both of things that are absent and also of things that are not existent.[2]

In this discussion, I will develop and qualify Wollheim's position. He himself tentatively links the "special capacity" noted above, to phenomena such as dreams, day-dreams, and hallucinations. This may be an apt linkage, but it is by no means the decisive one. For the phenomena that Wollheim mentions are specific instances of a more general and fundamental capacity – namely, imagination.

Now, the term "imagination" is of course used in many different ways. However, there is one usage that constitutes, as it were, the term's ontological potency, that is, something that is familiar, distinctive, and important, and that can thus lay claim to being paradigmatic of the term "imagination." This consists of the capacity to generate images – mental states which refer to sensible phenomena, through (in part) resembling or being iconic with them in specifiable respects. The great benefit of this capacity is that, as Kant puts it, it constitutes "the faculty of representing in intuition an object that is *not itself present*."[3] Indeed, Kant also characterizes imagination as "a blind but indispensable function of the soul, without which we should have no knowledge whatsoever, but of which we are scarcely ever conscious."[4]

In the main body of this discussion, I will argue that the twofoldness of pictorial art enables us to become conscious not only of imagination *per se*, but also of the specific characteristics that allow it to function as a necessary condition of experience. To show this I shall, in Part One, outline a general theory of the transcendental significance of imagination. (This account will derive from clues in Kant, but will also go far, far beyond what Kant himself would have countenanced.) In Part Two, I will use this account to develop and qualify some of the important ramifications of Wollheim's notion of twofoldness. (And again, it is possible that this may take us some distance beyond what Wollheim would himself assent to . . . but perhaps not.)

Part One

All animals have at least the capacity to attend to stimuli, to recognize prey and predator, to distinguish between possible mates and rivals amongst their own kind, and to distinguish between those creatures that are of their own kind and those that are not. They also have the capacity to follow familiar routes and tracks, and anticipate possible dangers.

These factors suggest that animals possess what Bergson calls "habit-memory" and the ability to apply what I shall call "protoconcepts."[5] Let me elaborate these two notions in turn. First, habit-memory. Since the animal can attend to phenomena through successive moments of time, and is able to find its way back to the burrow or nest, or whatever, we must assume it has basic retentional capacities. This assumption is also compelled by the fact that the animal can anticipate possible danger and modify its behaviour accordingly.

Now, this capacity to draw on past experience does not entail that the animal can recall specific facts from its own individual history. Rather, it has a habit-memory analogous to that of human experience. For example, in learning to ride a bicycle, or to tie one's shoelaces, it is the accumulating of experience rather than being able to recall individual events in the process of learning that are decisive in giving us the skill. One might, of course, recall spectacular disasters that were involved – and these may have salutary in-structive effects in the present, but these are not necessary in the acquisition and continuing exercise of the skill. In the case of animals, this is even more emphatic. One presumes that they have no capacity to recall specific facts about their past. Rather, experience is retained in a way that allows the formation of behavioural habits that enable the animal to negotiate its present environment and anticipate possible dangers.

The question arises, then, as to whether animal habit-memory involves imagination in the sense outlined in my Introduction. Now, it might be that the link between habit-memory and imagination in both animals and humans is, in fact, a very deep-seated one. For present purposes, however, I shall not develop this possibility. I shall be content, rather, to suggest that in animals, there is a power of imagination, which can, on occasion, intrude on its recognitional acts. To support this claim, one must note first that some animals, in sleeping, exhibit involuntary behavioural traits akin to those manifested by sleeping humans. This suggests that they might dream, and, if this is the case, we must assume that they have the capacity to generate imagery. If this is so, we would also be justified in assuming that this generative power served some cognitive purpose over and above providing the fabric of dreams; but the question is, *what* purpose? I would suggest the following. Earlier on, I noted how images of specific past learning-events can intrude in a salutary way on our present exercise of some skill. If animals can generate imagery, this may occur on similar lines. A locale where a predator was encountered in the past may provoke images of a creature of that type each time it is entered. Again, if an infant has gone missing, familiar features of the nest or burrow may stimulate the animal to generate images of infant creatures of its own kind. In these cases, the environment prompts the animal towards special care or urgency in its present orientation. The image gives an emphasis to factors that have a vital bearing on the creature's life-situation.

It is important to note that if this account is right, we must interpret animal imagination as *ostensively rigid*, that is, something that is provoked only by encounters with appropriate stimuli, rather than being summonable at will. This ostensively rigid non-volitional character also marks the second key term that I introduced at the start of this section, namely the "protoconcept." In so far as the animal can make the cognitive discrimination noted earlier, it has a capacity with limited kinship to human concept application. However, in contrast to humans, there is no evidence that would allow us to assume that this capacity can be employed in anything other than an ostensively rigid manner, that is, non-volitionally and in the presence of the relevant stimuli. Indeed, this embodies a deeper contrast with human powers of concept application. If an animal recognizes a prey or its mate, one presumes that the act of recognition is not one which distinguishes between this specific prey and prey *per se*, or between its mate and other past or possible mates. In human concept application, in contrast, the use of a concept is reciprocally structured. That is to say, an individual is recognized as an instance of a kind or class or whatever, and the kind or class or whatever is understood as a function of individual instances that are spread out across different times and places.

Given these points, we are now in a position to consider the conditions of specifically human cognition. How is it possible for us to apply reciprocally structured concepts in an ostensively non-rigid and volitional way? The immediate answer, of course, is through the acquisition of language and the use of signs. Through symbolic articulation our concepts are given a communicable and stable character that allows them to be used at will, and across many different situations and contexts including, most notably, those in which the objects articulated by the concept are not immediately present. But we must ask again, how this is possible.

It is instructive here to consider the following observations by Ernst Cassirer.

Only when we succeed, as it were, in compressing a total phenomenon into one of its factors, in concentrating it symbolically, in "having" it in a state of "pregnance" in the particular factor – only then do we raise it out of the stream of temporal change. . . . Everything that we call the identity of concepts and significations, or the constancy of things and attributes, is rooted in this fundamental act of finding-again. This is a common function which makes possible on the one hand language and on the other hand the specific articulation of the intuitive world.[6]

This pre-linguistic comprehension of the total phenomenon in one of its aspects is only intelligible as a function of imagination. Imagination is gradually released from its ostensively rigid animal form as the infant, through coordinating its bodily activities, is able to compose its environment into an arena of things amenable to volitionally repeatable inspections and manipulations. In playing with and exploring its environment, the infant gathers things together and takes things apart; it learns that a repeated action can bring the same results each time; it learns that some things can be done and some cannot; and if something cannot be done now, it might become possible if continued efforts are made. All in all, the infant learns crude practical rules through regularizing its activity to achieve desired effects.

This explorative establishing of order may initially engage imagination in a crude associative way. Moments of accomplishment or gratification provoke associated images from the past or fragmented imagery of possibilities (without, of course, being explicitly recognized in these terms). Such illuminations would enhance the child's coordinative activity. However, the more important point is that as the probings of and responses from its environment are repeated and become familiar, the capacity to generate images of items or situations becomes volitional rather than associational. The fruits of the infant's repeatable achievements *vis-à-vis* sight, dexterity, and bipedal mobility provide rules or skills wherein, it can at will, project the hidden or latent aspects of a thing or situation in imagination. The more, indeed, that the infant can generate such images, the more it is able to compose its environment into a field of means and ends. One might even go so far as to say that it learns a kind of crude categorical composition of the world. Notions such as unity, plurality, totality, reality, negation, limitation, and cause and effect are not learned initially as concepts, but rather as practical constraints and possibilities which, through repeated encounters guide the infant's activities and projections.

Imagination, then, fleshes out and enables the infant to negotiate that which is not immediately given in perception. This not only massively enhances its practical hold on the world, but also facilitates its cognitive grasp, by introducing the rudiments of symbolic articulation. It is this, of course, which the acquisition of language both refines and extends.

Given these points, one might reasonably conclude that the formation and application of concepts and the volitional exercise of imagination are reciprocally correlated – one cannot have the one without also having the other. If a being is to apply concepts in anything other than the ostensively rigid animal mode, it must be able, in imagination, to project different possible places, times, and contexts in which such applications might occur. When imagination is directed by concepts or descriptions its volitional character is, in turn, augmented. The conceptual or descriptive core enables it to project, and make concrete, very diverse possibilities of experience as alternatives to our present perceptual position and existential situation. Freedom and choice in any positive practical sense are informed by, and motivate such projections.

I am arguing, then, along the Kantian lines that imagination gathers up possibilities of perception, in a way that makes non-ostensively rigid concept application possible. The acquisition of such concepts reciprocally facilitates the exercise of imagination allowing it to become fully volitional.

This is the first transcendental aspect of imagination. The second also can be derived from Kantian insights. For insofar as the cooperation of understanding and imagination organizes the stream of sensations into a unified field of things, events, and possibilities, it also serves to give structure to our experience of time. In composing the phenomenal field the human subject must be attentive to the continuous succession of moments, to variations of size, shape, and intensity, to causal transformations, and to the modal characteristics of possibility, actuality, necessity (and their opposites) *vis-à-vis* an item or event's position in time. Through our practical and cognitive activity, in other words, imagination is, simultaneously organized in a comprehensible framework of present, past, future, and counterfactual possibility. If our capacity for projecting what is not immediately present were not organizable in these terms, we would not rise above crude ostensively rigid cognition.

Now, it is vital to note that this is not just a case of imagination being a necessary condition of our objective understanding of the world. For cognitive acts of objective understanding are acts of the cognizing subject. Indeed, as we saw earlier, to master the reciprocal structure of concepts entails that we comprehend their applicability in times, places, and contexts other than those which we might be presently inhabiting. This comprehension of other times and places of possible inhabitation opens out a sense of our own present, past, and future, and alternative routes that might have led to our present. Acts of objective cognition, in other words, and the unity of the cognizing subject are reciprocally correlated. Through applying concepts we simultaneously make the world intelligible in objective terms, and achieve consciousness of self. Imagination's directed organization of the temporal flow is at the heart of both dimensions. This is therefore, the second transcendental aspect of the imagination.

There is also a third. To understand it, we must first consider a feature of the image that has not been emphasized in the discussion so far. This consists in the fact that the image schematizes, that is to say interprets that which it is an image of in terms of some its sensory qualities, but not others. Now, the importance of this consists in a relation with memory. It is all too easy to think of memory in terms of faded pictures, or decayed sensory impressions, which are retrieved by present consciousness. The relation between our present context and memory images is, in fact, much more complex and creative. For the intentionally complex states that memories are of cannot simply be replayed in the present. They do not come ready-made in exactly defined frames. Indeed, if there were not an element of schematization involved – if memories could return with all the power of an immediately present perception – it is difficult to see how the present perception could be sustained in an intelligible continuous way.

Given the schematic core of memory-images, we might regard such imagery as a specific use of the imagination. *Remembering*, as opposed to simply recalling facts about our past, involves the generation of images that satisfy descriptions about events or situations that we have experienced. The vital point to emphasize is that such images are generated in the present and not simply retrieved. How we remember a past situation, and to some degree, what we remember, is given an specific character by the specific interests of our present circumstances. The factual basis of memory – even when it is veracious – allows for considerable stylistic and creative licence, in its generation of an answering image. Each time we remember the past, we do so from a new existential position. This means that in remembering the same fact from our past on different occasions, our iconic projection of how that fact occurred can vary. Each new present reconfigures our orientation towards the past, a point which is, of course, accentuated by the fallibility of even factual recall.

These considerations yield a quite specific notion of the self. It is a holistic structure that changes from situation to situation, even moment to moment. Determining how and what we are involves a continuing narrative, rather than mere description of chronologically successive experiences. It involves selective interpretation and valuation of past, future, and counterfactual possibility from the vantage point of the present. The imagination, with its schematizing and stylizing structure, is at the heart of this – let us term it – *fabric* of the self. This is the third transcendental aspect of imagination.

Part Two

I have argued so far, then, that the imagination has a transcendental significance in three respects. First, it is presupposed by our capacity to apply
concepts in a reciprocal and non-ostensively rigid way; second, it is presupposed as the basis of temporal unity in both our objective knowledge of the
world, and our knowledge of self; and third, it is presupposed as a core
element in the holistic and continuing narrative structure of experience. To
see how these transcendental aspects figure in relation to pictorial art let us
return again to Wollheim's notion of twofoldness, and, in particular, a disagreement that he has with Gombrich over its perceptual scope.

Gombrich's claim is that it is not possible to perceive what is represented
and the medium of representation simultaneously.[7] What is involved, rather,
is an alternation of perceived aspects as exemplified in the perceptual switches
which take place in seeing the duck/rabbit figure of gestalt psychology.
Wollheim's position, in contrast, is that the elements of twofoldness do,
indeed, must, permit simultaneous perception.[8] Now, it is important to note
how the question of varieties of pictorial representation has a bearing on this
issue. To show why this is the case, I shall unpack and develop a tripartite
distinction made by Kant.[9]

The distinction is between mechanical, agreeable, and fine art. In the
broadest terms, mechanical art is that which seeks to convey information in
visual terms, or to use such information as part of a strategy of persuasion
aimed at a specific viewing audience. It is the stuff of such things as instruc-
tion manuals, or advertizing. Agreeable art is that which aims simply to
please or amuse. We are dealing here with kitsch representations, or ones
whose functions are purely escapist.

Both these modes of representation share a common characteristic. If we
are to perceive them as pictorial representations as opposed to mistaking them
for realities, it is logically presupposed that we believe them to be pictures –
that they have a "made" character. However, in these cases the belief functions primarily in a dispositional sense. We know that they are representations, but their nature is such that our belief to that effect plays no significant
occurrent role in the process of perception. We engage with them, rather,
simply in terms of what they represent. If, indeed, we do attend to the
medium, this to some degree inhibits the representation's intended function.
For we are meant to be informed, persuaded, entertained, and so on, by the
represented subject-matter *per se*, rather than the way in which it is rendered.

This, however, brings us to artistically significant representation.[10] For Kant
– questions of aesthetic form aside for the moment – this has the characteristic of originality and exemplariness. Originality here should be taken to
mean a work's capacity to engage our attention through its refinement or

innovations in relation to the traditions of making in that medium. And exemplariness should be taken to mean the works embodiment of patterns and practices of production and composition which can be fruitfully developed by other artists.

The importance of Kant's notion of fine art has scarcely been recognized. For in affirming the importance of originality and exemplariness, he is indicating the way in which our reading of aesthetic form and representation, is actively mediated by what are, fundamentally, historical considerations. If a representation is aesthetically significant or original, this means that it differs in a positive way from other representations. It stands out from the norm established through our experience of other works. Interest here, accordingly, focusses on the way in which subject-matter is rendered – on compositional strategies, treatments of light and colour, conceptions of pictorial space, and the handling of light and paint. The work may stand out in these terms of course, simply on the basis of its contrast with our previous personal experiences and preferences. If, however, our perception is historically informed by a deep familiarity with the medium and its traditions, then the work may be all the more striking by virtue of its objective claim to originality.

In the case of the fine pictorial artwork, then, the belief that the picture is a picture – that it has been brought forth through human artifice – is forcefully occurrent. It is not a mere disposition or even an inhibition to our seeing of that which is represented (as in mechanical or agreeable art), rather it permeates our perception. Our orientation is primarily towards the twofoldness of the work. Wollheim is, therefore, right to affirm, that the elements of twofoldness are simultaneously perceived, but it is also vital to emphasize how this is made possible. Our awareness of the medium as a rendering of what is represented involves not simply perception, but perception informed and situated in quite specific, ultimately historical terms.

I am arguing, therefore, that in relation to mechanical and agreeable art, twofoldness is not to the fore. Gombrich's account of alternative perceptions of the two aspects may be loosely appropriate to these, bearing in mind that one of them – the subject-matter that is represented – is of primary significance. In the case of artistic representation, in contrast, twofoldness is the very basis of our perception. It is this fact, and its ramifications, that enable us to make linkages with the transcendental significance of imagination. I shall focus initially on the third aspect of this significance, namely, the image's function in the holistic core of experience.

A first point to note is that in affirming twofoldness, we are recognizing the fact that the representation has been made and composed. It is an image that has been volitionally generated by physical means, so as to satisfy the artist's intention to represent such and such a kind of subject-matter. Whereas this intention-directed volitional generation of imagery is meant to be overlooked in mechanical and agreeable representation, in artistic representation it is to the fore. This means that pictorial art exemplifies the ostensively non-rigid structure that enables the imagination to serve those transcendental functions outlined in Part One of this discussion. It also manifests another aspect of this structure – the one that marks imagination's decisive role in the narrative fabric of experience. For whilst the pictorial artwork is iconic with the kind of thing that it presents it does not – no matter how "naturalistic" the style – simply duplicate or clone that thing in visual terms. Rather, the image is manifestly stylized. We see it as a schematization or visual interpretation of its subject-matter. The term style is, perhaps, of paramount importance here, for to engage with a work's style in the fullest sense goes beyond formal considerations alone. It is to attend to how that which the picture is of, is *made manifest*. In perceiving style, in other words, we are perceiving twofoldness.

Let us take this somewhat further. In perceiving the work's style – as a volitionally generated, physically realized, intentionally directed image – we know that it was made. However, it was not made *ex nihilo*. In recognizing the work's stylistic distinctiveness we, at least tacitly, link it to precedents or the lack of them, in other works (by the artist or by others). We may also note the way in which some of the artist's stylistic traits – such as a hard edged articulation of form – are ones that characterize a more general school or movement, or even the sensibility of an entire historical era.

With this in mind, we can look back on the function of the mental image in the ongoing narrative of experience. Such an image – deployed in memory, or as a projection of the future or counterfactual possibility – interprets and stylizes its objects on the basis of the self's present existential interests, but, reciprocally, the interests of the present are a function of its inherited past experiences, its futural or counterfactual projections; and, indeed, a broader context of contemporary social attitudes, sometimes negotiated reflectively, but more often absorbed without awareness that the absorption has taken place. All these factors inform the generation of a present mental image. The pictorial artwork exemplifies their intersection. Indeed, it is precisely because we here focus on how the work stylizes, and its historical conditions and consequences that we are situated in the heart of the holistic experiential nexus, which shapes and is sustained by, the generation of imagery *per se*.

I shall now link artistic representation to the other two transcendental functions of imagination, namely its role in gathering up and giving temporal stability to the perceptual manifold.

In order to make this connection we must first recall what is at issue in Gombrich and Wollheim's disagreement over twofoldness. Gombrich holds that the perception of twofoldness is a kind of gestalt switch – from material base to representational content or *vice versa*. Wollheim in contrast holds that such properties can be seen simultaneously. Representation *per se* can form the object of a single perception. Now, in my foregoing arguments, I have lent support to Wollheim by linking the singular perception of twofoldness to specifically artistic representation. This support, however, must now be significantly qualified on two grounds. First, whilst the singular perception of twofoldness is appropriate to art, there are circumstances where twofoldness in Gombrich's dual perceptual sense can also be loosely appropriate. I say "loosely" here, because what I am talking about is not simply a radical switch from one perceptual emphasis to another but rather something much more subtle and dynamic.

It is the recognition of this that demands the second qualification to Wollheim's position. His notion of twofoldness is a useful working concept, but is logically more complex than his customary employments of it would suggest. In fact, it might be better to talk in this respect of *fourfoldness*. This is because representation's structure can be analysed in terms of four logically distinct aspects – (i) the physical or material base; (ii) the work's formal properties (e.g., line, shape, texture, mass, volume, light, and colour); (iii) physiognomic properties, that is, ones with specific ranges of emotional or psychological association; (iv) representational content.

For present purposes, the specific relation of twofoldness that holds between (ii) and (iv) – formal qualities and representational content – is of most interest. To enjoy formal qualities for their own sake is to enjoy complex relations of unity, diversity, reality, limitation, negation, and, overall, balance between these relations. The perception of them of is enormously complex and, in a positive sense, highly unstable. In an artist such as Jackson Pollock, for example, shape and form is often animated within a shallow optical space in a way that sets up strong formal rhythms. This invites the view to imaginatively continue the rhythms either backwards into the plane, or outwards to break its surface. Again, in works by artists such as Barnett Newman or Mark Rothko, extended bands of colour set up ambiguous figure/ground relations, and complex suggestions of presence, absence, and void. To perceive all these qualities in relation to one another involves strong changes of perceptual emphasis even at the purely formal level. In particular, there is systematic ambiguity as to which formal properties are to be seen as closely tied to the physical reality of the painted surface, and which are to be linked to those specific conditions of optical illusion that the work creates.

This ambiguity of reality and illusion at the formal level also extends to figurative works. One might, for example, distinguish between infrastructural formal qualities (line, shape, texture, mass, etc.) and superstructural formal qualities that are a function of the work's representational content.[11] Consider Manet's *Dejeuner sur l'Herbe*. This work can be appreciated in formal terms not only for its qualities of light and colour and the like but also for the way in which the particular disposition of human figures tends to compress the relation of foreground and background. Manet's use of representational content here serves a specific formal function that is loaded with psychological associations. A nominal outdoor "natural" scene is rendered claustrophobic and aggressively artificial. The manifest artifice of this formal strategy, indeed, is also rendered more insistent by the incongruity of a "picnic" scene where the male figures are attired in contemporary garb, whilst one of the female figures is naked.

Now, if a picture is of artistic merit, we are rarely content to negotiate its twofoldness just in terms of a singular perception of it (although this, as I have agreed with Wollheim is fundamental to our appreciation of it). Rather, we are also taken by the way in which representational content is *achieved* from the artist's handling of formal qualities, and the way in which such representational content functions, superstructurally within the formal structure. What all this involves is a close, more dualistic, perceptual attentiveness to the *emergence* of content from form, and their conditions of reciprocal dependence within the work.[12]

Such attentiveness involves a perceptual to-ing and fro-ing from a shifting and unstable level, to one which is, in a decisive sense, spatially and temporally fixed and fully articulate. This latter level is that of representational content *per se*. A picture is only a picture insofar as it individuates recognizable kinds of two- and three-dimensional visual items within a notional plane.[13] The basis of this is natural – based on resemblance – but it is also conventionally mediated to a high degree. Strong or fully realized perspectival accents are especially significant in such a context. For, whilst they do not "correspond" to the actual process of visual perception, they form a convention that enables virtual relations in a two-dimensional plane to be projected in a way that is maximally consistent with the systematic relation of visual items in the real spatio-temporal continuum.

The spatio-temporal coherence of such pictorial representation cannot be emphasized enough. Insofar as a picture represents recognizable kinds of things and relations in a perspectively accentuated space, it simultaneously articulates an implicit temporal horizon. The space can be notionally entered, and the viewer can take up different virtual positions – both spatial and temporal – within it. On entering such a virtual system and moving continuously through it, near objects would be reached before more distantly located objects. Indeed, the fact that, from an external viewing position, one thing blocks our view of another or has hidden aspects is, in neither case, taken as evidence that the hidden things or aspects do not exist. Rather, the situatedness of the visually accessible aspects within a system of perspectival accents

– however informal – offers cues whereby we can imagine ourselves moving
through this virtual space to occupy positions where what is hidden in relation
to the external viewing position would become visually accessible internally.

In Part One, I identified the way in which imagination enables us to project
the hidden aspects of things, or of states of affairs that are not immediately
given in perception. This projective capacity is essential for concept formation
insofar as to have a concept in the fullest sense entails that we can envisage
its possible applications in times and places other than that of its immediate
employment. In exercising imagination in this context, we, at the same time,
unify consciousness of self. For to project other times and places where a
concept might apply, is to project ourselves there as possible users of the
concept. (Consciousness becomes consciousness of self when it can conceive
occupying times and places other than the one presently occupied.)

Through stabilizing, and, in concert with concept-application, giving spatio-temporal unity to the perceptual manifold, then, imagination also gives
unity to the self. These transcendental functions enable experience to be
achieved. They allow the phenomenal flux of scattered perceptions to be
gathered up and systematized. Experience's achieved character is not something that is much remarked upon in adult life. However, it is, in symbolic
terms paramount in the dualistic version of twofoldness that I am currently
considering.

We will recall that to create and/or appreciate an artistic representation
involves attending to the emergence of representational content from formal
qualities, and to the function of the former in relation to the latter. This means
that we appreciate how the image achieves a virtual spatially and temporally
unified system of relations, from a more shifting and unstable zone. In such
an image we are presented not just with the immediately visible aspects of
the kind of subject-matter that is being represented, but also a system of
visual cues that enable the projection of hidden aspects and states of affairs –
or, to put it another way, a system of possible viewing positions within the
represented space. Such an image exemplifies transcendental imagination's
stabilization of the perceptual manifold and the unity of the self. If, accordingly, our perception shifts from this level to formal qualities and back again,
we symbolically trace the emergence of a stable experiential world from a
more unstable realm of phenomenal qualities. In one sense, time goes backwards in a symbolic replay of how experience itself emerges through the
powers of imagination. In another sense, the to-ing and fro-ing, from representational content to formal qualities, serves to disclose what the passage of
time hides, namely the fact that experience – even in its crudest sense – is
achieved. And this is the supreme significance of twofoldness in the sense of
perceptual dualism. It offers a kind of eternalization of the dynamic origins
of experience. In each life, experience emerges only once. In artistic represen-

tation it emerges always – or at least for as long as the representation survives and is appreciated.

Of course, in a philosophical analysis such as this, the phenomenon of experiential emergence can be described and analysed. Artistic representation, however, exemplifies the process at the ontological level of its occurrence, namely, the sensible. It is shown rather than said. Our criterion of showing here is perhaps best illustrated by reference to the *intuitive* illuminatory power of events and relations at the sensible level. When a person falls in love or forms friendships, for example, one can offer a reflective analysis of the reasons why this has happened. But such an explanation will be by no means the whole truth. The situations in life that provoke us to action or to emotional responses involve complex matters of appraisal that draw on different modalities of sense operating as a unified field. These appraisals themselves are not simply registered by consciousness, but draw on the subject's awareness of present, past, and possible physical and existential positioning. Reflective thought's explanation of such responses can only operate with very general reasons. Its abstractness cannot fully articulate the depths of our immediate sensibly grounded appraisals of the world. Yet, nevertheless, we are able to act on the basis of such appraisals. They give direction to experience. They are cognitive acts which embody an intuitive knowledge that draws on the depths of perception and experience.

The link between transcendental imagination and twofoldness in its dualistic perceptual sense, is of this intuitive order. It is one element in a complex network of responses that comprise different ways of aesthetically appreciating pictorial art. Pictures are intimately familiar to us. We are at home with them. They are a friendly part of our total rationalization of the world. But if we try to analyse why this is so, the answer is elusive. Very general notions such as "expression" seem applicable, without even quite illuminating what is involved. For what is involved here is a complex nexus of intuitive knowledge embodied in the artistic image. Some of it focusses on Wollheim's singular notion of twofoldness; other aspects focus on the dualistic version's relation to the transcendental imagination.[14] In the latter part of this discussion, I have presented this relation in a schematic analytic form. Its affective power, however, consists in the capacity to resonate intuitively with experience at its point of origin, and to make that resonation available indefinitely. This capacity is the province of artistic representation as a mode of *image-making*.

Conclusion

I have argued, then, that Wollheim's notion of twofoldness is of great utility in directing us towards some of the profoundest aspects of pictorial art. I have also indicated how Wollheim's approach requires some qualification if it is to fully encompass these aspects. I have, of course, offered rather more than a qualification of Wollheim's position by developing the significance of the transcendental imagination at some length. To some readers, this may appear to be a reflection of my own preoccupations rather than a studied response to Wollheim's philosophy, but Wollheim himself has observed how twofoldness has been interpreted primarily in terms of its perceptual or semiotic structure and that he is inclined to favour the former aspect.[15] My point, however, is that this aspect simply does not do justice to the existential depth and significance of twofoldness. To do such justice we need to develop the cognitive aspect of twofoldness without falling into the neo-linguistic reductionism of semiotic approaches.

I would suggest that the theory that I have proposed can form the basis of such a strategy. It is particularly unfortunate that Wollheim himself has not adopted something like it. I say this because whilst he does not use transcendental imagination as a working concept, he does explore cognate theories in *The Thread of Life* – most notably that of "experiential memory."[16] It is precisely themes of this sort that can and must be linked to artistic representation, if its decisive significance in human experience is to be properly understood. Wollheim's more general philosophical *œuvre*, in other words, opens up exciting possibilities for aesthetics. In this chapter I have tried to develop one such possibility.

NOTES

1. AO2, 213.
2. AO2, 217.
3. Kant, *The Critique of Pure Reason,* 165.
4. Kant, ibid., 112.
5. See, for example, Bergson, *Matter and Memory,* 89–105.
6. Cassirer, The Phenomenology of Knowledge, 114.
7. See, for example, Gombrich, *Art and Illusion,* 170–203.
8. See AO2, 213.
9. This is outlined in §§43–48 of Book One of Kant *The Critique of Judgement.*
10. The interpretation of Kant offered here follows that which is set out in more detail in Chapter 3 of Crowther, *Critical Aesthetics and Postmodernism.*
11. For more on the infrastructural/superstructural relation see Crowther, *Art and Embodiment. From Aesthetics to Self-Consciousness,* 18–20.
12. Some of the ramifications of this are developed acutely by Michael Podro in this volume.
13. I discuss this approach more in Crowther, The Logical Structure of Pictorial Representation.
14. There are, of course, other aspects as well. These are explored in detail in Parts One and Three of my *Art and Embodiment.*
15. In the verbal exchanges at the Wollheim conference held at Utrecht in 1997.
16. See especially TL, 104–121.

Part Two
Expression

Chapter 7
Wollheim on Correspondence, Projective Properties, and Expressive Perception

MALCOLM BUDD

Il est des parfums frais comme des chairs d'enfants, Doux comme des
hautbois, verts comme des prairies,
　　　　　　　　　－ Et d'autres, corrumpus, riches et triomphants
　　　　　　　　　(Charles Baudelaire, *Correspondances*)

From his earliest writings about the topic, the paper Expression,[1] for example,
through *Art and Its Objects*, The Sheep and the Ceremony and *Painting as
an Art* to Correspondence, Projective Properties, and Expression in the Arts,
Richard Wollheim has founded his conception of artistic expression on the
notion of correspondence – correspondence between the internal and the
external, a psychological or mental condition, on the one hand, and an item
in the environment, a portion of nature or an artefact, on the other. It seems
likely that throughout this time he has also thought of artistic expression as
being a function of projection – the projection of a psychological state onto
an object. But it is only in his more recent writings that projection has
emerged as the underlying motor of correspondence, and in these writings he
has articulated a theory of expression in art that combines the phenomena of
correspondence and projection. To examine this subtle and complex theory –
as given in *Painting as an Art* and further developed in Correspondence,
Projective Properties, and Expression (supplemented by AO2 and SC) – it is
necessary to extract it from the marvelously rich tapestries into which it is
woven. When the theory is isolated from the competing attractions of its
surroundings, certain defects in the design, gaps, or uncertain transitions and
an unwanted tension, become visible – at least, to my eyes. But the threads
that compose the theory appear to entwine in somewhat different ways and
to vary in salience across the different works, and in disentangling the threads
and weaving them into a self-standing design it is possible that my reconstruction will present only a distorted image of Wollheim's creation – or, at
least, of his vision. If, however, my reconstruction is accurate,[2] the theory
must, I shall argue, be both amended and amplified: one feature must be
discarded, one explicated, a certain argument must be provided, and the
tension I identify needs to be resolved.

In a nutshell, the theory is as follows. Correspondence is the core of artistic expression: A work of art expresses a psychological condition by corresponding to it; it corresponds to the psychological condition in virtue of possessing a certain perceptible property; the work possesses this perceptible property because the artist gave it this property in order that it would correspond to the condition; and a properly sensitive and cognitively endowed spectator is aware of the correspondence by undergoing an experience of a certain kind when confronting the work – an experience of the work as corresponding to the condition.

But the phenomenon of correspondence is not restricted to works of art. It pertains equally to the natural world. The judgement of a work of art and the judgement of some part of nature that it corresponds to a certain psychological condition have exactly the same content (CPE 155). The difference between the two judgements is just that, in virtue of there being a standard of correctness for the first judgement, given by the achieved intention of the artist (SC 7, PA 85–6, CPE 155–7), the first kind of judgement requires a larger cognitive stock than the second, if it is to be soundly based. This means that it is unnecessary to focus on works of art, rather than nature, in order to grasp the key element of Wollheim's theory of expression, correspondence, and its connection with the phenomenon of projection. Since this is my concern, I shall ignore the question whether the achieved intention of the artist is the appropriate standard of correctness for a judgement of correspondence about a work of art; I shall leave aside the question whether the theory identifies the most central or significant phenomenon of expressiveness in the appreciation of art, or of paintings in particular; and for the most part it will be a matter of indifference whether the item in the environment that corresponds to a psychological condition is thought of as a work of art or a portion of nature.

The fundamental question is, What is correspondence? Wollheim's answer is that correspondence is a relation between some part of the external world and an emotion, mood or feeling that the part of the external world is capable of invoking in virtue of how it looks (PA 82): The world seems to a spectator who perceives the correspondence to match or be of a piece with the emotion, and this experienced correspondence is liable to induce the emotion in the spectator under certain conditions. More perspicuously, for nature or anything else to correspond to happiness, melancholy, depression or terror, is for it to possess certain (relational) *properties*, properties of an unusual kind, namely *projective* properties. These projective properties are the previously mentioned perceptible properties in virtue of which an item that possesses them corresponds to a mood, emotion or feeling.

So the question becomes, What is a projective property? Wollheim's answer is that a projective property is a property that is identified through a distinctive, triple-aspect experience,[3] an experience that exemplifies a particular species of seeing, "expressive perception," a species that presupposes a certain psychological mechanism for dealing with emotions, feelings, and moods (emotions, in short).

This psychological mechanism is so-called complex projection.[4] But Wollheim's theory exploits, not the nature of the fundamentally unconscious (PA 84) process of projection, but one – at least one – of its consequences. The consequence of the complex projection of an emotion (E) onto the natural world exploited by the theory is that some part of nature (N) is experienced as having a property (P), a property different from the emotion E projected, the two properties being related in this way: nature is felt to be of a piece with the subject's emotion. That is: to experience N as possessing P in virtue of projecting E onto it is to feel it to be of a piece with one's E; and, more generally, to experience N as possessing P (whether or not as a result of projecting E onto it) is to feel it to be of a piece with E. And this requires an affinity between N and E, that is, features of N that make it a suitable object for the projection of E – ones that encourage and sustain such a projection.

The idea of expressive perception is therefore the key to the idea of a projective property, and so to the idea of correspondence. But what kind of perception is expressive perception? Expressive perception, the experience through which a projective property is identified – the form of seeing in which projective properties are experienced (PA 85) – is characterized, first, as being partly perceptual, partly affective: these constitute the first two aspects of the experience. Now, as a perception of the world this experience will have a representational content – it will represent the world as being a certain way – and as an affect it will be of a certain affective kind. So three questions need to be answered if we are to grasp the character of this experience (and so the character of a projective property): What is the representational content of its perceptual aspect, what is the nature of its affective aspect, and how are the two aspects related to one another?

I take the theory's answers to these questions to be as follows. First, the essential representational content of the perceptual aspect – that component of its representational content in virtue of which it is the perception of a projective property – is that the perceived world corresponds to an affective psychological condition – an emotion, feeling, or mood. Second, the affect is of the same nature as that of the corresponding psychological condition: if the corresponding psychological condition is melancholy, the affect is one of melancholy. And, third, the affect has a twofold relation to the appearance (or appearances) of the object it is directed towards:[5] (a) it is caused by the look of the object that possesses the projective property and (b) it affects the look of the object, it colours what is seen, it affects how what is perceived is perceived, so that expressed emotion and perception are fused or integrated (PA 82, SC 5). This second relation between affect and appearance implies that a part of the world has a different look when it is perceived with or through this affect from what it has when it is not so perceived: when it is not so perceived it does not seem to match the psychological condition. So its bare appearance differs from its appearance as clothed by or dyed with the spectator's affect: projective properties are laid over various features of the perceived scene or object – features that are such as to encourage and sustain the projection of the corresponding emotion.[6]

But there is also a further characterization of the distinctive experience definitive of a projective property: it reveals or intimates a history or origin, either that of the kind to which it belongs – how the kind of experience it exemplifies comes about – or its own, namely an origin in complex projection. This feature is the third of its three aspects.

At this point, it is necessary to take notice of a crucial difference in the nature of the theory as displayed in its various manifestations. In fact, on the evidence of the texts alone, an apparent shift in Wollheim's thinking about the connection between projection and correspondence might well be detected. Whereas The Sheep and the Ceremony represents expressive perception as, or as a result of, the projection of the subject's inner emotional state (or, rather, a constellation of such states) onto the object of perception, and maintains that the artist creates his work with the intention of exciting the spectator to project certain mental states onto the work, and *Painting as an Art* represents correspondences as being formed in projection, Correspondence, Projective Properties, and Expression acknowledges that in general the perception of correspondence is not a consequence of an immediately preceding act of projection. The apparently abandoned position, seemingly occupied by The Sheep and the Ceremony (and also, perhaps, *Painting as as Art*), represents the expressive perception of N as corresponding to E in this fashion: the look of N causes the subject (i) to experience E and (ii) to project E onto N, as a result of which N is experienced as corresponding to E. In other words, it presents the experience of correspondence that is integral to expressive perception as being the upshot of an act of projection carried out by the subject in front of the perceived scene.[7] But whether this position has been abandoned or whether it was never truly embraced, it is certainly not Wollheim's considered view, which is my concern.

With this clarification the supposed third aspect of the experience definitive of a projective property is now ready for examination. In fact, the idea that the experience of expressive perception intimates an origin in complex projection is crucial to Wollheim's theory, for without this idea the theory, as it stands, would not wed expression to projection: the notion of correspondence, explicable independently of the concept of projection, would bear all the weight and would be self-supporting. To see this, consider what the rationale might be for the introduction of the concept of projection into an account of expression. For Wollheim, the rationale could not be that it is intrinsic to expressive perception that the activity of projection is actually operative in it, for, as I have already indicated, Wollheim's theory (in its most recent incarnation) is *not* that the perception of expression or correspondence is itself a matter of the projection of a psychological state that the spectator is in when she encounters, or as a result of encountering, the perceived scene or object. On the contrary, most experiences of expressive perception do not themselves originate in projection – in the projection of a currently experienced emotion (CPE 149). And although a consequence of complex projection is the perception of something in the environment as corresponding to a psychological state, it does not follow that it is intrinsic to such a perception that it, or the kind to which it belongs, originates in complex projection – this would follow only if the perception of correspondence *must* derive from projection. But it is often the case that a certain type of event that is a consequence of one kind of phenomenon can just as well be a consequence of another kind of phenomenon: Although one result of the consumption of too much alcohol is a headache, the occurrence of headaches is not tied to the consumption of alcohol. So the concept of projection does not qualify for an essential role in an account of expressive projection merely because one way in which expressive perception can occur is in the aftermath of and as a result of complex projection. Another way of bringing out this point is to question what is meant by "the sort of experience they [expressive perceptions] exemplify." For as yet – in the light of any considerations that Wollheim has actually brought forward in his writings – there is no reason to concede anything more in general than that an experience of expressive perception is an experience of a kind similar in one respect to the kind of experience immediately brought about by complex projection: It is a perception of correspondence. In the absence of a compelling argument for the claim that the perception of an external item as matching a psychological condition is possible *only because and in virtue of* prior projection, the recognition of projection as an essential constituent of the analysis of expression is entirely dependent upon the intimation thesis. In sum: The rejection of the idea that the activity of projection must take place in or immediately prior to expressive perception, and the failure to eliminate the possibility that the perception of correspondence might be rooted, not just in projection, but in some other, independent psychological phenomenon, requires the introduction of the intimation thesis to bind expressive perception to projection.

But the thesis is problematic. It will be simpler to concentrate on the standard case, in which the intimated origin is, not the experience's own, but (supposedly) that of the kind to which it belongs. First: In what sense is it supposed to intimate that the origin of the kind of experience it exemplifies is the activity of complex projection? Presumably, for an experience to intimate something about itself the intimation must be an aspect of its phenomenology. But what form does the intimation assume? I take it that the answer to this question is that the intimation helps to compose the experience's intentionality: it is part of its thought-content or it is at least contained in the experience as a thought.[8] But if this is so, what is the precise content of the intimating thought? Perhaps the natural interpretation would be to construe it as something like this: "Experiences of this sort in general originate in complex projection." But it is worth noticing that the comparison with bodily pain that Wollheim brings forward to clarify the intimation claim (CPE 150) invites a different interpretation. A bodily pain that does not originate in damage to the part of the body in which it is felt is held to intimate, not how it came about, but how pain in general arises, namely from damage to the body. But if it does carry the general intimation it does so only by falsely intimating its own origin in damage to the bodily part in which it is felt: The difference between a pain that does and one that does not originate in damage to the part of the body in which it is felt concerns, not the nature of the intimation carried by the pain, but only the intimation's truth-value. So another interpretation of the intimating thought – an interpretation that would render the thought generally false – would be this: "This experience origi-nated in [is an immediate upshot of] complex projection." In fact, Wollheim's own suggestion is that the intimation is a matter of recognizing that the object of perception is something onto which we might have, or could have, pro-jected the corresponding inner state (CPE 153–4).[9]

Whichever interpretation is preferred, if the intimation is supposed to be contained in the experience as a thought, it seems untrue that it really is a characteristic of the experience of expressive perception that the experience intimates the origin of the kind it exemplifies – an origin in complex projec-tion, according to the theory. For this would require not only that anyone capable of expressive perception possesses the concept of complex projection – a requirement that many would regard as sufficient to render the character-ization untenable, but that Wollheim himself might not be too unhappy to embrace, given his commitment to some knowledge of psychoanalytic theory being inherent or innate[10] – but also that this concept is drawn upon by the subject and enters into her experience of correspondence between inner and outer. And this certainly seems contrary to the facts, at least on the supposi-tion that if an experience intimates something about itself this intimation must announce itself to us when we reflect on the experience in order to determine if it tells us this about itself. For reflection on the experience of expressive perception – at least, reflection on my own experience of the expressive perception of nature or the perception of the expressive properties of works of art – fails to reveal a thought concerning complex projection.

A final point about the intimation thesis: Even if there is a kind of percep-tual experience that possesses the intimation-of-origin-in-projection-aspect, it seems clear that there could be experiences otherwise intrinsically indistin-guishable that lack the intimation-of-origin-in-projection-aspect. And an experience lacking the intimation-aspect would appear to be just as good a candidate for the role of the experience definitive of expressive perception as one that possesses it. In other words, there seems to be no good reason why only a perception that possesses the intimation-aspect should be held to constitute a perception of correspondence. For it to be essential to a perception of correspondence that it possesses the intimation-aspect, the possession of this aspect would, it seems, need to play a significant role in expressive perception – a role not in fact assigned to it by the theory and, moreover, one that expressive perception appears not to require.

For these reasons, the characterization in terms of intimation appears to me to be wide of the mark.[11]

But the subtraction of the intimation-aspect from Wollheim's characterization of the experience of expressive perception would render it too thin to be enlightening. For any illumination of the experience would be entirely dependent on the specification of, first, its affective aspect and, second, the way in which this affect transforms the affectless perception, because the essential representational content of the perceptual aspect of the experience – that the perceived object corresponds to, matches, is of a piece with, a particular psychological state – is specified in terms of an unelucidated notion of correspondence or match.[12] Moreover, the transformation effected by the affect appears to be precisely that the perception becomes the perception of a correspondence between outer and inner.[13] Accordingly, any light thrown upon the experience derives solely from the characterization of the affect integral to it.

In fact, there is also a question mark over the affective aspect.[14] For there is an important feature of Wollheim's theory that I have not yet mentioned that stands in a somewhat problematic relation to a feature of his account already introduced. The additional feature is this. For many years Wollheim has insisted that it is unnecessary that the artist, in creating a work as an expression of an emotion, or the spectator, in appreciating it as an expression of an emotion – the artist being the original spectator of the work – should actually feel the emotion that the work expresses: It is perfectly possible for the artist not to be in the emotional condition expressed by the work or for the spectator not to be excited to that emotion; it is sufficient that each should be able to draw upon the emotion or upon memory of it (CPE 157, AO2 §17). Rather than being expressive of an emotion in virtue of having been produced in that condition and/or being productive of it, a work of art is expressive of an emotion because it is the sort of thing that one would make if one were feeling the emotion and/or something that would elicit the emotion in one in certain circumstances.[15] (Compare the idea that to experience a part of nature as being of a piece with an emotion requires the recognition that one might or could have projected that emotion onto that part.) But this means that the theory is faced with a dilemma. For either the affective element of the distinctive experience of a projective property is an actual feeling of the expressed or corresponding emotion, or it is not. But if it is, this contradicts the concession that the spectator who perceives a projective property need not actually feel the emotion expressed. So if the characterization of the distinctive experience of a projective property is to be preserved, the second horn of the dilemma must be embraced. But if the affective aspect of the distinctive experience of a projective property is not an actual feeling of the emotion expressed, what is this affective element and how can it fuse with the perception and colour what is seen?

What Wollheim needs is a sense in which an emotion can be present in a person – present in a non-dispositional sense – without the person actually feeling that emotion. He believes that there is such a sense. But in the absence of an elucidation of this sense a resolution of the tension in the theory by reference to it would be merely programmatic. Furthermore, even if an emotion can be non-dispositionally present in a person without her actually feeling the emotion, this would not be enough to reconcile Wollheim's commitments. For his theory requires the affective aspect of the experience of expressive perception to transform the perception from what it would be if stripped of the affect. It would therefore not be sufficient to identify a sense in which someone who does not actually feel the emotion might nevertheless have the emotion present in her in a non-dispositional sense – by thinking about or imagining undergoing the emotion, for example. What is needed is a conception of an emotion that someone does not actually feel on a certain occasion yet is present in the person in an occurrent sense that enables it to modify a perception from not being a perception of correspondence to being such a perception. And the difficulty in specifying the required conception – in explicating the idea of the occurrent realization of an emotion not actually felt and in establishing that it is suited to the required transformation of an affectless perception – is magnified by the indefiniteness in which the concept of correspondence is shrouded.

Part of the difficulty for Wollheim's theory presented by the tension within it derives from his attempt to construct a monolithic concept of expressive perception, applicable to both nature and art. In my view, not only is the perception of nature as the bearer of affective properties a different form of perception from the perception of works of art as being expressive of emotion, but there is no form of perception that is correlative with a significant conception of the artistic expression of emotion applicable uniformly across the arts: The variety of the artistic expression of emotion – the variety of the phenomena included under that umbrella notion – precludes this. However, even if the issue of a unitary conception of the artistic expression of emotion is left aside, the experience of, and response to, nature *as nature*, which includes the perception of nature as the bearer of affective properties, is markedly different from the appreciation of art – central cases of the perception of paintings as expressive of emotion, in particular – which is saturated with the understanding of works of art as products of the human mind. A partial resolution of the tension that threatens to tear the theory asunder would therefore be possible, at the expense of a principled bifurcation of the theory, by recognizing that the expressive perception of nature requires the beholder actually to feel the emotion she sees nature to correspond to; for it is only in the case of art that Wollheim has insisted that someone who perceives an external item as corresponding to an emotion need not actually feel that emotion. And this would not be a merely *ad hoc* manoeuvre, for an actual feeling of melancholy or happiness is, it seems, a constituent of the kind of perception of a landscape as being melancholy or happy that Wollheim has in mind. Furthermore, Wollheim himself appears to recognize that this is so. For, first, on at least two occasions where he introduces the notions of expressive perception and correspondence, each time in application not to art but to the natural world, Wollheim builds into his characterization of the expressive perception of some portion of nature the condition that the subject undergoes an emotional experience evoked by what lies before her: the position of both The Sheep and the Ceremony and *Painting as an Art* is that a landscape that is perceived as corresponding to happiness, melancholy, loneliness or despair is one that induces the emotion, an actual feeling, in the spectator, which feeling transforms the look of the landscape. And, second, Wollheim nowhere departs from this account of the expressive perception of nature by acknowledging the possibility of an appreciation of nature's affective qualities that is not founded on what a spectator actually feels in front of nature.

In conclusion: If the theory is to be viable, whether as an account of artistic expression or the perception of nature as the bearer of emotional properties (i) the characterization of any instance of expressive perception as intimating the origin of the kind of perception it exemplifies in complex projection must be jettisoned, (ii) an argument must be provided that establishes that the perception of correspondence is possible only in virtue of the perceiver having the capacity for complex projection (on pain of expressive perception not being tied to complex projection), and (iii) the notion of correspondence needs to be rendered definite by an elucidation of what it is for someone to experience an external item as corresponding to a psychological condition, and this elucidation must further an understanding of why an affect is an integral part of the perception of correspondence and of the affect's capacity to endow the perception with a representational content that it would otherwise lack. In addition, if the theory seeks to capture a central phenomenon of artistic expression, at least within the field of painting, and it remains true to the idea that one who perceives a work's expressive properties does not need actually to feel the emotions expressed by the work, the precise sense in which the experience of expressive perception has an affective aspect – one that does not consist in an actual feeling of the affect – must be clarified.

NOTES

1. Wollheim, Expression, reprinted in AM.
2. In the discussion that followed the presentation of this paper, Wollheim acknowledged the accuracy of the reconstruction that follows.
3. The experience is both *caused* by and *of* the projective property, as with other kinds of veridical perception (CPE 149).
4. For the distinction between simple and complex projection, see TL 214–5, PA 82–3, and CPE 150–2.
5. This affect is directed, we are told, not just towards the property itself, but towards "older or more dominant objects" (CPE 149).
6. Wollheim maintains that it is impossible to elucidate the required affinity between a part of nature and the corresponding psychological state, to spell out how nature must look if it is to be apt for the projection of that state onto it (CPE 154). But in general there is no insuperable difficulty in specifying the features that an item must possess if it is to be a suitable object of a certain kind of activity, and the reason Wollheim advances in support of his claim – that any convincing description of what it is about some aspect of nature that makes it suitable for the projection of a particular emotion would have to "upgrade" the mere affinity into the projective properties of which it is "the mere substrate" – is, I believe, not a compelling consideration. Nevertheless, items that possess projective property P might do so, it seems, not because each possesses the same set of features, but in virtue of indefinitely many differently composed sets of features.
7. In the discussion that followed the presentation of this paper, Wollheim – I believe rightly – dismissed this position as absurd, implying that (despite the appearances) he had never embraced it. Note that the account of complex projection in TL 214–5, reverses the relation between act of projection and experience of correspondence, presenting complex projection as being *triggered* by seeing or thinking of a part of the external world as matching or corresponding to an emotion.
8. For this distinction, see TL 38, 118.
9. Wollheim sometimes seems to equate the experience of N as being of a piece with E with the perceptual recognition of N as being apt for the projection of E.
10. In the discussion that followed the presentation of this paper, Wollheim confirmed (what I had taken to be) his belief that anyone capable of expressive perception possesses the concept of complex projection.
11. It is notable that the intimation-thesis is introduced into the theory only in CPE: There is no suggestion of it in any previous formulation.
12. As it stands, this might well not do justice to Wollheim's position, for he sometimes appears to construe "N corresponds to E" as being equivalent to "N is suitable for E to be projected on to it." But this equivalence would not be an equivalence of concepts, and the kind of argument necessary to support the equivalence is missing from every presentation of his theory.

13. Wollheim never attempts to make clear why the perception of correspondence should be made possible only through an affect attached to, integrated into, the perception, or how exactly the affect manages to transform a perception of something in the environment into one in which the item is seen to correspond to the psychological state the affect exemplifies.

14. In addition to the consistency problem identified below, there is a question about the rationale for insisting on an affective aspect to the experience of expressive perception. The rationale could not be that the suitability of an item to have E projected onto it can be recognized only by the item's encouraging the spectator actually to project E onto it, given Wollheim's position that recognition of that suitability does not itself essentially involve that projection. Perhaps the intended rationale is that the suitability of an item to have E projected onto it is recognizable only through the item's inducing in the spectator an affect of the same nature as E.

15. In AO (§16), there is the suggestion that a spectator who appreciates what a work expresses but who does not think of the work as being produced in that emotional condition or is not moved to that emotion, will think one or both of two thoughts: in lieu of attributing the emotion expressed to the artist, the spectator will see the work as being the sort of thing that she would make if she were feeling the emotion; and if the work does not cause the spectator to feel the emotion expressed, she will regard the work as something that would elicit the emotion in her in other circumstances.

Chapter 8
The Artistry of Depiction

MICHAEL PODRO

1. There are three aspects of depiction that we cannot think of as quite independent of each other: The first is its capacity to elicit recognition of its subject matter, the second is its possession of its own kind of cohesion and complexity in which the recognition of that subject matter is sustained, and the third is the way in which the complexity of representation is charged with expressiveness. On each of these issues severally, Richard Wollheim has substantially advanced our understanding, but he also has altered the style of philosophical discourse as it engages with the arts, and in particular the visual arts. That advance lay first in resisting a simplified epistemology that assumed that the experience of paintings, for example, would be explicable by assimilating it to other kinds of perceptual or cognitive achievement; insisting, on the contrary, that it was *sui generis* and that the task of the philosopher was to do justice to its phenomenology. But he also resisted the assumption that problems of philosophy and psychology could be disengaged from each other as belonging to distinct inquiries. Crucially, *Art and its Objects* became a pioneering work in developing the loop between perceptual engagement with works of art and philosophic reflection. It would be hard for anyone coming to the subject now to imagine how profound a change this was in Anglo-Saxon aesthetics. It was not, of course, that outside philosophy there was not very sophisticated discussion among artists and a demanding new literature, as in the writing of Ernst Gombrich and the discourse of psychoanalysis, but bringing them to a philosophic focus was another matter, and this was Wollheim's achievement. In this chapter, I shall take up rather than offer an exegesis of two lines of thought from within his aesthetics, while in so doing raise some questions about how Wollheim's own positions are to be understood. However, I take up his arguments primarily in order to bring together the three factors that I mentioned above: the nature of pictorial representation, the nature of the internal complexity of painting and what we understand as its expressivity.

I. 2. Let me start with a characterization of depiction, first its most general conditions, then some refinements, and then some comments. I take depiction to represent a subject which is recognized in it. Depiction, so I shall assume,

has two main conditions: (a) first our capacity to recognize through difference, and (b) second the intention to use the materially present object – say
the painted surface – to imagine what we recognize within it. To these two
conditions let us add two small refinements: (c) we are aware *that* there is a
difference between what we recognize in a picture and how things of that
kind would appear outside this depiction, although not the exact nature of the
difference, nor need we concern ourselves with making such similarity or
difference a matter for clarification; and (d) the imaginative use of the representation is limited to what the representation affords; we do not freely project
or associate round it but attend to what projections it corroborates or confirms
– confirms or corroborates through other aspects of the depiction or the
tradition in which it is made.

3. Now for some clarifications: (e) that depiction involves recognizing
through difference does not mean we make a comparison nor that we entertain a sense of similarity between what we see and the objects of some
previous experience or some possible experience outside depiction; while it
would be implausible to hold that similarity of some kind between objects
that we perceived under the same concept did not underlie our capacity to re-
use that concept, what we mean by recognizing is not seeing a similarity or
analogy. This is only worth reiterating here because the notion of analogy
will be of some importance to us later. One further clarification; (f) we use
the representation to imagine what we recognize in it. This sense of function
or purpose is a defining condition of depiction: depiction is not a matter of
some relation like resemblance between the material of representation and
the subject matter that it represents: we use the one to represent the other
whether to ourselves or to others. The fact that we may do this with unself-
conscious spontaneity does not alter this fact; unless we include the notion of
representing – to ourselves or others – what it is we recognize, all we would
have would be recognition not depiction. The relation of representation and
recognition in the case of depiction may look, superficially, circular: it might
be objected that saying we use what we recognize in the depiction – say a
landscape – to imagine a landscape; so the landscape has entered our account
twice. But the objection does not hold: if we merely recognize a scene when
we look at a picture we are hardly seeing it as – or using it as – a picture of
that scene. Indeed, the minimal description – saying that we are recognizing
a scene when it so happens we are looking at a canvas – will simply not tell
us at all how that more or less fleeting recognition fits into our world. The
experience gains such anchorage only when we use the look of the mountain-
ous scene that we recognize in the canvas to imagine such a scene.

Writers have sought a sense of depicting by observing how far we can
strip down the range of primary or secondary properties while still allowing
our ordinary concepts for the prepictorial world to gain purchase; but insofar

as they do so they are either using the resembling object like a picture (and so have smuggled in the notion of representation and so depiction) or must be taken as seeing the resembling object as just that: as having the property of resembling whatever it is it does resemble as the daughter may resemble her mother. At this point, someone might say that in seeing the mother in the cast of features of her daughter we are representing the mother to ourselves. This is perhaps the intuitive point that underlies a great deal of the resemblance-theory; we slide from seeing one object (or some kind of object) in another to treating it as representing the first object to ourselves. It is easy to see how one leads into the other, but the shift in purpose ought to be clear. (We might think of it as corresponding to the propositional shift from: "it is an aspect of x that she looks like y" to "I am looking at x to hold the look of y before my mind or to imagine the look of y, or to imagine y.")

4. Let me now take up the question of what this imagining may involve by following Wollheim's discussion of Gombrich's *Art and Illusion*, which has been pivotal for the literature of art for the last forty years.[1] Gombrich had argued that the capacity of painters to represent their subject depended on triggering the mechanisms that underlay recognition in ordinary perception, despite the limiting conditions of painting – for instance, paintings being flat and having a much narrower range of contrast between light and dark compared to that of our normal environment. For Gombrich, the feat of triggering such recognition – one sense of the term "illusion" – was distinct from any ordering or compositional achievement of the artist; indeed, they were two distinct demands that had to be reconciled. There were two components to Gombrich's position that, I believe, neither he nor his critics adequately distinguished: the first was that in pictorial representation, when awareness of the subject is elicited or prompted, we are forced to neglect the painted surface as such; the second and much more important thesis is that we are unable to discern *within our experience* the border between the "real" surface and the illusion of the subject that it prompts. Responding to the first thesis Wollheim argued that the very interplay of the material surface and what it represented was crucial to the art of the painter:

... the artist ... who exploits twofoldness to build up analogies between medium and the object of representation cannot be thought content to leave the two visual experiences in such a way that one merely floats above the other. He must be concerned to return one experience to the other. Indeed he constantly seeks an ever more intimate *rapport* between the two experiences. . . ."[2]

He later refined the point by saying that we should not talk of two experiences, but of two aspects of the object that figured within the same experience: the representational and the configurational aspects. So conceived, the relation becomes compatible with (even requires) Gombrich's second thesis –

the indeterminable border between surface and represented subject within our perception – but there is a crucial addition: for the transitions and relations between the medium and the represented subject provide the painting with an internal structure. It thus enables us to understand the relation between the representation of subject matter and the internal complexity of painting.

5. Let us fill out this point. Just as our seeing an analogy between two figures may lead us to see each differently in the light of the other or one as the transformation of the other or continuing the movement of the other – giving the depicted subject a structure it could have only in its depiction – a comparable structure arises out of the relation of the painted surface and the subject depicted on it, as each recruits the other to make our awareness of the other more replete, or more determinate or more nuanced. For instance, as the contiguous shapes on the surface delimit the forms of a body, the body may take on a distinctive character for us by our being aware of the paint laid on the surface to represent it; as we see one figure on analogy with another so we see the depicted figure and the laying on of the paint as forming – among other relations – a relation of analogy. This is not to say that seeing the figure in the paint is itself a case of perceiving an analogy – we simply recognize the figure within the depiction – but the figure once recognized is seen in a more replete or nuanced way by our awareness of the coincidence between the figure and the corresponding areas of paint; at the same time, those areas of paint, when we attend to them as such, are also seen differently by virtue of the subject that they represent; in this way the paint-figure relation is comparable to the way we see one figure on analogy with another – each term is seen in a more determined or nuanced way by connection with the other. We can adduce numerous forms of this kind of interaction, for instance, the way the drawn line, by virtue of the sense of its graphic impulse, may delimit the edge of a form as well as intimating its movement, so that we see the movement of the figure and its shape both analogized by the line. And these relations can gather with extraordinary complexity.

6. It might be objected that these are not cases of analogy; that while analogy is an appropriate term for the relation in which the two figures are seen "in the light of" each other, it is not an appropriate term in the case of the relation between areas of paint or lines and the figures we recognize in them. The reason why it may not be felt appropriate is because in the relation between areas of paint to the depicted figure we do not have two terms: the paint is subsumed within our perception of the figure, there is therefore no room to move, no way in which we can change the way we see one by reference to the other, as in the case of attending to one figure in the light of the other. But this argument assumes that our perception of the figure has saturated our sense of the paint, and that assumption is surely false. The painted surface, the procedures and morphology of the technique and its

material homogeneity do not disappear in our perception of the subject, but interplay with it; there are two terms, although not spatially discrete, and in attending to each we 'perceive' or recognize the configuration of the other within it. The point I am concerned about here is not limiting or extending the use of the term analogy but in using the more familiar notion of analogy to gain a clearer understanding of how one form or configuration illuminates another, the sense of their *rapport*. As with the functioning of metaphor, there is indeterminacy about the border of between the "tenor" and "vehicle" (to use one terminology) or between the primary topic and the expression used, and that indeterminacy is a condition of the mind's activity of finding or adjusting itself to the relation. It is within such complex transitions that the subject we recognize in depiction is sustained and explored. This is the central sense in which the subject is imagined in the picture and not merely glimpsed or elaborated in verbal association. Recognition is the starting point of an elaboration that does not simply return our experience to the prepictorial world but brings about a new system of relations in which the recognized subject is suspended and reconstituted. It is critically important and not only philosophically perspicacious to keep in mind the distinction between the functions of recognizing and representing, and giving each its place in an account of depiction, for depiction's mode of representing makes something new for recognition; we do not simply recognize through difference but variegate and differentiate in new ways what we have recognized.

7. How does this account of depiction correspond to that given by Wollheim?[3] There are two rather different readings (I shall refer to them as A and B) to which his recent position may seem susceptible. The salient difference between them is the implication we give to his central notion of "seeing-in."

(A) Depiction is regarded as depending on two principal conditions: first, the innate capacity for seeing-in and the corresponding twofoldness of its object; this first condition is not yet sufficient for representation, because that requires a further factor: a standard of correctness supplied by the intention with which the picture is produced – the intention as to how it should be seen or what it should express, assuming the artist fulfils his intention in his work. But it is not clear to me that we can have twofoldness or seeing-in without representation, because all we would have is seeing something that looks like or reminds us of or alludes to something else; he might possibly reply that this is all that is meant, and what must be added to get the sense of representation is the aforementioned sense of correctness. But why should a sense of correctness, of seeing the painting as it was intended to be seen, turn mere seeing a likeness of y in x, into treating the likeness as a representation? Why should we do this unless we have assumed the purpose of using likeness for representation in the first place?

(B) In a second reading of his thesis, we would take the capacity for "seeing-in" and the corresponding twofoldness of its object as already including the use of x to imagine y; that is, seeing-in would not only be a matter of recognizing the look of x in y but of using the recognition to imagine y. Wollheim's thesis holds that this is not yet representation, and his implicit reasoning I take to be this: in order to be a representation (as for an utterance to have a meaning) there must be a criterion of appropriateness, and that is provided by there being an intention that governs how the work is to be seen. This would meet the objection to our earlier reading, interpretation A; for now, "representation" in the sense in which I have used the term is already included in "seeing-in," although Wollheim withholds the use of the term until the further element, the criterion of correctness is included.

My sense of the matter is that only the second reading (B) is viable and intended; and only it allows the integration of configurational and representational aspects, the return of one to the other, described in the second edition of *Art and its Objects*.

There is a further issue of a more general kind. Wollheim sees no need for the notion of imagining in this basic account of depiction (reserving the notion for his important thesis about the internal spectator), while I cannot see how we can avoid using a notion of imagining as in imagining y in x or in recuperating the medium for subject for the purpose of imagining the subject, or seeing analogies between figures, so that we imagine one being transformed into the other or passing into the other. Depiction thus seems, through and through, to involve a mode of cognizance which our linguistic intuition leads us to call imaginative.

II. 8. I shall now turn to the relation between the development of recognition in the complexity of depiction and what we might call its inherent expressivity. How can the kind of complexity, in which medium and subject interact, be seen as expressive? I do not mean how can they bear one expressive force rather than another, but expressive in principle, as we might think that music was expressive in principle. Let us pursue the question through the theory of expression which Wollheim proposed in his paper Correspondence, Projective Properties, and Expression.[4] The account had two kinds of thrust: First, it was a causal account of how people come to have the propensity to perceive, in inanimate nature, correspondences to emotional states; second, it says something about the phenomenology of such perception. The argument proceeds, as arguments about expression traditionally do, by making the assumption that there are literal or objective qualities of the material world around us and in contrast to these objective properties there are some peculiarly inward properties of mood or feeling, and we project or spread these inward emotional properties onto the objective substrate. Wollheim's argument first of all offers an explanation of how the properties are generated for our experience of the world: At an early stage of infant experience, the rage and frustration or the sense of satisfaction experienced are projected onto the external objects, so that what is external is felt as of a piece with internal states, and this lays a psychological foundation, a capacity later to endow the insensate material world with expressive properties. As I understand the theory, while Wollheim assumes the painter can mobilize such complex projection (so providing a sense of correctness to our response to the affective properties of paintings), it is unclear how even in general the painter is thought to accomplish this expressivity *by means of his art*. What he does, as Wollheim tells us, he does while looking at his canvas to see what effect it produces, but expressiveness has not yet been related to what we know about the process of representation and its twofoldness. It might be thought that this is not something that could be explained in any general way, but this would leave expressivity and the complex art of representation unhappily unrelated. I shall attempt to modify Wollheim's account in order to meet this.

The source of the difficulty lies, I suggest, in the premise of the argument: that the emotive properties that are attributed to nature and by extension to painting are to be accounted for as a secondary (or tertiary) set of properties distinct from objective properties. What is in question is not whether we can make this distinction (we could hardly avoid it). Rather, the problem arises from assuming that the division between objective and expressive properties is psychologically prior to their fusion in projection and introjection. For we might think of our mental-conceptual hold on the external world as *starting out* with a perceived world which is highly physiognomic, only gradually being brought under the order of objective thought which filters out these 'animistic' properties. (Think of the neonate seeming to recognize its mother by smell or tone of voice – as evidenced by the fact that he or she relaxes as the mother comes into the room, or, later, the way the textures of one blanket rather than another seems to be felt as welcoming and reassuring.) This is not to see the inanimate world as possessing the properties of sentient beings, but it is to conceive of our being joined to the world in ways which are not yet determinate as between animate and inanimate, objective and non-objective. If we consider the matter in this way, then expressiveness in the inanimate world – as Wollheim's argument would also maintain – might be something of what remains, some of the residue, of an earlier relation to the world, but explained in part by our objectifying thought as not having saturated our perception.

9. And this way of considering expressiveness would suggest how expressiveness might be brought about by the painter's art and linked to the structures of depiction as considered above. For we might then argue that the way

in which we sustain and elaborate recognition through the interrelation of parts or aspects of the painting may also confirm and enforce the physiognomic or expressive properties. The natural world's latent expressive properties, those of the medium and those of the subject matter would be seen as recruited to, framing, confirming (or in tension with) each other.[5] We could as little conceive the inflexions of the line in a drawing by Raphael as without an expressive property and one that engaged with that of the figure it delineated as we could avoid seeing the figure's movement in the impulse of the line; the expressive quality would be diminished if we could not see these factors as recruited to and framing each other. This way of considering the matter would have the added advantage of aligning the expressivity of depiction with that of music and of poetry.

10. There is a further argument that Wollheim's paper suggests by the nature of its strategy (although not its detailed content), which I shall sketch out here because it gives some enforcement to the above suggestion. An aspect of early development that has a remarkable fit with the structure of depiction, with the relation between recognition of subject-matter and its complication in painting, is that of transitional phenomena,[6] and more narrowly, in such observations as those of Daniel Stern of how infant and mother respond to each other, not mimicking but varying each other's gestures, vocalizations, and movements – matching the excited rising voice with rising arm gesture, the infant banging and the adult nodding in time, the attunement going both ways and often across sense modalities. What the infant is thought to find in the interchange is both a *form* for its internal condition – a sense of itself – and a *response* to that condition.

11. How can this early situation be regarded as bearing upon what we have observed about depiction, its internal correspondences in which one form or aspect is seen in accordance with another or figuring within another? First, a rough sketch of the connexion: We might map the early transitional dialogue onto the way one motif, the recognized subject, is taken up into others, variations provided by reconstituting the subject within the medium and setting it within its play of analogies; this we may think of as corresponding to the gesture and variation of early interchange; our initial recognition seeks confirmation in the elaborations the painting provides. A painting in which we just recognized things would not serve this function. But, second, and more specifically, we assume that for the infant there is no determinate borderline between its own gesture or expression and the response which takes it up – which joins in with it and varies it. The transaction occupies a transitional space in which external and internal pass into each other; correspondingly, I want to say, depiction occupies a transitional space between literal presence and what is imagined in it. The relation in the both cases is strongly motivated: Our initial recognition of the subject within the painting

is something for which we seek confirmation in the elaborations that the painting provides, and we seek, in turn, corroboration for how we have perceived the elaborations as we move our attention between different aspects of the painting; that is, there appears to be an inherent urgency in sustaining that recognition and its extension in our engagement which would, in our analogy, correspond to our archaic urgency in sustaining communication with a responding other person. The structure and the urgency associated with it are not, of course, peculiar to art; rather it is an indication of how our engagement with works of art brings to a focus, reflects and reflects upon a fundamental feature of experience more widely conceived.

NOTES

The arguments of this paper are developed more fully with examples in Podro, *Depiction*.

1. See Gombrich, *Art and Illusion*; his further papers on this are republished in Gombrich, *The Image and the Eye*.
2. For this discussion, see Wollheim, Reflections on *Art and Illusion*; AO2, 224; see also his paper in the symposium on Kendall Walton's *Mimesis and Make Believe* in *Philosophy and Phenomenological Research*, vol. 51:2 (1991) and PA, 46ff. On Wollheim's position see Schier, *Deeper into Pictures. An Essay on Pictorial Representation* and Michael Podro, review in *Burlington Magazine*, Vol. CXXIV, Feb 1982, 100–02 and Fiction and Reality in Painting; Maynard, Seeing Double; and Budd *Values of Art. Pictures, Poetry and Music*, chapter II and Budd, How Pictures Look.
3. See PA, 45f, W-IPU and On Pictorial Representation in the present volume.
4. MD 144–58.
5. I am here taking up suggestions from Gombrich, *Meditations on a Hobby Horse and Other Essays on the Theory of Art*, 45–69.
6. Winnicott, *Playing and Reality*; The Theory of Parent-Infant Relationship; The Capacity for Concern. On infant-mother interchange see Stern, *The Interpersonal World of the Infant*; Trevarthen, Playing into Reality. Conversations with the Infant Communicator. (In Winnicott's famous account the infant is initially dependent and gradually gains independence from its mother. She initially responds to the infant's needs so that it feels as if its own urgencies had brought forth its satisfactions [the first illusion]; gradually the mother adapts less completely and there is a stage of partial disillusion and separation; separation becomes tolerable by means of a second illusion as some feature of the external world – the transitional object – becomes a substitute maternal presence, again enabling the infant to elude the realization of objective separateness. The transitional object is transitional in two senses: between mother and object and between the internal feelings and fantasies of the child and the externality of the object.)

Chapter 9
Style and Value in the Art of Painting

CAROLYN WILDE

The application of the concept of style to a work of art is a precondition of its aesthetic interest.[1]

In the first chapter of *Painting as an Art*, Richard Wollheim lays out his argument about the roots of meaning in the fine art of painting and says explicitly that the primary determinants of meaning in painting are psychological. It is this claim that puts Wollheim's work radically at odds with much other contemporary work in the philosophy of the visual arts which, in contrast, assimilates meaning in painting in various ways to meaning in language.[2] Although there is much I disagree with in Wollheim's presentation of his psychological account, my more positive purpose in this paper is to build on those parts that I am convinced by in order to extend Wollheim's remark above, or at least make more explicit what is perhaps already subsumed within it, and say that the application of the concept of style to a work of art is a precondition of its aesthetic interest *and value*.

The Matter of the Medium

Wollheim's insistence on a psychological account of meaning in the art of painting is connected with the sort of emphasis which he gives to the *making* of art. A painting, he forthrightly claims, is a work of art in virtue of the activity from which it issues, and in this activity the use of the medium and the realization of pictorial or painterly meaning are inextricably interconnected.[3] Painting is an activity in which certain brute materials, such as the plastic clays, minerals, and oils, are transformed into a medium and when used as the media of art such different materials have their own distinctive resources for meaning and expression. The process of painting is a process of more or less inventive attention to ways in which painterly or pictorial content can be realized through methods and techniques of handling these materials which manipulate the qualities intrinsic to them. Thus, the conditions of meaning in the art of painting are more than merely the conditions of pictorial depiction or of symbolic or iconological meaning, they also have essentially to do with what is particular to the material of paint as a medium of art.

Wollheim indicates that he takes his lead about the essential contribution of the medium in painterly activity from Stanley Cavell. In his essay *A Matter of Meaning It*, Cavell says this: "The home of the idea of a *medium* lies in the visual arts, and it used to be informative to know that a given medium is oil or gouache or tempera or dry point or marble . . . because each of these media had characteristic possibilities, an implied range of handling and result."[4]

Why Cavell put his point here in the past tense – it *used to be* informative – is not clear. Perhaps he has in mind the impoverishing effects of reproduction on artistic sensibilities. In reproduction, fine effects of the particular use of the medium are obscured or even altogether lost. What is central, however, is Cavell's emphasis on the different possibilities that characterize different media. For example, transparent waterbased pigments have different possibilities and limitations from opaque tempera or rich oils in depicting the various effects of light, such as lustre, luminosity, or glow. Silver point encourages precise attention to articulate structure and fine distinction of parts; thus, in this medium, light and shade is characteristically indicated in ways that conjure the hard edges of the world's surfaces. Charcoal, in contrast, does not allow of such precision of line but its facility for easy calligraphic energy spreading darkly over the surface plays upon a more indeterminate figuring of body and space and more dramatic sense of light and darkness. It is not just that these are different expressive possibilities, but also that these different materials require different representational conventions. An artist who has a skilled technique with silverpoint is exploiting the multiple ambiguities of the drawn line, between its use to trace a contour, define an edge, or indicate a direction of movement, none of which are representations of any visible lines in the world beyond the work, as well as to represent something that is itself linear, such as a wisp of hair. A painter has a good technique not if they have acquired schemas of representation, such as are taught in amateur manuals, but if they remain challenged by the possibilities of the medium's handling and specific effects. An artist who is alive to the materials can trade the limitations of one medium to produce certain effects against another and in so doing can not only bring different subject matter to our attention but also extend the ways in which experience and imagination can be made sensible. A traditional painter such as Titian is in this sense a master of his medium. Even the elusive expressivity of modern abstract painting trades upon our experience of such a tradition and is characteristic of more recent painters, such as Anselm Kiefer, for example, to ambiguously exploit expressive analogy in the use of the medium as a theme of the work itself, or even, as in Gary Hume's work, to wilfully deny traditional expectations in the use of the medium in ways which use a hand made process to mimic or even parody the technologically produced images of the contemporary world. The relationship between qualities of the marked surface and qualities of things depicted within it then, is indefinitely variable, and as subject to rhetorical inflexion as is any literary text.

One benefit of emphasizing the activity of painting in this way is that it reduces the temptation to describe painting as a simple process of copying or matching colours and shapes with some independently perceptible element of the world. Differences both in the visual qualities of each medium and in its handling as it is applied to the surface of the work provide different opportunities for exploiting visual and tactile analogies between qualities of the medium and qualities of things represented through its use. The process of painting can be described more actively as a process of constructing equivalencies between things of radically dissimilar nature, of making one thing, such as a smeared surface, stand for another, such as the surface of a pool or the side of a breast. Thus, the whole that is the painting makes its own demands for coherent integration, related to but independent from ways in which understanding what is seen in the world requires its own visual ordering. This not only shows how any notion of "seeing-in," of seeing things figured or represented in a marked surface has to be a constructive and active process, but, consistent with Wollheim's more general interests, it invites psychodynamic descriptions of those fine deliberative judgements involved in making one thing stand for another. To make or see equivalencies between the sensual qualities of paint and the sensible things of the world requires such psychological processes as substitution, compensation and reconstitution. Furthermore, it makes processes of abstraction more intelligible and central to all acts of painting, whether figurative or not, since processes of abstraction are endemic in the unstable relationship which is set up in any painting between the work its figured content.

In this essay, I want to emphasize the fact that the handling and use of the materials in directing and responding to its effects during the process of painting is manifest in observable stylistic qualities of the work. And I want to develop this claim in order to make the further, more specific claim, that it is the probity of this process of making, the process which generates style, which is a significant source of artistic value.

The Intentionality of the Work

What Wollheim means, more generally, by insisting that the proper account of meaning in painting is a psychological account is that meaning in painting depends essentially on the fact that a painting is a product of intentional activity. In agreeing with this starting point, however, we do not need to assume that artistic intention is something separable from what is presented in the work, nor that any statement of the artist's intentions, should they be presented independently from scrutiny of the work, have any over-riding authority about what is to be seen in it. The philosophical problem of intention in art is the question of what is legitimately and appropriately brought to bear in understanding what is to be seen in the work. Like any activity, describing a work of art as intentional is to place it in a context that makes it intelligible in terms of projects, beliefs, interests, and pleasures, all of which draw from a wider social and public understanding of such things, and that thus may not always coincide with the agent's own description or self understanding of the action.

There is, however, a major difficulty in the way in which Wollheim describes his psychological account of painterly or pictorial meaning in Section 8 of *Painting as an Art*. He says there that on a psychological account, "What a painting means rests upon the experience induced in an adequately sensitive, adequately informed spectator by looking at the surface of the painting as the intentions of the artist led him to mark it." And he then describes this marked surface as a *conduit* between the mental state of the artist and that of the spectator. The difficulty with this notion of a conduit however, is that it obscures the very thing that Wollheim elsewhere makes vivid. When something passes through a conduit, the conduit might channel and direct something but it does not participate in the constitution of that thing. The point about mental activity in the art of painting, however, as Wollheim so well illustrates in discussion of examples, is that the mental processes that constitute the attentive activity is not some separable optative thought on the part of the artist, to be somehow retrieved by the spectator, but is constituted in the material workings of the painting itself.[5] Painting is an activity in which complex psychological processes of attentive imagination and pleasure, are mobilized *within* the medium of paint in such a way that the sensuous qualities of the material and of its organization have an essential and dynamic relation to whatever is figured or represented in the work. Wollheim's own discussions of the paintings of Thomas Jones and Willem de Kooning in Chapter VI of *Painting as an Art* are rich descriptions of this process. But de Kooning's work, if looked at as a work of art rather than as a symptom of its author's pathology, is not a conduit through which we might retrieve his mental state. Rather, the accumulation of licked and swiped marks of fat and gaudy paint in de Kooning's *Woman* series is itself a presentation of a distinct, replete, and disturbing way of looking at a woman *through a method of art*. A style of painting is a method of looking, a method of looking that is publicly constituted through the materials of the art.

In his earlier work, *Art and Its Objects*, Wollheim had himself criticized that notion of artistic intention that was characteristic of certain Idealist theories of art for ignoring the significance of the medium. "The question arises," said Wollheim, speaking of Croce, "if we are asked to think of, say, paintings and sculptures as intuitions existing in the artist's mind, which are only contingently externalized, is this compatible with the fact that such works are intrinsically in a medium?"[6] Wollheim argues that since such a conception is not compatible with the fact that a work of art such as a painting is physically embodied in a medium, and since we are not to relinquish the fact that works of art are intrinsically so embodied, then the Idealist's conception must be false.

In reading these passages, I am reminded of an Idealist other than Croce who in fact makes similar points to Wollheim. In his *Lectures on Aesthetics* of 1915, Bernard Bosanquet says that the artist's imagination, "lives in the powers of his medium: he thinks and feels in terms of it; it is the peculiar body of which *his* aesthetic imagination and no other is the particular soul."[7] Bosanquet criticizes both Croce and Bradley for committing what he calls a profound error of principle by ignoring the essential part played by the qualities of the medium in the artistic process. In particular, he criticizes Bradley, who describes poetry as a more ideal art form that works with seemingly perfectly apt and transparent medium of language. The media employed in the visual arts, in contrast, being gross and physical and having independent qualities of their own, seemed to Bradley to be more like obstacles in the way of expression than apt instruments of it. This is, says Bosanquet, a false Idealism. "Things, it is true," he says, seeking to guard the truth of Idealism, "are not complete without minds, but minds, again, are not complete without things; not any more, we might say, than minds are complete without bodies. Our resources in the way of sensation, and our experiences in the way of satisfactory and unsatisfactory feeling, are all of them won out of our intercourse with things, and are thought and imagined by us as qualities and properties of the things."[8] If we try to cut out the bodily side of the world, he says in a way which prefigures Wittgenstein, we shall find that we have reduced the mental side to a mere nothing.[9]

Bosanquet's Idealism, then, is one that does accommodate the ways in which our intentional relationship with things is itself corporeal; what we intend to grasp we see as cold or hard or heavy or fragile, what we see at a distance requires an effort of attention, what is obscured we move ourselves in order to better see. These phenomenological facts about perception, as Merleau Ponty elaborates, are the stuff of painting. In the body of painting, we attempt to realize and negotiate the bodies, the surfaces, the textures, and the obscurities of the world. Although many of the reasons why painting is valued as an art worthy of serious attention are tied up with its complex relations with different conceptions of reality, a particular reason is that it engages us, through the seductive qualities of the material itself, in the mundane and yet infinitely strange material nature of things, which is both a source of deep pleasure and an unsettling mystery. Philosophical Idealism is also caught up with this mystery in its own abstracted way.

Bosanquet also emphasizes the way in which a work of art such as a painting embodies individual imagination: the work of art, he says, is the peculiar body of which that particular artist's aesthetic imagination and no other is the particular soul. The individuality of the artistic work and the way it gives unique expression to agency is something we have learned to value since at least the time of Vasari and the privileging of these qualities in Romantic art theory. Thus, we value what is singularly revealed through a process of artistic attention. The value of what is revealed in a painting is not merely identifiable with the value of whatever is the depicted content nor with the information it might usefully provide about it. (To think that it is often taken as a mark of philistinism, yet someone who cherishes the portrait or the view can often distinguish fine points of painterly presentation well enough.) A depiction of lemons may have no intrinsic interest; but a depiction of lemons by Chardin or Gris may have a great deal of value because of the way – the different way in each case – in which these ordinary objects are revealed or remade through individual and distinctive methods of painterly attention. Conversely, the seriousness or depth of content does not itself ensure the value of the work as a work of art. A painting can sentimentalize its subject-matter merely by borrowing stylistic effects that, in the hands of previous artists, have given it gravity. Thus, the particular way in which the subject-matter of any work is presented or revealed through the pictorial organization of the work and use of the medium is clearly important to evaluation in painting.

Probity in the Activity of Painting

Despite his curious talk of conduits in his account of the intentional activity of painting in *Painting as an Art*, however, Wollheim has two specific arguments about artistic intention and the use of the medium in those sections of *Art and its Objects* that criticize Croce, which are directly relevant for my own purposes of showing how artistic activity is related to artistic value.

First, says Wollheim, mental images could not be so articulated as to anticipate the physical pictures to be realized on wall or canvas, since this would involve not merely foreseeing, but also solving, all the problems that will arise, either necessarily or accidentally, in the working of the medium. This is not merely implausible, but, "it is even arguable that the accreditation of certain material processes as the media of art is bound up with their inherent unpredictability: it is just because these materials present difficulties that can be dealt with only in the actual working of them that they are so suitable as expressive processes."[10] This is followed by a second argument. Once we allow that the mental processes of artistic creativity are constituted within a medium, imaginatively or actively, then we have to recognize the extent to which the experience seems to derive its content from the nature of the artefact, and not vice versa, as the Idealist would have it. It is because the artefact is of such and such a material that the image is in such and such a conceived medium. It is plausible to believe, says Wollheim, "that the painter thinks in images of paint or the sculptor in images of metal just because these, independently, are the media of art."[11]

We have here two related claims about artistic production. The first is not simply that creative thought is intrinsically a process of thought imaginatively projected in terms of some specific medium, but that in being actively directed within a medium, the possibilities and constraints of the material itself moderate and redirect the working process. Already this brings with it a multitude of ways in which the artist can relate to the medium. It is not only a matter of how inventive or inhibited the artist is in the use of the medium, but, more fundamentally, the artist's relation to the process involves elements which are more generally thought of as aspects of character, such as how submissive, assertive, humble, flamboyant, careless, extravagant, courageous, or fastidious the artist is in working with the medium. It is these critical descriptions of the process of working that form the conceptual ground of artistic critical vocabulary. Again, however, the point is not that such descriptions are used of the work to infer to the artist's state of mind, but that they are used, constitutively, to evaluate the work. There are many examples where we read of the artist's humility before the unfolding work, as though the work were in some way imposing its own authority. This is a different way of putting Wollheim's more analytical point about the artist being his or her own spectator in the process of making the work. Appropriate responsive attention to the work as it progresses, I want to say, requires its own artistic virtues. A painter who is inattentive or indifferent to the limitations and possibilities of the medium, or adopts an habitual manner of control to achieve predictable effects, will produce a mediocre or hackneyed work. An artist who pushes against the restrictions of the medium may, on the other hand, make something that seems to advance the art and contribute to a new understanding of how we see things. Virtues of attention in the making of art are matters of probity. Probity in this context is not a matter of truth in the sense that the artist has to truthfully represent how something looks. Rather, it arises from the fact that the method of looking which constitutes the style of the work demands its own process of fine and appropriate attention during which the unfolding integrity of the piece is constantly vulnerable to such things as slight of hand, habit of eye, and to the temptation to make the whole process subordinate to some previous conception of the final appearance of the work.

In introducing the idea of artistic virtues in this way I draw no hard and fast distinction between moral and artistic virtue. For I see morality as an intrinsic component of practical thought in any context which requires fine and responsive judgement about the unfolding relation of means and ends. Indeed, that is, I believe, what morality, in any general sense, is. In this as in many other contexts a distinction can be made between doing a job well and doing it successfully. The successful artist is not always the good artist. I am not implying however that the good artist needs to be a good person, only that he or she needs artistic integrity. (The idea of a good person is far wider in scope than the good artist, since it relates to the much larger, treacherous and one chance work of living a life well.) Thus, although the structure of good judgement in action is the same in artistic and other contexts, its application is particular to context.

There is no one way of course that a painting can be done badly. In calling upon the notion of artistic virtue, I am not speaking of works which are merely incompetent, lacking skill, or expertise. Many amateur works that struggle with their own incompetence are vivid and delightful. I am speaking of works that, in one of many ways, either obscure incompetence through facile technique or misdirect the line of attention between the use of the medium and the realization of the work's content by mindlessly or cynically applying artistic formula. Such works may be commercially successful, may sell as evocations of Tuscan hillsides or as signifiers of some institution's cultural credentials, but they are in one way or another meretricious, and this is evident as a function of the work's style, that is, how its method of attention is structured through the effects of the medium.

Wollheim's second point is that in conceiving the artistic project the artist draws upon experience of established practices or activities in which certain materials have been previously used as artistic media. Clearly, the artist's stance to the traditions and genres within which they work is essential to the fact that a painting can be seen as belonging to a specific time or period. Just as one of the most difficult skills of living through social change and personal ageing is to be of one's time, one of the values of art in a culture that values change and development is to be actively alive to its time. Those works that are most impressively of their own times and may seem even to be in advance of it (which are not necessarily the most novel or sensational), are, I believe, the ones we call timeless. It is most difficult of course, to judge clearly of the work and values of your own time.

It is in these ways, then, that I believe that Wollheim is not only right about the importance of the role of the medium in the activity of painting, but that his arguments implicitly contain elements necessary to an understanding of how some paintings reward attention and command admiration more than others. But description of how some painting works and an evaluation of its pleasures are not two separate processes: describing the effects of the medium as they yield what is to be seen in the work is already to make an evaluation of it. As in any other process of judgement, however, since the process of description is complex and not clearly bounded, even though two critics may agree about much of what they see, what weight to give different elements or what wider or different contexts informs the experience of looking can make all the difference to the import and value they ascribe the work. Thus it is, that it is a moot point whether or not passages of crude and inept drawing are detrimental to the interest and aesthetic value of much contemporary painting – an agreement between two critics about these stylistic descriptions can be the ground of very different qualitative judgements, not because one might discount these features and the other does not, but because each place these same descriptions within a different conception of the work.

The Significance of Style

Style in painting is the same as in writing, a power over materials, whether words or colours, by which conceptions or sentiments are conveyed. Joshua Reynolds.[12]

Within art history the notion of an artist's personal style is commonly called upon as a tool of attribution and classification cashed out in terms of typical characteristics of handling, form, or composition. It depends on one's interests and purposes in looking at the work whether these same features are used for scholarly or commercial purposes of classification and attribution, whether they are used to form the basis of interpreting and evaluating the work, or even whether they are used diagnostically for psychological or therapeutic insight.[13] It is, however, important to distinguish between the need to explain the work and to understand it. The process of understanding is interpretative and evaluative, that is, it is judgement to the best sense of the work. In some cases, the work may be so shallow, confused, or hackneyed in its stylistic technique that it is not worth the attentive effort. Examples are to be found in any academic tradition. In speaking of the development of techniques of tonal modelling, for instance, Michael Baxandall vividly describes how technical lessons learned from Masaccio's work coarsened and vulgarized painterly practice in Florentine painting in the fifteenth century.[14] One of Baxandall's points here is that artists learned to paint in this impoverished way because it was teachable. Any individual style can of course always, to some extent, be generalized to become a standard method of artistic technique and this is one way in which a work can be impoverished through its own stylistic skill. Within an academic tradition, the interest that any one individual painter commands is a matter of the way they relate to those stylistic concerns that frame their practice form the broader context of their own interests and abilities.

In his discussion of style at the end of the first Chapter of *Painting as an Art*, Wollheim claims that individual style is distinct from the characteristics associated with it. He takes what he describes as a substantial or realist view of style: style, he says, is an underlying competence deep in the artist's psychology which causes these characteristics. On page 27 of *Painting an Art*, for example, he says, "Individual style is in the artist who has it, and though, in the present state of knowledge, it must be a matter of speculation precisely how it is stored in the mind, style has psychological reality." And, in an earlier writing on style, Wollheim wrote: "The force of the claim that style has psychological reality is that the style-processes that a correct style-description for a given artist presupposes are indeed part of that artist's mental store. He employs the schemata, he acts in accordance with the rules embodying them, and the disposition to do so has become for him a second nature."[15]

There are, again, some significant difficulties with Wollheim's psychological account. First and foremost it invites confusion between style and stylishness. A painter who applies a schema to shape the process of attention is more likely to be copying a style or relying on techniques, and one who relies on a settled stylistic disposition is unlikely to be open to the process of the work other than as a problem to be solved or a routine to be applied. These forms of artistic attention are more characteristic of the amateur, or of the slick facility of the commercially successful artist, than the creative artist. They are, in fact, characteristic of those sorts of picture making that Wollheim lists at the very beginning of *Painting as an Art*, such as "painters of Mediterranean ports, or painters of mammoth abstractions whose works . . . hang in the offices of exorbitant lawyers," who may be painters but are not *artists*.[16] The precarious position of the artist's self awareness of style is evident in our wary judgements of style and stylishness or, at the more theoretical level, in recurrent debates on Mannerism in painting. The point is that the artist's own attention to the style of the work during the process of production has to be in the right place. The style of the work, which is the product of the method of attention directed through the materials of the art and which embodies its meaning, is constituted in the process, it is not its aim. A painter whose *aim* or goal is to establish or forge a style, rather than establishes style in the process of other attentive interests in making a work, is a painter whose work is merely *stylish*. Similarly, the place of the artist's attention to style in making the work is often what distinguishes an original piece form one which is merely derivative, or, differently, an artistic work from a piece of graphic art. This is not to ignore that aspects of style can themselves become, as they have in much recent art, the subject of the work.

The insistence on the psychological reality of style, however, which I am not so much denying as recasting, can perhaps be seen as Wollheim's own allegiance to the humanist tradition that seeks to reject various sorts of determinist accounts of style, whether biological and evolutionary or historically materialist, and instead to explain style in terms of intention and agency. In this way, the question of the relationship between an individual painter's style and the style of the tradition or period in which that artist works is a special case of the more general question about the relationship between a person's subjectivity and the public structures of sense and order in terms of which personal experience is shaped and articulated. Within the field of intentional activity, art in particular focuses distinctions between the wider social or cultural conditions determining or shaping any action and the way in which agents themselves understand what they are doing. Like any agent the artist is always to some degree subjected to, or made subject within, the deeper determinations of the historical and cultural orders within which they work. But creative art is also the paradigm of an interplay between subjection and agency within a system of meaning precisely because it involves active reflection and intervention from within the conditions of social communication. This, I think, is the seed of truth within Romanticism of the idea of the creative artist as a symbol of freedom. It is this that enables art to be both a human practice that may transcends its time and a site of radical cultural critique.

Although explicitly or implicitly every artist works within a tradition, each artist's relation to their tradition is as unique as they way they handle the materials. This is not merely a matter of individual skill, but a deeper matter of perception. For how an individual artist relates and responds to the tradition in which they work, or to the work of other artist for example, depends on how they see them. The Cornish painter Alfred Wallis is valued because of his innocence and naiveté. Even he, however, was totally innocent of tradition; the Victorian prints of ships at sea that were common in seamen's cottages at that time provided him with a model. His work is fresh and original not because he naively copied the style or appearance of these works but because he strived to realize for himself something that had the equivalent force to articulate his own practical experience of ships and harbours. Other, more sophisticated St. Ives painters adopted some of his stylistic features, and in doing so the work in their hands risks becoming merely mannered and *stylized*, directed by a knowing conception of the look of the work to be produced. So although I am myself describing psychological elements in the formation of style, I do not think it helpful to see these in terms of sets of schemata somehow stored in the mind, but as intentional attitudes to the objects and materials which focus and shape artistic interest. Those painters who maintain responsiveness to materials, and whose style is a function of that attention rather than its aim, are the ones who produce the work we value most.

Thus, we can see why it is that we value authenticity and originality in painting and, thereby, why forgery is of moment to painting. A forger makes the artistic style of another painter into a productive goal.

Van Gogh's style, for example, has multiple and conflicting determinations. His method of seeing his subject brings together elements from his own distinctive interest in different sorts of works that do not themselves cohere together stylistically, such as the spatial organization of Millet's landscapes and the formal qualities of Japanese prints. The vibrancy of his later work is born of the struggle to bring these diverse and somewhat retrospective painterly interests into some harmony. (I speak of them as retrospective in so far as they are attempts to impose on present experience of the landscape something fabricated from past experience of art, unlike, say Cézanne, whose later style, although similarly conflicted, is engaged more directly with present experience: to that extent van Gogh's relation to his subject matter is more sentimental than that of Cézanne.) Van Gogh's work appears as it does, has the distinctive style it does, seeking to locate a specificity of time and place, because of his distinctive interests and capabilities. But a painter aiming to forge a van Gogh, even when not directly copying a painting but making a new work in van Gogh's style, merely copies the resulting effects of van Gogh's complex process, and thereby necessarily makes more homogeneous the very features of instability and risk which give life to the original work.

The formative elements of style themselves show the limitations of forgery. To forge a painter's style well, the forger needs not just to be able to copy a style, but to look in the same way as the original painter and to submit his own interests and manner of handling to those of the master. However, there is a limit to the extent to which this can be done, and for at least two reasons. First, a method of looking is a complex matter not reducible to any formula and always in some part unique to time and person. What is distinctive about the temporal modes of looking, of course, as is well known, may only be apparent later, when we wonder how people could have been deceived by a painting supposedly of some person in the eighteenth century, which has the features of a woman living in the 1930s. This is not only because women's faces change – in the cosmetic and expressive sense that styles of dressing and posing the face change – but more fundamentally because styles of depicting it do, of what parts and aspects are given salience in the process of depiction.

The second element setting limits to forgery, which returns us to the matter of the medium, is to do with handling. The processes of handling the instruments and the materials of art are somatic, they are the results, literally for example, of such obvious things as the shape, dexterity, weight, and use of the hand.[17] And in this respect no two people are alike. In painting an artist, unlike a skilled tradesman painter, who is trained to minimize individual effects, utilizes these essentially personal features, and we have come to value paintings to the extent that they are used well. Thus, although we might admire a forger who has both the intelligence and skill to mimic these elements, we also recognize that there is something impoverished or worthless about the work. It is not that we are being deceived by some person about the true provenance of a work, for that in itself does not tell us why provenance is important. A forged work aims to deceive about the subjectivity of the work, it is in that deeper sense inauthentic: It offers a falsely fabricated experience. Thus, it is that we value probity as a virtue in the art of painting.

NOTES

1. The remark is taken from an early work in which Wollheim discusses style in the context of anthropology, Aesthetics, Anthropology and Style: Some Programmatic Remarks.
2. Richard Wollheim, PA Section 8, p. 22. He says that these contrasting views, "include structuralism, iconography, semiotics and various breeds of relativism, which . . . have in common the belief, explicit or implicit, that pictorial meaning is primarily determined by rules, or by codes, or by conventions, or by the symbol system to which the meaningful picture belongs. I reject this belief. I do not deny that such factors can have a role to play in shaping, modifying, extending, meaning in certain cases, but I do deny that they are primary determinants of meaning."
3. PA 17.
4. Stanley Cavell, A Matter of Meaning It, *Must We Mean What We Say?*, 221.
5. This is of course not a minor point and would require more detailed attention. Our difference might be summarized by saying that, whereas Wollheim speaks of the work as a conduit between the artist and the spectator's mental states, and implies that there is some causal identification between the two mental states, I prefer to speak of the intentionality of the work as guiding the interpretative attention which the spectator gives to it. Since my aim here, however, is to extend those parts of Wollheim's presentation which I accept in order to speak about evaluation, I shall not take this further. The critical point has already been well made by Andrew Harrison in his review article of *Painting as an Art*, under the title, Conduits or Conventions? I thank Andrew Harrison for helpful discussion on many points in the essay.
6. Richard Wollheim, AO2, sections 22–23, p. 41.
7. Bosanquet, *Three Lectures on Aesthetics*, p. 302.
8. Ibid., p. 304.

9. My deepest unease with Wollheim's account of the psychological roots to meaning in painting have to do with this Wittgensteinian point. On page 22 of PA, Wollheim makes explicit what he means by a psychological account and says that "it is the kind of account that has quite rightly been chased out of the field of language, most notably through the influence of Wittgenstein." All I am able to do here though my use of Bosenquet is allude to the way in which Wittgenstein's arguments *are* equally applicable in this field of meaning in painting.

10. AO2, 43.

11. AO2, 43.

12. Sir Joshua Reynolds *Discourses*, Discourse 11, p. 32. Play on the spelling of the word "stile" in Reynold's text could lay a trail for thought about the extent to which different styles overcome the limits of the materials of art, or is the means by which, with the right kind of effort of attention, we move back and forth over the boundary between the two domains of work and world. If more attention were given to rhetorical items such as this in this essay, it would itself have a different style.

13. My point here parallels and is in agreement with that made by Svetlana Alpers in her essay, Style Is What You Make It. On p. 162, she says that there is a false dichotomy between period style and individual style, a dichotomy which cannot be bridged as long as we persist in speaking in stylistic terms which concentrate on the purpose of historical ordering. If we turn instead to a notion of style as a mode of making, we realistically link the maker, the work and the world.

14. Michael Baxandall, *Shadows and Enlightenment*, appendix, 148.

15. PS.

16. Wollheim includes these on his list of non-artistic paintings on p. 13 of *Painting as an Art*.

17. As I read in an exhibition catalogue, "Muller was ambidextrous, which could account for the liveliness of his style."

Chapter 10
Expression as Representation

ROB VAN GERWEN

According to Richard Wollheim, three ways of seeing are involved in behold-
ing a painting – that is, seeing-in, expressive perception, and the capacity to
experience perceptual delight (PA 45) – and the painter relies on the beholder
to use them in appreciating his paintings. Only the first two ways are relevant
to my argument. Seeing-in is the kind of perception adequate to representations of external objects. It is characterized by a specific phenomenology, that
is, *twofoldness*: We see something in a marked surface.[1] Expressive perception
is adequate to a painting's expression of mental or internal phenomena;[2] it
involves *correspondence* "[. . .] between some part of the external world – a
scene – and an emotion of ours which the scene is capable of invoking in
virtue of how it looks," and *projection*, "[. . .] a process in which emotions
or feelings flow from us to what we perceive" (PA 82). Do these distinctions
capture sufficiently the differences and similarities between representation
and expression? In what follows I develop a theory of expression's connectedness with representation, and divert from Wollheim's subtle considerations.
My most crucial departure from Wollheim's point of view lies in my characterization of the way in which representations address our senses, and my
insistence that expression follow suit in this type of addressing us (instead of
demanding a distinctly projective mode of perception). Wollheim thinks we
can see events in a painting that have preceded what is visible in it, but that
we have to project its melancholy expression.[3] It seems to me, however, that
in both cases an act of imagination is needed. My argument will start from
stock approaches to expression, and via an account of (naturalist) types of
representation such as depiction, go on to an account of expression in terms
of that account of representation.

Before all this, let us start with an intuitive grasp of the distinction between
representation and expression. The words "happy" and "desolate" obviously
mean different things; in a way, their meanings are even opposed. This
conflict of meaning, however, need not be an extensional conflict. When
looking at a picture of happy people dancing in the streets, we may yet find
the picture expressive of desolation without contradicting ourselves and this
may all pertain to the depicted events. The meanings of the two terms (taken

intensionally) may conflict, even while applying to the same extension: happiness may come qualified. Were we to think that the relevant terms are only applicable disjointedly, then one of our attributions would be inadequate: the dance would have to be either desolate or happy; it could not be both. This, however, is not what we have in mind when we find this happy dancing desolate. Applying "conflicting" terms to a single scene shows how complicated the task of understanding an event's expression can be, but does it prove that the applications of the two terms are different in kind? If we had a single term with which to describe the desolate variety of happiness, we might want to apply it.

The expressions involved in this example are of two types: the natural type, regarding the happiness in the faces and gestures of the dancing persons, where there is a direct causal connection between the expression and the mental events expressed – albeit that, here, this natural expression is depicted. The other type might be thought of as an environmental variety, which is at least a less straightforward and more complicated type of expression than its natural counterpart, but also one that introduces a wider set of circumstantial evidence, including thoughts and beliefs about events that may or may not in actuality be available to the dancing people – such as facts about the city's recent earthquake. Even though we may have to produce distinct accounts for these two types of expression, my point is that they are connected and mutually qualifying. They may differ in grade, but not in essence.[4] I am not neglecting the fact that my example involves a picture rather than its real-life counterpart. In fact, my point is that artistic expression, like the environmental type of expression, must be understood as a qualifier of what is depicted, and, therefore, as a representational means.

1. The Opposition Argument

According to what I take to be the best argument for opposing artistic expression to artistic representation, it is conceptually feasible to understand a painting that depicts happily dancing individuals as portraying the events in a desolate manner. Conceptually speaking, it seems all right to say that the mental or experiential dimensions of a painting's representation (its image, I mean) and its expression are of disagreeing nature, not only intensionally but even extensionally – if this distinction is available to one.[5] And this is so, supposedly, because expression is an aspect of the way the material of the work has been organized, whereas the subject represented in the image stands on its own – beyond the painted canvas, so to speak, in a distinct space – as do the experiences of its antagonists. Let us look at a classical example of the opposition argument. Nelson Goodman thinks that artistic expression is sufficiently characterized by taking it as metaphorical exemplification;

whether or not the metaphor in question is a psychological term is irrelevant, because expression is psychological by contingence only.[6] Goodman sees exemplification as a reference relation opposed to that of representation and, therefore, expression too is opposed to representation. I am unsure whether I understand this correctly, but if I do, I think it is not a viable position. According to Goodman, if you say that a work which expresses x-ness is x, then you are making a true assertion, since the work really possesses x-ness, albeit metaphorically. In part, this means that the expression of a work is not in the artist's control as much as its representation is.[7] Such difference in control is, however, at best a gradual matter. The representational and expressive effects of an artist's intervention may very well be effected by one and the same intervention. Wollheim's concept of "twofoldness" explains why a beholder sees represented depth in flat marks on the surface while empathizing with the way the artist put those marks there.[8] Therefore, we must consider our responses to a represented face and its natural expression-as-represented to be based on how the painted marks are placed on the canvas, as much as are our responses to the (artistic) expression with which this face is presented to us. The effort of *materially* marking off the expression and the representation within some single picture is wasted. So how can it not be wasteful to philosophically oppose the two? The reason the artist is less in charge of the expression of her work than she is of its representation is connected with the peculiar way in which both are recognized by the beholder. To understand why the recognition of expression should be "peculiar," we need a psychological account – one that Goodman has not provided, but Wollheim has.

The most notable of Goodman's problems in the area of expression is his inability to explain why we tend to use psychological terms to describe what is expressed – a fact that he acknowledges but dismisses as inessential. Expression terms supposedly are metaphors, and that is all there is to them. Well, let us suppose that we take a sad painting as a metaphorical exemplification – a metaphorical example – of sadness.[9] How can this painting make us want to apply the terms "is sad?" What metaphorical clues would be needed? I cannot think of any. What if we took the clues – if any were found – as literally applicable, and forgot all about metaphor? How could Goodman retort? He seems merely to repeat the mystery he set out to solve. The opposition between representation and expression is conceptual only. However, it is language "gone on holiday." It has no basis in the critical appraisal of works of art.

Like he did with representational seeing, in his later account of expressive seeing, Wollheim refers to a psychological phenomenon we are already acquainted with in more ordinary circumstances. The projection that Wollheim thinks is involved in our recognition of expression both in nature and in art stems from ways in which we have taught ourselves to handle our more negative emotions. To get rid of the fears that, for instance, we feel for a certain person, we project the fear onto him. In infancy, our projections often are plainly wrong, but when growing up they tend to become more and more appropriate to the other's objectives and expression. We no longer simply project our own state of mind onto the other, but, more complexly, ascertain the other's state as akin to ours. We take more care to verify our projections. The crucial question in the present context, of course, is: How do we ascertain the appropriateness of a complex projection of melancholy on to a natural scene or a painting, which clearly aren't sentient? According to Wollheim our relevant experience of the expressive thing or scene shows an affinity with previous similar experiences that involved melancholy. As Wollheim puts it, "When a fearful object strikes fear into an observer, as it does, it is not solely fear of that object. On the other hand, the experience reveals or intimates a history" (CPE 149). This account, subtle though it is, risks explaining expression as an experience of comparing a present perception with a set of previous ones – which falls victim to the argument that Wollheim himself developed, in Chapter 1 of this book, against the Resemblance accounts of depiction of Budd and Peacocke. Rather than explaining expression in terms of a comparison with something absent Wollheim should be held to insist on its perceptual nature. We perceive the expression of a work to pertain to the work, and to be part of it.

The positive side to the "opposition" argument is that it recognizes that *artistic* expression differs from the *natural* expression of real-life persons. However, it construes this difference wrongly. According to the opposition argument, depicted natural expression issues from within the depicted character, whereas artistic expression – being the expression pertaining to the work – issues from without, that is, from the hands and mind of the artist. Both in the production of a work of art and according to its appreciation, however, representation and expression issue from a single source: the artist's hands.[10] The difference between artistic and real-life natural expression lies in the absence, or, respectively, presence of the mental life that is expressed, but this distinction is unavailable with depicted natural expression. Due to this complication, artistic expression may need a different account, such as the following, which takes it as the expression of an (implied) "persona."

2. Persona Accounts

Bruce Vermazen, Stephen Davies, and Jerrold Levinson, to name only a few, think that in understanding artistic expression we empathize with a persona in the work. This seems to be a plausible alternative to the complex notion of an "affinity," which Wollheim (in PA 87 and CPE 152) places at the base of the correspondence between the expressive perception and its object.[11] The persona account allows us to group together the expressive elements in a work as resembling the natural expression of real persons (the mental life inherent in personhood being part of what "personas" have), while at the same time leaping out of the way of intentional fallacies by avoiding the identification of personas with real people, such as actors or authors.[12] We obviously sometimes empathize with personas in a work (e.g., with the characters played by actors), but how? And how do we do it where no explicit psychological narrative is involved, as in music? What – apart from the intuitions concerning a suitable persona that the expression of the music induces us to develop – introduces the persona to which the expressive elements are supposed to belong? It is as though iron filings, merely on account of our taking them as ordered by some specific magnet, will provide the description of a magnet. Up to a certain point, this may work if the filings are neatly laid out in a regular pattern, but if they aren't, why would one introduce a magnet as the ordering principle? Two answers are available. First, when introducing a persona (an implied magnet), we do not introduce full-fledged psychologies, but merely parts of a psyche, that is, those parts that correspond to what is expressed in the music. This answer takes us back to square one. The second answer is that introducing a persona is explanatory efficient. It structures the work in a meaningful way: elements will start falling into their right places. We need to find out what makes these "places" seem the right ones. Understanding problematic cases of artistic expression (such as musical expression) as a variety of character identification is a great step in what I think is the right direction, that is, taking expression as a kind of representation of the mental. However, as long as we have an insufficient grasp of how we recognize the mental events of (fictional, represented) personas, we seem to have gained too little. Reversely, an adequate understanding of our understanding of characters' mental lives may give us the glue to stick the persona account onto the problematic cases. We should develop the analogy between natural and artistic expression by making a comparison between expression and representation, and finding an alternative to opposing the two. Personas do not have real minds, and here philosophy is in need of some ontology of personas. I submit that the persona of some artistic expression is a product of the beholder's imagination which his imagination is induced to produce by "empty spots" in the work of art, and in the production of which it is guided by what is there to be perceived in the work (a tertiary quality, brought into existence by the work's secondary qualities).[13] This goes for understanding the character played by an actor or empathizing with his mental life, as well as for the harder cases of musical expressiveness. Stressing the constitutive role of the imagination helps us to see that expression is a disposition in the work to make a suitably equipped beholder procure an empathetic response. The matter of the absence of the mental from a work of art is my first argument for the position that artistic expression is an instance of representation. The mental is represented; some of its clues are there, but *it* (the mental) is not.

If a screenwriter wants a character to pick up a book, the script will tell the actor to pick up a book. The audience will see the character pick up the book. Greg Currie argues that the audience sees the actor, not the character, because characters do not have secondary qualities,[14] but this is puzzling, since visually there is *symmetry* between what the actor can be seen to be doing and what the audience is supposed to imagine the character is doing. We will not imagine the character to be bending in a different direction, or to be wearing a jacket that is different from the one the actor is wearing. We do, however, find an asymmetry between the mental lives involved. There is no need for the actor to feel bad whenever the script instructs him to act as though his character is in grief. If the audience is to imagine that the character is in grief, all the actor has to do is perform the external expressions he and the audience think accompany grief. He must present the clues, not the mental life itself. This asymmetry is instructive for us, because artistic expression is more fruitfully compared to represented natural expression (the clues of the mental performed by the actor) than to real-life natural expression. Taking the treatment of the material as one's clue for artistic expression and under-standing it as a natural expression of the artist, may seem a comprehensible enough next step to take in the case of painting, but it hardly is in the case of film. It is, however, in the case of film that things may become clearer. In the absence of the mental life as it is conveyed by a work, comparing artistic expression to natural expression by taking the work as an extension or symptom of the artist's mind, seems overstating the artist's intentionality. Instead, I treat it as functioning representationally. The relevant model for artistic expression is the representation of natural expression.

3. A Definition of Representation (its Naturalist Types)

To do that, however, some helpful definition of representation is wanted, that is, a definition that is successful in both the visual and the psychological regions of painting. I propose the following definition of naturalist types of representation, such as depictions. I take these naturalist types as basic, and my approach may tell you why. This is my definition of "representation":

Something which is perceived egocentrically is a representation of the naturalist type if and only if it while being perceived non-egocentrically, causes us to anticipate (in a postulatable world) the homomodal recurrence of some of the thing's properties.[15]

This definition attributes two characteristics. Representation involves, first, an anticipated homomodal recurrence, and second, non-egocentricity (not in the psycho-moral sense of selfishness, but in the phenomenological sense of centrally involving the body of perception). The perception of everyday life events, and of the thing hanging on the museum's wall (the painting), is relative to the position of one's body; it is, therefore, egocentric. However, the perception of a painting as an object of interpretation is not: art appreciation is non-egocentric. The term is Greg Currie's.[16] Although we can perceive non-egocentrically anything whatsoever, such as a chair's form, only in the case of representations are we intentionally induced to do so and to anticipate that certain of the properties perceived will recur in a different space and time. Such anticipation is homomodal if and only if it involves the exact same senses that would be needed to recognize the relevant properties in real life (or imagination). In depiction, both are visual. Sounds or smells cannot be represented pictorially. Cross-modal representation involves non-naturalist, conventional types of symbol,[17] such as description, most notably, but this is not my subject here.[18] As to the *recurrence* involved in representation, I use this term in combination with "anticipation" to replace "resemblance," in order to stress its psychology rather than its ontology.[19] The "recurrence" need not be actual as long as we imagine it to appear. The anticipation is meant "as such," that is, without the need for its satisfaction.[20] This meets Wollheim's minimal requirement and acknowledges the *perceptual* nature of representation (see Chapter 1, this book). It is also an alternative to saying that all that is needed to account for our understanding of pictures are our natural powers of perceptual recognition – as Greg Currie does (IM 85ff.). To account for representational recognition there is no need to answer questions about whether or not the image in the picture *tracks* the depicted – which will either be past or fictional – as it really is or has been, and whether our anticipation regards such tracking as causal (as in photography) or intentional (as in painting).[21] Goodman was right about the ontological problems connected with (actual) resemblance,[22] but wrong, again, by seeing the role of resemblance exclusively from an epistemological angle, neglecting its psychological – that is, anticipated – nature. We are not looking primarily for actual similarities in our appreciation of pictures; instead, we are *confident* that it *is* resemblances that are at stake. Expecting certain properties of a work to be recurrent from 'elsewhere' is more definitive of depiction than assessing the actuality of such recurrence is. Obviously, such anticipation is the achievement of the beholder. An adequate approach to artistic representation should be psychological.[23] If there happens to be an actual pictorial reference, then anticipation of recurrences is its psychological – that is, naturalistic – prerequisite. Further to this, *seeing* things *in* the picture, in

Wollheim's terms, presupposes our taking the thing on the wall as a picture; it presupposes our anticipating certain modalities of recurrence, the presupposition of which is of a general nature. Proposing the anticipation of kinds of recurrence as an explanans to seeing-in allows one to distinguish between kinds of "seeing-in." Wollheim's term is indiscriminate as to the sense modality that is addressed when something is "seen in" something. The paradigm case of seeing-in is the camel in the clouds. (Here the use of an optical term is unproblematic, but are there analogies for the other senses?) According to Wollheim, we can, for instance, see events happening in a still picture. I see why this proves the advantage of the seeing-in account over the seeing-as-account, but Wollheim's stretching of vision to imply elements that are not visually there I find unproblematic. Wollheim, however, prefers the stretching over allowing imagination a role in perception – he conceives of imagination as fantasy. I, instead, view fantasy as a subfunction of imagination, and imagination, the genus cognitive function, as a faculty operative within perception. Wollheim has to make sense of the point at which to stop implying what is visible in a painting even though it is not visually there. In the example he elaborates in Chapter 1 of this book, he seems to locate this stopping point in some or other intuition (and see my note 3). The challenge to my alternative – which explains how imagination is being activated by what is perceptually available – is how to make clear what our imagination is supposed to be introducing. Wollheim does not need to think my proposal to be an advance on his theory because it may seem to separate perceptual functions that he thinks cannot be separated, that is, vision and imagination,[24] but I will show how in the end my distinction does provide an advance, and why these separations have to be made in order to make sense of kinds of expression in art forms that involve other sense modalities.

4. Twofoldness and Non-Egocentricity

It may be obvious to us that, for instance, watching a film involves our eyes and ears only (apart from our imagination) and that nothing happening in the film can physically affect our bodies; but it was not at all obvious to those first film-goers who fled the auditorium in Paris thinking that Louis Lumière's train was going to run them over. They had no trouble recognizing the train, so they didn't miss anything remotely resembling pictorial conventions, but failed to see the train as depicted. At the general level of all types of representation, we find specifications of how we are to be addressed by its instances, that is, singular pictures (or otherwise). These general "conventions" form the second characteristic that I attribute to representation, that is, its *non-egocentricity*. Non-egocentricity distinguishes representations from real-life situations. Perceiving real-life events is egocentric: The perceiving person is in a spatio-temporal context shared with the things he observes. Moving his body normally brings about a relevant change in the world he perceives. Wollheim recognizes this but makes little use of it in his account of depiction. Instead, he thinks that a distinct species of seeing is involved. However, nothing special seems to be happening to vision, whereas something *is* going on with the way our other senses are used, that is, with our perception as a whole. Of our own free will we impose upon ourselves specific moral and epistemological constraints: We refrain from acting in accordance with what we understand we are perceiving, and tolerate the fact that the information gathered by our other senses is not contributing to our understanding of a painting. The thing on the wall and we who look at it are, together, in a different spatio-temporal context from that of the events represented in the picture. This is a logical point, not an empirical one. There is no gradual transition from small distances to large ones, to looking through binoculars, to, finally, looking at a painting. The break is between the last one and all those preceding it. Refraining from direct morally-relevant responsive actions in the case of a representation is chosen beforehand, that is, irrespective of what we are going to see in the particular painting, whereas choosing not to help a drowning child that we see through our binoculars, *is* morally significant. Disjunctively, abstaining from direct interference, non-egocentricity, and *pro tanto* anticipation of homomodal recurrence are necessary conditions for something to be a representation. Together they are sufficient.

How do we go about entering this non-egocentric world of which we form no part? Wollheim's notion of twofoldness captures this problem of transgression. "Twofoldness" pertains to the way in which the paint marking the surface of the canvas on the wall produces the meanings seen in the painting.[25] The artist's individual style (another of Wollheim's many contributions to aesthetics)[26] is what, both, forms the work's means of expression, and guides the beholder's stepping out of the egocentric into the represented, the non-egocentric. The marks that are painted on the canvas and exist in the beholder's space – who might touch or smell them – lead him towards the meaning of the painting that he cannot touch or smell but must enter *watching*.[27]

The non-egocentricity of represented events provides the clue to understanding the apparent discrepancy between what a depicted event looks like (which – symmetrically – "resembles" what the picture looks like), and what the picture expresses. In everyday perception, variations between the looks of a person and the meaning of his expression cannot possibly be as contingent as they can be in a representation, where a total independence of the mental life of the character from that of the actor may obtain. "Egocentricity" explains this: A real person's looks as well as mental life are equally present to the perceiver, whose responses may induce an expressor to adjust his expression. The expression and its perception are reciprocal. There is, however, no such reciprocity with regard to representations. For an adequate understanding of *artistic expression*, therefore, the logical thing to do is to compare it to representation and its non-egocentricity, rather than to egocentric expression – with which artistic expression only shares name and subject-matter – the experiential – but not the bodily and spatio-temporal characteristics.

5. Expression as Representation

Artistic expression, I submit, is a kind of representation: of experiential events. Its egocentric specifications are general and depend on the kind of representation it comes with. To perceive the artistic expression of a painting we need our eyes (and our imagination); for that of music our ears (and our imagination), and so on. Represented experiential events pertain either to the work's subject matter (or persona) or to the artist's stylistic variations, but whichever variety is at stake, it is the artist's variations in the material that intimate them – that is, suggest them and make them intimate to the beholder.[28] Clues ensuing from depicted natural expression are merely among the pointers available to the artist to steer our empathizing in relevant directions. As such, such clues do not form a necessary ingredient for an account of artistic expression. In line with the definition of representation given above, I propose this definition of expression:

Something which is perceived egocentrically is expressive of X if and only if it is a representation of X, and X is an experiential event, that is, a phenomenally conscious event.[29]

Something represents an experiential event if and only if it while being perceived non-egocentrically causes us to anticipate (in a postulatable world) the homomodal recurrence of experiential events.

If we want expression to answer to the first of representation's characteristics, that is, the anticipated homomodal recurrence, we should identify a perceptual modality specific to it. Neither one of our five senses is available because they would either be the one(s) responsible for the type of representation that the expression is mounted on (e.g., vision with painting) on account of which they cannot explain the need for a distinct notion for the conveyal of psychological aspects in the meaning of a work of art (Goodman might favour this outcome); or, alternatively, they would be different senses that would call for new phenomenological specifications that regulate the import of these senses, which specifications are not forthcoming. The perceptual mode responsible for our recognition of expression (empathy) – I take to be an act of imagination, and a mode of sensitivity as essential to our appreciation of works of art as it is to our understanding of people.

Natural, that is, egocentric, *empathy* can be contrasted with natural, that is, egocentric, seeing and hearing on account of the first-person privilege pertaining to the events perceived by it, such as those that are expressed in a sad face and desolate gesturing. I am not saying that the mental is not accessible from a third-person point of view; on the contrary, it is. However, it is accessible only to the point of *knowing that* a person is having some specific experience – which is a represented (possibly exclusively propositional) type of knowing – not of knowing *how* it would be for that person to have it. The arguments are familiar. Peter has lost his parents in a plane crash. Knowing the intentional object of his sadness and confusion, we may have a better understanding of the experience Peter is going through than Peter has, because, among other things, he is confused by his loss. Peter's first-person phenomenal awareness of the state he is in, however, should remain inaccessible to us. He is the one going through the turmoil, not we. As it is, by empathizing with Peter's first-person awareness we apply different concepts than we would if we were merely acknowledging his loss. In empathy, our imagination introduces some of our own personal memories and anticipations. By empathizing with Peter, we *associate* our own mental events with what we know (propositionally) that Peter is going through and guess is his psychological repertoire, and do not stop before having re-enacted an emotion which, we find, resembles in intentional structure and force – in phenomenology, Wollheim would say (see TL) – what we take Peter to be expressing.[30] Our access to Peter's mental life will be as appropriate as the many clues that emanate from his facial and gestural expressions. Such clues should have the type of coherence characteristic of a true theory: What the gestures tell us will be in accordance with Peter's face or grunting, and so on. And this holds over time as well: If Peter suddenly starts smiling and jumping about, this will affect our thoughts about his sadness. In short, natural expression addresses all our senses and is spatio-temporally complex, and, I surmise, this is so in a way that no representation will ever achieve. Needless to say, egocentricity is what explains the difference, because, lastly, and most importantly for distinguishing empathy from mere acknowledgement: We are in Peter's vicinity. This enables him to change his expression if he finds our responses inadequate to his fears, feelings or expectations: empathy implies second-person reciprocity.

Such reciprocity is absent from the appreciation of representations – due to the non-egocentricity of representations. The fact that in appreciating art our empathy is disconnected from our actions – we do not storm the stage to rescue the menaced heroine – does not go against the thesis that empathy is what it takes to understand expression; it merely symptomizes the non-egocentricity of expression. Nothing is wrong with the empathy, but something is with other parts of our perceptual apparatus. Because of non-egocentricity, in contradistinction with real-life empathy and the actions that surround it, our actions toward art works can achieve nothing in the range of preventing, enhancing, or changing the represented experiences empathized with.[31]

In artistic empathy, there can be no such thing because the mental life in question is in a different context from that of the beholder: It is represented. This is my suggestion: With artistic empathy the imagination is caused to actively constitute what is not present before the senses. An artist's individual style, consequently, if it is to be expressive, has to hold 'open spots' for the beholder's imagination to fill in, in order to produce the mental life that is expressed. The way I put it here seems wrong though, because artistic expression is not such as to make us cry whenever a character is in grief. In contrast, my account is not emotivist or evocational. Imagination is merely supposed by my account to expect a coherent homomodal recurrence of the mental. Hence, the second characteristic in my definition of expression. The anticipation is achieved by a re-enactment which, due only to its non-egocentric origin, will lack certain symptoms that are pertinent in its real-life, egocentric counterpart, such as direct constraints on one's agency. Artistically expressed mental states or events are produced by the beholder's imagination effected by the guidance issuing from what is sensuously present in the work (and what isn't, even though being expected), and are, therefore, as such not in any particular mind, nor do they belong to anyone in particular. Instead, the beholder merely does what he is supposed to do, much like the slavering of Pavlov's dogs upon hearing the bells (without the food).

This also answers a question about the intelligibility of my account: how can an experience that is caused by a work of art to appear in us, at the same time be represented in the work? This question exclusively addresses the concept of artistic empathy, or experiential representation, as though the understanding of depiction were immune to it. It isn't.[32] Perceiving a picture differs as much from everyday vision as artistic empathy differs from everyday empathy. When we understand that a picture depicts a house, we do not see a real house, even though somehow we succeed "naturally" to make the coloured spots on the flat surface before us into the three-dimensional object that is represented. In the cases of representations, the *phenomenalities* of perception and empathy are different, but their *phenomenology* of being addressed non-egocentrically is not. Natural empathy is a common aspect of perception, so there is every reason to suppose that the ability of non-egocentric address should function equally well in the case of artistic empathy as it does in the case of artistic vision. The intelligibility question, when applied to depiction, goes like this: how can a house that is caused by a picture to appear phenomenally in us, at the same time be represented in the work? A weird question. Isn't this what representation is all about?

According to Richard Wollheim, expressive properties, much like colours, are identified "through experiences that are both caused by those properties and of them" (CPE 149). This comparison supports my argument that both the pictorial and the expressive are elements in works of art that cause us to perceive these works in certain ways. However, there is a difference in indexicality between secondary qualities and expressive properties which calls for an approach like the one proposed here. I can bring out this difference by looking at the use of samples. Samples can be used as a proof of the existence of some specific colour. Colour samples derive their functionality from being available to a third-person perspective. This remark about samples obviously is neutral to the problem of the *phenomenality* of secondary qualities. The experiential, on the contrary, which I take to be expression's subject matter, is first-person privileged, such that if a *sample* of someone else's mental life were at hand instead of merely the word naming it, and if we might use it to establish whether the mental events exemplified really are there in some or other person, this sample would have to be exclusively first-person accessible. It would have to be (able to be) mine alone. The property that causes us to perceive an expressive property is not accessible in the same manner the pictorial is. None of the senses – because they allow a third-person perspective – would suffice to perceive the sample, and as a consequence, some distinct homomodality would be required for a naturalist representation of the experiential.

My approach enables us to see how, in the case of pictures, the basis of the difference between representation and expression lies in their respective subject-matters. The representation of a picture is its visually accessible aspect – that which conveys the visual aspect of the represented. It is perceived by the sense of vision. A picture's expression is the aspect that conveys an experiential dimension. It is perceived by the imagination – the power that has us perceive elements of reality that do not directly present themselves to our senses. Second, the account I am proposing helps us to understand why in practice we cannot locate the conflict involved in a *desolate* portrayal of a group of *happy* people. The desolation in the artistic expression changes the shade of happiness the represented character is depicted as going through, by changing the way we are to perceive it. Both expressive elements are perceived-cum-constituted by our imagination, which should explain why they mix. Perception is informed by the co-operation of the various senses and the imagination – whether we are talking about egocentric or non-egocentric perception. Above, I turned away from Wollheim's position because he attributed too much cognitive functionality to vision and isolated imagination by attenuating it to fantasy. It is by now evident how imagination can be functionally distinguished from the operations of (and data provided by) the senses, but as functioning integrally to perception. But I do not narrow imagination down to fantasy. And this correction should not remain inconsequential. Whereas it is perfectly intelligible, as Wittgenstein remarked, to think of *reports* about our own mental life as sophisticated expressions rather than as representations, in the case of worlds perceived non-egocentrically this distinction simply makes no sense. Here, expression should be taken as representation.[33]

NOTES

1. PA 46–80 contains an extensive discussion of these matters.
2. The discussion of expressive perception is in PA 80–89 and CPE. Like seeing-in, expressive perception presupposes certain beliefs, but, unlike seeing-in, "it also presupposes a deep part of our psychology, [...] a mechanism for coping with feelings, moods, and emotions" (PA 80).
3. Cf. Wollheim, who (this volume, 23–4) poses a set of questions regarding a classical landscape painting with ruins, arguing that at one point we can no longer see things in a picture. He thinks we might want to say that we can see the columns, can see that they came from a temple, can see that this temple was overthrown, but cannot see "[the columns] as having been thrown down some hundreds of years ago by barbarians wearing the skins of wild asses." What is it that we cannot see: the exact time-span, that the barbarians wore skins, that these were the skins of asses, or that these asses – before they were skinned – were wild? One wonders where, according to Wollheim, the borderline between seeing and imagining has been crossed. It is a long way from opposing the (Lessing's) claim that the visual is non-conceptual to claiming that we can see everything that is *readily* conceptualized – supposing that is where the borderline was crossed in this example. Also, all that we can see in a picture need not for that reason be depicted in it. Subtitles structure our perception of pictures in ways vastly different from how the picture itself structures our perception of it. This should be part of the conclusion issuing from a comparison of pictures to descriptions. Cf. Pictures and Language, MD 185–92, and Harrison, Chapter 2, this book. On the projective nature of expression, see CPE.
4. With this thought Bruce Vermazen started his Expression as Expression.
5. Which it is not to Nelson Goodman, one major voice in defending the meant opposition.
6. Cf. Goodman, *Languages of Art*, Chapters 1 and 2.
7. This position is also defended in Jerry Levinson's Musical Expressiveness.
8. In PA, Ch. I. What the Artist Does. Cf. also Podro, Depiction and the Golden Calf, and his chapter in this volume, Section II, for subtle criticisms.
9. Indeed, we are not interested here in "literal" cases of the depiction of a person's natural expression of sadness. So there will be no tears or saddened looks in our picture.
10. Paul Crowther (in *Art and Embodiment: From Aesthetics to Self-Consciousness*) takes this line of thought in developing an ecological definition of art, which

takes the artist's body position as its starting point. Wollheim, too (in Seeing-As, Seeing-In, and Pictorial Representation, henceforth SSPR), sees the work of art as the output of the artist's intentions; however, he does not equate this output with the artist's expression, but thinks the intentions introduce a notion of correctness in our perception. He rightly proposes a psychological view of the way we perceive expression.

11. Cf. Malcolm Budd, and, especially, Graham McFee, 155 *ff.*, this volume.
12. Cf. Levinson, Musical Expressiveness, for a survey of the arguments.
13. Cf. McFee, 158, this volume.
14. Currie *Image and Mind*, 9–12 (Section 1.5). Henceforth IM.
15. A definition of the genus of representation would change the "homomodal recurrence of some of the thing's properties" into something which includes imagination in a more independent role. See also Robert Hopkins, this volume, 231, n. 2.
16. IM 73. Currie takes the egocentricity of mirrors as an argument for their (genuine) transparency, as opposed to the non-transparency of photos. He is arguing here against Scruton's, Photography and Representation.
17. If, for example, music is to represent, it must on my account be taken to represent sounds, or its representing is delivered conventionally. Then again, perhaps there are other modalities involved with music apart from its sounds, which allow it to represent naturalistically after all. This latter point obviously needs elaboration, which I will partly provide.
18. Nor are they Wollheim's or McFee's (151, this volume).
19. This move is motivated methodologically: Ontological questions stem from an epistemological point of view – one that reduces the surface differences between types of representation to matters of their truth, asking questions about whether or not the represented exists. I have chosen instead an approach that is explicitly aesthetic in nature, because it enables us to analyze the differences that pertain to types and forms of representation long before the matter of their potential truth is at stake: people know that they are confronted with some specific type of representation, *and* know what is represented long before they know whether or not the represented is actually existent: aesthetics precedes epistemology.
20. Which is as far as I think the primitiveness of seeing-in goes. This also involves an approach of what Wollheim (PA 72–5, SSPR) calls paintings' "twofoldness."
21. For an excellent discussion of these epistemological matters, see IM, 53–6.
22. See Goodman, *Languages of Ar*, Chapter 1, and Goodman, Seven Strictures on Similarity.
23. And there is this extra advantage over Goodman in that from my aesthetic point of view we do not have to take pictorial representation as an instance of denotation. See also note 18.
24. I assume a Kantian notion of imagination as the mental power that brings before the mind things that are absent to the senses (as does Paul Crowther in Chapter 5, this volume, 85–6). Unlike fantasy, imagination is a power of perception in its own right. It – imagination – is not instrumental, is not obedient to the will, whereas fantasy is. Certain defects of autism testify to this (and I am proposing this – cursorily – as an alternative to the Theory of Mind option). An autistic person can be described (in terms of mind, not brain) as lacking the faculty of imagination. At a high level, autistics typically are unsuccessful in imagining what experiences other persons are having. Already at the lower level of taking in the data of the senses, autistics experience trouble selecting those data that conform to the concepts we use to describe the world. Imagination is a power of

perception, one more basic than fantasy. It is imagination which introduces the absent elements necessary to empathize with an act of expression.

25. Cf. SSPR. Cf. also Podro, Depiction and the Golden Calf.
26. In PS.
27. In keeping with Wollheim's insistence that the experience of expression be perceptual.
28. Cf. van Gerwen, *Art and Experience*, Chap. 7, for an account of intimation. Because different art forms employ different means of intimation, no monolithic theory of expression is forthcoming, as Budd argues (108, this volume).
29. A feeling of what it is like to experience some specific thing. Michael Tye recognizes as essential properties of consciousness that it must be possessed and that it entails a unique perspective onto the world. In *Ten Problems of Consciousness*, 10–25.
30. This does not commit me to the thesis that we can only represent what strikes the eye (cf. the discussion of this position in PA 64–5). However, when pushed sufficiently, we make this distinction between what can and what cannot literally be seen in a picture. We will point differently to things available through different means of perception. Cf. Currie, Imagination and Simulation: Aesthetics Meets Cognitive Science.
31. This ought to solve the so-called paradox of fictional emotion. Cf. van Gerwen, Fictionele emoties en representatie.
32. Cf. Graham McFee, this book, Chapter 10, 163, n. 5.
33. I thank Paul Crowther, Anthony Savile, Erik Benders, Alan Casebier, Berys Gaut, and the audience at the 1997 annual BSA conference in Oxford, for pushing me beyond some of my limitations.

Chapter 11
Wollheim on Expression (and Representation)

GRAHAM MCFEE

A major insight, present from the beginning in Richard Wollheim's writing on aesthetics,[1] is the connection of representational matters with expressive ones: an insight justly celebrated in the theme of this volume. As Jerrold Levinson puts it, in Wollheim's work: "Expressiveness is [...] treated quite on a par with representational content. [...]"[2] Pressure of space, and limitations on my intellect, mean that – in this chapter – I will be centrally concerned with expression only. But, before adopting that focus, a couple of remarks about representation clarify our issue and set the scene, as well as making the context of the discussion plain – both my context and Wollheim's.

The notion of representation is disposed to appear in three guises in the philosophical literature. The first, endorsed by Wollheim, recognizes the figurative and the depictional (especially in art) as representation; and, more accurately, as *pictorial* representation. The third, nowhere – to my knowledge – even suggested in Wollheim's writing, takes the term "representation" to refer to, for example, that relation embodied in language, where words are claimed as representations, and/or ". . . representation involves what Frege calls *thoughts*, which are identified by truth-conditions."[3] Whatever the linguistic virtue of such moves, they have no place in Wollheim's thought: and less in mine.

The *second* account of representation – which Wollheim embraces, and (twice: AO2 §12, §14; AM 26–7) characterizes in terms of stories from Hans Hofmann's studio – claims that ". . . the range of representational attributions . . . certainly extends well beyond the domain of purely figurative art" (AO2 §12: see also PA 62): and Wollheim discusses work both by Barnett Newman (PA 62) and by Rothko (MD 188: see also AM 128) in these terms. Be that as it may, the idea of pictorial representation is clearly sharper if we confine it to figurative (depictive) cases.[4]

Wollheim comes to consider these matters (in AO2 §§10–21) in the context of asking whether some properties regularly ascribed to some artworks are incompatible with the *weakened* physical object hypothesis; namely that ". . . *some* works of art are physical objects" (AO2 §9: my emphasis).

Like taking artworks as expressive (to which I shall shortly return), taking
them as representational – even, perhaps *especially*, in the sense of "depictive" – seems an invitation ". . . to deny the physicality of the canvas" (AO2
§12): and this is just where Wollheim's later way of stating the problem (in
terms of the *twofoldness* of representational seeing: AO2 213ff; PA 21, 46–7)
is irresistable.

Indeed (as AO2 §14 makes plain), Wollheim's primary interest here lies in
getting us to recognize that the difficulty of answering: "The first question of
aesthetics: . . . How does that (sensuous object) mean anything?"[5] is as much
a difficulty for representational properties as it is for (the more obviously
problematic) *expressive* ones.

A number of Wollheim's considerations here are negative: to defuse objections to the idea that physical objects could be expressive, or to clarify what
is implicit in taking them to be so.

Turning to his own account, Wollheim recognizes that the idea of artistic
expression has a connection to the expressiveness of human behaviour. But
such a connection is fragile: so a crucial issue here is whether or not ". . . the
whole concept of expression . . . [is] a conjunction of two elements, which as
easily fall apart as together" (AO2 §18 30 [46]). Yet, what are these elements
of the concept of expression here? For *expression* might be seen in two
distinct ways:

(a) ". . . in the sense in which a gesture or a cry would be expressive"
    (what Wollheim AO2 31 [47] calls "natural expressions").[6]
(b) ". . . because . . . it seems to us to match, or to correspond with, what
    we experience inwardly" (what Wollheim follows nineteenth-century
    usage in calling "correspondence" AO2 31 [47]).

These two are clearly different: so how is there *one* condition, expressiveness, captured by both?

We often refer to an expressive property by the same name as the original
psychological condition. The "doubling up," as Wollheim calls it (PA 84; MD
146), represents a way to characterize the "split" feared in *Art and Its Objects*;
a way to take the *correspondence* sense of the term "expression" as the key
one for aesthetics (PA 84, and see Budd, this volume 101. But concentration
on "doubling-up" can lead us to think of the expressive properties as somehow applied analogically or metaphorically.[7] And this, Wollheim insists (and
rightly), is mistaken. For such a position implicitly denies that ". . . expressive
perception is a form of seeing" (PA 85). And this thought is effectively
repeated at the end of his contribution here (Ch. 1, 27).

Throughout his writing, Wollheim's position is always guided by the
thought that ". . . art presupposes a common human nature, and . . . pictorial
meaning works through it . . ." (PA 8). So he emphasizes the powers and

capacities that come, as it were, with the anatomy and physiology – although recognizing that these supply only the preconditions for artistic experience. Thus, for instance, the seeing of representations is explained in terms of a characteristic kind of perception, *seeing-in*. Indeed, Wollheim's thought is *perceptualist* in the (quite) strong sense of taking artistic appreciation to be an activity that – if we have the right knowledge and training – we can all simply engage in: that it is a matter of learning to see, rather than to draw inferences. As he states it, ". . . perception of the arts *is* . . . the process of understanding the work of art" (MD 142).[8]

Wollheim's own account (in AO §45ff) treated art (and, by implication, *understanding* art) as a *form of life* in just this sense:[9] there was no more to be said about artistic expression, and for two reasons. First, the thoughts and so on about expressiveness in art might be unconscious thoughts. And in *Painting as an Art* (19: cited/quoted PL-A 219 – and see also PA 44) Wollheim stresses the need to see artistic intention so as to include *all* the "desires, thoughts, beliefs, emotions, commitments" that relate to the making of a work – where some of these are/may be unconscious.

Second, the concept of art here was esssentially a *regulative* concept: Ian Ground characterizes this idea by saying that, "[t]he concept of a work of art does not describe: it regulates" (27).[10] And, for that reason, *we* cannot fully describe *its* contours.

Recently, though, Wollheim's account has taken a slightly different form (without, of course, implying that he would necessarily give up or dissent from any of this). Indeed, Budd (this volume, Ch. 7, 104) urges that these "new" concerns were always implicit): he has found something more precise – and more psychoanalytic[11] – to say about the contribution of shared human powers and capacities.

What motivates this change (or, if Budd is right, this *re-emphasis*)? *I* find its explanation in Wollheim's rejection of three key *mis*-readings of the "form of life" idea, three related ways in which *his* ideas may be misunderstood or misrepresented. For the "form of life" idea might be:

- mis-read as externalist (PA 13–16) – notice especially his version of externalism explained as focussing on ". . . a property of the painting that has nothing to do with its being a painting, with its paintingness" (PA 15), both in respect of institutional definitions of art, and in respect of the "taxonomic" conception of, for instance, style, where the connection between internal and generative is most explicit (MD 181);[12]
- mis-read as not clearly *intentionalist*;
- mis-read as not clearly *realist* – two points here: first, the (mistaken?) "tendency" to regard Wittgenstein (whose term "form of life" is) as an anti-realist;[13] second, Wollheim's taking this issue as turning on whether central claims about artistic meaning/expression have ". . . truth-value,

independent of our means of knowing it."[14] Consider, in particular, the recognition-transcendence of, for example, ascriptions of intention, and especially unconscious intention (only "discoverable" [in principle] through psychoanalysis).

If this is right, we may justifiably take *these* as crucial characteristics of Wollheim's position as *he* views it; and therefore be unsurprised to find them foregrounded in *Painting as an Art*.

So, in contrast to the account of artistic expression given in *Art and Its Objects*, which imported the "form of life" account, the revised version is more thorough-going-ly psychological. As Wollheim puts it, ". . . artistic expression is invariably expression of an internal or psychological condition" (MD 154). Certainly, the same question continues to hold sway: how can a physical object be expressive?

In Wollheim's later position (PA, Ch. 2 §C; MD 151): "[a]t the root of expressive perception – seeing something outside us as expressive – is an act of *projection*." (PL-A 217).

In explanation of his account of projective properties,[15] Wollheim considers a melancholic for whom (in Wollheim's words: MD 151) "[i]nstinct compels him to project" his melancholy: there are two upshots, reflecting two kind of projection – which Wollheim calls *simple* and *complex* projection (also PA 82). In complex projection (the kind relevant to art), our melancholic person ". . . will come to look upon, and respond to, some part of his environment as melancholy" (MD 151).[16]

No doubt I could *not* in this way project (by complex projection) my melancholy onto a lake (or on to a painted canvas) were it not for some features or properties of the lake (or canvas). And Wollheim explains this in terms of an ". . . affinity between the inner condition of the person that is projected and the part of nature that it is projected onto" (MD 152); or (in his preferred expression) by claiming that ". . . nature, in its relevant parts, is felt to be . . . *of a piece with* the person's melancholy" (MD 151). More firmly, he defines *projective properties* as ". . . psychological predicates . . . applied to nature for reasons of correspondence" (MD 149), thereby bringing out the centrality of *correspondence* when, as Wollheim tells us, some theorists ". . . overlook attributions of correspondence" (MD 148). In this way, correspondence may be said to ". . . *rest* on the properties of nature" (MD 148: my emphasis).

But what is it to *rest* on properties in nature, or for there to be an *affinity* between a psychological state and a feature of nature? Certainly Wollheim conceives of the relation non-reductively: the feature in nature is "a substrate" (MD 154) for the projective property. Furthermore, it is important to avoid the mistaken assumption that, when we refer to a projective property, ". . .

there is no property of the object to which we thereby refer" (MD 148). There are really two aspects here. First, correspondence is ". . . a matter of the properties nature possesses" (MD 148): so that referring to the projective property is a kind of *indirect* referring to its "substrate." But second, and more important, complex projections are ". . . capable of generating new properties" (MD 152) – perhaps on the parallel with Grice's "sheep-dog?"[17] There we both find a use for a dog's behaviour and (associatedly) come to explain that behaviour differently: "a natural disposition . . . [to reconceive {the animal} in terms of its usefulness to us] . . . creates a new kind of entity," a sheep-dog.

So it is clear what is hoped for from such a view: that, as David Wiggins put it, ". . . the mind *lights up* the features of the world that engage with its sensibilities."[18] In this way, the outcome of complex projection can be seen both as person-related and as a feature of the "external world," a property appropriately ascribed to lake or to canvas.

Yet, granting the possibility of some sense of *affinity* here (between, say, melancholy and lake) seems insufficient: The difficulty lies in seeing how this creates new *properties* of the lake – and even ". . . properties of a new kind" (MD 154). To put this another way, *how* are such properties (". . . properties that are identified through our experience of them" MD 156) to be seen as *genuine* properties of objects, rather than being characteristics of the respond-ers? For a common-sense understanding of the term "projection" would imply precisely that properties *projected* onto the lake were not properties of the lake at all – rather, they were being "read into" the lake by the *projector* (and the same might be true for canvasses). Of course, this is not how *Wollheim* understands the idea of projection (although he recognizes the problem: PA 83): but how can he prevent his view *collapsing* into this one?

Wollheim responds by emphasizing that, when we come to consider art, the correspondence is *made*, rather than *found* (Wollheim's emphasis: MD 155).[19] And this is crucial to how expressiveness in art is to be understood, since ". . . the artist paints in order to produce a certain experience in the mind of the spectator" (PA 44). So, his central thought is that: "What is properly visible in the surface of the picture is a matter of what experiences appropriate information allows a sensitive spectator to have in front of it, provided only that these experiences cohere with, and are due to, what the artist intended" (MD 189; and see PA 89).

Notice, in passing, how this passage both reinforces and extends themes identified earlier: (a) its commitment to internalism; (b) [and relatedly] its intentionalism; (c) its realist overtones. Notice, too, its relating of artistic appreciation to a sensitive, *informed* audience; and also its *perceptualism*. But the crucial feature is that success is explained in terms of the fulfilled inten-tions of the artist. Thus, Wollheim claims:

... a work of art expresses an internal condition by corresponding to, or being of a piece with, it. Furthermore the perceptible property in virtue of which it does so is a property it has intentionally: the property is due to the intentions of the artist. The artist intended the work to have this property so that it can express some internal condition that he had in mind. (MD 155)

Later, Wollheim appeals to "... the fulfilled intentions of the artist" as offering a means to distinguish (at least in principle) a right and a wrong way to regard a certain artwork: "... the right way ensures an experience of art that concurs with the fulfilled intention of the artist" (PA 86, and this volume, Chapter 1, 26–7). But intentionalism can (or can seem to) locate the 'meaning' etc. of the work *outside* that work itself, especially when the meaning-bearing, expressive properties are projective ones, dependent to some degree on the *projector's* psychology. And must the relevant intentions be ones that artist actually *had*? Recall that the intentions can be unconscious, so it will be hard to *firmly* determine whether or not such-and-such was the artist's intention. In this case, he/she cannot say: perhaps the artist's psychoanalyst will know in twenty years!?

To meet such objections, Levinson offers Wollheim *hypothetical intentionalism* in which:

... the expressiveness inherent in a painting might be conceived to be that which we would most *justifiably ascribe to the artist as intended emotional communication*, on the basis of the perceptible features of the painting, a complete grasp of its context of production, and a full knowledge of the artist's intentions as to how the work was to be taken, approached, or viewed. . . . (PL-A 218)

But a view such as Levinson offers is insufficiently realist for Wollheim.[20] And Wollheim's realism (especially his commitment to the *psychological reality* of, for example, style) is a crucial feature, identified earlier.

As we have noted, Wollheim explicitly regards projective properties as genuine (if "unusual": MD 148) properties of the natural world.[21] In this sense, Wollheim sees himself as a *realist* about projective properties (as characterized earlier?).[22] Applied to painting, Wollheim's account "... still leaves as the bearer of meaning the visible surface of the picture" (MD 189): and this is a point on which Wollheim has been rightly insistent.[23]

Yet how is this *possible*? Why isn't this the aesthetic equivalent of, "With one bound he shook off his bonds"? (While I cannot say, what I offer is an explanation of what is required if one is to accept that it is not. . . .)

Wollheim's projectivist account of artistic expression is especially noteworthy for both its proximity to the *phenomenology of artistic experience*; and its dependence on what Wollheim calls "the hypotheses of psychoanalysis" (PA 8). Yet, the first of these advantages will be preserved on any account that does justice to that phenomenology, while the second visibly imports other contentious material: theses from psychoanalysis that even Wollheim, a staunch defender, calls *hypothetical*.

A brief chapter such as this cannot rehearse general objections to projectionism in the philosophy of understanding: and I certainly would not wish to dispute the insights of psychoanalysis (at least, I would not wish to debate them *with Wollheim*).

But what have we learned? As I have illustrated, the impact of Wollheim's argumentative strategy in *Art and Its Objects* is to make the central question one about how (if at all) expressive properties can be *genuine* properties of material objects, such as painted canvasses: that is to say, it reconstructs *general* questions about expressiveness in this form. And, as I have suggested, this strategy partly explains the direction of Wollheim's argument in *Painting as an Art*, and elsewhere.

Yet, does Wollheim's discussion of projective properties, as we have reconstructed it, *really* address the question taken as fundamental? For, rather than *explaining* expressive properties in terms of projective ones, it uses the term "projective properties" for the (bizarre) sort of "property" that offers, by definition, a "yes" answer to our initial question: ". . . projection itself must always remain less than perspicuous," Wollheim says (PA 85). So isn't this discussion a kind of *side-stepping* of debate? If so, it is *odd*, in that this conclusion is arrived at *through* introduction of additional theory: that is, through psychoanalytic concerns. Thus considerations of parsimoniousness suggest that *if* we can sketch an *equally* satisfactory account of artistic expression that does *not* import these additional "hypotheses," it should be preferred here: so the target is an account *just* as explanatory as Wollheim's. Can this be done? As we will see, features of Wollheim's own account may allow us another perspective on this matter. (Perhaps adopting such a strategy is impossible – perhaps progress requires a "genetic psychology" [MD 158] of a kind psychoanalysis provides. But suppose that this is not so.)

Then the danger of a projectivist account of artistic expression is precisely that it can over-rate *the artist's share*. So avoiding these problems requires focus – in ways Wollheim should approve of – on *the artwork itself*. But justice must be done to Wollheim's characteristic *perceptualism* about artistic understanding (and meaning), a perceptualism reaffirmed here (Ch. 1, 27). And such perceptualism may be explored from the point of view of critic as well as artist (as Wollheim does: for instance, CR; MD 132–43). For the "common human nature" (PA 8, quoted earlier) is presupposed by the critic's role too. So the expressiveness *of the object* should be accounted for by considering it from the point of view of *spectators*, a position apparently uncongenial to Wollheim. In perhaps its most memorable section, the first edition of *Art and Its Objects* famously ended with a rejection of investigations of the evaluation of art: "It will be observed that in this essay next to nothing has been said about the subject that dominates much contemporary aesthetics: that of the evaluation of art, and its logical character. This omission is deliberate" (AO2 153 [169]). The point is that the spectator's perspective conceived of *this* way is – somehow – inappropriate.

As Wollheim confessed, when including a discussion of evaluation in the second edition (AO2 227–8), this rejection was rooted in his recognition that the topic under consideration should be *the properties of artworks*. And that talk of the evaluation of art could readily degenerate into a focus on the spectator *rather than* the object. But what such *fierceness* could not easily accommodate was the degree to which the relevant *artistic*[24] properties were in fact *tertiary*[25] properties/qualities. By "tertiary qualities," I mean that, as Wollheim recognized in his talk of *"projective* properties" here, artistic expession requires more than would be given if "agreement in secondary qualities" were granted. For artistic properties are clearly "response-reliant" in *some* sense.[26]

Still, in Wollheim's discussion of projective properties, we have a principled basis for the *constraint* on adoption of the spectator's viewpoint; partly because, for the artist and the spectator, ". . . how the judgement is reached in the two cases is surely different" (MD 155). The spectator *finds* (rather than *creates*) the correspondence. But this is precisely the perspective from which it is easiest to see the public character (the objectivity) of expressive properties. And it may even accord with Wollheim's own view that ". . . this does not involve ignoring the view point of the spectator. It requires only rethinking it." (PA 43).

To move forward, let us ask (like good Wittgensteinians?)[27] what difficulty or perplexity we are seeking to unravel. By following Wollheim's path, we have identified the central perplexity as the possibility of expressiveness in, for instance, physical objects: how can, say, canvas with paint on it be moving? But notice three things: first, it is not as though we can really *say* how the behaviour of other humans is expressive (once *crude* empathy models are rejected). Second, art seems an easier case here than, say, the melancholy of natural landscape: the artworks are products of human intention. In this sense, they resemble actions or gestures. And, while we may be perplexed about *how* we can find human gestures expressive (as we may be puzzled about *how* we find certain sets of words or gestures funny),[28] we acknowledge *that* we do. Third, the issue is not one about our finding this or that artwork expressive: We know how *that* might typically be achieved – namely, through education about art (about the relevant traditions and categories, for instance) and through guided viewing of the work itself, perhaps in company with other works. It is the mere *possibility* of such expressiveness that is at issue. But we grant that there *is* such expressiveness: so where exactly is the problem? Of course, the problem comes when we try to *explain* the fact of the expressiveness of art in certain ways.

Wollheim's answer partly respects these considerations: the expressiveness of art engages projective properties as does the expressiveness of nature but, unlike nature, it is intentional. Also, Wollheim recognizes the direct connection between human expressiveness and artistic expressiveness (despite recognizing differences, too): we explain both in similar (for Wollheim, psychoanalytic) terms and, relatedly, if/when we endow an object or artifact with expressive meaning ". . . we tend to see it corporeally" (AO2 32–33 [48]).[29] Indeed, this point – with its associated concern with texture and so on – is one of Wollheim's bastions against formalism.[30] One feature of Wollheim's writing, especially his writing about painting, has been his commitment to what, following Stanley Cavell, he calls *the medium of painting*: ". . . a material worked in a characteristic way" (AM 122: see MWM 220–21, as Carolyn Wilde has emphasized, Ch. 9, 122). Thus, he comments tartly that: "Since the days of the great Heinrich Wölfflin, art-historians have tended to identify the objects of their enquiry with those properties of a painting which a good slide preserves" (PA 11). But Wollheim is never guilty of this. And one reason is that the connection with human expressiveness cannot readily be seen formalistically.

Furthermore, for Wollheim, issues concerning understanding are always issues relating to 'conditions of adequacy' for understanding, or to an appropriate "standard of correctness" (PA 89): and, through the connection with cognitive stock, to knowledge. Can we use Wollheimian materials – especially those concerning criticism – to give a Wittgensteinian dissolution of the problem of artistic expressiveness? While that cannot be achieved here, the direction can be suggested. The thought will be to offer a Wollheim-style account of expression, but without its dependence on psychoanalytic ideas.

Now, philosophers standardly talk about powers and capacities in terms of what must be *known* in order that the relevant power, and so on, be exercised.[31] For instance, discussion of the nature of criticism (and especially of the place of reference to the intentions of the artist) can be conducted in terms of the *cognitive stock* appropriate for criticism: That is, the critic's powers are treated (exclusively?) in terms of what he/she *knows*. This procedure is, of course, warranted by the important thesis that all perception (including, especially, that of critics) is concept-mediated. So the charge of misperception can be sustained by pointing to the employment, in the perception, of inappropriate concepts. But that does not do enough to characterize what can go wrong – and even less so what can go right – when critics confront artworks. Notice, for example, that if the perceptiveness of any perceptive critic of art were just a matter of the *cognitive stock* (of what the critic *knew*), the distance between him/her and us would become remediable, at least in principle: We could all acquire that cognitive stock, and with it that critical perceptiveness. That this is obviously not true should make us hesitate here.

So it is clear that, however revealing this talk can be, it leaves out something crucial. For me, Wollheim's fullest acknowledgement of this point – or what I *take* to be such acknowledgement – comes when he speaks of ". . . the concepts . . . the spectator has and mobilises" (W-IPU 48): hence the crucial idea is of *mobilizing concepts in one's experience*. The phenomenon referred to (the need identified) is familiar, I imagine, to anyone who has been taught a critical vocabulary for poetry but, at first, cannot see that this vocabulary informs the understanding of the poem – and then, quite suddenly, it does: the person can now mobilize those concepts in the appreciation of the poem. But talk of artistic appreciation requiring that *artistic concepts* be "mobilised in one's experience" employs the *term of art* as another way of stating the problem (or a part of the problem) about expressiveness.[32] For the work must be *found* expressive, by *me*, on the basis of *my* observation (etc).[33] So the expressiveness of (for example) the painting depends (minimally) on the possibility of creatures who can *respond* to it, finding it expressive.

One virtue of this *term of art* ("mobilise in one's experience"), derived from Wollheim, is that it treats what is required for artistic perception as a human power or capacity [NB "common human nature" PA 8], rather than as a *faculty*. For this ability to *see* artistic expressiveness and/or artistic value is just something that humankind has the capacity for: suitably trained, they can just *do* it ("In the beginning was the deed": quoting Goethe; CV 31; OC §402).[34] In particular, the essence of Wittgenstein's insight into the primacy of action is that we don't need to begin our explanation from some abstract ideas or images.[35] Identifying the requirement for *mobilization* is basically a way of explaining why there might be misfires here: and, even then, it really says no more than *that* the person cannot bring the concepts to bear – it does nothing to explain why this should be.

Furthermore, it is important to see the cognitive dimension implicit in this talk of expressiveness: that the expressiveness here is that of artworks, and only, or primarily, artworks can be meaning-bearing/understandable in the relevant sense.

But, to return, this is just the place where Wollheim's idea of needing to *mobilize concepts in one's experience* seems germane: we explain what power I lack (in contrast to the successful art critic) while granting:

(a) that the difference is not in what we *know* (not in our cognitive stock);
(b) that this is more than my inability to write attractive sentences about that artwork; and

(c) that the difference is not to be cashed out in terms of "faculty psychology."

This critic can (and I cannot) mobilize these concepts in his/her experience of the work. Notice two points: first, the difference here should be seen as *both* cognitive and affective – even when we have the same cognitive stock, there is a difference in what we can mobilize in our experience, which means in what we *can* or *do* experience! Second, there may be no better way to describe it than to point to the critic's successes and my failures: there may well be no informative way to characterize the differences here.

But our failure to have something more to *say* on this point need not be crucial. For the critic's understanding of a particular artwork might be seen as manifest in a whole range of different discussions/accounts of that artwork.[36] Insofar as those accounts are answerable to the perceptible features of the work, they are arguable: and if *I* cannot see them in the work (etc.), this is a limitation in *my* understanding precisely to the degree that *others* can see them. Like the line-drawings in children's books where ". . . representations of animals are masked in the contours of trees and vegetation" (MD 138), what can be seen in artworks need not be thought independent of the cognitive powers of those who look at the artworks: what the idea of *mobilizing in one's experience* can clarify is the extent to which this (cognitive) power should be thought of as a *power*.

To put that the other way round, we might view the contributions of *cognitive stock* and *mobilizing in one's experience* as differential explanations of failures to make sense of artworks: "He lacks the requisite cognitive stock," "She has the concepts, but cannot mobilize them in her experience." More exactly, we might think of these as diagnoses of relevance to aesthetic education: "He needs to learn more about . . ." (and then some filling about cognitive stock; locating the work in its appropriate tradition, for example); "She needs to be helped to see *these* artworks in ways we know she can see others," say – roughly as someone unable to see one aspect of a multiple-figure might be helped. So this account is positive in suggesting strategies for the development of artistic appreciation, or of aesthetic education.

Still, it may not seem to address the central issue. For how are we to identify the expressiveness ("what is expressed") in works? We now have the basic materials for my answer: The strategy, then, is both to do as well as Wollheim in characterizing expression and to do so within a framework of *reflective commonsense*. We have seen how failure to grasp the expressiveness of works might be seen as critical failure – explained via lack of appropriate cognitive stock or inability to mobilize that stock in one's experience of the artwork. And this in turn suggests a model for "critical rationality," although it is a (disappointingly?) case-by-case rationality.[37] For it suggests ways that

the expressiveness of works can be brought to others' attention: as we might
say, how the works might be explained to them.[38] And such "bringing to
attention" or explaining are here both well-exemplified and discussed – in a
broadly Wollheimian fashion – in the chapters by Svetlana Alpers and Michael Baxandall. Expressive works will be those that are "comprehensible"
(to use a term of Wollheim's: MD 174); and *comprehensibility* here might be
equated with critical success. Then expressiveness may plausibly be identified
with critical explanation: "expression is what explanation of expression explains!"[39] But, while this is not exactly wrong, it goes too fast, in at least
three ways. First, the place of informal as well as formal "critics" must be
recognized. Second, critical diversity must be acknowledged (at least in
principle): Diverse responses might be answerable to the features of that
work. And, third, there are "marks" of understanding other than verbal ones;
so that we may clearly understand without being about to say *what* we
understand, although it may turn out that others could say it for us – and we
respond, "Yes, that is my view exactly," or equally, "Well, something like
that. . . ."[40] When these points are in place, we can see how expressiveness
might be identified through critical discussion. We also see, appropriately,
that a contemporary master of such discussion is Richard Wollheim.[41]

  This conclusion is deeply congenial to me. In this way, my account is (or
is supposed to be) a kind of *quietism* (in one of the many senses of that
term):[42] It seems like "reflective common-sense." For, first, it preserves the
commonsense connection between understanding artworks (in particular, understanding them as expressive) and being aided in one's understanding by
others. David Wiggins speaks of ". . . mutual transparency between philosophy and practice":[43] It seems to me that Wollheim aims at this, especially in
his writing on art, and achieves it more fully than his theoretical writings
license. If we differ about this, I am sure it is partly explained by his modesty
and partly by his differing from me about the force of the appeal to parsimoniousness in theory construction (or, to put that another way, his commitment
to psychoanalytic theory). Second, this account reflects the fundamentally
fragile nature of the history of art: that each generation must come to see
works as expressive – and, as we saw earlier, Wollheim has developed the
kind of regulative account of art which explains this.

  Finally, I have offered, at the least, an alternative construction on some
aspects of Wollheim's works. If I could pursuade him to accept such a
reconstruction, I might then turn to areas of my greater "heresy": say, my
historicism, my institutionalism or my "robust sense of constructivity" (UD
311–13).

  In conclusion, I should add how very pleasant it is to be writing on
Wollheim's aesthetics, and having – as a result – to engage in the enjoyable

reconsideration of his writings that this project entailed. The contrast here is, first, with the pure purgatory (as his Ph.D. student) of writing extensively on some aesthetic problem – only to find that he had both anticipated *and refuted* my "solution," and, second, with my overwelming sense since then of his work as providing the stalking horse (or at least the agenda) for all of mine. Clive Bell urged that any person ". . . who would elaborate a plausible theory of aesthetics must possess two qualities – artistic sensibility and a turn for clear thinking."[44] Those of us who have encountered Richard Wollheim have been fortunate to be presented with the living exemplification that Bell was sometimes right!

NOTES

1. Throughout, reference to Richard Wollheim's works will use the abbreviations specified in the front of this book, with this difference: I will be giving section numbers with AO2 and, where appropriate, page numbers to the second and first [in square brackets] editions.
2. Levinson, *The Pleasures of Aesthetics*, 218, cited as Pl-A followed by page number.
3. Scruton, Notes on the Meaning of Music, 194.
4. As it was in McFee, Pictorial Representation in Art.
5. From Stanley Cavell, *Must We Mean What We Say?*, 228 note (cited as MWM). The problem is Hegel's (Hegel, *Introductory Lectures on Aesthetics*, §1 xxi (15): how is it that art ". . . pervades what is sensuous with mind?"
6. Wollheim speaks of natural expression as being ". . . coloured or influenced by what is appropriate" (AO2 31 [47]): In fact, plausible charity here suggests that we regard behaviour as genuine expression only when this is true (for otherwise the behaviour is unintelligible to us).
7. For example, Simon Blackburn, *Spreading the Word*, 171 relates projectivism and metaphor.
8. And earlier, "I cannot accept the view that perception of the work of art is primarily an evidence-gathering activity" (MD 141–2): I discuss this point in McFee, *Understanding Dance*, 138 – cited as "UD" followed by page number.
9. And note David Wiggins' use of Wittgenstein, *Philosophical Investigations*, §241, in Wiggins, *Needs, Values, Truth: Essays in the Philosophy of Value*, 205.
10. Ground, *Art or Bunk*, 9.
11. There are two points here: first, Wollheim's account of art always referred to aspects of human experience in terms drawn from the psychoanalytic: for example: "We may think of the concept [of art] as a protective parent. It is in its shadow that the vast oedipal conflict that is known as the history of art is fought out – a conflict in which the sons win, if they do, by becoming parents. Then they bear the concept that has borne them" (AM 151).
   Second, the accounts both of persons and properties (of "what there is in the world") imply far more than would be granted by some such accounts – psychoanalytic assumptions about the nature of the mind are imported. As we shall see, the account of *projection* here is understood in way in just such a way: a

commonsense view of projection is here being rejected. And Wollheim explicitly refers us to TL for a psychoanalytically-inclined account of persons and their powers. And I take Wollheim's own talk of "the hypothese of psychoanalysis" (PA 8) to endorse this point.

12. NB Wollheim's externalist opponent is the most extreme: Dickie's definition of art (PA 13–14; and Lecture I, note 1).

13. Consider, for example, Wright, *Wittgenstein on the Foundation of Mathematics*, esp. Chap. 2 and 12; Kripke, *Wittgenstein on Rules and Private Language*. (Note, too, this "tendency" in the early writing of Baker and Hacker and of myself.)

14. Dummett, *Truth and Other Enigmas*, 146.

15. Wollheim's clearest (and perhaps fullest) exposition here is in CPE, a paper that "... deepens the view of expression to be found in ... *Painting as an Art*" (MD 203); or perhaps "... develops further the account of artistic expressiveness found in *Painting as an Art*" (PL-A 219 note).

But is there a difference between the sorts of projection that give us secondary qualities and those which give us expressive ones? Certainly, if secondary properties are thought of as *real*, then either (a) they cannot be problematic vis-à-vis projection (McDowell, Wollheim) or (b) secondary qualities must be distinguished from the valuational properties of, say, artistic expression. Wollheim (MD 149: my emphasis) says that "... projective properties *resemble* secondary qualities" in certain respects: and cites McDowell's discussion. Grice certainly thinks in terms of value being "projected" (as does Hume?). And compare Blackburn, Reply: Rule-Following and Moral Realism, 174: "Moral judgements ... differ from judgements of secondary properties, with which they are sometimes compared". Hacker, Locke and the Meaning of Colour Words, 33–34) offers a view of the logical/conceptual priorities here; therefore an account of what any "analysis" must respect. But if this sort of answer works for secondary qualities, and if they are "response-dependent," why shouldn't a similar account work for valuational properties?

16. There will also be "... a change for the better in his interior condition" (MD 151) – this has a connection to Wollheim's contention that experience of projective properties is "... not a wholly perceptual experience ... [but instead] ... a partly affective experience" (MD 149). Nor has the relation to unconscious thought be weakened: "Projection is an internal act that we carry out under instinctual guidance ..." (MD 150) – therefore not necessarily conscious? Revealingly, Blackburn (*Spreading* ... 182) *contrasts* projectivism and perceptualism:

> The projective theory intends to ask no more from the world than what we know is there–the ordinary features of things on the basis of which we make decisions about them, like or dislike them, fear them and avoid them, desire them and seek them out. It asks no more than this: a natural world, and patterns of reaction to it. By contrast a theory assimilating moral understanding to perception demands more of the world. Perception is a causal process: we perceive those features of things which are responsible for our experiences. It is uneconomical to postulate both a feature of things (the values we have) *and* a mechanism (intuition) by which we are happily aware of it.

Even putting aside the reference to intuition, this (passive/causalist version) is clearly not Wollheim's account of the perception of artworks (or of artistic meaning). Moreover, accounts of this type have been criticized: for example, by Wright, *Truth and Objectivity*, 6–7, 108–39; Wright, Moral Values, Projection and Secondary Qualities, 1–26.

17. This is from Judith Baker's "Introduction" (8–9, 20) to Grice, *The Conception of*

Value; but, since it is paginated continuously with the Grice lectures, I regard it as part of the text.

18. Wiggins, Moral Cognitivism, Moral Relativism and Motivating Moral Beliefs: quote note 70.

19. Wollheim has another, related strategy, emphasizing ". . . the inherently developmental nature of projection" (MD 152), its connection to "intimations" of history, and so on (MD 149). Ultimately, Wollheim chooses to "bracket" (MD 152) both the question of how projection can ". . . alter the world" (MD 152) through the "creation" of projective properties and how it can have the kind of *intimated* "afterlife" (MD 152) presented. Evocative though this idea of the intimation of history may be, it makes sense to accord it little specific weight here, given Wollheim's (lack of an) account of it. (Note, though, a strongly psychoanalytic/ Freudian conception of the developmental history of persons at work here: compare Richard Wollheim *Freud* (London: Fontana, 1971), 196 on "history and the superego").

As was seen (Chap. 7, 104–5), Malcolm Budd's exposition – which, at the conference, Wollheim endorsed (see also chap. 7, 110, n. 2) – emphasizes *this* as the key strategy, despite Wollheim's explicit "rejection" of it (cited above); and then highlights this strategy's limitations. Yet, Wollheim clearly had put it aside, in favour of the one I discuss. Perhaps, as Wollheim suggested in conversation, some of the contributors knew his writings better than he did!

20. See McFee, Wollheim and the Institutional Theory of Art, 183: the reference is to the "style" paper in MD 179. Reference to Wollheim's realist inclinations invites or allows mention of another position, to contrast with Wollheim's. For there is, in the literature on the philosophy of understanding, a contemporary view that is called (directly by Blackburn, implicitly by Grice, *The Conception of Value*, 146–151) "Projectivism": and that addresses an issue germane to the discussion here – for it relates to the nature of "response-dependent" properties (see MD 156, quoted earlier), properties whose very *existence* seems to depend on there being creatures able to recognize or to perceive properties of that type. And it explains those properties as *projective*; as coming about because (to quote Hume, *A Treatise of Human Nature*, Book One, Part III, Section xiv, 217) ". . . the mind has a great propensity to spread itself upon external objects" – the citation to Hume is commonly made [for instance, Grice, *The Conception of Value* 107; 146] (see also Blackburn, Reply: Rule-Following and Moral Realism, 163 citing Hume's *Enquiry Concerning the Principles of Morals*, Appendix I. 246: ". . . gilding or staining all natural objects with the colours, borrowed from internal sentiment, raises in a manner a new creation" (Selby-Bigge/Nidditch 3rd Ed. [1975] 294). Central among such properties are those ascribing *value*, of which artistic expression might plausibly be seen as a variety.

21. Now, not all talk of "projection" should be seen as *projectivist* in this sense. For instance, MWM 52, quoted earlier giving exposition of Wittgenstein, talks of our ability to "project" words into contexts other than those in which we learned them: but he is neither endorsing not attacking such projectivism. Furthermore, Wollheim is not wedded to the same version of projection as Blackburn and Grice: Blackburn in two notes (in Blackburn, *Essays in Quasi-Realism*) associates his view with Grice's: "Grice's construction of value delineates processes strikingly similar to those suggested by my quasi-realist" (5); Grice's ". . . Humean Projection is identical with the line I endorse" (19)) – although it is perhaps not irrelevant that Wollheim is a Hume scholar, editor of a volume of Hume's work

(Wollheim, ed. *Hume on Religion*) Wollheim expressly likens projective properties to secondary qualities (MD 149), quoting with approval McDowell's account.
22. But, notice, both Grice and Blackburn think of their projections as creating "real"
properties in *some* sense . . . although (for Blackburn at least) not exactly ones
amenable to truth-valuation: as Wright, *Truth and Objectivity* puts it, Blackburn's
view is that ". . . moral discourse [and, by extension, artistic discourse] is not,
propertly speaking, assertoric" (11) – rather, its ". . . fundamental role . . . is not
to state anything but to express certain moral [aesthetic] attitudes." (7) But compare Blackburn, *Spreading the Word*, 180: Quasi-realism ". . . seeks to explain,
and justify, the realistic-sounding nature of our talk about evaluations . . ." For a
discusion of the relation of projectivism to quasi-realism, see *Spreading* . . . 180
note 5.5. Blackburn, Reply: Rule-Following and Moral Realism, begins by noting
that: "The projective theory indeed denies that the standard of correctness derives
from conformity to an antecedent reality." (175)
   In projectivism, ". . . an input of information [is used] to determine an output
of reaction" (175), so that it takes remarks as expressing ". . . *commitments*, as
opposed to . . . *judgements*" (177–8). Yet: "If quasi-realism is successful, the projectivist has a right to think of moral judgements as true or false, as reasonable
or unreasonable, and so on" (185).
   This "right" is just the issue: what *commitments* involved in, say, truth-
valuations are missing? For, as Dummett urged (Dummett, *Truth and Other
Enigmas*, xxii), a central issue here concerns, not whether the notion of truth is
employed, but ". . . what notion of truth is admissible."
23. For example, in CR (dates in terms of publication), he speaks of the creative
process as ". . . not stopping short of, but terminating on, the painted surface"
(AO2 185); in PA he calls some part of the world ". . . the bearer of projective
properties" (PA 83): and then expands this account to root artistic expression as
such; in Pictures and Language (1989), quoted above (MD 189); in CPE, quoted
earlier, on the *mistake* in thinking that reference to projective properties means
that ". . . there is no property of the object to which we thereby refer" (MD 146).
24. This artistic/aesthetic contrast, fundamental to my thinking on the arts, is clearly
articulated by Best (*Philosophy and Human Movement*, 113–16; *Feeling and
Reason in the Arts*, 153–63; *The Rationality of Feeling*, 166–175). See also UD
38–44; and my Art, Beauty and the Ethical, read in Antwerp, September 1996.
25. See Scruton, *The Aesthetic Understanding: Essays in the Philosophy of Art and
Culture*, 28–31; Pole, *Aesthetics, Form and Emotion*, 105–09.
26. And irreducible subjectivism in the dismissive, "anything goes" sense (UD 22–3)
is to be avoided by any plausible aesthetics. Wiggins, *Needs, Values, Truth:
Essays in the Philosophy of Value*, 191 quotes Hume's rejection, as ". . . an
extravagant paradox, or rather a palpable absurdity" (Of the Standard of Taste,
Essays 231), of the "anything goes" of subjectivism (compare *Essays* 230). But,
as Wiggins continues (193), Hume should, if consistent, ". . . never look to objects
and properties themselves": and this is precisely what Wollheim's commitment to
realism about artistic expression is designed to require.
27. Compare McFee, *A Nasty Accident with One's Flies*; also Baker, Some Remarks
on "Language" and "Grammar," urging that Wittgenstein: ". . . always sought to
address specific philosophical problems of definite individuals and to bring to
light conceptual confusions which these individuals would acknowledge as a form
of entanglement in their own rules. He did not make direct assaults on various
standard "isms" . . ." (129). That this is indeed Wittgenstein's view is contested

by, for example, Hacker, *Wittgenstein's Place in Twentieth-Century Analytical Philosophy*, 312, note 90.

28. Compare (and contrast!) Wiggins, *Needs, Values, Truth: Essays in the Philosophy of Value*, 195; and Wright, *Truth and Objectivity*, 7–11: If Wright is correct in thinking that most of us are not realists about funny-ness, how does the argument sustaining this position differ from that for our general *realism* about moral or artistic value?

29. Notice that here as elsewhere Wollheim is appropriately careful with the term "meaning."

30. In his discussion (AO2 §47), Wollheim returns to a related matter: what he calls *the bricoleur problem*, after the thought that human culture resembles ". . . a *bricoleur* or handiman, who improvises only partly useful objects out of old junk" (§23 43 [59]). The problem is ". . . why certain apparently arbitrarily identified stuffs or processes should be vehicles of art" (§23 43 [59]): why are ". . . certain processes or stuffs . . . already accredited as the vehicles of art" (§47 109 [124]). As Wollheim appropriately addresses this issue, it is confusing to press the art/ language parallel too far if one hopes it will be revealing about the expressive potentials of art media (see AO2 §50 115 [131]). For language is (in Dummett's expression in *The Seas of Language*) necessarily *both* a medium of communication *and* an instrument of thought. Whatever we make of the "communication" aspect, art is *not* centrally an instrument of thought. (As Wollheim puts it, ". . . internal employment . . . is a distinctive characteristic of language, to which there is no analogue in art" (AO2 §50 115 [131]).

31. As I put it:

> . . . the tendency within philosophy to discuss powers of persons in terms of knowledge (supposedly held by such persons. So that, here, we are asked to think about the critic's use of particular concepts in terms of his having (or not having) certain facts or truths internal or external to the work of art. In this way, the critic's judgement of the work may appear to be correspondingly reduced to his or her capacity to employ or, worse, to state certain truths." (UD 135)

In fact, this tendency is widespread.

32. NB Wiggins' talk of "<property, response> pairs" (Wiggins, *Needs, Values, Truth: Essays in the Philosophy of Value* 196) is just another way of stating the problem.

33. Is this a version of Wiggins' sensible – and hence misnamed – subjectivism [Wiggins, A Sensible Subjectivism?: see its dependence on ". . . our *actual* collectively scrutinized responses" (210); and note that he explicitly associates his position with Wollheim's (note 14, 194)]?

34. See McFee, Wittgenstein: Understanding and "Intuitive Awareness," 37–46.

35. As Wittgenstein, *On Certainty* (§471) puts it, ". . . its difficulty is to begin at the beginning. And not try to go further back."

36. Here, too, it should be noted, with Wollheim (AO2 185), that the term "criticism" is here being appropriated to do wider-than-normal duty: to encompass all the appreciative remarks we make about artworks.

37. See McFee, Davies' Replies: A Response, 182–3.

38. Concerning the idea of *explanation* in general (and, in particular, the varieties of explanations), see Baker and Hacker, *Wittgenstein: Understanding and Meaning, an Analytical Commentary on the "Philosophical Investigations," Volume I*, 69–85. Central here is the thought both that explanations might have more than one form and that they might not consist of words only.

39. Wittgenstein, *Philosophical Grammar* 69: "meaning is what explanation of meaning explains."
40. See Cavell, MWM, 92 on being "... browbeaten ... into amnesia."
41. In addition to the later chapters of PA, the clearest place to see this is in his writing for *Modern Painters*: in particular, I would mention Hans Hofmann: the Final Years *Modern Painters* Vol. 1 No. 2 1988 13–16; Hockney's Work in Perspective *Modern Painters* Vol. 1 No. 4 1988/9 12–20; Tiepolo at Fort Worth *Modern Painters* Vol. 6 No. 4 1993 32–35; Art and Ideas: The Shape of the Story *Modern Painters* Vol. 8 No. 3 1995. (Ed Winters, more than anyone else, emphasized this to me in his own perceptive discussions of Wollheim, as well as of art.)
42. For some discussion, see Wright, *Truth and Objectivity*, 202–30: better, it is standard Wittgensteinian "therapy."
43. Wiggins, *Needs, Values, Truth: Essays in the Philosophy of Value*, 330.
44. Bell, *Art*, 3.

Part Three
The Internal Spectator

Chapter 12
Viewing Making Painting

SVETLANA ALPERS

It's not necessary for me to say that I am not a philosopher. And perhaps it is also not necessary to admit that, though I am an art historian, I share Richard Wollheim's suspicions about the field: in particular, his suspicion of the linguistic turn, and of the interest in theory, as it is misleadingly called these days. On more than one occasion I have looked to his writing for his passionate and clarifying arguments against these views. Though I have more interest than he does in the historical situating of art, I, too, find it odd that the academic study is called art history with no mention, and indeed a great suspicion of, criticism. I am in sympathy with his confession of distance travelled and time spent in looking at art. Like Richard, I am a friend to as well as a lover of painting (to invoke terms he takes up in another context and to which I shall return).

But, I want to put a few questions, mark a few differences. I shall:

1) take up and press an opening statement in *Painting as an Art* about the artist as spectator of his work.
2) give an account of Rembrandt's *Bathsheba* and consider how this might or might not be characterized under a Wollheim account of criticism.
3) conclude with a brief remark on painting and friendship.

The opening statement in *Painting as An Art* that I wish to take up is this, "The artist is essentially a spectator of his work." As evidence, Richard offers paintings by artists including, among others, Rogier van der Weyden, Vermeer, van Gogh, Corot.

The statement is further explicated as follows: "It has been the practice for the painter to position himself in front of the support, on that side of it where he makes his marks, facing it, with his eyes open, and fixed upon it" (PA 39).

But is this what the paintings exhibit?

Each, it is true, features a support of some kind and an artist before it. But Roger's St Luke glances up from working at his silver-point drawing to look at his model (the Virgin).

Van Gogh fixes his eyes on the viewer, or more likely at himself in a mirror, but surely not on his canvas.

Vermeer leaves the matter open. Where does the back-viewed artist look? We cannot tell. Vermeer is unwilling to commit his painter to choosing between an address to the motif/model/world and an address to the canvas.

In the case of Corot, a spectator, finally, is depicted addressing the painting. But the spectator is not the artist. Corot is absent. In a mysterious displacement, it is, instead, his model whom he depicts as spectator of a landscape which, like the woman herself, was painted by Corot. Although the painting the spectator looks at on the easel is present, it is represented as having been painted in the past.

There is no question that in the course of making a picture, the painter does fix his eyes on the support/painting. And one can understand that this emphasis is essential to Wollheim's larger project, which has been to make the aesthetic attitude rather than the art object the proper concern of aesthetic philosophy.

But the artist's role as spectator is only part of his situation. There can, therefore, be a wilfulness about it when the painter isolates his address to the support. (Courbet's *Allegory*, where the painter turns his back on a crowded studio, is an example.) And there is a tension in the other instances about the singularity of the address. On the evidence of these pictures, we might want to expand the *ur* statement: The painter is essentially a spectator of his work, and a spectator of the world, and the maker of an object.

The curious object that Vermeer's painter is at work on registers the complexity. Look at the unformed hand with which the artist paints: it is unformed because not yet fully perceived and also because not yet fully described. It is, further, juxtaposed on the canvas in such a way as to press the relationship between the artist/his painting and his motif. For in its appearance against the canvas, the shadowed hand of the painter, with its stiff, extended cuff tinged in white, simulates the appearance of the shadowed cheek of the model with her stiff, extended collar tinged in white, which remains to be painted beneath the blue leaves. The image in the process of being put on the canvas, of which Vermeer shows the artist's hand to be a part, is a link between the artist and the world. The artist is represented creating what others have variously called a symbol (Milner) or a transitional object (Winnicott).

Let me return to the original statement: "The artist is essentially a spectator of his work."

If we take this statement seriously as, surely, we are meant to, it may be thought to de-emphasize three features of painting: the relationship between painting and the world (is not the artist also spectator of the *world/motif*); the object-*making* as distinct from the object-*viewing* that painting involves (is not the artist also a *maker* of his work); and, finally, the after-life of painting (isn't a painting later seen by spectators aware that the artist in the making of it had a relationship to it that they cannot share).

This third and final feature – which presses the difference between the artist and the spectator who comes after–can become evident when we at-

Rembrandt Harmensz van Rijn (1606–1669). *Bathsheba with King David's Letter*. Musée du Louvre, Paris. Oil on canvas. (With the permission of the Réunion des Musées Nationaux, Agence Photographique.)

tempt to reconstruct the creative process terminating on the work (the phrase is Wollheim's). As an example, I shall offer a canonical work, Rembrandt's *Bathsheba*.

Rembrandt's *Bathsheba* is normally viewed as a painting of a biblical narrative. Bathsheba was traditionally shown as welcoming David's attention. Display is of Bathsheba's pictorial nature. The biblical verses are taken as an opportunity to depict a bathing-beauty worthy of being seen and desired by a king. The subject is often identifiable by handmaidens grooming the feet and hair of a naked woman (see the painting by Jan Massys, also in the Louvre.) No letter is mentioned in the Bible and it was not regularly supplied by painters.

On Rembrandt's account, Bathsheba is neither welcoming, nor preening. In narrative terms, the moment Rembrandt depicts is a different one. Bathsheba has received the king's message, broken the seal, and read the letter. She is depicted after the event, lost in thought. She is contemplating, or so we may imply, her fate.

Seeing it as narrative enactment, we are not solicited by a woman's nude body. But spectators at the Louvre turn away in a certain discomfort. Why is Rembrandt's painting of a disembowelled ox hanging on the wall to the right more inviting? Perhaps it is embarrassing to be caught staring at the painting of a naked woman who is not represented as engaged in the display of her body; a woman, who does not seem to welcome or invite our attention?

There is an additional narrative element. As so often with Rembrandt, we sense we are in the presence of an individual. It is generally agreed that the features depicted are those of Hendrickje Stoffels, the woman who lived with him as his common-law wife. With this knowledge, we can describe this as Hendrickje portrayed as performing Bathsheba. The role in which Rembrandt cast her was singularly appropriate to them both – for like Bathsheba, Hendrickje was a woman to whom great trouble came because she was desired by a man outside of marriage. During the year Rembrandt signed and dated this painting, Hendrickje, five months' pregnant, was repeatedly called before the church council until she admitted the accusation that she was living with Rembrandt like a whore.

To see the painting as Hendrickje portrayed performing Bathsheba is to see it in a particular genre – an historical or historiated portrait such as, for example, the picture known as *The Jewish Bride*. In this instance, however, knowledge of the life of the person portrayed adds psychological specificity and depth to the depiction of the biblical narrative.

But is there such a seamless fit between the biblical narrative and the making of a painting which represents Hendrickje posing for Rembrandt? Let us now look at the painting not as an enactment of a biblical narrative, but among the studies Rembrandt made after nude models posing in the studio.

The basic studio situation was that which we find represented in a Rembrandtesque picture now in Glasgow: A female model, draped in a white garment is sitting on a fabric covered bench, her right leg extended, the foot resting on the edge of a platform that raises her above the artist at his easel. But Bathsheba's pose is different. In the Louvre painting, one is struck by the way in which the model's upper body is accentuated by position and light. It looks as if the artist had instructed his seated model to turn her upper body towards him as far as she could. Notice that we see her stomach and her breasts almost *en face* while her legs and face are depicted in profile view. Along with the lifting of her foot, it is this twisting of the torso that requires the model to use her left arm and hand to steady herself.

The pose was not new for Rembrandt. It is one that was repeatedly requested of models who posed for him in the studio. A woman had held it for him over twenty years earlier for the etching commonly known as the *Woman on a Mound*. The handling of flesh (a target of early criticism) and figural reversal distract one from noticing that here, too, stomach and breasts were turned out against the placing of the legs. This is clearer if we reverse the etching to see to see the model as he etched her. Rembrandt, on occasion, draws models in casual positions, at their ease and unaware, as it were, of being on view. But this pose is hardly a casual one. In the forward twist of the torso against the profiled legs (supported here by her right elbow in addition to left hand) there is an emphasis on modelling itself as a demanding act, a performance if you will. A woman holds her body in a pose to be studied by the artist.

Modelling in this active sense is a factor in the Louvre painting. But there are a number of differences. The gaze is averted, the head bent, the eyes lowered. This model does not look out. Though on just this point there is x-ray evidence that at an earlier stage of the painting she had held her head more like the other models – higher, with eyes looking out.

The studio scenario represented in the painting took place, of course, between Rembrandt as the painter and Hendrickje Stoffels as the model. One imagines that she took and held the required pose. At first her eyes looked out, head more erect. Then it changed. Perhaps she turned away. Perhaps Rembrandt asked her to. In either case, he registered the curious dislocation between the twist of the body and the averted, downward angle of the head which is now, however, more aligned with the position of the legs. While the illuminated upper body is present to the eye, the legs are curiously hard to make out. It is partly that they are minimized by position and by shadow (the right thigh is greatly foreshortened, and the left leg hidden by shadow.) But it is also that their placement is equivocal: Moving one's eye up from feet to knees it is impossible to say which leg is nearer, which farther away. They elude us.

Hendrickje is not depicted as wooing Rembrandt with her body or with her glance. But she remained to sit for him. He is enthralled with her as this and other paintings record. But his painting shows us a naked woman, lost in her thoughts, impossible, so it appears, for the artist to possess. Let us say that with her eyes averted, her glance downwards, Hendrickje is not represented as complicitous in the performances required of her as Bathsheba, and as model. For all his pictorial skill, Rembrandt cannot possess what he so loves. Hendrickje, one sees (and Rembrandt admits) has her own resources.

There are two or, possibly, three stages to the account I have given. The first sees the painting as a Bathsheba narrative. The second (and third) see Hendrickje in the studio: as a figure for portrayal (performing Bathsheba); and as a model posing nude. Under this studio description, Hendrickje is represented as resisting the roles given her by Rembrandt. To revise the earlier explanation of why the spectators in the Louvre turn away – her body is not unsettling because her mind is elsewhere. More fundamentally, her body is represented as eluding a comprehensive view.

In sum, the representation of Bathsheba can also be seen as the representation of a certain relationship between the painter and his model.

How might I account for what I have done in Wollheimian terms? I take it, to go back to a great essay, that I have been practising criticism as retrieval – a definition of that being a reconstruction of the creative process, inclusively construed (A02 185). Might I then, following the distinction offered in *Painting as an Art*, call the *narrative* Bathsheba the primary meaning (that is the textual meaning to Rembrandt with the inflection of Hendrickje as Bathsheba), and the relationship painter/model the secondary meaning (that is, what the making means to Rembrandt). But is a distinction between the two, between the narrative account and the model account, so neatly made?

And, is it meaning (the mental life of the artist) that I am retrieving or an historical process, an artist's performance or art-making through time. Furthermore, does not such a performance have a further history, an after-life in time. Is it not the introspective Bathsheba (the narrative interpretation) which disconcerts viewers who come upon the painting in the Louvre? Are the maker's and the beholder's share one and the same? Should one not admit, even as one seeks it, that there is a certain sublimity about a view which seeks to access and to isolate the painter's intentions? This is true whether one locates intentions in the act of painting, as I have, or, as Wollheim does, in the painter's mental life.

But there is a final twist. Rembrandt had Hendrickje pose in the studio and she was his model for Bathsheba. But he depicts her as resisting the roles assigned: The painting represents not his successful projection onto her, but someone who resists projection, someone he acknowledges as separate from himself. Such acknowledgement is rare for Rembrandt. Jan Six is another sitter who got away.

The point has greater reach. As it gets into painting, the world is surely the object of the artist's projection, a means of self-resolution. But the world is also external to the artist. The world as it gets into painting is also something understood because acknowledged. Considered this way, painting is not only a way of getting into and resolving oneself, but also a way of getting out of oneself.

Taking up Richard Wollheim's terms in the *Thread of Life*: Could one not say that painting's relationship to the world and our relationship to painting can be like friendship instead of like love (TL 278–80)? It can be the engagement of difference, respect for the singularity of another person or thing, the taking of an attitude, as well as the projecting, as one does on his account, in response to love.

Chapter 13
The Staging of Spectatorship

RENÉE VAN DE VALL

real pictures

In this chapter, I will apply Richard Wollheim's concepts of the "spectator of the picture" and the "spectator in the picture" to an artwork for which they seem hardly suitable: a piece of installation art. This exercise might be considered as a testing of these concepts under extreme conditions to discover their potential and their limits. Inappropriate as the experiment might seem, I think that it shows us some possibilities and impossibilities of Wollheim's theory of spectatorship that are also of interest for its application to paintings. Wollheim's distinction between the two kinds of spectatorship creates a separation between two different worlds that, as Wollheim stresses, should not be conflated. My objection to Wollheim's theory will be that this separation obliterates a third way of engaging the spectator that installations and pictures share.

In the Museum of Contemporary Art of Antwerp in September 1996, one could see an impressive installation by Alfredo Jaar. It consisted of a small round room, with dark floors and walls. The room was sparsely lighted. Inside were five columns of medium height. On closer inspection these columns turned out to be made of flat boxes, covered with black linen. A stack of four boxes formed one column. On the uppermost boxes of each column texts were printed in a white lettering. Each text described a photo – a photo that, as you understood, had been stored in that particular box. And each photo supposedly depicted a scene in or around one of the refugee camps in Rwanda: people waiting for food or medication, a priest who had fled from his village and who – even in the camp – was not safe, patients suffering from cholera or dysentery.

For instance:

Ruzizi 2 Bridge
Bukavu, Zaire – Cyangugu, Rwanda Border
Sunday, August 28th, 1994
The Ruzizi 2 Bridge is one of two bridges across the Ruzizi River that separates Rwanda from Zaire on the southwest border. At the peak of the violence, refugees fled Rwanda at the rate of 35,000 people per day. Now that this bridge has been closed for six days, the banks of the river are swelling with people waiting to cross.

So you found yourself bending over toward a column to read the text while trying to imagine how the photo inside would depict the scene described. Precisely because of this effort the scene became somehow more real than when it could have been seen in the usual way, as a newspaper photograph with a caption. Outside the room a text was printed that narrated the history of the mass killings in Rwanda. It ended with a quotation of V. Altaio: "Images have an advanced religion. They bury history."

The name of this installation was *real pictures*. It was impressive as a manifesto, but what made it successful as an artwork as well was its separating and contrasting of different levels of meaning. First, it compared different sorts of *representation*. (I use the concept here differently than Wollheim does, with an emphasis on the prefix *re*, for images or texts that describe or depict something that is not present.) So the work compared photographic with textual representation. This comparison was *presented* (without the prefix *re*) in a particular way: The installation showed a certain amount of columns made up of black boxes carefully arranged in a dark and sparsely lighted room. This presentation by itself evoked all kinds of associations: with gravestones and funeral parlours for instance. But there was something else.

As soon as you entered the room, it seemed as if an invisible hand directed your posture, your movements, your behaviour. It was, for instance, impossible to walk through this room fast, or to speak loudly. You were supposed to shuffle from one column to the next, in an enveloping movement, then to bend over toward the text and gaze attentively, and to whisper softly a remark to your company, if you happened to have anyone with you. The whole arrangement asked for a discreet, subdued, and attentive response, for a kind of behaviour belonging to the experience and the emotion you were supposed to feel. The installation formed a stage, where you, as an actor, were asked to perform the required experience. This aspect of the meaning of the work I would like to call its *mise-en-scène* or *staging*.

Alfredo Jaar's installation questions our attitude towards atrocious events like the massacres in Rwanda and about the way media coverage influences this attitude – not so much through its content, but through its *form*. As a press release accompanying one of Jaar's expositions makes clear, it is not photography as such, or even press photography as such, that the artist is questioning, but the way images circulate in present day visual culture. We are overfed, each time with new images that somehow each time seem to show the same. Each image disappears as soon as it has appeared: the next page, the next item, next day's newspaper brings again new ones. To quote the press release: "*real pictures* is a cemetery of images – those pictured have been disappeared by the very fact that their faces are those in our newspapers today, but not tomorrow."

These are true words. Yet, it is not this moralizing statement that makes the work convincing. The installation could have done without it. The crux of the work lies in what it makes us do. By withholding us the pictures that it suggests are present, it forces us to use our imagination and to visualize the scenes that the texts describe. The effort, and the concomitant emotion, succeed to bring you closer to what has happened and to make you realize how little an ordinary newspaper photo would have moved you. This tells you something about the usual relation of spectatorship and its non-involvement with the faraway events that supposedly are brought nearer by the press, television and other media.

Something else happens as well. By giving the work the form it has, evoking associations with tombs or funeral parlours, and moreover, by arranging the room in such a way so as to stage a certain manner of behaviour, Alfredo Jaar creates a form through which the emotions the massacres evoke can effectively be felt. The work stages a kind of physical and affective movement that resembles what we do when we are mourning. And strange as this might seem, this feels like a relief.

I think that the importance of the work lies not only in its comment on the press coverage of the tragedy in Rwanda and on the paradoxical effects of the abundance of visual information in mass media culture. What makes it interesting is also its implicit comparison between distinctive aspects of spectatorship, and even more implicit, distinctive aspects of subjectivity as well. By doing so, it reflects on how, in postmodern visual culture, our relation to the outside world is modelled. It makes clear what spectatorship in a broad, social and cultural sense is, by articulating different spectatorial roles. And in analysing these roles, we get some help from Wollheim's concepts of the spectator of and the spectator in the picture.

Spectatorship and Subjectivity

In *Painting as an Art* Wollheim states that some paintings have "a representational content in excess of what they represent. There is something that cannot be seen in the painting: so the painting does not represent that thing. But the thing is given to us along with what the painting represents: so it is part of the painting's representational content" (PA 101).

This representational content that is not itself represented is an unrepresented spectator: the spectator *in* the picture. This spectator has to be distinguished from the actual spectator, the spectator *of* the picture, who stands in the gallery space or in the church or wherever the picture is exhibited. The spectator *in* the picture does not stand in this actual space: he stands in the virtual space that is represented by the painting: the heavenly skies, nineteenth-century Paris, and so on. A crucial distinction between the two is one that is related to the twofoldness of pictorial representation. For the spectator in the picture, this twofoldness has been abolished: "The external spectator can be, and normally is, aware of the marked surface: he will move within the actual space to ensure that this is so. For the internal spectator the marked surface does not exist: it is not visible from the virtual space" (PA 102).

Wollheim repeatedly states that the two spectators should not be conflated; otherwise the meaning of the painting would change with each new spectator that comes along. The world of the internal spectator is imaginary: it is the world of the represented scene. The world of the external spectator is the perceptual world of the space in which the painting is hung.

The spectator of the picture identifies with this spectator in the picture, and by doing so, gains a particular access to the meaning of the painting. This is an act of centrally imagining: One imagines the scene from the inside, and from the particular viewpoint of the unrepresented spectator. Furthermore, for this viewpoint to contribute to our understanding of this painting, it should be more than just a point of view: the internal spectator should have a repertoire of characteristic attitudes or responses. This repertoire is somehow suggested by the painting.

If now we return to the installation by Jaar, we might say that a conflict between two kinds of spectatorship occurs. The first kind of spectatorship involved in this conflict might be compared with the spectator of the picture. It is the spectator for whom the marked surface exists. It is – in a broader, non-artistic context – spectatorship as it is usually understood: The observer at a distance of what is seen, taking in what is before him – the outside world or a representation of it – at a single glance. Of course he might see things "in" a visual representation, but not to the extent of loosing himself in this exercise. This kind of spectatorship implies the mode of vision that has recently been called "Cartesian perspectivalism." The name suggests an affinity with a particular modality of subjectivity as well: with the concept of the transparent, bodiless, autonomous subject usually associated with traditional metaphysics.[1]

However, the marked surface doesn't give this spectator what he wants. He wants an image, a photograph; what he gets is letters, texts. So what is called upon is his capacity to imagine the scene – even centrally imagine the scene, for instance in the role of the supposed photographer. The spectator of the picture forces himself in the role of a spectator in the picture to an extreme degree: He identifies with a point of view on a scene that can not even be seen. In this case, the adopted viewpoint is completely inward as there is no visual clue for it. But if the photo had been visible, the viewpoint would have involved a merging between the inner and the outer eye; a kind of vision that both colours and is coloured by what is seen, and is – at least intends to be – emotionally of one piece with what is depicted. It is expressive vision in

Wollheim's sense. The mode of subjectivity that matches this kind of vision is imaginative and empathic, but, one might add, liable to narcissist projection as well. One might think of Julia Kristeva's concept of the loving subject.[2]

But our spectator does more – responding to that aspect of the work's meaning that I have called its staging. He shuffles around, quietly and discreetly, speaks softly, in a space that is carefully arranged so as to solicit this behaviour. It seems as if his limbs know instinctively how to move in such surroundings, just as our voices hush automatically when we enter a cathedral. This is partly, but not only, a matter of convention. Some spaces impress us with a particular mood or demand, are designed in such a way as to make one physically act and feel elated or awestruck or depressed. The spectator called for by the work's staging is not an observer in front of, and hence outside his object. He is inside, but not because he cannot see. He is looking, but in doing so he is part of what he sees, physically and affectively engaging with his surroundings, which, in turn, responds to his movements. And the relevant mode of subjectivity is a receptive one: not autonomous, nor completely passive either; not transparent; not separated from its physical being. Merleau-Ponty's embodied subject might come to mind.[3]

For this third mode of spectatorial engagement, I do not find any clue in Wollheim's chapter on "What the spectator does." Wollheim allows for two possible ways of relating to the painting: actual perception or imaginative "seeing in." Accordingly, there are two kinds of space involved: the actual space in which the painting exists as a marked surface and the virtual space that is represented by the picture. Of course the two spaces interact: This accounts for the painting's twofoldness. But there is no concept for the painting or the space as it actually determines the physical and affective response of the spectator as an embodied being. When the spectator engages with the painting this engagement is thought of as an imaginative identification with a perceived point of view in a virtual space, not as a bodily involvement with what is seen in the actual space.

Now, it might be objected that shuffling around could be part of what an installation asks for, but that a two-dimensional work like a painting is not in any sense a stage. My reply to this objection is: Paintings form stages as well, first of all for the dynamics of our attention, which includes the movements of our eyes, but often our physical and affective behaviour in the space in which they are hung as well. Our attention is staged: triggered, caught, manipulated, distracted, guided by the visual dynamics of the painting – by the arrangement of its tensions and harmonies, its contrasts and relations, its clues and uncertainties. The painting plays a game with the attention of its beholder and thereby with his eyes.[4] Looking at it is a process in time, that includes the onlooker's body and the painting's material presence. And there are paintings for which this looking includes the way you approach them, for instance, because they so dominate the space in which they are hung that they stage your attitude and movements: for example, walking up an aisle and looking up in awe towards an altar piece.

To explain this third mode of spectatorship, it would not only be unhelpful, but also misleading, to make distinctions like those between the spectator in the picture and the spectator of the picture as hard ontological distinctions, relegating the one to the imaginary world of the represented scene and the other to the actual world in which the work is shown. The separation of these two worlds would make the staging of spectatorship inexplicable.

The Impossible Viewpoint

I will illustrate this point with some of Wollheim's own examples. Wollheim compares two kinds of pictures that are superficially related with regard to the point of view: Dutch seventeenth-century landscapes of Philips de Koninck or Jan van Goyen and the landscapes of Caspar David Friedrich. Although these paintings seem to have a lot in common, and in particular their high point of view, the Friedrichs present a point of view that is occupied, whereas the point of view of the Dutch landscapes is not (PA 131–6).

The spectator in the picture, according to Wollheim, should be more than just a point of view. His presence must make a difference for our apprehension of the picture. For this reason, there must be some suggestion of what Wollheim calls a *repertoire*, an indication of the kind of person this spectator is supposed to be, or of the kind of experience he is supposed to have. Furthermore, the point of view from which the scene is represented should be *occupied*.

And here my questioning starts. For how is this repertoire suggested by the painting to the actual spectator of the picture? And what makes us decide that a point of view is occupied or not? When Wollheim is comparing the Friedrichs with the Dutch landscapes, he takes their viewpoints as being there, given with the virtual space of the paintings. The only thing the actual spectator has to do is to discover them and, if they suggest an internal spectator, to identify with him. To explain the differences between the high viewpoint of the Dutch landscapes on the one hand and those of the Friedrichs on the other, Wollheim suggests that in the former the viewpoint is chosen because of the better view it gives of the scenery, whereas the Friedrichs have the high viewpoint to suggest a certain type of spectator. Therefore, the viewpoint of the Friedrichs is occupied, whereas that of the Dutch landscapes is not.

But wouldn't it be much more helpful to point out that in the Friedrichs one's attention is drawn strongly – sucked, one might even say – to a faraway point in the distance? One's attention transverses the represented space, initially ignoring what is in front or on the sides. By doing so, one's eyes focus upon an area in the center of the material surface and see its surroundings initially as blurred, vague, before they start to inspect them more closely. The detachment of the nineteenth-century nature painter – Wollheims identification of the spectator in Friedrich's pictures – relies on what the painting does to our eyes: It detaches them from their nearest surroundings and guides them straightaway to the horizon. Whereas in the Dutch paintings the swirls in the landscape and in the sky and the perspectival discontinuities make the eyes swirl as well, as birds circling up and down, back and forth over the hills and valleys.

The sense of detachment, rightfully stressed by Wollheim as belonging to the content of Friedrich's paintings, is, according to me, brought about by the compositional dynamics of the paintings, as it is to be seen by the actual spectator of the picture, looking at the picture plane with his actual, physical eyes. The way one actually focuses at the faraway center, while having – at first – the rest of the pictured scene at the edges of one's vision, largely contributes to this feeling of not-belonging on the one hand and of contemplation on the other. Of course, the virtual, represented space of the picture is part of this feeling as well. My point is not to deny this imaginary aspect but to stress that separating the physical from the imaginary and explaining the repertoire of the suggested spectator only in terms of the latter, is to miss something important. In this case the distinction between the spectator *of* and the spectator *in* the picture is misleading.

To this another question can be added: What does it mean that Friedrich's internal spectators are part of the represented space of the picture? Does that mean that they *might* have been represented, if Friedrich had decided to turn around the scene? Is the unrepresented spectator in the picture of the same fictional material, is he a spectator of the same level of being, as those spectators in Friedrich's pictures that happen to be represented?

Whoever is occupying this point of view, it is unlikely to be a human being of the same sort as the human figures that we often see in Friedrich's paintings. For one thing, the internal spectator appears, as Wollheim writes, to hang suspended in midair. Therefore, what he sees could not have been seen by any possible human figure within the painted scene. The spectator of these pictures might be partly imaginary, but he is not a spectator of the same representational order, part of the same fictional world, as the represented landscapes and what is in them. Not only is he not represented, as Wollheim says, but he is not even given along with the represented scene. If he is given along it is rather with the means of representation and the way these direct our eyes. This discontinuity between the represented scene and its internal spectator is another reason to state that the latter is not exclusively a part of the scene we *see in* the material surface, but also part of the way in which we attend to how colours and forms are displayed on the surface – If this distinction really makes sense here.

This does not imply that Wollheim's distinction is not useful at all. Ironically enough, it proves very helpful in some cases were it is not called for and where its merits have even been contested: in the case of those eighteenth- and nineteenth-century French paintings that are described by Michael Fried.[5] Fried describes a tendency in French painting starting with Chardin and Greuze of denying the presence of a beholder. The figures in Chardin's paintings for instance show no sign of noticing that they are looked at. They are absorbed in what they do. After Chardin, however, it seems to have become a problem to paint figures in such an absorptive state. They must be emphatically busy with highly important emotions or actions, to be convincing in their ignorance of the beholder. Fried relies largely on the writings of Diderot as evidence of the contemporary public's desire for their paintings to portray their human figures as being oblivious of the fact that they are being beheld. He describes this demand as a paradoxical one:

[Diderot's] conception of painting rested ultimately on the metaphysical fiction that the beholder did not exist. Yet paradoxically he also believed that only that fiction was able to bring the beholder to a halt in front of the canvas and to hold him there in the perfect trance of involvement that Diderot and his contemporaries regarded to be the experiential test of a completely successful painting. (Fried 1990, 8)

Obviously, this is a paradox only if one takes the beholder in the first sentence to be the same as the one in the second. The dramatis personae in a painting can only be oblivious of being beheld to the extent that the potential beholder forms part of their world. A possible unrepresented beholder in the represented space is indeed the kind of person the figures in the painting might or might not be aware of. Wollheim's spectator *in* the picture is a likely candidate of the kind of spectator these figures should ignore. The beholder that should be stopped in front of the canvas, on the other hand, is of a different order: He is Wollheim's spectator *of* the picture. Diderot, and Fried in his wake, treat the painting as if it were an actual stage. Indeed, the obliviousness of real life actors to their audience might be of that seemingly paradoxical kind that is noted. To say the same of the "actors" in a painting with regard to their real life public is incoherent.

Staging the Sublime

To conclude this chapter, I will now turn to the painting that I have already extensively described and analysed on earlier occasions.[6] My encounter with Jaar's installation and with installation art in general and my rereading of Wollheim's chapter on spectatorship have convinced me that I should revise my analysis. I present this revised version because the painting in question brings out very sublimely both the merits and the limitations of Wollheim's two concepts and makes clear in which way paintings and installations might resemble each other.

When Barnett Newman's *Vir Heroicus Sublimis* was exhibited for the first time, in Betty Parson's Gallery in New York in 1951, Newman put a short typewritten note on the wall with the following text: "There is a tendency to look at large pictures from a distance. The large pictures in this exhibition are intended to be seen from a short distance."[7]

For Newman, the position of the spectator was important for the appreciation of his pictures, because he wanted his pictures to have a spatial effect: "Anyone standing in front of my paintings must feel the vertical domelike vaults encompass him to awaken an awareness of his being alive in the sensation of complete space."[8] He wanted the spectator to have the feeling of one's own presence, a *sense of place*: "One thing that I am involved in about painting is that the painting should give man a sense of place: that he knows he's there, so he's aware of himself."[9] Newman succeeds in conveying this feeling through the staging of an interplay of visual orientation and disorientation by means of which different modes of spectatorship are made to conflict. The painting articulates a role for the spectator that divides him against himself. The sublimity of the painting rests upon its resolution of the conflict: upon the delight one feels in feeling a sense of place after all in what first appears to be a perceptual chaos. *Vir Heroicus Sublimis* stages a sublime experience by disorganizing one's sense of direction and making one feel lost in the overwhelming, burning redness of its field – and then giving one again a sense of direction, although on a different level of feeling. The mode of vision that gets defeated is the objectifying, detached way of looking with the concomitant sense of self as separate, selfdirecting and in control. The "sense of place" that one feels nonetheless calls upon a different mode of vision and a different sense of self in which the viewing subject feels physically, affectively and imaginatively engaged with his surroundings and receptive toward what these might offer. But how is this complex experience staged?

Newman's painting defeats the objectifying mode of spectatorship that tries to oversee the painting and to take it in at once from a distance. This is not only effected by the sheer size of the painting, as is often assumed, but also by the subtle handling of the *zips* (as Newman called the stripes in his paintings). The zips are not placed in a consistent way in front of, or behind, or in between the red fields. Each stripe has a different visual effect on the surrounding red colour. In some places the red field has a certain depth, as on both sides of the light cadmium red zips. Here the zips stand in the field, as a part of it, and enhance its depth. The red surrounding the dark brownish zip is flatter. The zip is seen either as in between or in front of the red, the red in the latter case continuing behind it. In the case of the ochre zip, both the red fields and the zip are seen as adjacent flat surfaces. The zip stands clearly in between the red fields. The white zip finally cuts through the red. On both sides the red hue is less intense than in the rest of the painting. So one does try to "see" figure and ground "in" the painting, but one succeeds only by looking at one of the different zips at a time.

Furthermore, the red hue comes toward you. The red is a dense, very tactile colour, almost like a mist filling the space in front of it. And the central field comes nearer than the two side panels. This is the kind of effect that works strongest when one does not really look at the painting, but is just turning around, or just entering the room, or leaving it. The same goes for the feeling the white zip evokes. This zip is different from the others, both in its dynamics within the painting, and in its relation to the viewer. It cuts through the red with an explosive tension and hurts the eyes; but by cutting through the suffocating red hue it also comes as a relief. In the disorienting organization of the painting, it serves as a point of orientation. It is not so much a visual point of direction, as you tend not to look directly at it, because it is sharp and forbidding. It is rather a point you are aware of without looking – a point of imaginative identification. However, one's connection with the white zip is not only brought about by imagination. The "being aware of without directly looking" is also a matter of the extended tactility which is an intrinsic part of embodied perception in space.

Wollheim has interesting things to say about Friedrichs *Rückenfiguren*. As in the usual accounts, he sees the *Rückenfigur* as a point of identification for the spectator – but not only.

This figure, or these figures [. . .] stand in some highly intimate relationship to the spectator in the picture. They are not he, but they have been cloned from him, so that he may be thought of as feeling himself drawn – drawn as it were, ahead of himself – deeper into the space to which he belongs; out of the unrepresented part into the represented part. The spectator of the picture, once alerted to what is taking place, responds. The shock of identifying with someone who is in effect precipitated into his, the external spectator's, field of vision sets up a signal. And the signal tells him to relinquish his identification and to pull back to a position from which the marked surface regains visibility. He retreats from imagination to perception – specifically to seeing-in. (PA 168)

In this chapter, I would like to suggest that in Newman's painting this double function of the *Rückenfigur* is divided. The red zips seem to be the extensions of the spectator in the picture. They draw you further into the represented space. It is two of the other zips – the brown and ochre ones – that act as barriers against the tendency to lose oneself in the represented space, by making the marked surface visible again.

But the white zip is again different. This zip proceeds into the unrepresented space *in front* of the picture – a space that is not part of the picture as a material surface, nor of the represented space, but is yet somehow suggested by the painting. Again: How are we to understand this space in front of the painting? As a virtual space, suggested but not represented by the picture? Like the space in a Friedrich, that seems to continue toward the spectator, because the landscape seems to run on under the point of view from which it is represented? Or is it the actual space of the gallery, as it is animated by the picture?

Wollheim makes a further distinction between paintings that embody an unrepresented spectator and paintings that embody the illusion that a represented figure enters our space (PA 185). The white zip might be compared to such an illusory invader – if its effects would indeed be illusory. But are they indeed a form of making us believe? The presence of the white zip in the actual space cannot be compared to a belief, right or wrong. When we feel its nearness, both as a sharp and blinding light and as a welcome interruption of the burning red field, we actually perceive it – by feeling with our eyes and seeing with other senses than our eyes alone. The white zip's tactile and affective qualities respond to our way of engaging with the visual dynamics of the painting – dynamics that include its acting upon the space in which it is hung. Walking around in such a space is not the thing the spectator of the picture does until he identifies with the spectator in the picture. It is what one should do to experience the painting: to come closer and to retreat; to immerse oneself in the glow of the colour and retract oneself; to face it and to look away; to focus and to unfocus – all these movements, both physical and imaginative, have to be performed be able to become what it wants you to be. In this respect, a painting can be just as spatial as an installation. And precisely this spatial way of engaging the spectator tends to be lost in between the terms of Richard Wollheim's otherwise enlightening distinction.

NOTES

1. See Jay, *Downcast Eyes. The Denigration of Vision in Twentieth-Century French Thought*. At this place I will not discuss, let alone challenge, the notion of Cartesian perspectivalism and the problematic connection of the Cartesian Ego with central perspective in painting. I use the notion here purely descriptive, as a rough but workable indication of one of the several ways in which we relate ourselves – visually – to the outside world. The different modes of vision I distinguish here are probably not exhaustive. Neither are they phenomenologically exclusive, even if the theories that have most effectively conceptualized them in many respects do oppose each other.
2. See Kristéva, *Histoires d'amour*.
3. For my reading of Merleau-Ponty, I have profited from Crowther's *Critical Aesthetics and Postmodernism* and *Art and Embodiment. From Aesthetics to Self-Consciousness*.

188 RENÉE VAN DE VALL

4. In this respect, my comment on Wollheim's theory of spectatorship parallels Michael Baxandall's argument in Chapter 17, this book.
5. In, for instance, Fried, *Absorption and Theatricality. Painting and Beholder in the Age of Diderot*. For the discussion between Wollheim and Fried see Wollheim PA 364–5, n. 34 and Fried, *Manet's Modernism or the Face of Painting in the 1860s*, 344–5, n. and 512–3, n.
6. See Van de Vall, *Een subliem gevoel van plaats. Een filosofische interpretatie van het werk van Barnett Newman* and Van de Vall, Silent Visions: Lyotard and the Sublime.
7. See O'Neill, ed. *Barnett Newman: Selected Writings and Interviews*, 178.
8. In an interview with Dorothy Seckler in O'Neill, ibid., 250.
9. In an interview with David Sylvester in Auping, *Abstract Expressionism: the Critical Developments*, 144.

Chapter 14
Presentation or Representation

SUSAN L. FEAGIN

At first glance, it seems obviously true that *trompe l'oeil* paintings are picto-rial representations, and also that they are among the clearest examples, or exemplars, of pictorial representation. It has widely been taken to be a serious defect in Richard Wollheim's analysis of pictorial representation that it entails that *trompe l'oeil* paintings are *not* pictorial representations. Wollheim, nev-ertheless, accepts with unflinching candor what others take to be a *reductio ad absurdum* of his analysis. "Obvious truths," distressingly, sometimes turn out to be neither obvious nor true, and I believe this is the case for the view that *trompe l'oeil* paintings, as such, pictorially represent their subject-matter. In what follows I argue that, whatever problems there are with Wollheim's account of pictorial representation, its implications for *trompe l'oeil* are not among them. In fact, it is necessary to make the distinction in function between *trompe l'oeil* and pictorial representation in order to understand and appreciate the full power of each. In the first section, I describe some exam-ples of *trompe l'oeil* painting that are clearly not pictorial representations. Some of these examples reinforce the distinction between *trompe l'oeil* and painting as an art, though others make it look like *trompe l'oeil* painting can be practiced as an *art*, even if not for the purposes of pictorial representation. In the second section, I explain why a painting may be both a highly effective *trompe l'oeil* painting and a pictorial representation of the same subject. Again, I introduce some examples to show how a painting designed and crafted to take on both roles has rich potential to explore the oppositions and contradictions between the two.

I: *Trompe l'oeil* is not Pictorial Representation

As Wollheim uses the term, "pictorial representation" refers to a specific subclass of pictorial representations, that is, those produced by painting, and specifically by painting practiced as an art. In this paper, unless otherwise indicated, "painting" and "pictorial representation" are used in this way. According to Wollheim, "[i]f a picture represents something, then there will be a visual experience of that picture that determines that it does so. This

experience I call the 'appropriate experience of the picture'."[1] This criterion
is necessary, he says, in order to preserve the perceptual, and even more
narrowly the visual, status of the pictorial arts.[2] The "appropriate experience"
is defined both in terms of its phenomenology and in terms of artists' intentions.[3] Phenomenologically, the experience has two aspects, the configurational and the recognitional. Though separable logically for the purpose of
analysis, they are fused phenomenologically in an experience that has, as it
were, its own gestalt.

Pictorial representations are artifacts, and are therefore defined at least
partially in terms of the intentions of their maker, especially intentions about
how the artifact is to function.[4] Thus, the appropriate experience of a pictorial
representation must "tall[y] with" the painter's intentions.[5] *Trompe l'oeil*
paintings are also artifacts, and, unlike pictorial representations, they are
intended to "fool the eye," to create an illusion, that is, to look as much as
possible like whatever it is that they imitate or mimic, what I sometimes refer
to as the painting's subject-matter. To the extent that a *trompe l'oeil* painting
is successful, the spectator's experience will *not* contain a configurational
component, the component that is responsible for one's experiencing the
painting as painted rather than as what it is supposed to mimic.[6]

The Dictionary of Art discusses *trompe l'oeil* under the general heading of
"illusionism," which is characterized as a function of paintings when "the
intention is that something should seem not so much represented as substantially present."[7] This terminology, that the function of painting is presentational rather than representational, is particularly apt. "Faux finishes" are
examples of illusionism; one can even buy kits for painting a surface in such
a way that it appears to be marble, granite, or some other material. That this
type of painting is, per se, more of a craft skill than an art is a point in favor
of the view that the function of *trompe l'oeil* painting is different from the
functions of painting considered as an art.[8] The practice of *trompe l'oeil*
painting, however, is not restricted to the amateur or to the arena we might
be tempted to call "craft." Numerous churches and palaces in Europe contain
trompe l'oeil painted surfaces that look like marble pilasters and columns,
with *trompe l'oeil* inlays of semi-precious stones such as lapis lazuli and
malachite. Some artists even raise the stakes with bravura design schemes
that intersperse painted columns, pilasters, and so on with real ones, challenging spectators to determine which are which when they are literally side-by-
side. These painted surfaces are neither pictures of nor pictorial representations of marble or marble pilasters. Rather, they are *presented as being*, for
example, marble pilasters.

Illusionistic interior wall paintings in ancient Rome were prized for making
a room feel larger and more open, even though painters lacked the geometric
techniques such as those developed in early fifteenth-century Florence for

rendering objects in a systematic and orderly fashion in pictorial space. Once these techniques were developed, *quadratura*, the practice of painting whole rooms, including ceilings, with illusionist effects and integrating actual architectural elements into the design scheme, became the "in" thing, a "must have" for anyone wanting to display their social status and power. Andrea Mantegna was something of a *wunderkind* at this type of painting and his ceiling for the *Camera degli Sposi* in the Palazzo Ducale, Mantua, is *tour de force trompe l'oeil*.[9] He painted the shallow yet still concave dome to create a visual illusion of a much higher dome with a central oculus, where people and cherubs gather around a circular balustrade that seems to open up to the sky. Pictures of this ceiling are widely reproduced, but they typically include only the central oculus and balustrade, and not the lower parts of the dome on which Mantegna painted unbelievably elaborate *trompe l'oeil* marble subjects (ribbons surrounding eight wreaths encircling portraits, held up by children, and divided up into segments by a network of stylized vines) with *trompe l'oeil* gold mosaic backgrounds. Every inch of the ceiling is covered with *trompe l'oeil* painting that creates illusions of space, including background areas one would ordinarily experience as flat or as extending to an indefinite distance, but which here are given a specific shallow depth in the form of *trompe l'oeil* gold mosaics.[10]

Central to Mantegna's effort are values that are also central to the Renaissance. Though one might expect an updating of the Roman use of mosaics as part of the Renaissance classical revival, *gold mosaics* used as a background are associated with Byzantium and its religious tradition. Mantegna appropriates them for domestic and secular, decorative purposes. In the Byzantine tradition, mosaics were valued as being more dazzling, durable, expensive, and prestigious than fresco painting, which was virtually the only pictorial alternative. They definitely carried prestige value: any church that could muster the money would sport mosaics rather than fresco. There is thus a certain irony that Mantegna's *painting* of *trompe l'oeil* gold mosaics carried prestige value, though we all know that different kinds of activities and objects are more highly valued at some times and not others. Perhaps the most important point of all is that illusionism, as a function of painting, was prized in the Renaissance, though anathema to Byzantine pictorial practices.[11]

Mantegna treated gold mosaics as he did marble, as something to be presented *trompe l'oeil*. The difference, as manifested here, between the two cultural traditions is not between two functions of pictorial representation, but between two functions of painting. Gold backgrounds in Byzantine painting were to aid worshipers in moving beyond the material world towards spiritual reality. The physical yet illusory space defined by *trompe l'oeil* gold mosaics is crucial to Mantegna's vision; it cannot be achieved through a pictorial representation of gold mosaics.[12]

Around 1508, Raphael was commissioned by Pope Julius II to decorate his private *stanze* in the Vatican where we can again see how Byzantine gold mosaics were appropriated for Renaissance purposes. The *Stanza della Segnatura* acquired its name because it was for a while used as a Papal Court of Justice. Its wall paintings, such as the *School of Athens*, have unfortunately tended to overshadow the ceiling, where Raphael painted allegorical figures symbolizing different branches of learning, separated by *trompe l'oeil* marble borders with a classical theme. The background is *trompe l'oeil* gold mosaic; indeed, the entire room is another *tour de force* exercise of *trompe l'oeil* painting.[13] The *trompe l'oeil* gold mosaics are decorative, yet they also establish a visual link with Byzantine culture, in particular, Justinian's legal code, quotes from which appear in the ceiling. Byzantium flourished under Justinian's rule, and it is not merely a happy coincidence that the technical means for making mosaics were in fact perfected during his reign.

In 1902, Pierpont Morgan commissioned Charles McKim of the McKim, Mead, and White architectural firm to design a building to house his library, a superb and vast collection of incunabula, first editions, leather book bindings, and other objects garnered from all over the globe. Morgan certainly had catholic tastes when it came to art and artifacts, if not in religion. McKim retained H. Siddons Mowbray to design the interiors of the neoclassical structure, whose paintings on the dome of the rotunda are "virtually direct citations of Raphael's famous vault decorations for the *Stanza della Segnatura* in the Vatican."[14] It is safe to assume that Morgan was not burdened with an excess of humility, and that he appreciated comparison of his library and his status as antiquarian and collector of books and precious objects with the pope's. Certainly Mowbray himself could do worse than to play the role of Raphael! Indeed, it is likely that both Raphael and Mowbray used their own classical and archeological knowledge to conceive and design the rooms in ways that would embody the ideals (and, *sotto voce*, the humors) of their respective patrons. There was a veritable renaissance of *trompe l'oeil* painting in the nineteenth century in Germany and America, not so surprising in an era known for its neoclassicism. Mowbray's painting relates to his own era's renaissance of classical traditions, interpreted in their own way, similar to the way Raphael's painting is related to his. The significance of these comparisons emerges when one identifies the functions of these *trompe l'oeil* paintings as presentational, with their accompanying values, rather than as representational.

Four features of *trompe l'oeil* distinguish its function as presentational and not representational. First, *trompe l'oeil* has the function of presenting itself *visually* as something it isn't, so what it presents itself as must be something that can be seen. Thus, it is grounded in what can be seen. Wollheim grounds pictorial representation in what can be "seen in," in part because it is possible to pictorially represent things that *cannot* be seen, such as a general type of thing rather than just a particular thing. Second, *trompe l'oeil* paintings and pictorial representations have different functions and hence different criteria for success. The phenomenology of a visual experience of a successful *trompe l'oeil* painting is characterized in terms of what the painting mimics (what the painting presents itself as being). However the phenomenology of the visual experience of a successful pictorial representation is to be characterized, it certainly will not have illusion as a necessary condition.

Third, there is no temptation to require the perceiver of *trompe l'oeil* to be especially informed, experienced, or prompted so as to be able to experience it as intended.[15] People who know virtually nothing about art typically do perceive and enjoy the illusions of *trompe l'oeil* painting, and identifying its function as presentational accounts for this fact. In contrast, Wollheim's requirements for a spectator who wishes to have the appropriate experience of a pictorial representation can be quite extensive. Finally, related to the third point, there is no single perceptual experience, "the appropriate experience," that determines the content of a *trompe l'oeil* painting any more than there is a single perceptual experience that identifies the object in front of me as a piece of wood or as a chair. In general, the more numerous and less restricted the range of perceptions one has of a *trompe l'oeil* painting where it does "fool the eye," the better the *trompe l'oeil* painting.[16]

These four differences between pictorial representations and *trompe l'oeil* painting help explain why one should not take the latter too seriously. Plato did, though he had a broader agenda: to show the inadequacy of perception as a source of knowledge. He also wrote about painting from within a tradition that seemed to hold that the ability of painters was to be measured largely, if not exclusively, in terms of how deceptive their paintings could be. Deception, though a possible and at times actual goal, is tangential to the fact about human psychology that is central to *trompe l'oeil* painting: *what one knows to be true cannot always be made to penetrate the phenomenology of one's visual experience.* At least some human processing of visual stimuli is relatively "modular" or "encapsulated," that is, not penetrable by "higher order" cognitive states such as beliefs or expectations about what one is seeing. For example, one may know that the lines in a Mueller-Lyer illusion are the same length, even though one cannot help but experience one as shorter than the other. *Trompe l'oeil*, trading on and grounded in this psychological fact, produces engaging and amusing visual effects, visual puzzles and paradoxes, and a concomitant enjoyment in and amazement at a painter's skill and virtuosity.

II. Dual Purpose *Trompe L'oeil*

The four differences between *trompe l'oeil* painting and pictorial representation explained above, along with the cognitive impenetrability of certain types of visual experiences, motivate drawing a distinction between functions of *trompe l'oeil* painting and functions of pictorial representation. Nevertheless, it is possible for a painting to have both presentational and representational functions simply because a very high degree of success in the former is compatible with success in the latter. Success in *trompe l'oeil* painting is a matter of degree. If there is any tiny little thing within the painting itself that gives away that it is a painting and not what it presents itself as being, the painting will also be able to support a visual experience with a configurational aspect, the sort Wollheim requires for a pictorial representation. It is not a problem – any more than it is a problem with many, many other objects that have multiple uses – that one cannot have both sorts of experiences at the same time.

It has been pointed out *ad nauseam* that a perfect *trompe l'oeil* painting – one that is completely undetectable as such – is virtually impossible. Even if true, this fact does not place a limitation on *trompe l'oeil*; quite the contrary, it provides an opportunity for artists to use the ontological wobble set up by a painting's dual functions to play with ideas about appearance and reality, percepts and concepts, spirituality and physicality, paradoxes of self-reference, visual puns, and the relation of the work in question to other works of art and the history of art. Though we tend to associate artists' self-consciousness about the nature of what they do as artists with the modernist tradition in the arts, the fact is that painters have unquestionably played with such ideas at least since the Italian Renaissance and very likely back to ancient Rome.[17] The following examples illustrate some of the possibilities.

Raphaelle Peale's painting *Venus Rising from the Sea* combines a highly successful *trompe l'oeil* with a pictorial representation of what the *trompe l'oeil* mimics.[18] A napkin appears to be pinned to a ribbon swagged across the top of the painting, covering all but a rather impressionistic depiction of a woman's long hair and raised arm at the top and a foot at the bottom. The napkin, pins, and ribbon are all *trompe l'oeil*. A friend, with whom I was visiting the museum one afternoon, and who would be the first to admit that she knows nothing about art, gazed briefly at the painting and then turned to move on. Since skillfully produced *trompe l'oeil* effects tend to delight just about everyone, I was puzzled by her lack of a reaction and said something vaguely about how extraordinary the painting is. She responded, "Well, I guess they've had some complaints."

Aha.

As Wollheim says, sometimes a simple suggestion to look again is all a spectator needs to be "suitably prompted," and in taking another look she realized she had been fooled. The painting all of a sudden looked different. She was amazed, amused, and she marveled at the painter's skill. It is hard for me to believe that Peale would not have welcomed both responses to his painting, each fulfilling a particular function he intended it to have: as a *trompe l'oeil* presentation of a napkin pinned up to cover the painting and as a pictorial representation of the same. A painting may support both experiences, but in less successful *trompe l'oeil* paintings it is difficult to recapture the innocence of the original *trompe l'oeil* experience once one has "seen in" what is pictorially represented. *Venus Rising from the Sea* is among the more successful easel paintings in this regard, since the illusion is easily recoverable. In fact, when displayed on an easel in a roped-off corner of the room, it cannot be seen closely enough or at a sufficiently acute angle to tell, on the basis of the phenomenology of the visual experience, whether the napkin is painted or real.

In *Painting as an Art*, Wollheim says that *trompe l'oeil* paintings are not pictorial representations because, as *trompe l'oeil* paintings, they do not invite attention to and inspection of the painting's surface.[19] Yet, paintings with dual functions may do so, and painters may quite intentionally draw the spectator's attention to the surface to show that *even then* they have the painting skills to successfully maintain an illusion. Raphaelle Peale took the dare, so to speak, by signing his name on the selvage of the napkin, wittily presenting himself as the painter of the napkin rather than as the painter of the entire painting.[20] Peale's signature is just one example of how features *internal to the painting*, even features spatially internal to the *trompe l'oeil* parts of a painting, may draw one's attention to it as a painting when the painting has both representational and presentational functions.

I am also convinced that one reason Peale's painting can provide an experience having a configurational component of the sort required for a pictorial representation is that the portion of the painting representing the napkin is static, and, even if one doesn't realize it, the lack of motion can have a psychological effect on the perceiver. It was wise for Peale to choose a type of napkin that is relatively thick and heavy, so that its immobility is less of an issue than if it were, for example, a fine, delicate linen handkerchief, which would be more likely to move slightly with the breezes created by moving spectators. In this case, the immobility of the painting would have weakened its effectiveness as *trompe l'oeil*. Temporal features are sometimes an important limitation of a *trompe l'oeil* experience, since the painting does not change through time in ways some real things do.

It is also possible for something spatially *external to the painting* to "suitably prompt" a spectator to treat the painting as a pictorial representation. A frame, for example, invites attention to the surface by marking off a particular portion of one's visual field as an object for attention.[21] But not all paintings are framed or marked off as an object separate from the floor, wall or ceiling. The Italian baroque reveled in *trompe l'oeil* ceiling painting; one of the most spectacular examples of which is Andrea Pozzo's ceiling painting in the church of Sant' Ignazio of the *Entry of St. Ignatius into Paradise*, though no one will ever be deceived as one can be with the Peale. To experience the illusion one must stand at a particular point marked on the floor; under ordinary conditions one will approach the painting from angles that reveal its status as painted. Temporal factors are at work here as well. Unless one believes that a miracle occurs as one looks up and that time stands still in a freeze-frame of the exact moment St. Ignatius enters Paradise, the perceived immobility contributes to the configurational component of an experience of it.[22]

Years ago, so the story goes, a visitor to the Nelson-Atkins museum ran to one of the guards gasping that someone had splattered water on the marvelous *trompe l'oeil* still-life of flowers and insects by Jan van Huysum.[23] What the visitor saw, of course, is paint that was applied to look like water droplets. The entire painting may be seen as both presentational and representational, and those small portions of the painting serve both as presentation and representation in a special way. To see that area of paint as *trompe l'oeil* one will see it as a droplet of water resting on the surface of the painting. Conversely, to have the defining experience of that area of paint as a pictorial representation of a drop of water one will see it as a representation of a-drop-of-water-resting-on-a-leaf. Thus, not only paintings but *portions* of paintings may function representationally and presentationally.

Painters have exploited the distinction between the function of *trompe l'oeil* painting and the functions of pictorial representation to raise questions about appearance and reality, truth and deception, the durable and the ephemeral. They have produced visual puns, paradoxes of self-reference and puzzles about the nature and value of painting by strategic uses of *trompe l'oeil*, long before Picasso and Braque played with ideas about representation and reality in attaching bits of paper, among other things, to their paintings. We are familiar with twentieth-century paintings (as well as photographs, sculpture, and performances) that assiduously deny the importance of the hand of the artist, and deny along with it artistic values of self-expression, individual genius, and virtuoso technique. Others reassert the value of skill and craft: Zeke Berman's photographs of carefully constructed spaces which are perspectivally odd; Duane Hanson's sculptures that appear to be real people, parts of which are real clothing; and even David Parson's "signature" dance, where utter darkness is punctuated by a sequence of precisely timed lights which reveal the dancer positioned in mid-air so that he never appears to touch the ground. Such questioning is often taken to be a characteristic of modernism, but one does not have to wait until the twentieth century to find painters being reflective about their skills in a way that affects what and how they paint. *Trompe l'oeil*, doubled up with pictorial representation, both asserts and denies the powers of the painter, powers revealed in the different sorts of visual responses appropriate to each. In a very different context, Immanuel Kant proposed that the experience of the sublime is both painful and pleasurable. Through the strategic use of *trompe l'oeil* along with pictorial representation, spectators can be led both to applaud and question the nature of art and skills of the artist, as well as our own powers of perception and capacities for knowledge.

NOTES

This paper is reprinted here from the *Journal of Aesthetics and Art Criticism*, 56: 234–40, by the kind permission of the editor.

1. Richard Wollheim, in this volume, 14.
2. Ibid., 14.
3. Ibid., 19, 26–7.
4. There is more slippage than there ought to be in the way "painting," "picture," and "pictorial representation" are used. I adopt the following practice in this paper. To my ear, "picture," as in "This is a picture of . . . ," more naturally refers to the entire painting rather than to a portion of it. "Pictorial representation" may also describe the painting as a whole, yet items in the painting, such as flowers, insects, people, and so on, may be pictorially represented. A painting identified overall as a picture can have a variety of functions. It may contain painted portions whose functions are presentational or both presentational and representational. A *trompe l'oeil* painting is identified as such when its function is presentational.
5. Wollheim, this volume, *38*. I share the general dismay of so-called intentionalists that "intention" has come to be used to characterize this position. Fortunately, for the purposes of this paper, intentions in a rather straightforward sense are involved, that is, intentions with respect to how the painting is supposed to function.
6. Curiously, "recognition" does not capture the character of the experience for *trompe l'oeil* painting either. In ordinary usage, "recognizes" is veridical, which the *trompe l'oeil* experience is not. The recognitional aspect of the appropriate experience of a pictorial representation, however, *is* veridical since it will correctly register what the painting represents.
7. Turner, ed. *The Dictionary of Art*, 134.
8. A large number of artists, critics, and theorists make this distinction. I offer here a quote from Thomas Moran, painter of the American sublime, who was accused of painting panoramas that did not actually exist: "The literal truth counts for nothing; it is within the grasp of any one that has had an ordinary art education. The mere restatement of an external scene is never a work of art, is never a picture" (quoted by Watts, Moving Mountains, Sec. H, 6.)
9. Mantegna used single point perspective, though other perspective systems can do the trick.
10. See Stokstad, *Art History*, 668, for a colour plate of the entire ceiling.
  Interestingly, the *trompe l'oeil* gold mosaics are not painted in the strictest sense. They are produced by applying gold leaf, the same method used to create the gold backgrounds in Byzantine icons and early Renaissance altarpieces. The gold leaf is then incised to create the mosaic effect. This method of covering a surface is close enough to painting (and much closer than some other methods of

making pictures, such as photography) to be treated as painting. Andre Grabar's monumental book on Justinian goes so far as to discuss *actual* mosaics under the heading of painting! See Grabar, *The Golden Age of Justinian*, chapter two, "Painting."

11. It deserves emphasis that the choice of medium, painting or mosaics, does not determine one's visual goals or purposes. Each medium comes with its own constraints on and opportunities for achieving various goals. Mosaics can be and have been used for illusionistic purposes.

12. It is possible to pictorially represent gold mosaics; see, for example, Giovanni Bellini's pictorial representation of a mosaic apse ceiling in his altarpiece for San Zaccaria, Venice.

13. Pictures of the ceiling reveal the red bole that was used under gold leaf in order to affix it, a dead giveaway that these are not real mosaics, and sufficient to raise some question about whether these are *trompe l'oeil* mosaics or whether they are actually pictorial representations of mosaics. I side with the former, mainly because there is nothing in their visual context, as there is with Bellini's painting, that indicate they are representational. It would be useful to know whether the red bole was exposed with the initial incising and whether it was visible to those in the room.

14. Guide to the Period Rooms, published by the Pierpont Morgan Library, no date. Barbara Savedoff alerted me to the possibility that the ceiling decoration was not real mosaics but *trompe l'oeil*. Rebecca Gantwerk, Public Programs Coordinator, Pierpont Morgan Library, confirmed that the ceiling was *trompe l'oeil*, and explained that Raphael's ceiling is the source for the painting.

15. There are exceptions. Leonard Pardon, a decorative painter whose commissions have included work in Buckingham Palace, painted a different marble faux finish on each of twelve nine-by-five-foot panels for the sultan of Brunei. One would have to know more about the variety of marbles in the world than the average person to perceive and recognize the success of Pardon's work. See *Architectural Digest*, Sept. 1997, 249.

16. Andrea Pozzo's ceiling painting of the *Entry of St. Ignatius into Paradise* in the church of Sant' Ignazio, Rome, is one exception.

17. See, for example, White, *The Birth and Rebirth of Pictorial Space*.

18. The painting is owned by the Nelson-Atkins Museum of Art in Kansas City, Missouri. The museum added "A Deception" to the title, though it appears that Peale did not himself title his painting in this way. If he had, his intention could hardly have been deception! See Goheen, ed. *The Collections of the Nelson-Atkins Museum of Art*, 115.

19. PA, 62.

20. Painters sometimes tease the spectator with little clues or "in jokes" from the artworld, which make its interpretation more complicated. For example, the non-trompe l'oeil parts of the painting are thought to be taken from a painting by James Barry, *Venus Rising from the Sea*. Are these areas also *trompe l'oeil* painting, that is, of Barry's painting? Suppose that Peale picked this painting because it is sufficiently obscure that spectators, even highly educated ones, would be highly unlikely to know of the visual similarity. If his copying is considered *trompe l'oeil* painting, one would have to have special knowledge to experience Peale's painting as *trompe l'oeil*. To answer these questions, one needs to consider if and when copies, replicas, or forgeries of paintings are *trompe l'oeil* paintings, issues that extend beyond, way beyond, the scope of this paper.

21. Some frames are part of the work (whose identity, then must not be described *simply* as a painting). In other cases, the frame may act as an external prompter, reinforcing the idea that the fundamental identity of *trompe l'oeil* is illusion and not deception. A similar situation exists with respect to whether varnish is part of the painting. One can make a very good case that it is part of some paintings, or at least that the artist would have expected it to be part of the presentation of the painting. Smooth, glossy varnish on some still lives, for example, contributes to the configurational aspect of the experience.

22. Wollheim's criteria for the visual experience that defines what a painting represents, as I understand them, do not allow for temporal qualities to play a role in that experience (presumably adding to the configurational component) as I suggest they do in this example, in the Peale painting discussed earlier, and in still life paintings with a *vanitas* theme discussed briefly below. One might want to consider how a temporal component might be added to Wollheim's account.

23. See Goheen, 66, for an image of the van Huysum.

Chapter 15
The Case for the Internal Spectator: Aesthetics or Art History?

CAROLINE VAN ECK

Among recent aesthetic theories on the visual arts, *Painting as an Art* stands out not only because of its conceptual richness and sophistication, but also because it is built on the double ability to look very well at paintings and to put into words what is seen. It not only forces the reader to think about painting, it also offers numerous ways of looking at pictures. One of the most interesting among these is Wollheim's case for the internal spectator. This is both an illustration of his sophisticated ability to look and to present a theory based on that capacity, and a complex issue, which raises a number of questions about what can be seen in pictures and the ways it is transformed into a theory, the character of Wollheim's argumentation, and the relation between the concept of the internal spectator and art-historical notions such as that of the implied spectator.

1. Wollheim's Case for an Internal Spectator

Wollheim's introduction of the distinction between the internal and the external spectator is entirely in line with the aim of *Painting as an Art*, which is to study "the conversion of the materials of painting into a medium, and the ways in which this medium could be so manipulated as to give rise to meaning" (PA 7). His strategy in arguing for the existence of an internal spectator as a means of privileged access to the meaning of a limited category of paintings may be described as follows. To begin with, Wollheim briefly describes the phenomenon under discussion, viz., that some paintings possess a representational content that is in excess of what is represented (PA 101). He then clarifies this phenomenon with the help of a psychological analogy: Every visual experience is of "something; but the subject having the experience, although an integral part of the experience, is not perceived." After some refinements drawn from this analogy, he reformulates his thesis: some paintings contain an internal, unrepresented, spectator in the picture, who in the strongest case must be able to see everything that the painting represents, in the way the painting represents it. In the second stage of the argument, Wollheim introduces a new analogy, which will prove to be something more than an analogy: the distinction between central and a-central imagining. This is an elucidation of the implications of the meanings of the concepts he is using for what he is saying, resulting in the formulation of a new analogy, this time between pictures that contain an unrepresented spectator and the mental act of centrally imagining. In the act of centrally imagining, a protagonist is selected (from whose viewpoint the imagined events are seen), and endowed with a repertoire. This analogy is then used to understand what is going on in paintings with an excess of representional content: The painter who endows his work with an internal spectator may be thought of as working in the same two stages, and the internal spectator must be assigned a repertoire so that he can fulfil his function, which is to allow the external spectator distinctive access to the content of the picture. That is, centrally imagining is not just an analogy used to understand paintings with an excess of representational content, but is partly constitutive of that excess, because these paintings contain an internal spectator whose role is similar to that of the protagonist in an act of centrally imagining. In the fourth stage of the argument, the nature and function of the internal spectator are illustrated by discussing two groups of paintings: Caspar David Friedrich's landscapes and Manet's paintings with one or more figures. Wollheim starts with showing how one may become aware of the difference in representational content by comparing the pictorial uses and effects of the high viewpoints (and the aesthetic privileging based on it) chosen in landscapes by Philips de Coninck and Caspar David Friedrich. He then argues that Friedrich chose to create a hiatus between what is seen and where it is seen from in order to make the physical viewpoint correspond with the spiritual viewpoint of the pietist nature-artist, who here acts as the internal spectator.

In the case of the Manet paintings, pictorial phenomena are also described and analyzed in psychological terms. Through his use of frontality, the averting of the eyes of the persons depicted and his handling of the relation between the figure and the surrounding space, Manet almost forces the external spectator to assume and identify with an internal spectator who in vain tries to attract the attention of the figures portrayed. Here Wollheim stresses the importance of the pictorial as the basis for the creation of meaning by means of an internal spectator: "The only way in which an artist can endow an internal spectator with . . . a repertoire is through the way in which the artist depicts whatever it is that this spectator confronts us with. What the internal spectator sees or thinks or feels must be reconstructed from how the represented figure is represented" (PA 164).

2. What Can Be Seen in The Picture and the Case for the Internal Spectator

This very perceptive and subtle analysis raises a number of questions, both about the conceptual economy of Wollheim's account of the internal spectator and about the way in which features of particular paintings are perceived and conceptualized. In particular, questions and doubts are raised when one tries to apply Wollheim's concept of the internal spectator to categories of paintings he does not consider, such as those based on the use of linear perspective; or to clarify the relation of his internal spectator to an analysis of the role of the spectator that at least at first sight seems to be very close to Wollheim's internal spectator, viz., the concept of the implied spectator, which was explored by the art historian John Shearman in another series of Bollingen Lectures, held a few years after Wollheim's.[1]

Whereas Wollheim's introduction of the internal spectator is based on an experience of excess of meaning, Shearman's analysis of the implied spectator is based on one of incompleteness. In Shearman's interpretations of Renaissance works of art, what is represented as happening involves the imaginative participation of the spectator. In Verrocchio's *Christ and St. Thomas* in Or San Michele, Christ is shown as having stepped through a closed door (the niche), St. Thomas as approaching Him from "our" actual, Florentine space from the group of Apostles, to whom we, the actual spectators, belong by implication (*ill. 1*). That is, to say that the spectator in the street finds himself in the same position as the Apostles, is to say that the subject of Verrocchio's group is completed only by the imaginative presence of the spectator in the narrative. The relationship between work of art and spectator is transitive, in the sense of "taking a direct object to complete the sense, passing over to or affecting something else, operating beyond itself."[2] By looking at what is going on in these works of art, and studying their composition, the spectator realizes that their composition is based on the acknowledgement of the presence of a spectator. The spectator is drawn imaginatively into the work of art, forced to take part in imagination in the situation represented. On the one hand, the meaning or impact of the work of art is thus completed; on the other, the spectator succeeds in understanding the work of art by imagining him- or herself to be a participant in the situation represented.

In Leonardo's painting of the *Angel of the Annunciation*, the spectator shares the salutation of the angel with one unique, but absent person because in this version we do not look at the angel and Mary in profile; instead, the Angel frontally addresses the spectator who is forced by the handling of pictorial space and the gesture and look of the Angel to identify with Mary imaginatively. While standing in front of the painting and trying to follow what is happening, we become the Virgin for a moment – and realize the differences that separate us poor sinners from her.

Both the Verrocchio and the Leonardo are instances of works of art whose relation with the spectator is fully transitive: Their subject is completed by and in the spectator. A further development in this transitive mode can be

Illustration 1. Verrocchio, *Christ and St. Thomas*. Or San Michele, Florence.

found in works of art which assume the fiction of a continuum between the painted space and the real, that is, in this case, the liminal space (i.e., that zone of the real space which lies at the threshold of the painted space, but is not part of the painted space). Giovanni Bellini's San Giobbe Madonna, now taken from its original architectonical frame, in the Accademia in Venice (*ill. 2*) is an instance of this further development. Here, the group of saints and the spectator are mutually accessible to each other. The use of linear perspective serves to situate the picture and the spectator into one spatial and psychological continuum, as the way the feet of the saints seem to protrude into "our" space, and the drastic foreshortening of the tiled floor show. Yet, despite this mutual accessibility, there is very little contact between the figures depicted and the spectator. Saint Francis is the only figure to address the viewer both by look and gesture; the other figures all look away at something the spectator does not see, and their attention seems to be engaged by some hidden topic.

Now we might argue that this is a case where it is apt to assume an internal spectator. Something is going on here over and above the situation represented, but is given with the representation. This feeling is based on the averted looks of the Madonna, the musicians and the Saints, with the exception of Saint Francis. Given the location of the painting, the movement and gesture of the Madonna and the careful blurring of the barrier between real and pictorial space, it does indeed seem logical to centrally imagine this scene from the viewpoint of a protagonist, and to give him the identity of a visiting pelgrim who is accepted into the sacred company. But Wollheim would probably deny that this is a case of a spectator in the picture, because of the illusion of spatial continuity conveyed by the use of linear perspective. There is no gap between pictorial and real space, and therefore no need to assume an internal spectator besides the external spectator. However, when one stands in front of this altarpiece and becomes aware of the relation between real or pictorial space that is difficult to convey in a reproduction, the composition of the figures and the handling of space suggest a representational content in excess of what is represented.

Conversely, one might wonder whether Caspar David Friedrich's *The Cross in the Mountains* is not rather a case of an implied spectator, although it is cited by Wollheim as an instance of the hiatus, typical for Friedrich, between what is seen and where it is seen from, and is on that basis included in his list of examples of paintings with internal spectators (*ill. 3*). From the lack of foreshortening in the way Christ and the mountain top are represented one has to conclude that the scene depicted could only be visible from a point of view in mid-air. But is this a case of implying, that is staging, the spectator in mid-air by the lack of foreshortening, or of ignoring the spectator in the "real world?" Does it suggest all sorts of meanings through the gap between

Illustration 2. Giovanni Bellini's *San Giobbe Altarpiece*.

Illustration 3. Caspar David Friedrich *The Cross in the Mountains*, 1808
(Tetschen Altarpiece, Oil on canvas.) (With the permission of Gemäldegal-
lerie Neue Meister, Staatliche Kunstsammlungen Dresden.)

the viewpoint from which the picture was made and the viewpoint of the external spectator? Is this the opposite of the implicit acknowledgement of the position of the external spectator as demonstrated in the foreshortening of the tiled floor in the San Giobbe altarpiece, which is also suggestive, but in the opposite way, viz., by bridging the gap between the painter's viewpoint and that of the spectator, of meanings over and above the representational content of the painting?

To answer these questions, we must return to Wollheim's argument for the internal spectator and examine in what ways it is connected with actual paintings and what can be seen in them. Wollheim's case for the spectator in the picture contains two unknown quantities: the phenomenon that some paintings have a representational content in excess of what they represent, which is a feature of the paintings that Wollheim wants to give an account of, and the concept of the internal spectator, presented by him as the explanation of this feature. Both give rise to a number of questions. To begin with, what precisely is the nature of the feature of some paintings that they have a representational content in excess of what they represent? As Wollheim explains, there is something in these paintings that cannot be seen, so the painting does not represent that thing; but it is nevertheless given to us along with what the painting represents, and therefore it is part of the representational content of the painting. He then draws an analogy with the mental process of centrally imagining in order to clarify the distinction between what a painting represents and its representational content.

Now, instead of following Wollheim's psychological elucidation of excess of representational content, I propose to pause for a moment to take a closer look at the paintings Wollheim cites as instances of this phenomenon. What is the matter with these pictures that he describes as excess of representational content? The first group of paintings, landscapes by Caspar David Friedrich, have in common a very high viewpoint, and, correspondingly, a lack of connection between the viewpoint from which the landscape is represented, and that of the external spectator. This gives the impression of the landscape continuing under the feet of the external viewer and consequently causes a feeling of spatial disorientation by which one is at the same time drawn into the world of the painting and rejected from it because one does not have firm ground under the feet, so to speak; or, as in the case of the Tetschen altarpiece, the external viewer is made to reflect on what the selection by the painter of the very high viewpoint conveys about this cross and the viewer's relation to it. Whose viewpoint is represented, and what does it imply about the importance of this cross that this viewpoint is chosen? One might explain these pictorial features in terms of an internal spectator, but it is not necessary to do so: we can also give an account of what distinguishes these paintings in terms of handling of pictorial space and the relation between internal and

external viewpoint. In other words, it all depends on how we define representational content: as consisting exclusively of the event, scene or plot depicted,
or as including not only the what of the representation, but also the pictorial
means by which it is represented: handling of space, composition of the
figures, manipulation of the viewpoint, and so on.[3] Since these are part of the
how, instead of the what of representational content, they cannot be seen in
the painting in the same way as we see a cross or the sea, ships, or trees in it;
but when we consider the way such objects or situations are conveyed, we
look at the pictorial means of representations, which are just as well part of
the painting, rather than given along with what the painting represents, as
Wollheim puts it. In other words, the hypothesis of an internal spectator is
one way of putting into words what distinguishes Friedrich landscape paintings from his Dutch predecessors, but not necessarily the only one.[4]

The second group of instances of an internal spectator discussed by Wollheim consists of Manet's single-figure paintings. They all have in common
that the persons depicted do not look, or only absent-mindedly, at the external
spectator; and some of them exhibit some sort of ambiguity in the handling
of space: in *Madame V. in the Costume of an Espada* for instance, the relation
between foreground and background is ambiguous. Wollheim here develops
his case for the presence of an internal spectator even more in psychological
and psycho-analytical terms than in the case of the Friedrichs. It is a marvellous account, which gives new drama and importance to paintings that often
are so easily dismissed as merely impressionist accounts of Parisian life; but
again, the question is, what precisely is the matter with these paintings? And
is the assumption of an internal spectator the only way of accounting for it?
In all these paintings the figures do not look, or not with full attention, at the
external spectator; they seem to be preoccupied (*Le Repos* and *Emile Zola*),
to have something in mind (*Woman with a Parrot*), to be struck by a sudden
and arresting thought (*The Street Singer*), or to falter in what they are doing
(*The Tragic Actor*). That is, they are given facial expression and gestures that
do not make their minds or characters accessible to the external viewer, but
instead stress the gap between them. They are very present, but at the same
time inaccessible. Manet breaks with the traditional aim of portrait painting,
which is to reveal the character of the sitter by means of a more or less
codified handling of gesture, dress, looks, and selection of body posture.[5] The
external spectator is both drawn to these paintings by the wonderful handling
of texture, and closed out by the absent air of the sitters. This almost inevitably puts the external spectator in the role of somebody trying to attract the
attention of the sitter, and that is the role Wollheim gives to the internal
spectator in these paintings. But again, if we widen the concept of representational content to include the pictorial means by which these sitters are
represented, it becomes unnecessary to assume the presence of an internal

spectator. We might assume some unrepresented object of attention in the pictorial space instead, or notice the spatial ambiguities and reflect on the ways these stage our ways of looking at these pictures. As in the Friedrich paintings, pictorial space and viewpoints are manipulated in such a way that they first attract and then disorient the external viewer's attention. Access to what is represented is first promised, and then denied. Both processes are suggested by pictorial means, and there is no absolute need to build an interpretation in psychological terms in the way Wollheim does, however fascinating and illuminating that may be.

In both groups of paintings, Wollheim's analysis tends to concentrate on the representation of content seen in terms of situations, events or personal interaction between the figures depicted. This last point also may be put differently, namely in terms of how the internal spectator is endowed with an identity and a repertoire. Wollheim shows the logical necessity of these endowments within the conceptual framework of his case for the internal spectator. But he is much less clear about the way in which identification and endowment is connected with what is actually to be seen in a painting. In the case of the Friedrich paintings, the interpretation begins with a description of the hiatus between what is seen and where it is seen from and the effect on the spectator of the landscape running under the point of view from which it is represented. It then moves on to the question why Friedrich did all this, and the proposed answer that he did it because it fitted in with his vision of the nature-artist that Friedrich wished to capture; and to do so, Friedrich introduced the nature artist into the painting as viewer or internal spectator (PA 136). In the next stage of his argument, Wollheim asks how Friedrich did this; what would the repertoire of the internal spectator be, and how would Friedrich indicate it? Wollheim answers the question about the nature of the repertoire by quoting a remark of Friedrich about the need for the painter to be able to paint not only what he sees outside him, but also what he sees within him. The question about the way Friedrich indicated the repertoire of the internal spectator is answered by arguing that Friedrich aims at two things in populating his landscapes with rivers, trees, the sky, and so on: "He aims at showing us what the internal spectator sees, but he also aims at showing us the expressive manner in which the internal spectator sees what is before him" (PA 139).

From the way of representing these objects, we are able to reconstruct, with the help of any background information we may need, that repertoire. But Wollheim does not prove that such an internal spectator is indeed present, or that there is a necessary ground for endowing that spectator with such or such a repertoire; the whole argument rests on Wollheim's hypothesis that Friedrich wished to capture the vision of the nature-artist, which is subsequently taken for granted (PA 136 and 139). We are presented not with an argument *that* there is indeed an internal spectator in Friedrich's paintings, but with an argument that such an assumption would fit in with what Wollheim takes to be the artist's intentions.

Similarly, in the discussion of the Manet single-figure paintings, Wollheim moves from the proposition that they share a psychological subject-matter (PA 141) to the statement that this type of painting corresponds to "the most fundamental conscious aim of Manet's work" (PA 142). He situates this group within the context of Manet's other works and that of fellow painters such as Degas in order to grasp more clearly what distinguishes them. Next, he identifies a specific problem Manet had in painting them, according to Wollheim, of how to convey in a single-figure painting the sense of psychological disconnectedness that in his group of pictures he was able to convey by the way in which he represented the relations between the figures peopling these scenes. According to Wollheim, Manet's solution was not strictly perceptual, but needs the involvement of the spectator as well by making him imagine an internal spectator (PA 160). In the next sentence Wollheim's suggestion has become "Manet's ruse." The evidence Wollheim provides for this proposal is a reversal of the reasoning followed in the case of Friedrich: Here it is not the chosen point of view that serves as evidence for an internal spectator with a fixed point of view but rather the absence of such a point of view. The centralized or near-centralized composition Manet used suggests the possibility of a mobile, prowling internal spectator who in vain tries to attract the attention of the figure. Two other pictorial features, the frontality or nearfrontality and the treatment of the background, are also presented by Wollheim as circumstantial evidence for the presence of an internal spectator. In these cases, the handling of space draws the external spectator into the role of a prowling internal spectator.

In assigning an identity and repertoire to the internal spectator to these paintings, Wollheim again stresses that an artist can only endow the spectator in the picture with a repertoire by means of the way in which he has depicted whatever it is (PA 166). Arguing for the functional identity of two varieties of background, one highly cluttered (as in the *Street Singer*), and one a monochrome ground which lacks all differentiation between flat and upright, Wollheim then suggests, on the force of the observation that such an equation of the undifferentiated and the cluttered is characteristic of the way figures appear to us in our dreams, a connection between the internal spectator and the nocturnal dreamer. However, in this very complex and wide-ranging account of the role of the fore- and background in Manet's single-figure paintings, Wollheim does not explicitly propose an identity or repertoire for the spectator in these paintings. Instead, he discusses the movement between the lure into the painting and the recall to twofoldness, or the dialectic between imagination and perception.

To resume, we could say that in both groups of examples the argument moves away from a demonstration that these paintings possess an internal spectator to a consideration of the manner in which such an internal spectator would function, how the painter might have intended to endow the painting with it, and the problems it is supposed to solve according to Wollheim. In other words, the discussion has shifted from an argument that x is the case to an exploration of the how and why of x, and the conditions of the possibility of x. Thus, in the case of the Friedrich landscapes, Wollheim does not present his arguments for assuming such an internal spectator, or more in general for interpreting what is a spatial phenomenon, based on an ambiguous handling of the viewpoint, but investigates how Caspar David Friedrich could have indicated the assumed internal spectator.

3. Aesthetics or Art History?

Now the question is, of course, why Wollheim does this. It is my hypothesis that this shift becomes understandable when we consider the case for the internal spectator not as an analysis of a feature of a particular group of paintings, but as a way of analysing the way in which their meaning arises as a psychological process. This has everything to do with the nature of the task Wollheim has set himself in *Painting as an Art*: to give a psychological account of pictorial meaning, which "roots meaning in some mental condition of the artist which, when it finds outlet in the activity of painting, will induce in the mind of the spectator a related, an appropriately related, mental condition" (PA 357).

That is, Wollheim's project is not art history, but rather the objective study of art: an account informed by the experience of paintings, psychology and philosophy of the way in which the materials of painting are transformed into a medium, and the way in which this medium could be so manipulated as to give rise to meaning (PA 7). His interest lies not with the traditional pursuits of art history, such as iconography, stylistic analysis or the study of works of art considered as material culture, because for him traditional art history is hopelessly vitiated by its positivist approach to the past, with its "overestimation of fact, rejection of cause and failure to grasp the centrality of explanation" (PA 9).

In order to argue this I will return to John Shearman's discussion of what looks at first sight a rather similar topic, that of the implied spectator. As we have seen, Shearman is concerned with Renaissance works of art whose subject is completed only by the imaginative presence of the spectator in the narrative. On the one hand, the meaning or impact of the work of art is thus completed; on the other, the spectator comes to understand the work of art by imagining him- or herself to be a participant in the situation represented.

Their composition acknowledges the presence of an implied spectator, and can only be understood if we take into account the actively engaged attention of such a spectator. In this last respect, Shearman's implied spectator appears to be similar to Wollheim's internal spectator.

In investigating the relation between works of art and their spectators, Shearman roughly follows the same procedure in each interpretation: First he describes the work of art in question, focussing on the way in which its composition, handling of the figures, perspective or actual location in space can be described as being based on the acknowledgement of an actively looking spectator; next, he provides historical evidence (varying from textual sources such as Franciscan manuals on devotional practice to historical material about the original location and context of the work of art); finally he sometimes offers some conceptual elucidation of his way of interpreting, mainly using linguistic or grammatical analogies such as the concepts of "neo-Plinian reading" (following through with the eyes what is represented as going on), of transitivity, or that of "predicating the composition" upon the presence of the spectator. But he gives very little attention to this last aspect of his project; as one reviewer remarked, the mode is "autobiographical" rather than theoretical.[6]

Shearman does not distinguish between internal and external spectators. In fully transitive paintings, the implied spectator becomes a participant of the situation or events depicted, in most cases only in spatial or compositional terms (manifest for instance by the handling of foreshortening, as in the *San Giobbe Altarpiece*), but sometimes as well in terms of plot (as in Leonardo's *Angel of the Annunciation*).

Yet, it is interesting to see what happens if we apply the theory of the one to understand one of the more intriguing cases of the other. I have in mind Friedrich's *Tetschen Altarpiece*, discussed by Wollheim to illustrate the role of the internal spectator, and Bellini's *San Giobbe Altarpiece*, cited by Shearman as one of the fullest cases of transitive composition based on the acknowledgement of an implied spectator. Does it make sense to say that the internal spectator in the Friedrich is in fact an implied spectator, or that the implied spectator in the Bellini is in fact a spectator in the picture? As a close look at the examples discussed by Shearman shows, the implied spectator is in fact a compositional device, a pictorial strategy based on the manipulation of perspective, the staging of the way the figures in the painting are located and address the viewer. This is very evident in the *San Giobbe Altarpiece*, where the way in which the tiled floor is foreshortened, and the feet of the saints seem to protrude over the edge of the pictorial space alert the spectator to the strategies used by the painter in order to create the illusion that the viewers and the painted figures share the same space. In the *Tetschen Altarpiece*, the manipulation of viewpoint creates the opposite illusion: because of the gap between the painter's viewpoint and that of the external spectator, the latter feels excluded rather than acknowledged by pictorial means, and as we have seen, this manipulation of the sense of spatial connection between the viewer and the scene depicted makes the viewer think about its meaning. This is a case not of an implied, but of an excluded spectator, and as such serves as the vehicle for a realization of meaning in excess of the representational content.

By contrast, the *San Giobbe Altarpiece* seems to come very close to the cases of an internal spectator discussed by Wollheim. Something is going on here over and above the situation represented, but is given with the representation. This feeling is based on the averted looks of the Madonna, the musicians and the Saints, with the exception of Saint Francis. Given the location of the painting, the movement and gesture of the Madonna and the careful blurring of the barrier between real and pictorial space, it does indeed seem logical to centrally imagine this scene from the viewpoint of a protagonist, and to give him the identity of a visiting pelgrim who is accepted into the sacred company. Yet, there is a difference with the cases of an internal spectator Wollheim discusses, and that has to do with the accessibility of the situation represented in the *San Giobbe Altarpiece*. Precisely because Bellini has succeeded in creating the illusion that the barrier between real and pictorial has been lifted by means of linear perspective and a number of subtle pointers that the world of the painting protrudes into the world of the viewer, the spectator does not have to make the imaginative leap needed in the cases where there is an excess of representational content to gain access to what is being represented. The spectator does not have to identify imaginatively with the situation, but rather to ask a number of factual or historical questions about the original location of the painting in the church.

In other words, this brief comparison between the spectator in the painting and the implied spectator shows that the first is part of the psychological process of making sense of a picture, of trying to grasp its meaning, whereas the second is part of an art-historical analysis of certain compositional features of the painting itself. Thinking about the role of the implied spectator also makes one aware of what is going on and of the meaning of a painting, but in pictorial, not psychological terms. The use of an implied spectator is a pictorial strategy to make the viewer of the painting feel that the painting is addressed to him or her. It is a way of attracting and involving the viewer's attention;[7] whereas the use of an internal spectator is an imaginative act of the viewer in those cases where he or she feels that access to the meaning of the painting is initially denied through the suggestion, by pictorial means, of a gap, a hiatus, or an absence. It is not, or not exclusively, an exploration of varieties of pictorial composition, as Shearman's implied spectator is, but part of Wollheim's psychological account of the ways in which meaning is constituted. Wollheim's discussion of the internal spectator is not an exercise in art history, as Shearman's investigation of the implied spectator is, but a way of showing why paintings matter.

NOTES

1. Shearman, *Only Connect . . . : Art and the Spectator in the Italian Renaissance. The A. W. Mellon Lectures in the Fine Arts 1988*.
2. *Oxford English Dictionary*, quoted by Shearman, ibid., 33.
3. Wollheim's definition of the pictorial phenomenon that leads him to assume an internal spectator is rather focused on objects: "There is something that cannot be seen in the painting: so the painting does not represent that thing. But the thing is given to us along with what the painting represents: so it is part of the painting's representational content" (PA 102).
4. On this topic, see also Renée van de Vall in this volume, Chapter 13.
5. See Boehm, *Bildnis und Individuum: Über den Ursprung der Porträtmalerei in der italienische Renaissance*.
6. Gombrich, Review of: Only Connect. . . .
7. Hence Gombrich's (ibid.) suggestion that the rhetorical term "apostrophe" (addressing onself directly to the audience) would be a much better description of what Shearman has called transitivity.

Chapter 16
The Spectator in the Picture

ROBERT HOPKINS

1. Pictures are marked surfaces that convey a certain content, or, put another way, that represent something or other. When we appreciate pictures, we are aware of them both as marked surfaces and as representing certain things, and our appreciation reflects that dual awareness. Thus there are at least three sorts of reason we might give for appreciating a picture. We might cite the way the surface is marked, or the content the picture conveys, or the way the latter emerges from the former. Here I want to concentrate on the second sort of reason, valuing the picture for what it represents.

There is a superficial, but nagging, problem concerning the value of pictures *qua* representations. It stems from the fact that every picture fundamentally conveys the same sort of content. For every picture represents some object or objects, in a suitably broad sense of the term; the properties those objects enjoy; and states of affairs of which those objects form constituents. Furthermore, all these aspects of the represented world are represented from a certain perspective on them. I intend this last notion to be purely spatial – there is a point, spatially related to those points the picture depicts, from which the picture presents those other points and the items which occupy them. For convenience, I will say that all the features of pictorial content mentioned so far constitute a *scene*. Thus, my claim is that, fundamentally, pictures represent scenes.

Why should this make problematic our appreciating pictures for their content? The difficulty is not that it turns out that every picture represents the same thing, and that there can thus be no reason to value any one picture over any other. The differences between the various scenes different pictures represent provide ample room for preferences between them. Rather, the problem begins with the question whether pictures can represent anything other than scenes, anything in addition to the features of the world listed above. For if they cannot, one might wonder why we should bother looking at the pictures rather than devoting our visual attention to scenes themselves, either the very scenes the pictures represent, if they are available, or scenes suitably similar to those represented. It seems that at least in answering this question, our appeal to the pictures' having the content they do will be of limited use. We must either resort to mere considerations of convenience, as we can if it is not even the case that some suitably similar scene is to hand; or appeal to the other two kinds of reason for caring about pictorial art – the qualities of the marked surface, and the way those qualities give rise to the picture's content.

I do not say that this problem goes deep. But deep or not, it can be side-stepped if pictures are indeed free to convey contents other than the mere representation of scenes. Consider the situation if, in particular, they can represent scenes along with *reactions* to them, on the part of some implicit observer of the world depicted. These reactions might be of thought or of feeling. They must concern the scene, but might also involve broader currents of ideas or affective disposition. Were this possible, appeal to what a picture represents could readily explain the interest of the picture over the corre-sponding scene. When we confront scenes face-to-face, while we may react to them ourselves, we never confront a representation of some possible set of reactions. Thus, looking at pictures offers, as looking at the things depicted would not, the chance to explore how someone else might react, to be initiated into another sensibility.

Many have been tempted by something like the thought just articulated. Certainly art historians have sometimes appealed to related ideas. In this chapter, I want to consider the best developed account of the putative phe-nomenon. It is that offered by Richard Wollheim in Chapter 3 of *Painting as an Art*.[1] Wollheim thinks that some pictures contain an internal spectator, an implied viewer of the depicted scene, through whose eyes we are to see it. His account of quite what this involves is both detailed and illuminating of the aesthetic interest of the phenomenon. So, if right, it provides part of a solution to the problem of pictorial value outlined above. Only part, because Wollheim thinks that only a subset of aesthetically valuable pictures contain internal spectators. For those outside of that set, we would need to explain their value in other terms. This in no way diminishes the interest of Woll-heim's view, since the problem is unlikely to admit of a single solution of any kind, let alone one appealing to the sort of idea sketched above and which Wollheim's account makes precise. However, before I can expound Wollheim's view, I need to provide some background. More precisely, I need to say a little about the more basic forms of pictorial content, as Wollheim understands them.

2. According to Wollheim, there are two such forms of content. I will call them *depictive* and *expressive* content. Roughly, the former is a matter of what the picture depicts, the latter a matter of any emotions or moods it expresses. Each essentially involves a particular perceptual response on the part of viewers of the picture. For depictive content, the relevant response is "seeing-in." For expressive content, it is what Wollheim calls "expressive

perception." Both perceptual responses are distinguished by their phenomenologies. Seeing-in essentially involves both an awareness of the marks before one on the canvas, and an awareness of some absent object, the item depicted. Expressive perception involves one's visual experience being "permeated" by emotion, or some other affective state. Both these perceptual states can occur in response to something other than a picture. We can see things in damp patches on a wall, and expressively perceive low-lying marshland (seen in the flesh) in the light of some emotion or mood. Since there is in these cases no depictive or expressive content, such content requires more than simply that the appropriate perceptual response be elicited. What is further required is that the response be subject to some "standard of correctness." That is, something, usually the intention of the artist, dictates that is it *right* to respond to the picture with some particular response of the given type, and not another: right to see one thing, rather than another, in it; or to see the picture in the light of one emotion, and not another.[2]

A picture's depictive content is simply, to use the terminology of Section 1, a matter of the scene the picture represents. Since Wollheim thinks that paintings can also exhibit another kind of content, what I am calling expressive content, we might wonder whether the problem posed above is not already partly solved. If pictures need not merely depict scenes, but can also express certain emotions, then, even setting aside all but the *content* of pictures, encountering them offers satisfactions which looking at the corresponding scenes would not. However, this conclusion is too hasty. Since Wollheim accepts that expressive perception can occur not only before pictures, but when we confront objects in the flesh, it seems that nothing yet said guarantees a difference between encounters with pictures and encounters with the scenes they depict. Of course, objects encountered in the flesh don't have expressive *content*, for all that we may perceive them expressively. But since our response to expressive content is just expressive perception, it is not yet clear how this difference could provide a reason for valuing the painting that is not also one for valuing the object painted.

However that may be, Wollheim provides the materials for a quite distinct solution to the problem of Section 1. For, he thinks that, in addition to depictive and expressive content, pictures can exhibit a third kind. It is this proposal I want to consider.

3. In PA, Chapter 3, Wollheim makes the following claim, which I have broken into components for ease of discussion. Some pictures,

(1) represent[3] (have as part of their content) (PA 101)
(2) someone viewing the depicted scene
(3) more or less from the point from which it is depicted (PA 102, 183)

(4) with a repertoire of psychological states and dispositions to think, act and feel
 (a) at a minimum that repertoire involved in being an *embodied* viewer (PA 130), but perhaps
 (b) some more distinctive psychology
(5) who is distinct from the person in the gallery looking at the picture, (PA 183–5) but
(6) with whom that person imaginatively identifies, with the result
(7) that the viewer of the picture is left responding to the picture differently, in ways both perceptual and affective, and thus understanding the picture in a new way. (PA 129, 183)

How does Wollheim argue for this position? Naturally enough, he appeals to examples, offering insightful readings of particular paintings by supposing them to contain an internal spectator. But how more precisely does he do that? Which features of these paintings does he appeal to in seeking to render plausible his claims about them? It is here that the seventh and last aspect of his view, as I characterized it, rises to prominence. For therein, according to Wollheim, lies the point of a picture's containing an internal spectator. Number 7 above describes the function of the spectator in the picture, and the best way to argue that there are such spectators is to show them doing what they are supposed to do. Given the importance of number 7, it is worth making as clear as possible. Wollheim says that the "function of the spectator in the picture is that he allows the spectator of the picture a distinctive access to the content of the picture" (PA 129). But what is the content thereby accessed? Is it content of the two central kinds Wollheim has already described, depictive or expressive content, or is it something new? In proposing that there are internal spectators Wollheim precisely suggests that there is a third form of pictorial content, but access to that can hardly be what he has in mind. For the function of representing an internal spectator cannot be that it provides a new form of content for the viewer to grasp, on pain of trivializing talk of function altogether. The grasp on the picture which recognition of the internal spectator permits must thus be a grasp on *other* aspects of the picture's content. And it doesn't really matter what these are – depictive, expressive, or of other, not yet characterized, forms, provided that grasping the content in question requires imaginative identification with an internal spectator of the depicted scene. The role of the internal spectator is as a *route* to other content, and the justification thus provided for supposing there to be such spectators is not hampered, but helped, by supposing that content of many different forms is thereby made accessible.

However, if the internal spectator is itself to form part of the picture's content, then the route to other aspects of the picture's meaning which it provides cannot be one which the viewer takes merely on a whim. It might be that viewers respond to certain pictures by imagining in the ways listed above, but that will be of no more than psychological significance unless those responses are "licensed" (PA 129) by the intentions of the artist. This complicates the case that Wollheim must make, but not unmanageably. He merely needs to show that, if we do respond to his chosen paintings by imagining in the ways listed above, and thereby come to see the picture in a new and satisfying light, then it is likely that the artist intended it so to be seen, and intended that we take this route to seeing it that way.

To make his case, Wollheim discusses various paintings by Friedrich, Manet, and Hals. His treatment of these pictures is as subtle and interesting as the more theoretical claims they exemplify are provocative. But do the two sets of claims, the readings of the paintings and the theory that prompts them, interlock as tightly as Wollheim would want? Must we, if we are to make sense of these examples, accept the theoretical machinery on offer? Or can we accommodate the phenomena with rather less? These are the questions I want to examine. I consider two positions antagonistic to Wollheim's, to see how his examples put pressure on them, and at precisely which points.

4. I start with the position that gives least ground to Wollheim. According to this view, there is no need to suppose that any picture has a spectator in it, nor to appeal to any imaginative engagement on the part of the external spectator, in order fully to account for pictorial content. For, this view claims, depictive and expressive content, together with the standard modes of access to those contents, seeing-in and expressive perception, unaided by imaginative identification and the like, can accommodate all the salient phenomena. What grounds are there for rejecting this minimalist position?

At this point, of course, we must turn to examples. Let's consider Wollheim's chosen Manets (PA, Figures I and II). These, I think, are in one respect his strongest examples, but in another his weakest. Their strength lies in the fact that they obviously possess some feature which we need to work to accommodate. Their weakness is that it is not clear that we need internal spectators to do that work.

If I allow myself to simplify enormously Wollheim's rich and subtle discussion of these paintings (PA, Ch. 3, §§C–D), and if I try to frame the phenomenon he adduces in the most neutral possible terms, the result is this. Manet's single figure pictures, like his group portraits, show people who, although generally vital and engaged with life, are temporarily distracted from it, and from the contact with others that forms its core. They are preoccupied, momentarily beyond reach. Now, why might these pictures pose a problem for minimalism?

Suppose the minimalist were forced to deny that the momentary distractedness of Manet's figures could be part of the content of the paintings at all.

That denial would be sufficiently implausible to cast serious doubt on her view. We could force it on the minimalist if we could argue that momentary distractedness is not the sort of property which can be seen in a surface. For then the distractedness cannot be part of the paintings' depictive content, and since it is hardly plausible that it is part of their expressive content, minimalism could not place it in content at all. However, this approach is handicapped by the fact that, as Wollheim himself notes (PA 64–7), what can be seen in a surface is pretty much tied to what can be seen face-to-face, and the fact that it is highly debateable what this latter limitation amounts to. Wollheim himself, in criticizing Lessing, appeals against an unduly restrictive conception of the possible contents of vision (PA 65), and it is arguable that any conception broad enough for Wollheim would also allow that we can see the very features Manet attributed to his figures.

Happily, another, and better, reply is open to Wollheim. He need not say that the represented distractedness constitutes a sort of content beyond those minimalism recognizes, provided he can persuade us that the only route to that content lies along paths not open to the minimalist. That, after all, was the strategy which emerged from our discussion of the role of the internal spectator. And it will certainly bite against the minimalist, since her claim is not just that depictive and expressive content are the only kinds of pictorial content there are; but also that seeing-in and expressive perception are the only licensed means of recovery of a picture's contents. How might we pursue that strategy here?

In answering this question, let me, so as not to prejudge the theoretical dispute to follow, speak loosely for a while. To see the distractedness of the depicted characters, we must discover the difficulty of engaging with them. Moreover, and here is the crux, that discovery can only be made by attempting, and failing, to engage the figures *visually*. We come to see the momentary absence of the woman with parrot, or of Mademoiselle V. in her Espada costume, through, continuing to speak casually, seeking out her gaze and failing to find it. Moreover, in so failing we realize that this is no accident of how the character stands to us. To move around her, aligning our line of sight with hers, would no more guarantee the contact we seek. It would merely leave the glassy stare directed at us, rather than passing nearby.

Now, this talk is unacceptably casual, and it is a serious question, which will be our central concern in what follows, how best to articulate the points it might be making. But unless such talk is rejected as altogether meaningless, its appropriateness forces us to abandon minimalism. For the only clarification available to the minimalist is quite implausible. She must construe talk of unsuccessful attempts at visual engagement as meaning failure to *see* something or other in the marked surface. For since expressive perception is clearly not what the last paragraph confusedly describes, seeing-in must be its topic. And since seeing-in is a way of seeing the picture, it does not leave room for engagement, or unsuccessful attempts to engage, with *the figure* depicted. But this way of taking the above is quite inappropriate. The attempted visual engagement is not a matter of trying to see something in the canvas – seeing the figure therein is a prerequisite of trying to engage with her, not what one thereby seeks. Thus the minimalist can make no sense of the phenomenon here, and so much the worse for her.

5. We must, it seems, abandon minimalism. But must we therefore adopt Wollheim's account? There seems to me to be one, and probably only one, tenable position lying between the two. This accepts that we must add to the minimalist's resources. To make sense of talk of attempted visual engagement we must, like Wollheim, appeal to the imagination. We must accept Wollheim's claims that appreciating some pictures requires us *imaginatively* to engage with the depicted scene; that that imagined engagement is, at least in part, importantly visual; and that the artist's intentions license such imaginings. What we will try to resist, however, is his suggestion that in such imaginings we identify with some represented other, an internal spectator. Rather, the imaginings in question exclusively concern us, the viewers of the picture. It is ourselves we imagine engaging with the scene.

This is a position Wollheim himself discusses (PA 102, 185). There are the materials in what he says for three, perhaps interrelated, objections to the proposal. They exploit the apparent unsuitability of the external spectator for the allotted role on three counts: her psychology, her location and her identity. Let me briefly state each in turn.

The first objection focusses on Wollheim's insistence on the importance of repertoire. If some paintings need to be understood by seeing the depicted scene through the eyes of someone with a specific psychology, there are two reasons why that person should not be the external spectator. For when the external spectator imagines *herself* engaging with the depicted scene, she is likely, on the one hand, to import too much of her own psychology, in the way of either the peculiarities of her own psyche or those of her age. Such aspects will be at best irrelevant to understanding the content the artist imbued the picture with, and at worst a hindrance to it. But, on the other hand, the viewer is also likely to bring too little to understanding of the picture, in the way of those distinctive positive aspects of repertoire that, Wollheim claims, are integral to some pictures. She will, in short, be bound to see the depicted scene through her own eyes, and it is unclear then what point there could be to the imaginative engagement, since it can only reinforce the way she sees the picture when relying on seeing-in and expressive perception alone.

The second "objection" is more of a question. It demands clarification of the imagined spatial relation between the external spectator and the depicted scene. Imagining engaging with that scene presumably requires imagining

being located in the same space as the depicted things. So does the viewer of
the picture imagine the depicted object as in the space she in fact occupies,
or does she imagine herself in the space the object is represented as occupying? Until this question has been answered, the proposal is incomplete.

The third objection presents Wollheim's "basic reason" for rejecting the
proposed view (PA 185). This is that if appreciating a picture requires the
viewer to imagine something about herself, and if her so imagining forms
part of the picture's extended content, then that content changes from one
viewer to the next, and in ways that the artist, in ignorance of who would see
the painting, could not possibly have anticipated in his intentions for the
work. But then the picture's content would alter without the artist's intentions
licensing this change, and that is to infringe a fundamental principle governing pictorial content of any kind.

6. Since it presents the least difficulty, let us deal with the question of
imagined location first. Wollheim makes it plausible that the imagined engagement with the depicted scene that we are taking to be important to some
pictures need not be limited to imagining that scene from the point from
which the picture presents it. In the context of the Manets, I noted the
possibility of imagining moving so as to try to meet the figure's gaze, and
Wollheim suggests (PA 162) that, for at least some pictures, such imagined
movement would be in the space represented as surrounding the distracted
figure. If the current proposal is to accommodate such phenomena as this, it
should be that the external spectator imagines herself in the represented space,
when imagining engaging with the objects which occupy it.

However, this way of resolving the second difficulty may only seem to
highlight the third. That, at least, seems to be Wollheim's view (PA note 35).
So let me try to tackle the issue of content change next. First let us step back,
to see what the core of the problem might be.

The key difficulty here seems to be this. As I noted earlier (Section 3), the
external spectator's imaginative responses to the picture will have nothing to
do with its content, unless those responses are licensed by the artist's intentions. But on the current proposal the key response essentially involves the
spectator's identity – she is to imagine *herself* engaging with the depicted
objects. Since the artist can have no knowledge of who the spectators will be,
the response cannot be underwritten by artistic intention in the way content
requires. So the proposal, the accusation claims, is inherently unstable: Either
the spectator's imaginings have nothing to do with the picture's content, or
they concern, not the spectator herself, but a, quite distinct, spectator *in* the
picture.

If this is the heart of the problem, there are grounds for hope. For we find
the same pressures at work elsewhere in the pictorial realm, and there they
do not prove irreconcilable. In the case of depictive content, as in that of

imaginative engagement with the depicted scene, for there to be content the spectator must respond in accord with the artist's intentions. She must see in the picture whatever it is the artist intended her to. But here, as there, the artist can have no knowledge of who will see the painting, and therefore whose response his intention needs to concern. The problem that confronts the proposed middle way of accommodating imaginative engagement with the depicted scene finds an exact parallel in the realm of depictive content.

Now, of course, in the depictive case content *could* be set merely by the intended responses of a subset of viewers, a set small enough and accessible enough for the artist's intentions explicitly to concern each of them. At the limit, one might suggest that the only response essential to content is the artist's own. But it seems to me quite clear that this is standardly not the case, and in some instances (such as where the artist herself is blind) could not be so. So the problem remains, at least in the standard cases – how can the artist's intention govern the responses of those of whom she has no knowledge?

The solution here is quite simple. The key intention on the artist's part is, in a sense, open-ended. She intends *whoever* sees the picture to see therein what she has depicted. This is perhaps a little simplistic. It may be that a better specification of the intention is that the depicted scene be seen in the surface by whoever (i) sees the picture, (ii) is in general capable of seeing things in surfaces, and (iii) knows what the depicted objects look like. But we need not quibble over details, it is the form of the intention which matters here, not its filling out. Again, no doubt the intention need not be completely successful, for the picture to have depictive content – no matter if not every suitably qualified viewer in fact gets the pictorial point. As long as some do, the picture depicts what those people see in it. But, again, quite how to negotiate the complexities here is incidental to our concerns. For the point is that, if something like this solution to the problem works in the case of depictive content, a parallel solution will work in the case in hand. The intention licensing the external spectator's imaginings about herself is this: Whoever sees the scene in the picture is to imagine herself seeing that scene face-to-face, and engaging with it (in whatever ways the particular picture renders appropriate). This is an intention the artist can have, and which can be more or less fulfilled by the responses of the various viewers of the picture, without placing impossible demands on the artist's knowledge of those viewers.

I hope that Wollheim would accept something like this account of the intentions governing depictive content. He may even accept that something parallel does indeed hold in respect of imaginative engagement with the depicted scene. Where he will balk, I suspect, is at the claim that this amounts to a solution to the third problem facing the proposal in hand. For, after all, the person who sees the appropriate things in a picture does not enter into its depictive content, only what she sees in the surface does so. Open-ended intentions are fine for picking out the set of people whose responses determine a picture's content, but not for determining that content itself. And when Wollheim offers his "basic reason" against letting the external spectator do all the work here, it is as reason for thinking that "the spectator of the picture could not conceivably be part of the picture's content, hence could not conceivably be the spectator in the picture" (PA 185). So has the problem really been solved?

It has, provided that we are clear about one further difference between Wollheim's account and my own. It is no part of the current proposal that there is a spectator in the picture, or, more particularly, that there is an internal spectator identical with the external one. Rather, my view attempts to accommodate the phenomena without multiplying the varieties of pictorial content, properly conceived, at all. Imaginative engagement with the depicted scene is licensed by the artist's intention, and is essential to grasping certain aspects of pictorial content, such as the distractedness of the Manet figures. Such licensed imaginings may make various novel aspects of content available to the viewer; and their doing so may be essential to those aspects being part of the picture's content. But, for all that, the imagined engagement is not itself represented, not even in an extended sense.

Is this aspect of my disagreement with Wollheim merely verbal, a dispute over whether to use the word "content" to describe licensed imaginings? I don't think so. Wollheim's original objection was that if the external spectator were the spectator in the picture, an important principle governing content would be infringed. I have not merely dodged that charge by eschewing claims about pictorial content; I've tried to show how the imaginings essential to understanding the picture can be licensed by an open-ended intention on the artist's part. If the resulting account of the pictorial phenomena remains unacceptable, because there is some further principle it infringes, we have yet to be told what that principle is.

7. All this leaves the first, repertoire-based, objection quite intact. In effect, that objection had three elements. It suggested that the external spectator's imaginings about herself would import irrelevant features of her psychology into the attempt to understand the picture; would omit key positive elements of the distinctive psychology through which the picture is in fact to be understood; and would as a result of these twin faults undermine the point of imaginative engagement altogether, reducing it to a mere repetition of that contact with the picture that seeing-in and expressive perception already afford.[4] These are serious charges. What can be said to rebut them?

The first thing to note is that, even if the twin accusations of irrelevant egocentricity and inadequate empathy could be proven, it would not follow that there was no point to the imaginative engagement the position describes. For even if the external spectator imagines engaging with the depicted scene while having precisely the psychology she in fact enjoys, the forms of engagement her imagination allows for readily outstrip those available in seeing-in and expressive perception. That this is so is, indeed, the lesson of our discussion of the Manets. The imagined unsuccessful attempt to engage visually with the depicted figures deepens our sense of how they are, in ways that the comparatively passive processes of seeing-in and expressive perception cannot provide. Since that discussion made this plausible without appealing to any particular psychology for the imagined protagonist, any normal external spectator could expect these benefits even if she did import her own psychology into the imagined scenario.

However, there are anyway grounds for scepticism about the two more basic charges. Taking that of irrelevant egocentrism first, it is simply untrue that the external spectator's imagining herself engaging with the depicted scene will inevitably leave her imagining engaging with it idiosyncrasies, contemporary *Weltbild* and all. *Pace* Wollheim's observations about the plenitude characteristic of central imagining (PA 129), imagining may be indeterminate in many and varied ways, including the nature of the imagined protagonist. The viewer of the picture will exploit such indeterminateness in imagining engaging with the depicted scene.

Moreover, she will do so for good reason. For, since the point of such imagining is to understand the picture better, and since the spectator is fully aware that peculiarities of her person or time can only obstruct her in that goal, she will set aside those of her features that are likely to be thus obstructive. In deciding quite what to set aside, she has just the same resources at her disposal, and just the same opportunity to make use of them, as Wollheim's imaginer, seeking an internal spectator as the target of his imaginative identification. Since in this respect the two positions seem evenly matched, the charge of egocentricity comes to naught.

What of the last accusation? This claims that the external spectator will be hampered from imagining a protagonist with that distinctive positive repertoire which is, in some cases, "inscribed" (PA 130) into the painting. Again, however, it is very hard to see why this should be. For, along with indeterminacy, imagination exhibits what we might call *autonomy*: it is free to represent things as they in fact are, or as they are not. Exploiting this, the external spectator can imagine herself engaging with the scene while having a repertoire she does not in fact possess. Nor can the problem be that in practice she will never grasp what repertoire it would be appropriate to attribute to herself, if not the one she really displays. For, again, her position in this respect precisely matches that of Wollheim's external spectator. The two put the epistemic resources available to them to work in the context of different imaginative projects, but the resources, and the demands made on them by the project, are in each case the same.

8. What has emerged is that there is no substance to any of Wollheim's objections to the position lying between minimalism and his own account. That middle position is at least tenable. But if so, there are at least some grounds for thinking that it is the position we should adopt. Let me explain.

Suppose I ask you to imagine what it is like to be crushed by an enormous weight. You might, I suppose, do this by imagining the experiences of some other person meeting that fate, and then imaginatively identifying with the sufferings that person undergoes. But it would be far more natural simply to imagine yourself being crushed. And, I suggest, this is because, quite generally, where an imaginative project requires us to imagine certain experiences, attitudes or actions, we normally imagine ourselves in those situations, rather than someone else in them, with whom we then identify. My claim is not that we cannot do the latter. I am not promoting some form of the thesis that imagining necessarily concerns oneself.[5] I claim only that doing what I have described is the default option, that which, as a matter of psychological fact, we go in for, unless we are coaxed into doing otherwise.

Given this, we should expect this default to hold when we engage with pictures, and in particular with those pictures Wollheim discusses. There too what we naturally imagine, if we imagine anything of this sort at all, is simply *ourselves* confronting the depicted object. As I have argued, imagining in this way allows us to reap the benefits, in terms of a deepened understanding of the picture, which form Wollheim's central concern. So why think that we reap those benefits by any means other than those we standardly deploy when imagining experiences, attitudes, etc. quite generally? Unless something particular to our confrontations with these pictures drives us to imagine in the more complex way Wollheim has described, we will just do what we normally do.

Of course, our psychology might be quirky, so that we do in fact respond to pictures with more complex imaginings, to everything else with more straightforward ones. Equally, it could be that the painters of the pictures Wollheim discussed intended us to imagine in the complex, identification-involving, manner. But there is no reason to believe that the first possibility here holds, and little more reason to accept the second. It is far more likely that our psychology is uniform, in this respect, whatever prompts our imaginings. Equally, it seems likely that the artists of these pictures were like us in this regard. For them too, imaginings concerning themselves provided the default. If so, it is likely that, having themselves responded to their canvases in this way, they intended and expected us to do just the same.

9. Faced with the challenge the middle position presents, Wollheim might try one last response. This would be to suggest that there is no difference of substance between it and his own view. True, when he provided arguments against that rival, he presumably considered it to differ from his position, and in objectionable ways. But any success I may have had in arguing against those objections perhaps just serves to show that there aren't really interesting differences between the two positions after all. Let's consider this response.

If the thought that the two positions are really one has any force, it derives from the aesthetic importance of the phenomenon which the two views attempt to describe. The idea must be that, whether we imagine a repertoire and patterns of engagement for an internal spectator with whom we identify, or whether we imagine ourselves equipped with that repertoire and engaging with the depicted object in those ways, is all the same from the point of view of reasons for appreciating the picture. Either way, our experience of the picture is complicated and deepened. Either way, the satisfactions which pictures offer, merely through representing what they do, are multiplied.

In effect, the response encourages us to divide the elements in Wollheim's thinking into two groups. On the one hand, there are those elements which the middle position accepts – that licensed imagining goes on; that it is imagining someone, with a certain psychology, engaging with the depicted scene; that it leads the viewer to understand the painting differently. Roughly, these were elements (2), (3), (4) and (7) in my original exposition (Section 3). On the other hand, there are those elements the middle position rejects– that the imagined protagonist is someone other than the viewer of the picture, and that these imaginings form, in whole or part, some novel form of content for the picture. These rejected elements I labelled (1), (5) and (6) above. The response's claim is then that this division between the elements is also the dividing line between those of Wollheim's claims which capture the aesthetically important aspects of our imaginative interaction with the paintings he discusses, and those that are of no consequence for pictorial aesthetics. So the middle position and Wollheim's view agree on everything that is of aesthetic significance and disagree only over the theoretical – and aesthetically irrelevant – details.

10. To assess this response we need, of course, to consider the aesthetic issues Wollheim's discussion raises. I suggest that the best way to do this is to return to the problem framed at the beginning of this chapter. That was to explain how a picture's representing what it does can be of aesthetic interest. Although this is not a problem Wollheim explicitly addresses, it is not unreasonable to ask how far his views help us to solve it. For he is certainly concerned, in *Painting as an Art*, to offer an account of what there is to value in painting, and the problem merely provides a way of focussing one aspect of that question. I will argue that Wollheim is too optimistic about the extent of our imaginative engagement with pictures, and thus that he is not as well placed to solve the problem of Section 1 as he might have hoped. At the end, I will relate these claims to the issue between Wollheim's view and the middle position, and in particular to the question whether their differences matter to the aesthetics of painting.

Before beginning, it will help to introduce a last piece of terminology. In considering the aesthetic issues, we are, for now at least, prescinding from the dispute between the middle position and Wollheim's view. It would help, therefore, to be able to talk about our imaginings in a way neutral between those two positions. We can do this by adopting Wollheim's term "the protagonist" for that person, whatever their identity, we imagine engaging with the depicted scene. Wollheim claims that the protagonist is a spectator internal to the picture, the middle position claims that he is the viewer of the picture himself. But both accept that there is a protagonist, and that he is imagined engaging with the depicted objects.[6]

From the perspective of the problem framed in Section 1, one element in Wollheim's view is particularly important. This is the claim that at least some pictures "inscribe" a distinctive positive psychological repertoire for the protagonist. (this was (4b) in my original summary). As I noted from the first (Section 1), one way to solve the problem is to appeal to the idea that pictures can represent, not just scenes, but reactions to them, and thus, as I put it, "initiate us into another sensibility." Now, Wollheim's views offer a way to give substance to that solution, but only if he makes the claim about a distinctive positive repertoire. If some paintings require us to imagine some protagonist engaging with the depicted scene, they may indeed allow us to explore sensibilities other than our own, but only if the psychology of the protagonist we are imagining is substantially different from ours.

It is not that, without positive repertoires, Wollheim can offer nothing by way of solution to the problem. He can certainly provide something, just not nearly as much. In the absence of a distinctive repertoire, our protagonist's engagement with the scenes is that of an embodied viewer, and certainly someone free of the idiosyncracies of our own repertoires, but little more can be said about his psychology than that. For, as I noted in discussing Wollheim's repertoire-based objection to the compromise view I favour (Section 7), imagined engagement can enrich our understanding of a picture, even if the repertoire imagined as guiding that engagement is just that of an embodied viewer. We have an example of such engagement in the case of the Manets discussed above. There the imagined protagonist is just someone, embodied and sighted, but little more. To the extent that we find illuminating Wollheim's careful discussion of these examples, a crude summary of which I offered in Section 4, we have reason to consider that he has provided part of an answer to our initial problem. By imagining a protagonist in the depicted space, trying to catch the subject's attention, we discover an aspect of the depicted woman, her momentary absence from life, which would otherwise lie hidden from us. What the painting thus offers us through these imaginings is a subtle way of grasping one of Manet's points. The point grasped is of aesthetic interest, but so, quite plausibly, is the particular process of recovering it. Only a very narrow notion of which satisfactions count as aesthetic could lead one to deny this.

However, as I have said, the inclusion, in the case of some pictures, of positive repertoires for the protagonist would greatly increase what we could offer by way of solution to the problem. And it is a disappointment, therefore, that the claim that some pictures do indeed inscribe a positive repertoire is precisely the claim Wollheim does least to establish. For many of his examples do not press at the crucial point. The discussion of Hals (PA, Ch. 3, §E), like that of Manet, makes no mention of a substantial repertoire. Instead, we are again here in the realm of Wollheim's limiting case, the protagonist who is simply an observer, albeit not a "disembodied eye" (PA 130). If Wollheim is to push us beyond that realm, the burden of his argument must fall fully on the Friedrich discussion, and in particular on the case of *Afternoon* (PA 138–40). Wollheim's treatment of this picture is intricate, but – and I can do no more than assert this here – it seems to me to leave key questions unanswered.

My claim is not that it would be impossible to inscribe a positive repertoire into a picture. It is hard to convince oneself either that such a thing could be done, or that it could not. As Wollheim himself notes, any such inscription must depend on the way the scene visible in the canvas is depicted (PA 164). Given this, deciding whether such inscription is possible would require us to settle obscure questions about the way in which possessing a distinctive repertoire might alter how the world is seen to be (how the affective "permeates" the perceptual), and about whether such alterations in the seen world can be captured in the depictive content of a picture. My claim is rather that Wollheim has not argued convincingly that inscription of a distinctive positive repertoire ever occurs. Even if one were to decide on theoretical grounds that a positive repertoire could be inscribed, this would still leave open the issue whether any actual paintings do inscribe such things. And surely pictorial aesthetics is centrally about why we should value the art painting is, not about reasons for caring for it as it merely might be. So what is needed, for Wollheim to complete the solution to our problem which he has begun,[7] are clear examples of such inscriptions. I do not know whether such examples are there to be had. In this respect, then, my discussion of Wollheim's contribution is inconclusive.

11. Where does all this leave matters? Insofar as Wollheim fails to establish that pictures ever do inscribe positive repertoires, his discussion in chapter three of *Painting as an Art* does not live up to its promise of solving the problem posed in Section 1. As I noted in the last section, even without positive repertoires, Wollheim can contribute something to that solution; but making good the claim about positive repertoires would take us a long way towards a satisfactory response to the challenge Section 1 posed. But the question how far Wollheim's discussion satisfies the demands of aesthetic inquiry connects with the earlier dispute between his position and the middle view developed in Sections 5 to 9; and this in two ways. I will close by outlining them.

First, the less imposing the aesthetic consequences of Wollheim's observations about our imaginative responses to the paintings he discusses, the larger loom the supposedly "theoretical" differences between his position and the middle view. The earlier response on Wollheim's behalf (Section 8) sought to belittle those theoretical differences in the face of the views' shared consequences for the aesthetics of painting. But the fewer and less significant those consequences, the harder it is to share that perspective on the situation. The theoretical differences regain some of their prominence – and they, of course, favour the middle position.

Second, although the issue whether positive repertoires are ever inscribed is logically distinct from that of whether we should prefer the middle position to Wollheim's view, psychologically the possible positions here come in pairs. If one accepts Wollheim's more extensive theoretical machinery, one is more likely to be optimistic about the prospects for inscribing a positive repertoire. For, having accepted that sometimes we engage in licensed imaginings about an implied internal spectator, it is natural to take the issue of the nature of that spectator, and in particular his psychology, to be open. A distinctive positive repertoire then seems as live a possibility as any other. If, on the other hand, one prefers the leaner framework I have defended, the land looks to lie quite differently. The imaginings some pictures provoke in their viewers concern those viewers themselves. Of course, they know, in imagining engaging with the depicted scene, to set aside their foibles and idiosyncracies. Equally, it is not ruled out from the first that they are to imagine themselves with distinctive dispositions, of thought or feeling, which are not in fact theirs. But the rest point, as it were, is that the viewer imagines herself engaging while having only features common to all viewers. If she is to imagine otherwise, she must be given clear signals as to what she is to incorporate. Inscription of a positive repertoire is not excluded, but we will want firm grounds, in any given case, for thinking that it occurs.

So Wollheim's theoretical extravagance, as it seems to me, encourages optimism about what there is to appreciate in pictures, my parsimoniousness prompts a more pessimistic view. Of course, neither attitude is a substitute for argument on the matter of whether positive repertoires are in fact inscribed. But, in the absence of the convincing examples for which I wait, perhaps limning the temptations particular positions expose us to will help keep our heads clear for the argument, when it comes.[8]

NOTES

1. London, Thames and Hudson 1987. Throughout I refer to this edition.
2. Since I discuss these two forms of content largely to set them aside, what I say is very brief. For more on depictive content, see PA Ch. 2, §B and, for critical discussion Hopkins *Picture, Image and Experience,* 14–20, 37–8, and Budd "On Looking at a Picture." On expressive content, see PA, Chapter 2, §C and CPE.
3. Wollheim denies that the implied spectator is "represented" (PA 101). However, what a picture represents, in his sense, is what I am calling its depictive content. As I use the term, representing is the genus, the species of which include depicting, expressing, and any other kind of content a picture may have. Thus, for me, the implied spectator is not depicted, but is represented.
4. In discussing minimalism, we conceded for the sake of argument that the distractedness of the figures could be *seen in* the paintings, and argued that it could be so only through imaginative engagement with them. This is why I here contrast imaginative engagement, not with seeing-in and expressive perception *tout court,* but with seeing-in and expressive perception unaided by imaginative engagement.
5. For critical discussion of this thesis, see Williams, Imagination and the Self.
6. I talk of the protagonist as "he" simply for grammatical convenience. Obviously, on either Wollheim's view or my own, the protagonist might be masculine, might be feminine, or his gender may simply be irrelevant to the imagined engagement with the depicted scene the picture invites.
7. I noted in Section 1 that this solution could at most be partial. My point here is that even this partial solution is, as it stands, incomplete.
8. Thanks are due to Malcolm Budd, Dudley Knowles, Philip Percival, Monique Roelofs, Anthony Savile, and Richard Wollheim.

Chapter 17
A Word on Behalf of
"the Merely Visual"

MICHAEL BAXANDALL

Chapter 3 of Richard Wollheim's *Painting as an Art*, The Spectator in the Picture, is preceded by the fascinating last three pages of Chapter 2, which seem to throw an immediately necessary light ahead on what follows.

These three pages (PA 98–100) are the section of the book in which Wollheim writes on visual delight. It is the section in which he invokes Proust on Chardin and our own everyday domesticity, and on the pleasurable to-and-fro between them, in which (as Wollheim insists) expressive perception is implicit – "projection controlled by a great artist". From this Wollheim modulates into locating visual pleasure in the reciprocal relation between experience of worked paint and experience of an image. The first he associates with a close view, the second with a more distanced view. And it is the section that ends with reproof of Lessing for too narrow a sense of the visible, as something presuming what is called the "disembodied eye." Real pleasure in painting draws on synaesthetic associations, memory of smell, taste, hearing.

Since these pages have so framed and coloured my reading of Chapter 3 and "The spectator in the picture," I shall continue to let them do so here.

Chapter 3 is a marvellously rich account of how we let a picture take imaginative possession of us, or how we take imaginative possession of a picture, or both. The succession of incremented formulations of central imagining, the careful stipulations about plenitude and cogency and the balance between lure and embellishment, and the accreting instances – from Friedrich, Manet, and Hals – lead to the full-blown drifting internal spectator of the later pages.

The issue the last pages of Chapter 2 prompt me to raise is: What, quite, is the visual system's active intervention in internal spectatorship? If any? What is it doing, apart from such things as intermittently insinuating the wholesome check on "lure" of "embellishment?" Is it even possible that we might perhaps pursue the imaginative part of the enterprise on the basis of memory of the picture? or is the immediate engagement of eye and stimulation necessary? Above all – since I am an art historian – has this any part in the art criticism that would be the extension of Wollheim's aesthetic?

To declare the specificity of what I am referring to I shall give a hostage and refer to it, in most cases, not as "visual" (since this word can become limp) but as ocular – ocular in the sense that it derives from properties of the organ, the eye, early vision, and from the contrivances of the mind to work with those properties. But in a way I shall be brooding on Wollheim's sense of the word "access" – as in the phrase "full access to the content of the picture."

For much of Chapter 3, one can accommodate the unobtrusiveness of the ocular, its effective bracketing off (as a constructive force) within and around visual delight, by telling oneself that that is a matter of level of description. It could be being covered by or subsumed, or absorbed into, the imaginative experience Wollheim is concerned with. He has simply chosen to give his account of things at this descriptively high or perceptually late or psychologically fully integrated level, because that is what interests him. But in his final reformulation he suddenly comes near to closing this escape off.

He has been dealing with a possible counter-argument (with which I am not concerned) to his construction of the total spectator and he says:

What the [counter-argument] clearly assumes is that any contribution that identification with an internal spectator makes to pictorial understanding is bound to be fundamentally perceptual. Throughout this lecture I have been contending that this is not the case, and that at least as important as the perceptual contribution is the affective or emotional contribution.

In point of fact pictures that contain an internal spectator are likely to be ordered in this last respect. [I am not sure about the emphasis here – WHETHER *ordered*, in this last respect OR ordered in this *last* respect.] In some cases the affective contribution that identification with an internal spectator makes to pictorial comprehension will be much greater, in other cases it will be comparatively less, though it will always be sizeable. (PA 183)

Then he introduces the drifting spectator, and he finishes:

The test for any proposed location [sc. for the internal spectator's drift] always remains whether the fruits of centrally imagining a spectator at that point can or cannot be fed back into the pictorial understanding of the picture. (PA 183)

My problem with this is certainly not the idea of the internal spectator's drifting, which within Wollheim's descriptive system seems necessary and powerful. Nor, in the first instance or as such, is it the relative valuation of perceptual and affective. Rather, it is the implication of relative valuation here at all – the sense that, in the context of pictorial understanding, the perceptual and the affective are each of a kind to be separated in such a way that they can be weighed against each other for their relative importance of contribution to the pictorial understanding. In other contexts the demarcation could no doubt be legitimate and useful. But this is the "pictorial understanding."

This is, perhaps, not the sort of point that lends itself to argument, being in the end a matter of what one finds important or interesting. But I can make a few remarks about a picture, and try to let a position work itself out.

Wollheim has made Manet very much his own in this context, so I will take a Chardin – Chardin's *Return from the Market*. I hope it is a picture that admits some sort of central imagining – I think so – but it is aligned at a slight angle to the set of single-figure paintings of Manet that are at the centre of Wollheim's account of the requirements of the Internal Spectator picture.

Part of the "lure" of the picture is that the central figure of the blue girl has an extraordinary nervous inner movement about it. Perhaps this is partly the gestural highlit left edge, by which Chardin has chosen to put his signature. Perhaps it is also that there are also so many rotated and reduced and reversed self-similarity-type echoes of the total form of the girl and her shopping bag within the figure and outside it, at least down to the scale of that red bow.

But it is partly a matter of the woman's left foot that, unlike her right foot, is inconspicuous and (I would suggest) disappears except when we actually look at it, fixate it. But, I would also suggest, this left foot – that is to say the foot to our right – is non-obviously placed. When one does not see it the general character of the figure might suggest a foot rather further over, I think. It comes as a surprise every time one sees it. There is an analogous though lesser effect with her left hand on the loaf of bread.

What is the strictly ocular contribution to this? As we all know, we see pictures or anything by moving the eye several times a second in such a way that the central hyperacute part of the retina, the fovea, covering an arc of about two degrees, is directed to successive points. We scan. But we use the information from the less acute peripheral part of the retina as well as that from the hyperacute fovea.[1] At the start of the fixation the attentive processing focus is on the foveal centre of ocular fixation. If the cognitive appeal of the object fixated is limited, the focus of attention shifts elsewhere, into the periphery, and this plays a part in determining the location of the next fixation. But the movements are determined by a complex set of intrinsic dispositions and both involuntary and voluntary reactions, of which higher-level promptings such as interest and attention are only part.

I would suggest Chardin's control over our projection, something of which Wollheim speaks, lies partly in this. He places distractors like the bowl in the left foreground. This bowl intermittently draws fixation by appealing on all levels – from being a puzzlingly placed object, a refugee from the dresser, to just being bright and sharp. But (just as important) it is also likely *not* to be a long-term retainer of attention through the length of a fixation. It is nice, with that lustre, but not itself cognitively demanding – a canonical view of a regular easily objectified form. The bowl is a sort of generous rather than

Chardin, Jean Baptiste Siméon (1699–1779). La Pourvoyeuse, 1739, Oil on canvas, 47×38. (With the permission of the Réunion des Musées Nationaux, Agence Photographique.)

possessive attractor of fixations and part of its pictorial effect is to instigate non-foveal takes of other parts of the picture. We see the girl without her left foot because distractors like the bowl ensure a range of low-definition peripheral takes of her. Thus partly movement. Thus partly lure.

Another point, a point about the relation between picture surface and image. In this painting the third dimension, the sequence from far to near, is resolved into two dimensions by spreading across the plane, far to near being from left to right. This introduces ambivalences: in fully 3D perception the girl looks to our left (to *her* right) as in reverie or listening; but there is also an insistent secondary 2D perception in which she addresses, even perhaps looks at, the far backroom.

And the back room has various kinds of uncertainties of scale and space – how big is the water-urn on the right? is there a step down into the room? that sort of thing – that are characteristic of mental imagery, visual imagination or visual memory. It may be that a sense of this picture that has not at some time in some way involved however briefly some sense of the backroom scene being in the blue woman's mind has not fully accommodated it, is incomplete.

But it is precisely the perceptual relation of flatness vis-à-vis virtual space, the way it is preliminarily announced or set up – through the ambivalence of the woman's address and so on – that insists on synaesthetic projection. She is listening/looking/visualizing). (It also, by the way, has the effect of rendering the rectangular ambience into an expansive surface framework of verticals and obtuse angles, plus just one contracting acute angle above the small girl in the doorway – again an invitation to expressive perception.)

Behind all this, again, is a straight ocular circumstance. It is not, as Wollheim suggests, in distant and near viewing that the primary conversation between perception of worked paint surface and perception of image is located. Rather, its basic and continual presence is in the simultaneous work of the mind on both fine and coarse channels of information – which, in fact, derive not only from fovea and periphery but also from separate fine and coarse channels of information from the fovea itself. Actual locomotion by the spectator between closer and more distant viewing positions is only a crude reduction of this. At any one moment fine vision is seeing paint, coarse vision is seeing image, so to speak, though it is not really as simple as that.

So, what am I pleading for? Obviously I have a worry about, first, a quarantining and, second, an attenuation of the specific richness of the experience of pictures. But there is very little point in arguing over emphasis, and in any case I certainly do not want to quarantine or attenuate the affective and the imaginative. But perhaps one can go back to the matter of the level of description and ask whether Wollheim would not allow criticism, if it wants, to describe as much as it can of the imaginative activity he associates with the Internal Spectator in terms of the ocularly based visual cues and constraints that prompt and control them – at a lower level, as it were. That would at least acknowledge two characteristics of pictorial meaning that – since time has run out – I have no choice but to state as axiomatic.

The first is that the visual perceptual process we go through while looking at a picture is, in its detail character and gait, one enactment of the humanity represented in the picture. Basic critical decorum demands that our comprehension of the picture should cohere with that character – in the case of this Chardin (say) jittery, ambiguous, entrapped. Imagination or affect that lose immediate contact with the ocular cues and constraints can become wilful and arbitrary.

The second is that, while our expressive perception and projection are controlled – not to say manipulated – by a picture like this, they are not controlled in such a way that the inner or psychological life of the picture is fully specified, exhaustively specified, in (as it were) the psychological-narrative domain or register. It is in some degree open here to inflection and completion from our individual experience. One of the dangers of art criticism is the critic's preempting or aborting, with some scenario determined by his personal experience, of the spectator's own final burst of projection. In short, the critic can be seen as having his prime business with the ocular cues and constraints – establishing the score, so to speak, rather than giving one more performance.

NOTE

1. This point has been made with particular clarity by Julian Hochberg in, for instance, Hochberg, Art and Perception, particularly 230–33, and Some of the Things That Paintings Are, particularly 27–30.

Part Four
Reply

Chapter 18
A Reply to the Contributors

RICHARD WOLLHEIM

I should like to begin by expressing my gratitude to the contributors to this volume, and I am embarrassed by the kind things that they have found to say. Fortunately for its readers, they have also substantial criticisms to make of my ideas, and it is to these criticisms that I shall address myself. I shall not presume to answer the criticisms: I shall at best indicate how I believe that they can be met where they can be met. In doing so, I shall more or less follow the divisions of the volume itself, simply noting at the outset that there are two main lines of criticism: one is that I go too far, the other is that I do not go far enough. At least one critic suggests that I go about the required distance, but in the wrong direction.

Communication and *Trompe l'oeil*

I observe that three contributors to this section – *Harrison, Savile, Wilde* – note with some surprise my rejection of the connexion between pictorial art and communication. To many, the connexion seems self-evident, and further it appears to fit well with my insistence that, in the case of meaningful works of art, there is a match, or tally, between the artist's intentions and the experiences of an appropriate spectator.

However I believe that the disagreement between myself and my critics on this topic is largely terminological, and that is why I begin with it. In fact, I shall first dispose of the terminological issue, or what I see as such, and then I shall take up a more detailed disagreement with Savile.

What I mean by communication is the attempt, or, more narrowly perhaps, the successful attempt, on the part of an agent to instil certain beliefs, or – a weaker version of the same idea – certain speculations, or suggestions, or hopes, or suspicions, into the mind or minds of an audience. The agent may identify the audience with which he intends to communicate to varying degrees of specificity, but he must identify it with sufficient specificity for it to make sense for him to try to adapt the means of communication he uses so as to achieve the success he desires. Specifically he must, if there is to be

communication, adapt how he puts things to the cognitive stock that he
believes his audience to possess.

To bring my conception of communication into sharper focus, we may
contrast two kinds of strategy that an agent might employ when he addresses
the outer world. One is when he presupposes a certain cognitive stock on the
part of his audience because he is interested solely in an audience that can be
identified by the possession of such a cognitive stock, the other is when he
presupposes a certain cognitive stock because he has reason to believe that
the audience he is interested in happens to possess just that stock. On my
view of the matter, it is only in the second case that the agent is engaged in
communication.

So much for the different ways in which my critics and I think of communication.

Now I turn to *Savile*, and I greatly admire the ingenuity of his attempt to
find a place for communication within the essence of art by speculating that
the communicative role of art can be invoked to explain how art persists in
human culture, and why it does not die out, like many another fad. More
specifically, Savile suggests that it is the connexion with communication that
allows the historical transition to be effected from the status of craft to that
of art.

Now I am susceptible, as Savile understands perfectly well, to the idea that
aesthetics can, indeed must, find a place for such diachronic hypotheses
within it. My uncertainty is whether the conception of communication that
Savile uses when he characterizes what it is that the artist can offer the patron
or client in bargaining for the survival of art is the same conception of
communication that I use. The uncertainty arises because, though Savile, in
the example of Richard I and Blondel, correctly points out the weakness of
an earlier formulation of mine, he is operating without benefit of how I am
now inclined to restate what for me is crucial to communication.

My own sense of the matter is that what, on Savile's *Just So Story*, the
artist has to offer should not, and, on my view of the matter, would not, be
thought of as communication, and for this reason: that, once the patron or
client starts to think of art as valuable or interesting, he will be prepared to
see that he has whatever cognitive stock is needed for him to understand the
work of art. In that way, the artist is, at any rate over time, relieved of what I
have taken to be the burden that falls upon a communicator: the burden of so
expressing himself as to take account of the audience's cognitive stock.

A subsidiary reason why communication seems to me more loosely connected with art than Savile thinks is that it is generally held that a sufficient
condition for communication to occur is when the audience succeeds in
inferring the artist's intent from what the artist has said or done, even if this
falls short of fulfilling his communicative intent. However an artist could not

find this satisfactory. He will want the audience to *grasp* his meaning, which is for me always a matter of having some appropriate experience: mere uptake is not enough. This seems to lead to the conclusion that, however much art there may be that is communication, nothing is art in virtue of satisfying the communicative pattern.

Another issue that is a topic common to two respondents is that of *trompe l'oeil* paintings, and the question whether they are or are not representations. It is my view that they aren't. Levinson maintains that I am obviously wrong in thinking this, Feagin maintains that I am right, but certainly not obviously so. For my own part, I have tended to treat my view more as a fall-out from my general thesis that representation can be understood in terms of seeing-in, and not so much as something important in itself. I have liked the view for one consequence, for from it it follows that the kind of painting that those who equate representation and illusion would put at the very centre of representation is not even a case of representation.

If *trompe l'oeil* paintings are not representations, what are they? Feagin says that they are *presentations*, and she lists four conditions of what it is to be a presentation. I shall return to the detail of these conditions in a moment. Meanwhile I must point out that these conditions do not, singly or conjointly, establish what Feagin claims for them. They do not establish the central difference between presentation and representation, which is that representation, though not presentation, depends upon a convention. (This has nothing to do with the usual sense in which it is argued that representation that is, representational meaning, is conventional.) A representational painting is one made by a painter who intends the spectator to look at it a certain way, and the spectator, knowing that he is to look at it this way, and finding that he can, does so. There is nothing analogous in the case of *trompe l'oeil*. Indeed, not only is the spectator of a *trompe l'oeil* painting better off if he doesn't know the intentions of the artist, it is arguable that knowledge of them is incompatible with appropriate perception. In certain circumstances, the *trompe l'oeil* effect, just like – to use Feagin's example – the Muller-Lyer effect, will survive knowledge of the facts of the case, but that is not the same as saying that the *trompe l'oeil* painting itself can still be perceived as it was intended to be. Arguably being seen as successful illusion falls short of what *trompe l'oeil* aims at.

As to Feagin's specific conditions upon *trompe l'oeil*, I am not certain that I get the point of the third and the fourth. Surely the spectator who is appropriately taken in by Mantegna's handiwork in the Camera degli Sposi has to have some knowledge about the Gonzaga family, though – and this may be Feagin's point – none about Mantegna and his attitude to antiquity. And I should have thought that there was an appropriate experience required of such a spectator, though – and again this may be Feagin's point – the spectator should not be aware of the requirement. The appropriate experience is close to what used to be called the "standard experience" of seeing the Gonzaga family face-to-face in the location and perspective Mantegna feigns.

Levinson has two stabs at the issue of *trompe l'oeil*.

The first I believe to be largely irrelevant. Starting from the well-known fact that most, indeed virtually all, *trompe l'oeil* paintings fail, Levinson points out we end up looking at *trompe l'oeil* paintings not *as trompe l'oeil* paintings, but as ordinary representations. We pay as much attention to their surfaces as we do to the surfaces of ordinary representations, hence they have, at least on my reasoning, as good a claim to be representations as any other kind of painting. This, it seems to me, is irrelevant, for, if *trompe l'oeil* paintings are thought to present any special problems for the theory of representation, it can only be, as Feagin recognizes, when they are viewed in a way that accords with what the genre demands.

Levinson's second stab at the issue takes us to the heart of what he has to say in, as he agreeably puts it, "friendly interrogation" of my theory of representation. Accepting my general linkage between representation and seeing-in, Levinson contends that, if I am to uphold my account in all cases, I should adopt a weaker account of seeing-in than that which I go for. For, according to him, though it is true that, sometimes when we look at representations, our experience involves twofoldness – he calls these cases of "pictorial seeing" – sometimes, or in cases of what he calls "simple seeing-in," it does not. In cases of simple seeing-in, the pictorial surface must have some causal effect upon the viewer, but the requirement that the viewer should attend to the surface goes unsatisfied. Levinson distinguishes between the two kinds of case thus: Twofoldness is to be insisted upon only when the representation before us is a work of art, and we set out to look at it *as* a work of art. Engagement with other visual representations, such as (Levinson's list) "postcards, passport photos, magazine illustrations, comic strips, television shows, or movies," to which we should now add *trompe l'oeil* paintings, does not call for twofoldness, and insisting that it does, by including twofoldness in the definition of seeing-in, is correspondingly wrong.

On a completely trivial level, what Levinson advocates is unobjectionable. For clearly the term "seeing-in," which I took over from Richard Damann, is not so linguistically entrenched that redefining it by removing one condition from it cannot be faulted: It constitutes no affront to the language.

Nevertheless any such terminological change might expect to encounter opposition from someone sympathetic to my general project on grounds that it fails to grasp the nature of that project. Indeed it might be thought to assume that project dead. For, in linking representation with seeing-in, I did not simply have it in mind to link representation with a term of a somewhat free-floating nature. My aim was to link a kind of art with a term *only in so far as this term picked out a certain perceptual capacity.* This capacity, which we humans at least possess, has been overlooked both by theorists of art and by perceptual psychologists, and what is distinctive of it – or so I claim – is that those experiences which instantiate this capacity involve twofoldness.

If my project succeeds – and this is a basic reason why any cavalier dismissal of it is to be regretted – it would achieve four things. In the first place, it would fix the scope of representation in a non-arbitrary way: that is, by insisting that representational pictures are those which call for the exercise of a particular perceptual faculty. Second, it would vastly enlarge the scope of representation, and thus increase the interest of the field, by getting it to include, for example, abstract painting, which, on reflexion, we can see call for the same kind of perceptual engagement. Third, it would establish that the very same perceptual faculty that allows us to identify what a representation is also allows us, given certain further information, to identify what any particular representation is of, or what it represents. And, finally, since this further information must be perceptual, or is about what the representation looks like, my project would vindicate one of our most basic intuitions about pictures, which has come under heavy fire in recent times, namely that pictorial representation is, both in general and in particular, a perceptual phenomenon.

But in point of fact it turns out that Levinson's redefinition of seeing-in, which takes one condition (twofoldness) out, and seemingly substitutes nothing for it, does not have the consequence feared of it. It does not incapacitate seeing-in as a perceptual faculty, nor does it reduce it to mere seeing face-to-face. For, not merely does Levinson at the last moment come up with a substitute for twofoldness, but, for my part, I find it hard to see how what he comes up with substantially differs from twofoldness. For he tells us – and I quote his words – that, when our perception of pictures involves twofoldness, that is, it is a case of pictorial seeing, the spectator "attend[s] to the surface as [he] views it and is affected by it": but that, when twofoldness is not involved that is, it is a case of simple seeing-in, the spectator engages in "a kind of *as-if* seeing that is both occasioned by visually registering a differentiated surface and inextricably bound up with such registering." "Attending to"/"registering": if the disagreement between us is located in the fine grain of this contrast, I doubt that it is a topic that will retain the interest of readers of this volume for long.

Representation

I move now to the topic of representation proper.

Harrison claims that, if I had pushed the concept of twofoldness further, or as far as it needs to go, I would no longer have the stark contrast between how pictures gain meaning and how language gains meaning. He writes, "My contention is that if we take what he [Wollheim] tells us about 'twofoldness' seriously what it implies is then at odds with *how* he contrasts pictures with language. Faced with that choice we should choose "twofoldness'."

Let me say at the outset that, if Harrison were right, I would find the consequence of his argument reason enough to abandon the concept of two-foldness. For, attractive as I find the concept, the contrast between the two kinds of meaning, linguistic and pictorial, is for me more compelling. Fortunately, for all the subtle things that he finds to say along the way, Harrison does not to my mind make good his basic claim.

He does not do so for two reasons.

First, Harrison does not have in mind the concept of twofoldness that I employ. And that he doesn't is not for reasons that would still keep us on track. That is to say, he does not think that the problem for which I invoke twofoldness requires a different solution from that which I offer, so that, preferring to stick to my word for the solution to my problem, he associates the word with a different concept. No, from the beginning Harrison invokes twofoldness as the solution to a quite different problem from mine, so his concept and mine diverge from the start. He changes the subject.

Let me explain.

I use twofoldness to pick out the distinctive experience that is required to fix the content of representational pictures. In consequence, this enables me to use twofoldness to explain what pictorial representation is. Harrison does not believe that representational content is fixed by experience, even in the somewhat complex way in which I think that it is: he prefers a view according to which the key factor is what he calls "structural analogy." In consequence, it is barely surprising that he has no use for a conception of twofoldness that picks out a characteristic of experience. (He says, and here he anticipates *Levinson*, that, in the case of what he calls the merely *depictive function* of pictures, by which he means representation outside the context of art, two-foldness in my sense is irrelevant: in his words, it "falls away." It is only, according to Harrison, with representational *works of art* that twofoldness is in place.) It is then, not simply that Harrison, in discussing twofoldness, changes the subject, as I have accused him. As he sees it, he saves it. That is, he saves twofoldness for something worthwhile. Exactly what this is is not all that clear to me. But what is clear is that he uses twofoldness to refer, not to a feature of experience, but to a difference that turns up both in language and in art: that is to say, the different perspectives of speaker/artist and hearer/ beholder.

Second, when Harrison thinks that twofoldness, carried appropriately far, obviates the need for the sharp contrast that I make between how language gains meaning and how pictures gain meaning, the contrast that he wants to attenuate seems not to be that which I am concerned to vindicate. He displays, it is true, some interest in the contrast that I am concerned with, but not, as far as I can see, to the point of producing arguments that actually *meet* my arguments.

Oddly enough, what Harrison says, in the last and (to my mind) most interesting section of his essay, about drawing, and how drawing operates, specifically the way in which a line can fulfil a number of different representational functions without our being able to attribute these discretely different functions to discretely different aspects of the line, seems to me, not only the core of what he has to say about the similarity of language and pictures, but pretty close to the core of what I have to say about their dissimilarity. For me, the telling point is that, in language, meaning rests on structural features, in painting – and, I would say, in art generally, including the literary arts – it does not.

Roelofs also thinks that I do not take my account of representation far enough: though her sense of where this would be is markedly different from Harrison's, since she is in principle totally favourable to an experiential account of representational meaning.

Roelofs believes that I need to attach to my account what she calls "a perceptual hypothesis." She thinks that such a hypothesis is necessary if we are to have a characterization of seeing-in that is "experientially and explanatorily adequate."

Let me say, not for the first time, that I do not know that it is right to expect of an account of seeing-in that it should be experientially adequate. I discuss this in On Pictorial Representation. As for explanatory adequacy, I feel that the insistence that a spectator of a representation must, in addition to perceptual experience, hold to a recognitional hypothesis, or a hypothesis about what is there to be recognized in the picture, takes us further from, rather than closer to, the kind of account that will explain representation as experientially grounded.

(Let us put to one side the question whether representations, hence experiences of representations, can have non-conceptual content, for that may be no more of a problem for Roelof's account – even though that account is explicitly stated in terms of conceptual content – than it is for mine that relies on seeing-in unsupplemented.)

The question that Roelof's supplementation of seeing-in by a perceptual hypothesis is required to solve is how to ensure that the content of the spectator's experience coincides with, (more specifically) does not fall short of, the representational content of the picture he is looking at. The addition of a perceptual hypothesis is designed to bring it about that the spectator's experience is what in my lecture I call "the appropriate experience."

So how, according to Roelofs, does the hypothesis that she thinks necessary function in the mind of the spectator? There are two possibilities. One is that, as Wittgenstein might have put it, the spectator *sees according to the hypothesis*: the other is that he doesn't, and that the hypothesis is a mere cognitive accompaniment to his perception.

Let us consider the second possibility first. The spectator has a perception of the picture, and holds to a hypothesis about what there is to be recognized in the picture. Now, if this hypothesis is necessary, as we are told that it is, this can only be because the experience that the spectator has is not the appropriate experience. For the experience must fall short of the content of the picture by an amount equivalent to that for which there is need for the hypothesis. Indeed our doubts might go deeper, and we might wonder whether, despite his adherence to the perceptual hypothesis, the spectator is an adequate spectator. For, if he is, what is preventing him from seeing in the picture what the hypothesis asserts is there to be seen?

So let us turn back to the first possibility, which is that the spectator sees the picture according to the hypothesis. This, I take it, ensures that the experience that he has is the appropriate experience. In such an eventuality, the spectator's experience is, as it stands, adequate to the content of the picture, and the only role that I can see for the perceptual hypothesis is that it helped to bring this about. The perceptual hypothesis is at best causal of the experience that determines the meaning of the picture: hence, *contra* Roelofs, it is not constitutive of the meaning itself.

Crowther seems to think that, as far as my purposes are concerned, I take twofoldness far enough, but that, if taken further, it would allow us to set the perception of pictures within a larger philosophical anthropology. It is this that allows Crowther to say, "Wollheim's philosophical *oeuvre*, therefore, presents exciting possibilities yet to be realized." I admire the ambitious nature of Crowther's project, and am flattered by his attempt to bring my work within its orbit, but I remain sceptical of this attempt in so far as it depends on thinking of seeing-in as a form of imagination: a view that Crowther shares with (in this volume) *Podro*, and, to some extent, *van Gerwen*. There must, of course, be some usage of imagination that makes this view true, but I am uncertain that it is a useful usage.

Let me briefly state the problem of how imagination stands to the perception of pictures as I see it.

Suppose that we look at a marked surface of sufficient complexity, or above what Harrison calls "the mesh." Then we might (one), while looking at the surface, imagine something, alternatively (two) see something in the surface. I believe these to be two radically disjoint possibilities, and there are four major differences that separate them.

One, imagination is more connected with the will, seeing-in considerably less so.

Two, seeing-in is more responsive to the detail of the marked surface, imagination very much less so, and, in some cases, not at all.

Three, seeing-in requires that we continue to fix our eyes on the marked surface, whereas imagination does not. With imagination we can shut our eyes, and it can continue unhindered.

Four, there are identifiable ways in which, when we are engaged in seeing-in, we can change perceptual gear, and can supplement seeing-in with imagination, and these ways do not seem capable of redescription as cases where we supplement imagination with imagination.

Of the authors who connect seeing-in with imagination, Podro has more of an argument than Crowther for doing so. For Podro ingeniously claims that, if seeing-in is to be more than a matter of one thing's reminding us of another, the something extra must be a matter of how we use the reminding thing: We use it, Podro argues, to represent to ourselves the thing that we are reminded of. And that is an exercise of the imagination.

The considerations that I list above are likely to leave me unconvinced of the conclusion of this argument, but, as to the argument itself, I do not see why Podro should think that, if seeing-in is not fortified by imagination, it is merely a case of seeing something that reminds us of something else. Nor do I see why, when seeing-in is fortified by imagination, imagination is adequate for the element of recognition that the perception of representations requires: unless, of course, one just *calls* anything that has this adequacy "imagination." (With imagination, one is always dangerously close to the stipulative.)

Neither Podro's *A* nor his *B* seems to me a correct interpretation of seeing-in, the former containing too little, the latter too much.

Returning finally to Harrison and his proposed fourfoldness, I should like to point out that I have, in *On Formalism and its Kinds* (Fundacio Antoni Tapies: Barcelona, 1995), tried to say what I find problematic about the general idea of a "formal quality."

Now to the limits of seeing-in, and to Levinson's doubts about the way I try to fix these limits. I feel that Levinson is not altogether understanding of the strategy I use.

I start from the fact that my theory of representation needs a distinction between what it is to see some specific thing in a picture and what it is to infer something about a picture from what we see in it. Only the first gives us what the picture represents: the most that the second can give us is information about what may more broadly be called the representational content of the picture. At this point, my strategy in On Pictorial Representation was to try to elicit the needed distinction from the distinction between what it is to be able, and what it is to be unable, to see some specific thing in a picture on the grounds that the latter distinction is more accessible. It is more accessible because it can be assigned an operational counterpart: that is to say, we can be said to see some specific thing in a picture only if the thought of that thing as in the picture can make a difference to how we see it, or if we can see something in that picture under some description essential to that thing. And in the lecture I tried to illustrate this by showing my audience Poussin's *St. John on Patmos*, and at the same time giving them pieces of increasingly precise information about the ruins that litter the landscape. I then tried to get them to gauge, on the basis of their own reactions to a mere slide, whether there was a point, and, if so, where it was, at which a spectator would be unable to use the information provided him to colour his perception of what the picture represented, or to see what he saw in the picture under the description that the latest piece of information suggested.

Levinson objects to this procedure on the grounds that it makes the limits of seeing-in too empirical. I cannot agree. I give a principle for dividing possible from impossible experience in a certain domain. But, since the principle is a principle that governs experience, I thought it no bad idea to try to activate, even if only imaginatively, the domain of experience in which the principle holds. That, I take it, is just what a thought-experiment attempts.

Levinson's desire to argue from all this to a multiplication of kinds of seeing-in – and possibly a multiplication of kinds of pictorial repesentation – is not a project in which I have any desire to follow him. It seems neither necessary nor attractive, though, of course, identity of phenomenon is always consistent with difference in instantiation.

Finally, Levinson is critical of my suggestion of fulfilled intention, as opposed to intention *simpliciter* as the criterion of what a picture represents. I think that his criticism rests on a misunderstanding. He writes:

What it is for the pictorial intentions of the artist of P to be *fulfilled* cannot be specified apart from what suitable spectators are *enabled* to see in P. Such intentions are fulfilled if viewers are in fact enabled . . . to see in P what the artist intended to be seen there. The artist's *fulfilled* intention cannot be thought of as an independent condition to which viewers' responses can be held accountable, but can only be understood in terms of the responses of appropriately primed and backgrounded viewers being the ones they were intended to be. (35–6)

Levinson's argument, at least as we have it, flounders on an ambiguity. What is it of which he claims that it "cannot be specified apart from what suitable spectators are enabled to see" in a picture? On one reading, the answer is: *whether* the artist's intention has been fulfilled. I see no particular reason to dispute this claim, nor do I see any bad consequences: indeed this fits in with, even if it exaggerates, my basic argument. On another reading, the answer is: *what it is for* the artist's intention to be fulfilled. Then the claim would be serious, for it would, as Levinson perceives, completely trivialize my argument, but I see no reason to accept the claim. Critics of my theory of representation could offer coherently different iviews of what it is for an artist's intention to be fulfilled.

When Levinson concludes that the standard for correctness for representation is "not the *fulfilled* intentions of the artist," but "merely the intentions *simpliciter* of the artist for a certain sort of seeing-in, given they are capable of being complied with by the picture's intended viewers," he is, as he seems mostly to recognize, recapitulating my theory. That in this matter he finds it relevant to distinguish between my theory as expressed in "Imagination and Pictorial Understanding" and as expressed in *Painting as an Art* is something finer than I can take in.

Expression

Let me begin with a powerful objection – nevertheless based, I believe, on a misunderstanding – that *Wilde* raises against my account of pictorial meaning. (A similar objection is made by Harrison.) The objection holds for every variety of pictorial meaning, though it has a particular relevance for expressive meaning, and it is that I traduce at once pictorial meaning itself and my view of it by talking of the work of art as a conduit between the artist and the spectator. For such a view, it is said, denigrates the work of art in that it turns it into an object the interest of which for the spectator is exhausted by the fact that it allows the spectator to reconstruct from it the intentions of the artist.

But three points.

First, in talking of the work of art as a conduit, more specifically as a conduit between the artist's intentions and the spectator's experiences, I was saying something about what the work of art *is*, or how it functions. I was not saying anything about how the spectator should treat, or regard, the work of art. I was not saying that the spectator should treat the work of art *as*, let alone *solely as*, a conduit.

Second, though it is not so clear to me what it is for a spectator to treat a work of art as a conduit, two other things are clear to me. It is clear to me what it would be to treat a work of art solely as a conduit, and it is clear to me that this would be inimical to its functioning as a conduit, or, more specifically, as the kind of conduit that I envisage a work of art to be. To treat a work of art solely as a conduit is to be interested in its appearance solely for what this tells us about the intentions with which it was made. And, if we do this, we are highly unlikely to see the work as it was intended, for it is highly unlikely that part of the intentions with which it was made was that it should be seen in a purely inferential way. To put the last point another way: If we treat the work of art solely as a conduit, part of what is supposed to pass down the conduit will get blocked or distorted.

Third, and in amplification of the last point, I have claimed that it is required of the spectator that he should see the work in accordance with the artist's intentions, but not necessarily that he should be, in any prior way, aware what the artist's intentions are. He will need to become aware of them only when doubt sets in about the rightness of his perception.

I am grateful to Wilde for obliging me to make these points clear.

I believe that an altogether separate issue between Wilde and myself is the appropriateness or otherwise of applying causal notions to persons and their works. Wilde, like Wittgenstein, appears to think that this is anti-humanistic. I see no reason to believe this.

A further issue on which I disagree with Wilde – and possibly with *Alpers*, though here it might be divergence rather than disagreement – is that I think that intentions are located in the artist, even if, in many cases, there is no satisfactory way of referring to them except through the works in which they are fulfilled. In fact, I do not grasp the intelligibility of any other view.

I turn now to expression itself.

Three of the contributors who concentrate on expression – *McFee*, *Podro*, and *van Gerwen* – expressly connect the issues of expression and representation. But they do so in different ways, and to different ends.

Van Gerwen links representation and expression by divorcing expression from natural expression, and then thinking of it as the representation of the mental. To make this plausible, van Gerwen reworks the notion of representation, which he explicates in terms of three factors.

First, vision. I agree here.

Second, the expectation that some of the properties that are looked at will, or perhaps just could, recur in a different space and time, but homomodally, or directed to the same sense-modality.

Third, non-egocentricity, or, more specifically, non-egocentric vision. Non-egocentric vision occurs when a spectator sees something, and does not relate what he sees to his own body, or to the space that his body occupies. Strictly speaking – and this is important for van Gerwen – non-egocentric vision is not a form of vision characterized from the inside, or by reference to certain internal, or phenomenological, features of experience, as, say, seeing-in is. What for van Gerwen makes vision non-egocentric is certain kinds of constraint, "moral and epistemological," that we, the viewers, choose to impose upon what we do, or are inclined to do, in response to what we see. What is distinctive of these constraints, van Gerwen insists, is that we impose them *a priori*, or in advance of knowing what we shall see. In this respect, they contrast with, say, the *a posteriori* constraint that we might impose upon our jumping into the sea to save a drowning child once we see the waves towering above us.

When van Gerwen turns from representation proper to expression, he preserves the same general account, except that, in re-employing the notion of the homomodal, he has something to say about the relevant modality. The candidate he selects is empathy.

Rather than follow van Gerwen's ingenious theory in detail, let me express my reservations about his attempt to resolve the nature of aesthetic perception by appeal to non-egocentricity: that is to say, by denying the motivational force we allow such perception to have, while thinking of the perception itself as normal. For, if we consider carefully one situation where an appeal to such constraints seems to do the trick – that is, when we inhibit our desire to storm the stage in order to rescue the heroine, which van Gerwen cites in a slightly different context – it ought to be clear that even here the constraints by themselves, or without reference to the nature of the perception, don't explain everything. For, in the theatre, it isn't that we see the heroine normally, and then stop ourselves from acting upon it. On the contrary, it is precisely because we don't see the heroine face-to-face, but see her-in-the-actress, that we don't raid the stage. It is our non-normal perception of the actress that tells us that raiding the stage would not advance our aims. The performance would be disrupted, and the heroine would still be in danger. The constraints follow from the nature of the theatre, which, like the nature of representational painting, is grounded in a special kind of perception that it calls for, and in terms of which it can be partially explained.

If van Gerwen assimilates expression to representation (at least as he sees it), *McFee* may be said to assimilate – or to experiment with assimilating – representation to expression (at least as he sees it). Attracted (to some degree) by the machinery that I use to explain representation, van Gerwen postulates something broadly parallel to explain expression. Daunted by the machinery that I seemingly invoke to explain expression, McFee suggests that not even in the case of representation is there a clear need for such explanatory *impedimenta*.

As I understand him, McFee proposes that, in both cases, instead of pursuing the hopelessly complex phenomenology of an ever-elusive experience, we should simply introduce into our theory whatever it is in the way of psychological background to that experience that will explain why the experience is credited with enabling the spectator to do what he is held to do. And his view is that, in the case of representation and in that of expression, all that we need refer to is cognitive stock and the ability to mobilize that stock, or to apply it in suitably different ways to the experience of the work.

My suspicion is that why McFee thinks that this will take the place of a phenomenological account is because of the comparatively modest view that he takes of what it is that the experience enables the spectator to do, or of the role that the experience plays in our transactions with art. For McFee seems exclusively preoccupied with the way experience gives us knowledge of what a work of art either represents or expresses. In consequence, he overlooks another, and very important, role that experience of the work plays. Closer attention to this further role would almost certainly have made the case for coming to grips with the nature, or the actual phenomenology, of the experience seem stronger. What I have in mind is that, in addition to its epistemic role, or providing evidence for the representational or expressive meaning of the work of art, the experience is also partly constitutive of this meaning. And that, as I have emphasized, is because the meaning of a work of art derives, not just from the intentions of the artist, but more specifically from his *fulfilled* intentions. And an artist fulfils his intentions when the work that they cause him to create has the power to produce in an appropriate spectator an experience that tallies with those intentions.

We now ask, Why does the fact that experience is, not only evidential for, but also constitutive of, representational and expressive meaning make it more important than ever to investigate its nature? One brief answer is that it is only by considering the nature of the relevant experience that we can determine the scope of the meaning which it carries.

I must add that the argument that I use against McFee, of being short on phenomenological description, has often been used against me by those who think that I under-describe the experience of seeing-in. In On Pictorial Representation, I have tried to come to grips with that issue in a way that what I have said in answer to Roelofs recalls.

Budd does two things. He criticizes my account of expressive perception, finding it wrong *in toto*, and he offers a partial diagnosis of why I go wrong.

The diagnosis is not offered as a deep diagnosis. For my mistake, or part of my mistake, according to him, is that I try to offer a monolithic account that covers both our expressive perception of art and our expressive perception of other things, such as nature. But Budd cannot mean that, if I had confined the scope of my account, it would have stood a better chance of being right, since he in effect finds the account incoherent. His criticism is more of the order that anyone who attempts something so over-ambitious as I do will end up talking nonsense. That may be so, but I find it deeply implausible to think that a common account is not a natural objective. Certainly the two differences that Budd cites as distinguishing between the expressive perception of art and that of nature – namely, (1) that the latter requires, whereas (at least according to me) the former does not, an actual, or "primary," experience of the emotion expressed, and (2) that the expressive properties of art, as opposed to those of nature, have been intended as such, and are perceived as such, by the human mind – are differences that appear to call at least as loudly for a difference within a common explanation as for a difference of explanation.

Budd thinks that my account is wrong on at least three counts.

(1) it claims, in advance of supporting arguments, that any instance of expressive perception intimates the origin of expressive perception itself in complex projection.
(2) it claims, once again in advance of supporting arguments, that the perception of correspondence presupposes the power of complex perception.
(3) the notion of correspondence, and that of the perception of one external thing as corresponding to some internal state, are indefinite, or imprecise.

I shall confine myself to two broad observations on Budd's methodology.

Many of Budd's arguments consist in charging that the concepts I use in elaborating my theory are imprecise, or indefinite, and, in consequence, that the theory I advance is merely programmatic. I have little difficulty in conceding these charges, and I regret that they hold. However I wonder whether all philosophical theories of expression and perception are not merely programmatic, and the inadequacies of the concepts used may simply reflect the fact that these are early days. Such admissions might easily lead me on to look to Budd for assistance in removing these shortcomings were it not for my being brought up against the fact that Budd and I have clearly very different starting-points.

So, what is this difference in starting-point? I see it like this: Characteristically I set out to consider the phenomenon of expression, and our experience of it, and there seems to me one factor that stands out. Let us call it A. I then look for some explanation of A, and I think that I find it in B, which, for all the obscurity that attaches to it, seems to have support in experience.

Budd appears to take A on trust from me. But the lack of conviction with which he does so, and the difference between the two of us, manifest themselves as soon as he turns to consider B. For he treats whatever implausibility that (as he sees it) attaches to B as also detaching plausibility from A: Indeed he begins to treat the plausibility of A as entirely dependent on that of B. For an example of this strategy, consider the way in which Budd treats the relations between correspondence and expressive perception, and his conclusion that expressive perception is the "key" to correspondence.

I doubt if there is any way in which disagreements between Budd and myself can find resolution until he discloses what *he* takes to be the *donnees*, albeit the obscure *donnees*, of our attributions of expression to works of art. Since, as far as I can see, Budd shares my belief that expression is experientially grounded, I am unwilling to think of him as entirely quit of this obligation, however enticing the pleasures of neutrality may be.

Podro is more forthcoming on this last topic, and he thinks that there is a real disagreement between us in that I think of our perception of expressive properties as somehow coming after our perception of objective properties, and he reverses this ordering. We humans start off, he contends, with "a perceived world which is highly physiognomic, only gradually being brought under the order of objective thought."

Do I disagree with this?

The truth is, I don't know. More helpfully, I disagree with it only if it turns out to be incompatible with my claim that expressive properties originate in projection. As far as that determination is concerned, the onus, I am inclined to say, is on Podro. There certainly are ways of taking his words so as to make them compatible with my claim. I doubt if I can make much sense of his suggestion that there is a primordial way of seeing the world, which at once is animistic, and precedes projection: the more so because I believe that projection starts from the beginning of life.

The Internal Spectator

Of those contributors who focus in on the account of an internal spectator to be found in Lecture III of *Painting as an Art*, *Hopkins* is clearly the most sceptical, and I start with him.

Let me start by observing that Hopkins is a good kind of adversary for me because, as he shows clearly in his criticism of the "minimalist" position, he clearly distinguishes between perception and imagination, while embracing the idea that, in front of a painting, we can profitably recruit imagination to supplement perception along the lines I suggest. He further agrees with me that, for this supplementation to aid understanding, the way the imagination is exercised must be "licensed," and that means for him, at least part of the time, "licensed by the artist."

Where Hopkins and I begin to disagree is when I think that, in certain interesting cases, licensed imagination takes the following very specific form: the spectator, that is, the external spectator, identifies with, that is, centrally imagines, an internal spectator, who has been placed in the represented space by the artist, and endowed by him with a repertoire, which therefore serves as a constraint upon what he, the internal spectator, can be imagined as doing or experiencing. Hopkins is averse to this suggestion, and thinks in contrast that what the external spectator is required to do – and he thinks this holds in all cases – is to imagine *himself* in the represented space. Hopkins calls his account a "middle view" because it allows imagination in but keeps an internal spectator out. Instead the external spectator is the protagonist of all his licensed imaginings.

I shall confine myself to two comments on Hopkins's discussion. Both comments suggest that he hasn't fully accepted the realism of my suggestion, or that it is a suggestion about a certain strategy that certain painters have adopted. Alternatively he may feel that my suggestion is so implausible that he charitably reinterprets it. But I would like to bring the differences between our approaches out into the open.

In order to do so, I start with the fact that Hopkins thinks that his middle view has an initial plausibility over my view. Why does he think this? Why does he think that a view that attributes to an artist less complex intentions is more plausible than one that attributes more complex intentions? There seem to be, implicit in his text, two different answers, which in turn correspond to two different conceptions that Hopkins has of the nature of the disagreement between us.

One answer is that a hypothesis that attributes simpler intentions to an artist has greater plausibility because that is what artists' intentions are like: They just do not have the complexity that the hypothesis of an internal spectator posits. This corresponds to the view that there is an empirical disagreement between us, and the relevant fact of the matter is the nature of the intentions that artists form.

A second answer is that Hopkins thinks that the middle view is *prima facie* more plausible on what might be thought of as Ockhamite grounds. This is what he suggests when he writes, "My view attempts to accommodate the phenomena without multiplying the varieties of pictorial content." Such an answer corresponds to a view of the disagreement between us as theoretical, as though either there was no fact of the matter about what intentions motivated an artist, and we had only to order the outcome in the most parsimonous manner, or there is a fact of the matter about what goes on in the artist's head, but we have no access to it.

Rightly or wrongly, I suppose the issue to be of the first kind. Hence, in so far as he is discussing my proposal, Hopkins cannot, except at the margin, introduce Ockhamite considerations. For that is to ignore the realism of my proposal. By contrast, Hopkins supposes the issue to be of the second kind, and either supposes that I do also, or thinks that it is more plausible to treat me as if I did. In Section 8, where he talks of "default" explanation, Hopkins treats the internal spectator hypothesis as I do it, and he finds against me. But, let me say dogmatically, I am not convinced by his discussion.

The truth is that Hopkins does not capture my two strongest reasons for preferring my account to his. He does not capture my two strongest reasons for thinking that an artist who wanted to recruit imagination to the understanding of his picture would rather go my way than his middle way.

The first reason is that what a middle-way artist would be asking the spectator to imagine himself doing is something that he, the spectator, cannot do, hence (for this is the same thing) cannot imagine himself doing – though he could *try to* imagine himself doing it. The impossible thing is for the spectator to enter the represented space, given, that is, that he doesn't belong there, or hasn't been put there by the artist. For I take it that a represented space is partially identified by its inhabitants. Add a figure, and the identity of the space changes.

The second reason is that, if *per impossibile* the spectator did imagine himself entering the represented space, why should we think that his doing this would thereby add to his understanding of the picture at issue? For, even if his entry into the space didn't alter the represented space, as the last reason assumes, a picture representing that more populated space would be a different picture from one representing the less populated space – and what the imaginative project that Hopkins favours would advance is surely understanding of the former, merely possible, painting rather than what is desired, which is understanding of the latter, or actual, painting.

I must point to a possible tension within what I have been saying in response to Hopkins. It raises an important issue. Initially I suggested that what is between us, or whether an artist is likelier to have intentions of the sort I propose or of the sort Hopkins proposes, is a purely contingent matter, with the weight of evidence on my side. But have I not then introduced metaphysical considerations when I suggested that an artist *couldn't* form intentions of the sort that Hopkins is convinced he will have, and *must* form intentions of the sort I propose?

My resolution of the tension is briefly this: An artist is certain in the fulness of time to evolve a theory of his art, and this theory will contain a number of modal truths about what is possible, and what is not possible, within the general matrix of his art. Once he does so, then the intentions that he goes on to form will be modified by such a theory.

Van Eck struggles with a very real problem about the internal spectator, but I believe that she fails to solve it, because she looks for an answer involving a stark contrast, which is what she supposes the problem demands, whereas I supect that the answer will turn out to be a matter of pointing to some differences of emphasis.

She asks what distinguishes the kind of inquiry that *Painting as an Art* exemplifies from that pursued by traditional art-history, and she tries to locate an answer by contrasting my treatment of the internal spectator with John Shearman's treatment of the implied spectator.

Let me dispose of one suggestion that van Eck pursues, which is, I believe, based upon an unimportant misunderstanding. Van Eck tries out the idea that the internal spectator, as I conceive of him, is connected with an excess of representational content, whereas the implied spectator, as Shearman conceives of him, is connected with a paucity of representational content. But nothing substantive can be built on this. For, (1) I don't speak of an excess of representational content as such. I speak only, as van Eck herself recognizes, of representational content in excess of what is represented: that is, you can't see the internal spectator in the picture – any more, it might be said, than you can see the implied spectator in the picture. So neither is represented: but both are, I take it, part of the representational content. And, (2) the excess that I talk of comes about only when the internal spectator is counted in, whereas the paucity that Shearman talks about arises only so long as the implied spectator is counted out. In other words, there is, at least in respect of excess and paucity, little to choose between us.

Van Eck is right to suggest that I am concerned with aspects of a picture that give rise, alternatively reinforce, its meaning. But I do not see that this stands in sharp contrast to what art historians do, nor is it remote, as she suggests, from issues of composition. In one respect, van Eck is surely right. An interest in how paintings acquire meaning will always go beyond merely establishing the existence of a certain item in a painting: It will focus on how that item functions, or is used. And that is because meaning is a matter of use: use by the artist.

The damaging suggestion that van Eck makes, in more places than one, is that there is something optional about what I say. What I say may be, she suggests, "fascinating and illuminating," but there is "no absolute need" to accept it. In so far as this is not just a hyperbolic way of saying that I might be wrong, it arises out of a failure to recognize the character of merely persuasive arguments, such as, for instance, the inference to the best explanation, which I use at several points. If some state of affairs, which is not in itself improbable, could explain better than anything else can the existence of something for which we have firm evidence, then this gives us reason to believe in that further state of affairs. To say that it is optional whether we accept such arguments illuminates one aspect of them: they are not deductively sound. But it obscures another aspect of them: they, or some of them, are as strong as they need be.

I take it that the core of *van de Vall*'s case is not, as she might seem to suggest, the narrowly textual argument that I have so defined seeing-in and identification with an internal spectator as to make them exhaustive of forms of attention to pictures, thus squeezing out any third form, but the more substantive claim that there is a third form of attention, for which there is presumably place in my scheme of things, and I should reinstate it at the trivial price of redefining some of my terms. What is objectionable for van de Vall is that the only kind of spectator that I allow for is one coincident with an embodied eye, hence a spectator whose contribution to the understanding of painting consists entirely in perceptual experiences and visual imaginings. What I have left out is any kind of spectatorship that involves manoeuvering some part of the body other than the eye so as to get into some interesting relationship of a non-ocular kind with the pictorial surface or the represented scene.

I am sure that it would be right of me to concede something, but not everything, to van de Vall. This is because our fields of interest do not perfectly overlap. What I say, and its limitations, derive directly from my characterization of painting as an essentially visual art. By the same token, her emphasis on what we might call the "full-body" spectator comes initially from her concern with installation art, which inherits some of its characteristics from sculpture. However I do not take this to be the end of the matter. For there have been, over the centuries, over the decades, a number of serious paintings that demand that their spectators behave in a way related to, or derivative from, ways in which the spectator of sculpture has traditionally been expected to react in front of a work. I have to confess that van de Vall, by invoking the ever-daunting example of Barnett Newman, makes me feel better about this oversight than I otherwise would.

Baxandall's subtly entitled essay is in effect a pull in the opposite direction. For he queries whether I have not, in describing the phenomenology of identification with an internal spectator, allowed the whole process to get too dissociated from vision, from the visual. And, by the visual, Baxandall has two things in mind. First, there is the seeing that the internal spectator might be imagined to do. And second there is the seeing that the external spectator is required to do in order to determine what the picture instructs him to imagine the internal spectator seeing, and also feeling, thinking, imagining.

At this point, Baxandall in effect takes up a question that other contributors to this volume have taken up, though generally in a more sceptical fashion, van de Vall, van Eck, and Hopkins all feel that I should have said more *in general* about how an internal spectator's repertoire is inscribed in a painting. Baxandall hopes that I might be able to say more *in particular*. And I must add that he has, in *Patterns of Intention*, set some admirable examples of more or less just this.

Let me say something autobiographical about how I came by the whole idea of an internal spectator. The truth is that I first found myself in a position to advance, for certain paintings, the hypothesis of an internal spectator in the course of going round the great 1984 Manet exhibition at the Metropolitan Museum. What happened was that, time and time again, I discovered that I was engaging in imaginative enactments of a kind that might be expected to follow in the wake of my explicitly locating an internal spectator. Yet I had done no such thing. That being so, I trusted that my eyes had not deceived me, and that the repertoire that I was following with such conviction was one for which my perception of the painting had given me some warrant: some implicit warrant, that is. Later, in writing up this whole process, I tried to recapture the fleeting experiences that must have influenced me. In attempting to do this, I knew that I was going against everything that an educated late twentienth-century eye characteristically finds in Manet's canvases. I agree with Baxandall that I could have done it better.

Alpers makes me aware of a carelessness with which I expressed myself. For, in saying that the artist is essentially a spectator of his own work, I did not mean that his being a spectator of his own work is the whole of his essence. I meant only that it is part of his essence. After all, there must be some work of his that he has made if he is to be the spectator of it, and he must have been the spectator of some world if he was to make the work. And these two things – looking at the world, and making the work – must be essential activities of him as a painter.

However, once the account of the artist's essence has been amplified in the required way, I feel as perplexed as I believe Alpers to be over how to relate a story of the sort that she tells about the making of Rembrandt's *Bathsheba* to this account. Alpers has two suggestions to make.

The first suggestion is that stories like this, though they make no contribution to pictorial meaning, tell us a vital fact about painting: a fact of a sort upon which painting's capacity to bear meaning, both primary and secondary, ultimately depends. They show us that painting is an activity that is carried out *in the face of* a neutral, recalcitrant, mind-independent world. Hendrickje Stoffels's suitability to model the part of Bathsheba and her reluctance to do so created for Rembrandt a situation that epitomized the dilemma that painting essentially confronts, and he constructed his painting around this fact.

The second suggestion is that the way Rembrandt filtered one narrative – the Biblical narrative – through another narrative – the studio narrative involving Hendrickje – endowed Rembrandt's painting with something that not every painting possesses: secondary meaning. For we can see in certain difficulties that Rembrandt had with a woman, and by implication with women, and which he worked his way through in the course of painting *Bathsheba* – the demands that he made upon her, and his willingness or otherwise to accept her rejection of those demands – no small part of what painting this painting meant for him. And this, it will be recalled, is how I think of secondary meaning.

Alpers's essay brings home to me two facts. The first, which is not altogether unwelcome, is that the notion of secondary meaning, as it is to be found in *Painting as as Art*, is a very mixed bag. More work, as they say, needs to be done. The second, which is decidedly welcome, is that a theory of pictorial meaning such as *Painting as an Art* expressly set out to provide may very well be not all that there is to a philosophical theory of painting.

Bibliography

Alberti, L. B. 1966. *On Painting*. New Haven, London: Yale University Press (trans. with an Introduction by John R. Spencer).

Alpers, Svetlana. 1987. "Style is What You Make It: The Visual Arts Once Again." Lang, B., ed. *The Concept of Style*, Ithaca NY: Cornell University Press.

Auping, M. 1987. *Abstract Expressionism: The Critical Developments*. New York: Abrams.

Baker, Gordon. 1992. "Some Remarks on 'Language' and 'Grammar.' " *Grazer Philosophische Studien* 42: 107–31.

———, and Peter Hacker. 1980. *Wittgenstein: Understanding and Meaning: An Analytical Commentary on the 'Philosophical Investigations,'* Vol. I. Oxford: Blackwell.

Baxandall, Michael. 1985. *Patterns of Intention*. New Haven, London: Yale University Press.

———. 1991. "The Language of Art Criticism." Kemal, S. and I. Gaskell, eds., *The Language of Art History*, 67–75. New York: Cambridge University Press.

———. 1995. *Shadows and Enlightenment*. New Haven, CT: Yale University Press.

Bell, Clive. 1987 [1947]. *Art*. Oxford: Oxford University Press.

Bergson, Henri. 1978. *Matter and Memory*. London: Harvester (trans. N. M. Paul and W. S. Palmer).

Best, David. 1978. *Philosophy and Human Movement*. London: George Allen & Unwin.

———. 1985. *Feeling and Reason in the Arts*. London: George Allen & Unwin.

———. 1992. *The Rationality of Feeling*. London: Falmer Press.

Blackburn, Simon. 1981. "Reply: Rule-Following and Moral Realism." Holtzmann, S. and C. Leich, eds., *Wittgenstein: To Follow a Rule*, 163–87. London: Routledge & Kegan Paul.

———. 1984. *Spreading the Word*. Oxford: Oxford University Press.

———. 1993. *Essays in Quasi-Realism*. Oxford: Oxford University Press.

Block, Ned. 1981. "What is Functionalism?." Block, N., ed. *Readings in Philosophy of Psychology*, Chap. 3. Cambridge, MA: Harvard University Press.

Boehm, Gottfried. 1985. *Bildnis und Individuum: über den Ursprung der Porträtmalerei in der italienische Renaissance.* München: Prestel.

Boghossian, Peter, and Dick Velleman 1989. "Colour as a Secondary Quality." *Mind* 98: 507–49.

Bosanquet, Bernard. 1915. *Three Lectures on Aesthetics.* London: Macmillan.

Budd, Malcolm. 1992. "On Looking at a Picture." Hopkins, J. and A. Savile, eds. *Psychoanalysis, Mind and Art,* 259–80. Oxford: Oxford University Press.

———. 1993. "How Pictures Look." Knowles, D. and J. Skorupski, eds., *Virtue and Taste,* 154–75. Oxford: Blackwell.

———. 1995. *Values of Art. Pictures, Poetry and Music.* London: Allen Lane.

Cassirer, Ernst. 1956. "Vol. 3 – The Phenomenology of Knowledge." *The Philosophy of Symbolic Forms,* New Haven, CT: Yale University Press (trans. R. Mannheim).

Cavell, Stanley. 1969. *Must We Mean What We Say?* New York: Charles Scribner's Sons.

Churchland, Paul. 1984. *Matter and Consciousness.* Cambridge, MA: MIT Press.

———. 1986. "Perceptual Plasticity and Theory Neutrality." *Philosophy of Science* 55(2): 167–87.

Crowther, Paul. 1993. *Art and Embodiment: From Aesthetics to Self-Consciousness.* Oxford: Clarendon Press.

———. 1993. *Critical Aesthetics and Postmodernism.* Oxford: Oxford University Press.

———. 1994. "The Logical Structure of Pictorial Representation." *Acta Philosophica, Filozofski Vestnik* XV: 199–210.

Currie, Gregory. 1995. "Imagination and Simulation: Aesthetics Meets Cognitive Science." Davies, M. and T. Stone, eds. *Mental Simulation,* 151–169. Oxford: Blackwell.

———. 1995. *Image and Mind.* New York: Cambridge University Press.

Dummett, Michael. 1993. *The Seas of Language.* Oxford: Oxford University Press.

———. 1978. *Truth and Other Enigmas.* London: Duckworth.

Eldridge, Richard. 1985. "Form and Content: An Aesthetic Theory of Art," *The British Journal of Aesthetics* 25: 303–316.

Empson, William. 1961. *Seven Types of Ambiguity.* Harmondsworth: Penguin Books.

———. 1977. *The Structure of Complex Words.* London: Chatto and Windus.

Fodor, Jerry. 1975. *The Language of Thought.* Cambridge, MA: Harvard University Press.

———. 1983. *The Modularity of the Mind.* Cambridge, MA: MIT Press.

Fried, Michael. 1988 [1980]. *Absorption and Theatricality. Painting and Beholder in the Age of Diderot.* Chicago: University of Chicago Press.

————. 1996. *Manet's Modernism or the Face of Painting in the 1860s.* Chicago: University of Chicago Press.

Fry, Roger. 1926. *Transformations: Critical and Speculative Essays on Art.* London: Chatto and Windus.

Goheen, E. R., ed. 1988. *The Collections of the Nelson-Atkins Museum of Art.* New York: Harry N. Abrams, [in association with the Nelson-Atkins Museum of Art].

Gombrich, Ernst. 1963. *Meditations on a Hobby Horse and Other Essays on the Theory of Art.* London: Phaidon Press.

————. 1993. "Review of: Only Connect . . . ," *New York Review of Books* 40(5): 19–22.

————. 1986. *Art and Illusion.* 5th ed. London: Phaidon Press.

————. 1982. *The Image and the Eye.* Oxford: Phaidon Press.

Goodman, Nelson. 1972. "Seven Strictures on Similarity." *Problems and Projects,* 437–46. Indianapolis: Bobbs-Merrill.

————. 1978. "The Status of Style." *Ways of Worldmaking,* Indianapolis: Hackett, 23–40.

————. 1985. *Languages of Art.* Indianapolis: Hackett.

Grabar, A. 1967. *The Golden Age of Justinian.* New York: Odyssey Press.

Gregory, R. L. 1966. *Eye and Brain: the Psychology of Seeing.* New York: McGraw-Hill.

————. 1970. *The Intelligent Eye.* New York: McGraw-Hill.

————. 1987. "Perception as Hypotheses." Gregory, R. L., ed. *Oxford Companion to the Mind,* 608–11. Oxford: Oxford University Press.

————. 1987. "Perception." Gregory, R. L., ed. *Oxford Companion to the Mind,* 598–601. Oxford: Oxford University Press.

Grice, H. P. 1991. *The Conception of Value.* Oxford: Clarendon Press.

Ground, Ian. 1989. *Art or Bunk.* Bristol: Bristol Classical Press.

Hacker, Peter M. S. 1976. "Locke and the Meaning of Colour Words." Vesey, G., ed. *Impressions of Empiricism,* 23–46. London: Macmillan.

————. 1996. *Wittgenstein's Place in Twentieth-Century Analytical Philosophy.* Oxford: Blackwell.

Harris, R. 1996. *Signs, Language and Communication.* London: Routledge.

————. 1996. *The Language Connection.* Bristol: Thoemmes Press.

Harrison, Andrew. 1973. "Representation and Conceptual Change." Vesey, G., ed. *Philosophy and the Arts,* 106–31. London: Macmillan.

————. 1978. *Making and Thinking.* Indianapolis: Hackett.

————. 1988. "Conduits or Conventions?" *Art History* 11: 439–45.

————. 1991. "A Minimal Syntax for the Pictorial." Kemal, S. and I. Gaskell, eds., *The Language of Art History,* 213–39. New York: Cambridge University Press.

————. 1992. "Style." Cooper, D., ed. *A Companion to Aesthetics*, 403–07. Oxford: Basil Blackwell.

————. 1997. *Philosophy and the Arts. Seeing and Believing*. Bristol: Thoemmes Press.

Hegel, Georg W. F. 1993 [1832–45]. *Introductory Lectures on Aesthetics*. Harmondsworth: Penguin.

Hochberg, Julian. 1978. "Art and Perception." Carterette, E. C. and M. P. Friedman, eds., *Handbook of Perception, X, Perceptual Ecology*, 225–58. New York.

————. 1979. "Some of the Things That Paintings Are." Nodine, C. F. and D. F. Fisher, eds., *Perception and Pictorial Representation*, 17–41. New York.

Hopkins, Robert. 1998. *Picture, Image and Experience*. Cambridge, UK: Cambridge University Press.

Hume, David. 1969, [1740]. *A Treatise of Human Nature*. Harmondsworth: Penguin.

Jay, Martin. 1993. *Downcast Eyes. The Denigration of Vision in Twentieth-Century French Thought*. Berkeley: University of California Press.

Kant, Immanuel. 1952 [1793]. *The Critique of Judgement*. Oxford: Oxford University Press (trans. J. C. Meredith).

————. 1973. *The Critique of Pure Reason*. London: Macmillan (trans. N. Kemp-Smith).

Keynes, G., ed. 1957. *The Writings of William Blake*. London: Nonesuch Press.

Kripke, Saul A. 1982. *Wittgenstein on Rules and Private Language*. Oxford: Blackwell.

Kristéva, Julia. 1983. *Histoires d'amour*. Paris: Éd. Denoël.

Levinson, Jerrold. 1996. *The Pleasures of Aesthetics*. Ithaca, NY: Cornell University Press.

Lopes, Dominique. 1996. *Understanding Pictures*. Oxford: Clarendon Press.

Lord, Catherine. and J. A. Bernadete. 1991. "Baxandall and Goodman." Kemal, S. and I. Gaskell, eds., *The Language of Art History*, 76–100. New York: Cambridge University Press.

Lormand, Eric. 1996. "Non-Phenomenal Consciousness," *Noûs* 30:242–61.

Marr, David. 1982. *Vision*. New York: Freeman and Company.

Maynard, P. L. 1994. "Seeing Double." *Journal of Aesthetics and Art Criticism* 52: 155–67.

McFee, Graham. 1985. "Wollheim and the Institutional Theory of Art." *The Philosophical Quarterly* 35:179–85.

————. 1990. "Davies' Replies: A Response." *Grazer Philosophische Studien* 38: 182–83.

————. 1990. "Wittgenstein: Understanding and 'Intuitive Awareness.' " Haller, R. and J. Brandl, eds., *Wittgenstein: Towards a Re-Evaluation*, 37–46. Vienna: Hölder-Pichler-Temsky.

———. 1992. *Understanding Dance*. London: Routledge.

———. 1994. "Pictorial Representation in Art," *British Journal of Aesthetics* 34: 35–47.

———. 1996. "A Nasty Accident with One's Flies." Inaugural Lecture, University of Brighton.

O'Neill, J., ed. 1990. *Barnett Newman: Selected Writings and Interviews*. New York: Knopf.

Peacocke, Christopher. 1987. "Depiction," *Philosophical Review* 96: 383–410.

Podro, Michael. 1987. "Depiction and the Golden Calf." Harrison, A., ed. *Philosophy and the Visual Arts*, 3–22. Dordrecht: Kluwer.

———. 1993. "Fiction and Reality in Painting." Reprinted in Kemal, S., ed. *Explanation and Value in the Arts*, 43–54. New York: Cambridge University Press.

———. 1998. *Depiction*. New Haven, CT: Yale University Press.

Pole, David. 1983. *Aesthetics, Form and Emotion*. London: Duckworth.

Rey, G. 1983. "Concepts and Stereotypes," *Cognition* 15: 237–262.

———. 1993. "Sensational Sentences." Davies, M. and G. Humphries, eds., *Consciousness*, 240–57. Oxford: Blackwell.

Rock, I. 1984. *Perception*. New York: Scientific American.

Rosch, E. 1978. "Principles of Categorization." Rosch, E. and B. B. Lloyd, eds., *Cognition and Categorization*, 27–257. Hillsdale, NJ.

Rosch, E. and C. B. Mervis 1975. "Family Resemblances: Studies in the Internal Structure of Categories." *Cognitive Psychology* 7: 573–605.

Schier, Flint. 1986. *Deeper into Pictures. An Essay on Pictorial Representation*. Cambridge, UK: Cambridge University Press.

Scruton, Roger. 1983. *The Aesthetic Understanding: Essays in the Philosophy of Art and Culture*. New York: Methuen.

———. 1993. "Notes on the Meaning of Music." Krausz, M., ed. *The Interpretation of Music: Philosophical Essays*, 193–202. Oxford: Clarendon Press.

Shearman, J. 1992. *Only Connect. . . . Art and the Spectator in the Italian Renaissance – The A. W. Mellon Lectures in the Fine Arts 1988*. Princeton: Princeton University Press.

Smith, E. and D. Medin 1984. "Concepts and Concept Formation," *Annual Review of Psychology* 113–38.

Smith, E. and D. Medin, eds. 1981. *Categories and Concepts*. Cambridge, MA: Harvard University Press.

Stern, D. 1985. *The Interpersonal World of the Infant*. New York: Basic Books.

Stokstad, M. 1995. *Art History*. New York: Harry N. Abrams.

Trevarthen, C. 1993. "Playing into Reality. Conversations with the Infant Communicator," *Winnicott Studies* 7: 67–84.

Turner, J., ed. 1997. *The Dictionary of Art*. London: Macmillan.

Tye, M. 1995. *Ten Problems of Consciousness*. Cambridge, MA: M.I.T. Press.

van de Vall, Renée. 1994. *Een subliem gevoel van plaats. Een filosofische interpretatie van het werk van Barnett Newman*. Groningen: Historische Uitgeverij.

———. 1995. "Silent Visions: Lyotard and the Sublime." *Art & Design, Profile No. 40*: 10.

van Gerwen, Rob. 1996. *Art and Experience*. Utrecht: Department of Philosophy.

———. 1998. "Fictionele emoties en representatie." *Feit & Fictie* IV: 13–26.

Vermazen, Bruce. 1986. "Expression as Expression," *Pacific Philosophical Quarterly* 67:196–224.

Walton, Kendall L. 1990. *Mimesis as Make-Believe: On the Foundations of the Representational Arts*. Cambridge, MA: Harvard University Press.

———. 1992. "Seeing-In and Seeing Fictionally." Hopkins, J., ed. *Psychoanalysis, Mind and Art*, 281–91. Cambridge, UK: Blackwell.

Watts, J. D., Jr. 1997. "Moving Mountains." *Tulsa World*, 28 Sept.

Weitz, Morris. 1970. *Problems in Aesthetics*. London: Collier MacMillan.

White, J. 1987. *The Birth and Rebirth of Pictorial Space*. Cambridge, MA: Harvard University Press.

Wiggins, David. 1987. *Needs, Values, Truth: Essays in the Philosophy of Value*. Oxford: Blackwell.

———. 1991. "Moral Cognitivism, Moral Relativism and Motivating Moral Beliefs." *Proceedings of the Aristotelian Society, Suppl.*, LXV: 61–85.

Wilde, Carolyn. 1987. "Painting, Expression, Abstraction." Harrison, Andrew, ed. *Philosophy and the Visual Arts*, 29–50. Dordrecht: Reidel.

———. 1992. "Richard Wollheim." Cooper, David, ed. *A Companion to Aesthetics*, 447–9. Oxford: Basil Blackwell.

———. 1994. "Painting, Alberti and the Wisdom of Minerva," *British Journal of Aesthetics* 34: 48–59.

Williams, Bernard. 1973. "Imagination and the Self." *Problems of the Self*, 26–45. Cambridge, UK: Cambridge University Press.

Winnicott, D. W. 1991–(1960). "The Theory of Parent-Infant Relationship." *The Maturational Process and the Facilitating Environment*. London: Karnac.

———. 1991 (1963). "The Capacity for Concern." *The Maturational Process and the Facilitating Environment*. London: Karnac.

———. 1991 (1971). *Playing and Reality*. London: Routledge.

Wittgenstein, Ludwig. 1969. *On Certainty*. Oxford: Blackwell (trans. D. Paul and G. E. M. Anscombe).

———. 1974. *Philosophical Grammar*. Oxford: Blackwell (trans. A. Kenny).

————. 1976 [1953]. *Philosophical Investigations*. Oxford: Blackwell (trans. G. E. M. Anscombe).

Wölfflin, Heinrich. 1932. *The Principles of Art History*. New York: Holt (trans. M. D. Hottinger).

Wollheim, Richard. 1961. "Reflections on Art and Illusion." *Arts Yearbook*. Reprinted in AM, 261–89.

————. 1963. "Art and Illusion," *British Journal of Aesthetics* 3: 15–37.

————. 1964. "On Expression and Expressionism," *Revue Internationale de Philosophie* 18: 270–89.

————. 1966. "Form, Elements, and Modernity: Reply to Michael Podro," *British Journal of Aesthetics* 6: 339–45.

————. 1968. "Expression." Vesey, G. N. A., ed. *Royal Institute of Philosophy Lectures 1966–67*, 227–44. London: Macmillan.

————. 1968. *Art and its Objects: An Introduction to Aesthetics*. New York: Harper & Row.

————. 1970. "Nelson Goodman's Languages of Art," *Journal of Philosophy* 67: 531–9.

————. 1972. "On Drawing an Object." Osborne, Harold, ed. *Aesthetics* 121–44. Oxford: Oxford University Press.

————. 1973. *On Art and the Mind*. London: Allen Lane. (AM)

————. 1979. "Pictorial Style: Two Views." Lang, B., ed. *The Concept of Style*, 129–45. Philadelphia University of Pennsylvania Press.

————. 1980. *Art and its Objects, Second edition*. Cambridge, UK: Cambridge University Press. (AO2)

————. 1983. "On the Question 'Why Painting Is an Art?'," *Proceedings of the Eighth International Wittgenstein Symposium* 10: 101–106.

————. 1984. *The Thread of Life*. Cambridge, UK: Cambridge University Press. (TL)

————. 1986. "Imagination and Pictorial Understanding," *Proceedings of the Aristotelian Society, Supplement* 60: 45–60. (W-IPU)

————. 1987. "Aesthetics, Anthropology and Style: Some Programmatic Remarks." Greenhalgh, Michael and Vincent Megaw, eds., *Art in Society*, 3–14. London: Duckworth.

————. 1987 (1979). "Pictorial Style: Two Views," Lang, B., ed. *The Concept of Style*, 129–45. Ithaca, NY: Cornell University Press.

————. 1988. *Painting as an Art*. Princeton, NJ: Princeton University Press.

————. 1991. "Correspondence, Projective Properties, and Expression in the Arts." Kemal, S., ed. *The Language of Art History*, 51–66. New York: Cambridge University Press.

————. 1991. "The Core of Aesthetics," *Journal of Aesthetic Education* 25: 37–45.

————. 1993. *The Mind and its Depths*. Cambridge, MA: Harvard University Press. (MD)

————. 1995. *On Formalism and its Kinds*. Barcelona: Fundacio Antoni Tapies.

————, and J. Hopkins, eds. 1982. *Philosophical Essays on Freud*. Cambridge, UK: Cambridge University Press.

Wright, C. 1980. *Wittgenstein on the Foundation of Mathematics*. London: Duckworth.

————. 1988. "Moral Values, Projection and Secondary Qualities," *Proceedings of the Aristotelian Society, Supplement* LXII: 1–26.

————. 1992. *Truth and Objectivity*. Cambridge, MA: Harvard University Press.

Index

Index

(kinds) of, 44, 45, 105; visual, 13, 57, 189, 200, 217
explanation, 167n
expression of: emotion, 108; environment, 136; events, 136; internal phenomena, 135; pictures, 147; self, 196
expression, 101–11, 125, 151–63, 252–6; as comparison, 138; as disposition, 139; (contingently) psychological, 137; defined, 144, 146; facial and gestural, 145; intended, 254; natural and artistic, 139, 140, 252; as projection, 4, 6, 10, 101; and/as representation, 9, 119, 135–50, 252, 254; and response, 137; two elements, 152
expression, artistic, 4, 101, 109, 138 144, 146, 152, 154, 158, 160, 164n, 166n; and individual style, 9; non-egocentric, 146
expression, natural, 152; depicted, 136, 138, 140, 144; causally connected to mind, 136; egocentric, 145; of real persons, 139
expressive perception, 102, 104, 105, 106, 107, 135, 137, 152, 154, 217, 219, 220, 221, 224, 225, 232, 236, 237, 254, 255; affective, 103, 107, 110, 111; and its object, 139; 'key' to correspondence, 255; of nature, 109, 254; ordinary, 65; perceptual, 107; phenomenological vs. causal account, 117; projective, 42
expressive, 139; experience, perceptual, 8; gesture or cry, 152; possibilities, 122; process, 127; vision, 180
expressiveness, 57n, 69, 112, 117, 155, 157; its explanation, 159; of physical objects, 158; of pictures and music (and poetry), 119, 139; its possibility, 158
external and internal, pass into each other, 119
external spectator, 5, 6, 10, 25, 71n, 133n, 179, 180, 184, 201, 204, 207–8, 212, 219, 221–5, 227, 228, 247,

256; acknowledged, 212; actual, 182; intended (addressed), 8, 212, 243, 251; disoriented, 209; embodied, 228; engaging, 177, 181, 257, 260; experience, 17, 18, 251; identity, 222; repertoire, 10, 25, 155, 221, 224, 253; viewpoint (position), 157, 158, 185, 207, 213; non-involved, 179; suitable (appropriate), 7, 13, 15, 16, 18, 24, 25, 26, 27, 34, 35, 36, 38, 39, 102, 124, 139, 155, 160, 194, 195, 223, 230, 241, 250, 254; third mode, 182
externalism, 153, 164n
eye: disembodied, 229, 232; embodied, 259; immediate engagement, 232; moving, 234

facile technique, 128
facture, 41, 53, 55, 56; *see* making of art
fantasy, 8, 51, 148, 149n; and imagination, 142
Feagin, Susan, 7, 10, 243–4
fiction, 34, 51, 52, 141, 183
figuration, 151, 184
first-person privilege, 145, 147
flatness, 236
Fodor, Jerry, 71n
foreshortening, 204, 212
forgery, 9, 198n; its limitations, 132–3
form of life, 153; three misreadings, 153–4
form, 129; total, 234
formal critics, 162
formalism, 159
fourfoldness, 94, 249
fovea, hyperacute part of retina, 234, 236
frame, 42, 68, 195, 199n
Fried, Michael, 184, 188n
Friedrich, Caspar David, 6, 182, 183, 187, 201, 208, 209, 211, 229; *Rückenfiguren*, 186; *The Cross in the Mountains* (Tetschen altarpiece), 204, 206f, 207, 212

imaginative: enactment, 260, engagement (its scope), 202, 221, 223, 224, 225, 227, experience, 233; perception, 73n; recurrence, 141; repertoire, 227; response, 222, 230; subjectivity, 181; use of the representation, 113
imagined: events, seen, 201; spatial relations, 221, 222
imagining, 61, 66, 219, 226; as higher-level thinking, 63, 64, 69, 71n; central *vs.* acentral, 6, 25, 26, 180, 200, 201, 204, 207, 213, 225, 232, 233, 234, 256; engaging with the depicted, 221, 222, 227, 228, 230, 256, 258; indeterminate, 225; seeing, 24, 29, 32, 37, 60; undergoing an emotion, 108; visual, 259
immobility: perceived, 196
indexicality, 147
individual style, 4, 5, 9, 129, 130, 131, 134n, 143, 146; its psychological reality, 4, 7, 130, 131, 156; as competence, 130; as second nature, 130; *see* accounts of style; style
infant: *see* children
inference, 16, 22, 62, 66, 68, 153, 249, 251; to the best explanation, 259; perceptual, 35
information, 32; visual, 32, 37; channels, 236
Ingres, Dominique, 22, 34
installation art, 177–9, 180, 181, 260; and painting, 185
institution of art, 77, 79, 80, 82
institutional theory of art, 79, 153, 162
intelligibility question (*re* depiction), 147
intention (intentionality), 46, 117, 123, 154, 190, 257; artistic, 126, 140, 153; located in artist, 252; metaphysical, 258; open-ended, 223, 224; simpliciter, 250, 251; vs. natural (causal), 141, 159; *see* artist's intention
intentional object, 44, 45, 46; fallacy, 139; structure and force, 145
intentionalism, 35, 153, 155, 156, 197n; hypothetical, 156

intentionality of experience, 106
interest: in a picture, 46; artistic, 132; higher-level, 234
interference: direct, 143
interior wall painting, 190
internal spectator, 5, 8, 10, 25, 26, 96, 179, 180, 186, 187, 200, 202, 204, 207, 208, 210, 211, 212, 216–30, 232, 233, 234, 237, 256, 257–9; identification with, 259, 260; function, 218; repertoire, 180, 182, 201, 209, 210, 218, 224–30, 256, 260; prowling, 210; unrepresented, 179, 183, 200, 201, 231n
internalism, 155
interpretation, 27, 41, 62, 67, 74n, 90, 129, 133n, 198n, 209, 212; charity, 163n; psychological, 213; visual, 93
intimating a kind (history) of experience, 104, 105–7, 110, 138, 165n, 255; its truth value, 106
intimation (representation of experiential), 144, 150n
introspection, 41, 44, 45, 46, 48, 54, 71n
intuition, 13, 15, 97, 117, 135, 142, 164n, 245; in the artist's mind, 125
isomorphism, 32, 67, 71n; structural, 28; a degree notion, 28; causal precondition of seeing-in, 29

Jaar, Alfredo, 177–9, 180
Japanese prints: formal qualities, 132
judgement, 129, 158; responsive, 128

Kant, Immanuel: on imagination, 8, 85, 86, 89, 91, 92, 98, 149n, 197
Kiefer, Anselm, 122
Kirchner, Ernst Ludwig, 34
kitsch, 91
Klee, Paul, 34
Kooning, willem de, 124
Kristeva, Julia, 181

landscape: as melancholy, 109; Dutch, 182; painting, 1, 183; "with ruins," 23–4, 34, 142, 148n, 250

mobilizing: cognitive stock in experience, 160, 161, 253
model (sitter), 54, 208; and painter,
174–6
Modernism, 194, 196
Modularity theory, 63, 74n
Monet, Claude, 18
monolithic theorie of expression, 108,
150n, 254
morality, 128
motivation, 83, 253
movement, 236; physical and affective,
179, 259; imagined, 222
movies, 31, 140, 142, 244
Mowbray, H. Siddons, 192

narrative, 174, 211, 212, 261; biblical
173; of Bathsheba, 174, 176
naturalist, 22; representation, 135, 140;
of the experiential, 147
nature: *as nature*, 108; its affective
qualities, 109; its expressiveness,
159
neoclassicism, 192
Newman, Barnett, 10, 94, 151, 260; *Vir
Heroicus Sublimus*, 185–7
non-communication thesis, 83; weak,
strong, 83
non-ocular contribution, 259

objectivity, 211
objects: ordinary, 126; sensuous 152;
viewing, making, 172
ocular contribution, 233, 234, 236, 237;
attracted fixation, 234, 236
of a piece: nature with emotion, 103,
107, 118, 154, 156
onomatopoeia, 58n
ontology, 149n, 183
Opposition argument (*re* expression),
136–8
opticality, 142; of pictorial art, 13; *see*
ocular contribution
orientation, 186
original, 91, 92, 132; vs. derivative, 130
ostensively rigid (or not), 87, 91

pain: bodily, 106
paint: sensual qualities, 123
painter, 122; his aims, 130; hypothetical, 75; viewpoint, 213; who is no
artist, 130; *see* artist
painterly: activity, 122, 123; presentation, 126; interest, 132
paint-figure relation, 115
Painting as an Art, 101, 104, 109, 153,
154, 157, 200, 211
painting, 112–20, 121, 132, 141, 176,
197n; adding bits of paper, 196; concept of, 77; different aspects, 120;
its dilemma, 261; experience *sui generis*, 112; internal coherence, 8,
112, 115, 117, 119, 123, 186; limiting condition, 114; lured into, 210;
mode of representing, 116; portions,
196; size, 185; twentieth century,
196
painting: as activity, 128; as art, 189;
visual, 260
Parmiggiano, 22
Patterns of Intention, 260
Peacocke, Christopher, 7, 17–8, 27n,
59, 62, 67, 71n, 73n
Peale, Raphaelle: *Venus Rising from the
Sea*, 194–5, 198n
perception of pictures, 91, 141; no
second-person reciprocity, 145
perception, 64, 68, 118, 147, 186; actual, 181; affectless, 107, 108;
causal, 164n; concept-mediated, 159;
of correspondence, 104, 105, 107,
108, 109, 117, 255; its depths, 97;
its different means, 150n; embodied,
9, 141, 186; everyday, 114, 141, 143;
fully 3D, 236; general account of,
13, 63; higher-level, 74n; as
hypotheses-forming, 72n; and imagination, 26, 142, 210, 248, 256; as
inferential, 72n; of nature (vs. art),
108; (non-)egocentric, 140–1, 143,
252, 253; of paintings (pictures),
109, 146; permeated by affective,
229; psychology of, 3, 20, 46, 56;

perception (*cont.*)
  representational, 2, 7, 9, 137; sec-
    ondary, 2D 236; straightforward, 85;
    of subject, 116; veridical, 110; *see*
    twofoldness; expressive perception
perceptual: apparatus, 146, 197; contri-
    bution, affective, 233; features, 156,
    161; solution, 210; stimuli, low-
    level, 63, 66
perceptualism, 153, 155, 157, 164n,
    233
periphery: low-definition, 234, 236
Persona accounts (*re* expression), 138–
    40
persona: no full-fledged psychology,
    139; ontology, 139; dramatis, 184
personal, 155, 164n; features, minimiz-
    ing vs. utilizing, 133; experience,
    155, 237
perspective, 95, 187n, 212; linear, 202,
    204, 213; as a rhetorical device, 10;
    single-point, 197n; spatial, 215
perspectivism: Cartesian, 180, 187n
phenomena, 64
phenomenal, 59, 60, 61, 69, 72n, 89,
    147; flux, 96; integration, 60; con-
    sciousness, 65; first-person, 145; in
    perception and empathy, 146
phenomenology, 45, 69, 145, 217; of
    experience (of painting), 19, 20, 48,
    54, 112, 156, 190, 253, 254; general
    specifications, 144; of non-egocentric
    address, 146; of seeing-in, 24, 31,
    44, 62, 64, 68, 73n, 74n, 135; of
    (simple) perception, 42, 43, 141, 193
philosophy (analytical), 49, 39, 78, 79,
    83, 97, 112, 159, 255; anthropology,
    248; of painting, 261; and psychol-
    ogy, 211
photography, 31, 47, 244; newspaper,
    179; (non-)transparency, 149n
physical, 94; and spiritual, 194; embod-
    iment, 125; nature of canvas, 152;
    object, weakened thesis, 151
physiology and anatomy, 152
Picasso, Pablo, 34, 196

pictorial: art, 151; effect, 236; means, 208,
    209; "mesh," 7, 47–8, 52, 55, 56, 58n,
    248; narrative, 43, 53; organization,
    126; reference, 141; shapes, 65, 207;
    significance, 21, 22; structure, 14
picture, 197n, 227; as communication,
    45; as imaginary window, 42, 44;
    flatness, 68; psychological life, 237;
    representational, 245; surface, 9,31,
    32, 64, 65, 66, 69, 236 transitional
    space, 119; vs. description, 148n
Pictures and Language, 49–54
Pierpont Morgan library, 198n
pigments, 122
Plato, 193
pleasure, 124, 129
Podro, Michael, 8, 55, 58n, 72n, 73n,
    74n, 248, 249, 252, 255–6
poetry, 160
point of view: external, 208; high, 201,
    207; in mid-air, 204; manipulated,
    208, 211, 212; occupied, 182; physi-
    cal vs. spiritual, 201
Pollock, Jackson, 94
portrait, 174, 175, 208
postcards, 31, 244
postmodern, 179
Poussin, Nicolas: *St. John on Patmos,*
    250
Pozzo, Andrea, 195
pre-linguistic, 88
presence (absence), 90, 93, 94, 174, 178,
    208; of expressed mind, 138, 143;
    imaginative, 202, 211; literal 119;
    one's own, 185; of represented mind,
    140; of spectator, 184, 212; substan-
    tial, 190; to the senses, 85, 89, 90,
    146, 147
presentation and representation, 10, 178,
    190, 243; functions, 192, 194, 195,
    196, 197n
probity, 127; as a virtue, 133
problem: artistic, 130; of attitude, 64, 69;
    of bricoleur, 167n; of coherence, 60–
    2, 66, 67, 69; of location, 64, 69,
    70n, 71n